Mark Twain's
Own Autobiography

Mark Twain in Dublin, New Hampshire, 1906. (Courtesy of the Mark Twain Memorial, Hartford, Conn.)

Mark Twain's OWN AUTOBIOGRAPHY

The Chapters from the
North American Review

Edited by
Michael J. Kiskis

Second edition

The University of Wisconsin Press

The University of Wisconsin Press
1930 Monroe Street, 3rd Floor
Madison, Wisconsin 53711-2059
uwpress.wisc.edu

3 Henrietta Street
London WC2E 8LU, England
eurospanbookstore.com

5   4   3   2   1

Printed in the United States of America

Library of Congress Cataloging-in-Publication Data
Twain, Mark, 1835–1910.
   [Autobiography]
   Mark Twain's own autobiography : the chapters from the North American review /
edited by Michael J. Kiskis.—2nd ed.
       p. cm.—(Wisconsin studies in autobiography)
   First published in book form under title: Mark Twain's autobiography. 1924.
   Includes bibliographical references and index.
   ISBN 978-0-299-23474-4 (pbk. : alk. paper)—ISBN 978-0-299-23473-7 (e-book)
   1. Twain, Mark, 1835–1910. 2. Authors, American—19th century—Biography.
3. Humorists, American—19th century—Biography. I. Kiskis, Michael J. II. Title.
III. Series: Wisconsin studies in autobiography.
PS1331.A2   2009b
818'.409—dc22
[B]
2009010516

For James Martine and John Gerber

Acknowledgments

I began reading and writing about Samuel Clemens almost thirty years ago while a graduate student at the State University of New York at Albany. I studied with John Gerber. When John died, I managed to obtain a vintage poster of Mark Twain that hung in John's office—it's a distinctive pencil drawing with a detailed face and eyes. It now hangs over my desk, a daily reminder of my beginnings with Mark Twain that resonates with the debt I owe to those whose work I have come to respect and admire.

There have been a few score of others who have helped me with their advice, guidance, and friendship. Decades in the vineyard of Twain studies is a long, long time. I have been able to keep my head in the work because of the people laboring along with me. There are too many for a brief paragraph, though let me mention a few: my thanks especially to Laura Skandera Trombley, Gary Scharnhorst, Ann Ryan, Kerry Driscoll, Tom Quirk, Dennis Eddings, and David E. E. Sloane. In Elmira I want to thank Barb Snedecor who has given me opportunities to expand my thinking and Mark Woodhouse and Charlie Mitchell for their steadfast humor and good company. I treasure all of you.

This second edition would not be if not for the interest of Sheila Leary, the director of the University of Wisconsin Press. We had lunch several years ago, and our conversation prompted this new edition. We met at a small bed and breakfast in Elmira, New York, called The Painted Lady. Sam Clemens would like that (it has a particularly striking billiard room). I suspect that Katy Leary, too, would smile. Bill Andrews, the general editor of the Wisconsin Studies in Autobiography series, was again supportive, and I appreciate his continued thoughtfulness.

I thank my wife Ann Cady. The "Livy" to my "Sam," Ann has been a partner in this work and has been patient with me as I grumbled my way through it. I became interested in questions of domesticity and Sam Clemens some years ago. Ann has helped me become more conscious of what "home" means not only to the depth and resilience of scholarly work but also, and more importantly, to the stability and peace of everyday life. Bless her, she keeps me humble—and warm. No mean feat.

Contents

ix

Contents

Abbreviations

Full bibliographical information for the works listed here will be found in the Selected Bibliography.

CTSSE	*Collected Tales, Sketches, Speeches, & Essays*, 2 vols. Edited by Louis J. Budd.
HHT	*Mark Twain's Hannibal, Huck, and Tom*. Edited by Walter Blair.
MTA	*Mark Twain's Autobiography*, 2 vols. Edited by Albert Bigelow Paine.
MTB	*Mark Twain: A Biography*. By Albert Bigelow Paine.
MTL	*Mark Twain's Letters*, 2 vols. Edited by Albert Bigelow Paine.
MTLs	*Mark Twain's Letters*. Vol. 1, *1853–1866*, edited by Edgar Marquess Branch, Michael B. Frank, and Kenneth M. Sanderson. Vol. 2, *1867–1868*, edited by Harriet Elinor Smith, Richard Bucci, and Lin Salamo. Vol. 3, *1869*, edited by Victor Fischer and Michael B. Frank. Vol. 4, *1870–1871*, edited by Victor Fischer and Michael B. Frank. Vol. 5, *1872–1873*, edited by Lin Salamo and Harriet Elinor Smith. Vol. 6, *1874–1875*, edited by Michael B. Frank and Harriet Elinor Smith.
MTN	*Mark Twain's Notebook*. Edited by Albert Bigelow Paine.
MTP	Mark Twain Papers, Bancroft Library, University of California, Berkeley.
NAR	*North American Review*.
N&J	*Mark Twain's Notebooks & Journals*. Vol. 1, *1855–1873*, edited by Frederick Anderson, Michael B. Frank, and Kenneth M. Sanderson. Vol. 2, *1877–1883*, edited by Frederick Anderson,

Lin Salamo, and Bernard L. Stein. Vol. 3, *1883–1891*, edited by Robert Pack Browning, Michael B. Frank, and Lin Salamo.

SCH   *Sam Clemens of Hannibal.* By Dixon Wecter.

SMTHL   *Selected Mark Twain–Howells Letters, 1872–1910.* Edited by Frederick Anderson, William M. Gibson, and Henry Nash Smith.

Foreword to the Second Edition

I feel a special satisfaction and gratitude in publishing this new edition of Mark Twain's autobiography to mark the hundredth anniversary of his death in 1910. Satisfaction and gratitude because, through his will, Samuel Clemens left a legacy that lifted my own forebears out of poverty and servitude and gave them a chance at higher education.

My great-great-aunt, Catherine Leary, better known as Katy (or Katie) Leary, worked as a valued servant and family companion in the Clemens household from 1880 until shortly after Samuel Clemens' death in 1910. Clemens mentions her frequently in his correspondence and is often cited as saying "Why, Katy . . . she's like the wallpaper, she's always there."

Katy's memoirs, as told to Mary Lawton (a family friend of the Clemenses), were published in 1925 as *A Lifetime with Mark Twain: The Memories of Katy Leary, for Thirty Years His Faithful and Devoted Servant*. The book is still in print, and scholars have mined it for details and perspectives on Clemens' habits, family life, and social circle. Social historians, too, have taken an interest in Katy herself as an example of the American servant class in the nineteenth century. And creative writers have made Katy a character in a one-woman play and even an episode of the television program *Touched by an Angel*.

But both scholars and family members believe that Mary Lawton, who transcribed and edited Katy's stories for *A Lifetime with Mark Twain* in Katy's old age, exaggerated in casting Katy's stories in stereotypic language of an uneducated, Irish-born housemaid.

Robert Agan interviewed Katy's niece Marguerite Leary Conway in the 1970s. She had lived as a girl in Katy's New York boarding house in the years following Mark Twain's death. Marguerite (my great-aunt Peg) told Agan, "She was a very intelligent person who had experienced so much in thirty years in the Clemens household. Her grammar may have included 'aint's' and a double negative now and then, but she did not speak in the vernacular as recorded by Mary Lawton. Many people who knew my aunt and enjoyed her stories of the Clemens family urged us to protest, but my brother and I decided we were the only ones concerned, so we did nothing about it."

Who was Katy Leary, and what became of her after the deaths of most of the Clemens family? Katy was not born in Ireland, but rather in Elmira, New York. She was one of five children of immigrants Fenton (or Fintan) Leary and Margaret Connelly, who had fled the great Irish famine of the 1840s. They came from Skibbereen in County Cork, which in 1846–47 was the site of some of the most harrowing suffering, disease, and mass starvation in the whole of Ireland, described at the time by witnesses as "a state of distress horrible beyond description." Arriving in America, Fenton and Margaret settled in the Irish neighborhood on the working-class south side of the river in Elmira. They lived among Margaret's Connelly kin; the present-day Elmira city park named for Katy Leary borders Connelly Avenue.

In Elmira, Fenton and his sons Bat (Bartholomew) and Denis worked as laborers and stonemasons. The daughters—Mary, Katy, and Maggie—learned fine sewing and dressmaking. Mary Leary was hired to work as a live-in maid and seamstress in the well-to-do Elmira household of Charles Langdon. His sister, Olivia Langdon, married Samuel Clemens, and when the Clemenses established a home in Hartford, Connecticut, they hired Mary's younger sister Katy to be their own seamstress and live-in maid.

Over the next thirty years in the Clemens household, Katy, whose formal education lasted only to her fourteenth year, was encouraged to borrow and read classic and contemporary works from the Clemens family library. She heard Sam Clemens' storytelling and the witty debates among the varied visitors to the Clemens home. And, she traveled with the family in the United States and Europe, sometimes accompanying the Clemens daughters to museums, concerts, and plays.

When Samuel Clemens died in 1910, Katy was fifty-four years old. In accordance with his will, she received $10,000 from his estate and was able to move into a large house at 37 West 97th Street in Manhattan. She took in boarders, including Claude Beuchotte, a Frenchman who had been Sam Clemens' butler in his last years and, according to the U.S. census, was then working at a hotel. Katy's parents, brothers, and sister Maggie had all died before the turn of the century, but she invited her older sister Mary to move from Elmira to live with her in New York City. She invited her widowed sister-in-law, niece, and nephew as well.

Katy's younger brother Denis had been the only sibling to marry. A stone-mason who later operated a saloon, he died in 1898 at the age of forty-one. He left a widow, Katharine Warren Leary, and two children, six-year-old Warren Denis Leary and three-year-old Marguerite (Peg) Leary. For a time, Katharine continued to operate the saloon at 200 Fulton Street in Elmira, not far from Connelly Avenue.

While in high school, young Warren was fortunate to receive a letter of recommendation for employment from Samuel Clemens. In 1910, according to the U.S. census, eighteen-year-old Warren was working as a telegraph operator in Elmira while finishing school. The move to Manhattan, at Katy's invitation, meant financial security for Katharine and young Peg. No longer needing to support his mother and sister, Warren was able to think of college as a possibility, but he needed to accumulate some savings. Equipped with his telegraphy skills, he took a job with Standard Oil, walking their pipeline to check for leaks. If he found any he was to shinny up a telegraph pole, tap in, and send a Morse code message to headquarters. He walked that pipeline from New Jersey across Pennsylvania to the Ohio border.

Warren was the first of his family to get a college education. He enrolled at the new Pulitzer School of Journalism at Columbia University, which opened in 1912 and was the world's first school of journalism. He started his journalism career at the *New York Herald* and the *New York Tribune*. Younger sister Peg Leary enrolled after high school at the Pratt Institute in New York to study domestic economy (home economics). She became a teacher in the New York public schools and married a lawyer, Jim Conway, a former tenant at Katy's boarding house.

Warren and Peg could not have imagined in 1925 that Katy's memoirs would endure over time as a source for scholarship. Indeed, today the Mark Twain House and Museum in Hartford, Connecticut, and the Center for Mark Twain Studies at Elmira College in Elmira, New York, both include in their public presentations details about the Clemens family servants (especially Katy Leary and another long-time servant, George, the African American butler).

In recent years, I have been fortunate to receive a private tour of the kitchen and servants' quarters at the Mark Twain House in Hartford, to spend the night at Quarry Farm in Elmira, and to pore over documents at the Mark Twain Archives at Elmira College. Those experiences brought me to the realization that Mark Twain's death, and the legacy that he left Katy Leary in his will, marked a turning point in my own family's history. I would like to think that Mark Twain—a journalist, author, and investor in a typesetting machine, who opened his personal library to his servants for their pleasure and self-education—would take satisfaction in his key role in launching several generations of Learys into careers as writers, journalists, and publishers.

Sheila Leary

Director, the University of Wisconsin Press

Introduction to the Second Edition

PROLOGUE

The autobiography Samuel Clemens constructed is held together not by facts, nor plot, nor sequence, nor point of view, nor even by editorial fiat. The material is unified by Clemens' singular voice as it vibrates between rage and reverence, affection and hatred, joy and sorrow. It is held together by a voice at once truthful and fraudulent, but always genuine. And Clemens' honesty remains intact because this is the way he thinks about, sees, and interprets his past.

SAMUEL CLEMENS' LIFE

Samuel Langhorne Clemens was born on 30 November 1835 in Florida, Missouri. He was the sixth of seven children and spent the first seventeen years of his life in and around the Mississippi River and the family's home in Hannibal, Missouri. Sometime after his father's death in 1847, Sam was placed as a printer's apprentice: that began his sixty-year relationship with journalism and writing.[1] The printing trade continued Clemens' education by allowing him access to a variety of writing styles and to myriad opportunities to read and practice a brand of untamed humor. It also guaranteed him a trade that he could use to support himself during his first trip out of the Mississippi Valley in 1853 when he headed east to experience the excitement and the frustration of life in New York City, Philadelphia, and Washington, D.C.[2] That trip east was the first that took him far away from Hannibal and foreshadows his adult interest in the literary centers of the East.

After he returned home he continued to work as a printer (most often for his brother Orion) until he decided in 1857 to head to New Orleans in the

hope of finding passage to South America where he could earn a fortune
trafficking in coca leaves. His hopes dashed (there were no ships traveling
to Brazil), he became a "cub" river pilot, eventually earning his professional
license in 1859. Soon after the start of the American Civil War, which made
it more dangerous to be a Mississippi River pilot, Sam served very briefly as
a member of the Marion County Rangers (a regional and Confederate mili-
tia band) until he turned his attention west and, with Orion, who had been
named the new Secretary to the Nevada Territory, crossed the American continent by stagecoach. He found no prospects in silver mining but did settle
on a trade in journalism and a pen name—Mark Twain. In 1867 he toured
the Mediterranean as part of the Quaker City cruise, which would lead to
his first book, *Innocents Abroad*. During the next forty years he traveled
extensively; ultimately, he spent a decade living in Europe, made a fortune,
declared bankruptcy, circumnavigated the globe, and remade his fortune. In
all, Sam Clemens lived in Virginia City, Nevada; San Francisco, California;
Buffalo and Elmira, New York; Hartford, Connecticut; a series of European
cities (among them London, Paris, Florence, and Vienna); New York City;
and Redding, Connecticut. He adopted a variety of professions: printer, cub
reporter, steamboat pilot, silver miner, journalist, correspondent, lecturer,
novelist, entrepreneur, publisher, and, finally, celebrity and sage. He was
known by most Americans and a by good part of the world as a humorist; he
was also a sharp and cutting moralist.

Clemens married Olivia Langdon ("Livy") of Elmira on 2 February 1870
and remained devoted to her throughout his life. Their life together was a
potent mix of happiness and sorrow.[3] They shared flush times during which
they lived in a showcase home in Hartford, Connecticut, became well established in the social order of that city and spent summers at Quarry Farm in
Elmira.[4] They shared the discomfort and embarrassment of bankruptcy after
Clemens' investments in the Paige typesetting machine and his running of
the Charles L. Webster & Co. publishing firm soured.[5] But they also shared
the credit for repaying the debts that grew out of those failures and for a
triumphant return to the United States in 1900 after years of financial exile
in Europe.

The couple also rejoiced in their children: Langdon was born during the
first year of the Clemenses' marriage on 7 November 1870; Olivia Susan
(Susy) was born on 19 March 1872; Clara Langdon was born on 8 June 1874;
and Jane Lampton (Jean) was born on 26 July 1880. All but Langdon were
vibrant in their youth. Clemens' literary life was enhanced and energized by
the family's time together; however, as time passed there was also the heavy

burden of heartbreak. Never a hearty child, Langdon died at the age of eighteen months from diphtheria. Susy died from spinal meningitis in 1896 when
she was twenty-four years old (her death came at the end of the world tour
which would free the family from oppressive debt). Olivia died from heart
failure in Florence, Italy, on 5 June 1904. Jean, the youngest, suffered from
epilepsy and spent a good part of her young womanhood separated from the
family. She was found dead on the morning of 24 December 1909 in Clemens' home in Redding, Connecticut. She was twenty-nine. Samuel Clemens
died on 21 April 1910 in Redding. Clara Clemens was the only child to survive both her parents: she died on 19 November 1962. Her daughter, Nina
Gabrilowitsch, was born in August 1910 four months after Clemens died. She
died on 16 January 1966.

EDITORS AND EDITIONS

When he died, Samuel Clemens left a chaotic collection of manuscripts that
he identified rather loosely as "my autobiography." This material, composed
over the forty years from 1870 to 1910, offers a variety of literary forms: character sketches, remembrances, occasional essays, diaries, dictations, even letters. Clemens seems to have used some of the materials as an exercise to
prepare for his longer fiction; several pieces of his short fiction grow directly
out of his married life and can be matched—almost verbatim—to portions
of his autobiography. He used a considerable portion of his autobiographical manuscripts for his one sustained effort to offer an autobiography to the
public—the series "Chapters from My Autobiography," which appeared in
the *North American Review* during 1906 and 1907.[6]

A number of editors have worked with and shaped the autobiographical
material, yet no editor has yet composed a definitive edition of Clemens'
"Autobiography."[7] Realistically, for any full and ordered text to be properly
identified as *the* autobiography, the myriad materials could be arranged only
by Clemens himself. By definition, an *auto*biography can be organized and
planned only by the writer: the writer—the self—steers a clear course and
decides the manuscript's final shape, structure, plan, proportion, and emphasis. Because they operate without such explicit authorial direction, advice,
and consent and can, in the end, make only a good faith effort to establish
authorial intention, editors create biography. Their choices for a text are
substantial, but editors are affected by their own time and critical contexts
that intrude on the self-portrait; their perspective infiltrates and often alters
the self that is disclosed in the narrative. This is even more complicated in

Clemens' case because of his shifting intentions for the autobiography and his, at times deliberate, at times unconscious, dissembling as he creates and recreates his past. Clemens' self-description, self-reflection, and self-analysis (when there is any) are bound to be flawed, but his flaws are part of the process of composition and presentation. Subsequent editors have based their decisions on their perception of his life; we get the editor's interpretation of the life, not necessarily Clemens'.[8]

At first blush, Clemens seems not to have been particularly concerned about the influence of later editors. After all, he had relied heavily on the help of various editors during his lifetime (including Bret Harte, Mary Mason Fairbanks, Olivia Clemens, and William Dean Howells). It seems reasonable to assume that he would consider any future editor as one more helper and that such a helper would be necessary since Clemens announced that his "autobiography" was not to be published until after his death. By publishing material as "Chapters from My Autobiography," Clemens advertised that these "chapters" were only a part of the whole story and that more material would come out later. Clemens, in fact, gave a series of interviews throughout the 1890s that played on his plans to publish the autobiography one hundred years after his death: "Chapters from My Autobiography" would keep readers interested in and alert for any future publication. That could help assure future sales, which was a concern Clemens felt keenly toward the end of his life when he saw the profits from his writing as the one sure bequest he might leave Jean and Clara.[9]

Clemens' actions and instructions betray a deep concern over control of the autobiographical materials.[10] Clemens left very specific instructions regarding the form he envisioned for the autobiography and the publication of the remaining text. Those instructions are aimed at his editors. Clemens was most concerned that the material be presented in the order in which it was composed. The form would follow the drift of his interests. He described the process in 1904: "Start it at no particular time of your life; wander at your free will all over your life; talk only about the thing which interests you for the moment; drop it the moment its interest threatens to pale, and turn your talk upon the new and more interesting thing that has intruded itself into your mind meantime" (*MTA* 1:193). While this mandate is mirrored in his practice of composing autobiography, it has had only partial success in influencing later editions of the autobiographical materials. Truth be told, Clemens himself seemed unable to conform fully to the instruction when he began to fashion a text for publication: he compromised when he developed the materials for the chapters published in the *North American Review*.

To formalize his instructions, Clemens penned two sets of directives to his "editors, heirs, and assigns." The first appears in manuscript immediately after the preface which he wrote in Florence in 1904. The "preface" is Roman numeral I; the directives are II and III.[11]

I

In this Autobiography I shall keep in mind the fact that I am speaking from the grave. I am literally speaking from the grave, because I shall be dead when the book issues from the press. I speak from the grave rather than with my living tongue, for a good reason: I can speak thence freely. When a man is writing a book dealing with the privacies of his life—a book which is to be read while he is still alive—he shrinks from speaking his whole frank mind; all his attempts to do it fail, he recognizes that he is trying to do a thing which is wholly impossible to a human being. The frankest and freest and privatest product of the human mind and heart is a love letter; the writer gets his limitless freedom of statement and expression from his sense that no stranger is going to see what he is writing. Sometimes there is a breach-of-promise case by and by; & when he sees his letter in print it makes him cruelly uncomfortable & he perceives that he never would have unbosomed himself to that large and honest degree if he had known that he was writing for the public. He cannot find anything in the letter that was not true, honest, respect-worthy; but no matter, he would have been very much more reserved if he had known he was writing for print.

It has seemed to me that I could be as frank & free & unembarrassed as a love letter if I knew that what I was writing would be exposed to no eye until I was dead, & unaware, & indifferent.

II

My editors, heirs, & assigns are hereby instructed to leave out of the first edition all characterizations of friends and enemies that might wound the feelings of either the person characterized or their families & kinship. This book is not a revenge record. When I build a fire under a person in it, I do not do it merely because of the enjoyment I get out of seeing him fry, but because he is worth the trouble. It is then a compliment, a distinction: let him give thanks & keep quiet. I do not fry the small, the commonplace, the unworthy.

From the first, second, third, & fourth editions all sound & sane expressions of opinion must be kept out. There may be a market for that kind of wares a century from now. There is no hurry. Wait & see.

III

The editions should be issued twenty-five years apart. Many things that must be left out of the first will be proper for the second; many things that must be left out of both will be proper for the third; into the fourth—or at least the fifth—the whole Autobiography can go, unexpurgated. (MTP‡)

The other set of directives, in script, appears on the cover page on which "Autobiography of Mark Twain" is typed:

To heirs & assigns:

1. Whereas about a twentieth part of this autobiography can be published (in serial form, not book form) while I am alive, no large portions of it must see print in any form during my lifetime.

2. Words of mine which can wound the living must wait until later editions. This book is no revenge-record.

3. It will be noticed that I have marked certain chapters which are to be kept suppressed, sealed up, and unprinted for a hundred years. These must not be shown to anyone, but kept sealed—as I shall leave them. (MTP‡)

These demands are related less to a concern for the feelings of those Clemens fries—a concern he rarely felt in his personal, business, or political dealings—than to economic and financial worries. His instruction that editions be released at twenty-five year intervals is most likely a ploy to extend the copyright and, therefore, the profits from the manuscripts.

Clemens' directives underscore his belief that editors will play a primary role in delivering his text to the public, a responsibility each editor has taken very seriously. The list of editors is formidable: Colonel George Harvey, Albert Bigelow Paine, Bernard DeVoto, and Charles Neider. Each shaped Clemens' material to suit a particular purpose. Colonel George Harvey, editor of the *North American Review*, received Clemens' enthusiastic support during the preparations for "Chapters from My Autobiography," which began with the issue for 7 September 1906 and ran until December 1907. Part of Clemens' enthusiasm can be attributed to Harvey's reaction to the autobiography. On 4 August 1906, Clemens wrote Mary Benjamin Rogers[12] that Harvey had just left after spending three days with him in Dublin, New Hampshire: "He has been exasperatingly indifferent about my Autobiography, and he came up here as calm as Marjorie Fleming's mother-turkey, to see if he could find a chapter in it good enough for his literary section. He found twenty-four-to start with. . . . That's the kind of fulsome flattery that I like" (*Mark Twain's Letters to Mary*, 39). Clemens also liked the $30,000 that Harvey paid for the chapters.[13]

A day earlier, 3 August 1906, Clemens had written to William Dean Howells informing him of the deal with Harvey. That letter also refers to Harvey's role as editor: "The Colonel has done some wonderful editing of the MS. He has selected five 5,000 word installments, & placed them together so cleverly that the seams don't show, & each seems to have been written by itself" (*SMTHL*, 391). The first seven chapters (7 September through 7 December 1906) present a brief history of the Clemens family and lead to Clemens' marriage to Olivia Langdon. They then move on to events that took place either in the Clemenses' Hartford household or during the years spent in and around Hartford. The remaining chapters (21 December 1906 through December 1907) meander through the years, introduce personalities from Clemens' childhood, and describe his experiences in the West and in Europe. They introduce Olivia Clemens and the Clemens children, Jane Lampton Clemens, and Orion and Henry Clemens, as well as a variety of supporting players. A portion of the text is punctuated by headings that identify the dates on which certain sections were composed (a few of which are inaccurate), and there are also dates, in parentheses, beside the text in various places. Thus the reader is given some sense of the chronology, even though a strict chronological sequence is not part of this plan.

It is tempting to give Harvey credit for editing the series; however, Clemens did direct the development of the chapters—there are scraps of paper on which he not only identified sections of the autobiography he had with him in Dublin but also indicated specific sections he wanted to weave into the chapters. The editing may have been collaborative. No doubt Harvey would have been an ideal source for editorial advice, but Clemens was rarely able to give full control of a manuscript to anyone (except perhaps Howells). It is also difficult to think of Clemens relinquishing control of the materials while he was still alive, especially since he seems to have drafted the directives in a bid to maintain control after his death.

After Clemens died, his daughter Clara Clemens Gabrilowitsch and Albert Bigelow Paine were awarded control over the manuscripts.[14] In his two-volume edition *Mark Twain's Autobiography*, which was published by Harper & Brothers in 1924, Paine did attempt to follow Clemens' approach, an approach that touted the non-chronological sequence of thought. Paine presented the material in the order in which it was composed and eventually included twenty-two fragments: "The Tennessee Land" (1870); "Early Years in Florida, Missouri" (1877); "The Grant Dictations" (1885); "The Machine Episode" (1890); "Jane Lampton Clemens" (1897–98); "Early Days" (1897–98); "Playing 'Bear'" (1897–98); "Herrings" (1897–98); "Jim Wolf and the Cats" (1897–98); "Macfarlane" (1897–98); "Old Lecture Days" (1898); "Ralph Keeler" (1898); "Beauties of the German Language" (1898); "Viennese Procession" (1898); "Comment on Tautology and Grammar" (1898); "Private History of a MS that Came to Grief" (1900); and chapters added in Florence, which include "Villa Quarto"; "A Memory of John Hay"; "Notes on 'Innocents Abroad'"; "Stevenson, Aldrich, etc."; and "Henry H. Rogers" (1904). The last section of the first volume and all of the second volume are devoted to "The Final Dictation, Beginning January 9, 1906, Present Mr. Clemens, Mr. Paine, Miss Hobby, Stenographer."

In the note which precedes the section titled "Early Fragments: 1870–1877," Paine stops to point out how Clemens' comments on form and chronology influenced the edition: "The various divisions and chapters of this work, in accordance with the author's wish, are arranged in the order in which they were written, regardless of the chronology of events" (*MTA* 1:1). Actually, Paine dated some of these "divisions and chapters" incorrectly; for example, the sketch of Jane Lampton Clemens is dated 1897–98, though evidence suggests it was composed soon after her death in 1890.[15] He also included sections that should not be part of the autobiography at all, such as "Macfarlane,"[16] and chose not to use others that might properly be included, especially from the series of autobiographical dictations. Paine concluded his two volume compilation with Clemens' comments of April 1907, though the dictating sessions continued through 1909.[17] He conformed to Clemens' restrictions by publishing the pre-1906 fragments along with only those dictations composed between January and April 1906 and by deleting from both a few passages that might be considered offensive or troublesome.[18] That work seems aimed at shaping Clemens' public image, at assuring that readers will see Clemens in a complimentary, even flattering light.

In contrast to Paine's relatively chronological presentation, Bernard DeVoto and Charles Neider completely rearranged material to suit their own thematic and narrative purposes. In his introduction to *Mark Twain in Eruption: Hitherto Unpublished Pages about Men and Events*, DeVoto writes: "I should not care . . . to commit the irrationality . . . of discussing Mark Twain's books as what they are not rather than what they are. Providence owed us no obligation to make him the kind of autobiographer who could anatomize his soul. If his autobiography is not a document of his inner life, it is nevertheless rich with reminiscence" (xxii). DeVoto made ample use of that reminiscence, but he introduced an artificial structure by tying selected pieces together within nine major headings: "Theodore Roosevelt," "Andrew Carnegie," "The Plutocracy," "Hannibal Days," "Two Halos," "In a Writer's Workshop," "Various Literary People," "The Last Visit to England," and "Miscellany." He chose this plan as a reaction against Clemens' and Paine's organization. Without imposing this structure, he wrote, "I should come out with something as shapeless as the published portion, which had always seemed to me an annoying book" (vii).

That final comment is telling and demonstrates DeVoto's personal agenda as it trumps Clemens' notion of what an autobiography should be. In effect, DeVoto's book is neither *an* nor *the* autobiography. It is a collection, an anthology of arbitrarily allied comments and sketches. DeVoto's annoyance led him to reject Clemens' plan. His desire to gain an audience, to "interest many people and add much that was characteristic and something that was new to our picture of Mark Twain" (viii), prompted him to impose his own thematic form on the material. Yet, in a demonstration of the strength of Clemens' voice, even though DeVoto rejected the form that Clemens had hoped would convey some of the informality and geniality and heat of conversation, the collection of sketches and characterizations and outbursts that make up *Mark Twain in Eruption* still offers readers a chance to experience the flashes of energy that signal Clemens' creativity.

On the other hand, Charles Neider rejected all previous plans for the materials with his edition of *The Autobiography of Mark Twain.* In his introduction Neider wrote: "To put it briefly, Paine either did not envision the possibility of a true autobiography or did not care to undertake to make one. The same can be said of DeVoto. Both said in their introductions that what they were presenting was not really autobiography but a kind of table talk. To both men I owe thanks because they gave me the opportunity to do the exciting job which remained to be done" (ix–x). The problem of course lies in Neider's method and structure: he essentially reframed the story by placing it within a rough chronological order—not the chronology of composition but the chronology of Clemens' life.

In a 1936 comparison between the materials presented by Albert Bigelow Paine and the *North American Review,* Delancey Ferguson called attention to the problems resulting from an editor's intrusion into the autobiographical process.[19] Ferguson concentrated on passages (at times words and expressions, at times sentences and paragraphs) that Paine removed from the *North American Review* text before presenting it in the 1924 collection. Ferguson makes a strong case for regarding Paine's changes as an intrusion into Clemens' story. Ferguson points out: "With [Clemens], as with Dickens, when a book was printed he was through with it. He was, however, almost a fanatic in his insistence upon careful proofreading. Hence it is as difficult to believe that the North American Review text does not represent what Mark Twain meant to say as it is to picture him making the trifling deletions and niggling, 'pussy-footing' alterations which this collation has revealed" (45–46).

To carry Ferguson's point still further, it becomes obvious that Neider's work presents another and more serious problem of editorial intrusion, for here we have the wholesale reordering of Clemens' thought. An example will help to put this in perspective. *The North American Review,* Chapter

III, published 5 October 1906, is a combination of three days' dictations: 1, 2, and 5 February 1906. The February 1 dictation ends with a reference to Langdon Clemens which is used to introduce the chronology for Susy Clemens' birth and the story of her death: "Our first child, Langdon Clemens, was born the 7th of November, 1870, and lived twenty-two months. Susy was born the 19th of March, 1872, and passed from life in the Hartford home, the 18th of August, 1896" (580). The dictation then progresses through the tale of Susy's suffering and death while Clemens waited alone in England for news. Neider's chapter 37 (190) opens with the February 1 mention of Langdon's birth. The difference is that Neider uses this opening statement to move on to Clemens' confession of guilt over Langdon's death: "Our first child, Langdon Clemens, was born the 7th of November, 1870, and lived twenty-two months. I was the cause of the child's illness. . . . I think it is most likely that I have never confessed until now" (190). In the sequence of the dictations, Clemens did not "confess" until 22 March 1906. The original chronology is more reflective of Clemens' tendency to sidle towards confession and pronouncements of guilt. Neider makes this confession more direct and, therefore, less characteristic of the man he hoped to describe. This is a telling example. Clemens spent the days before the "confession" wandering through a variety of memories, many of them about Susy and her place in Clemens' heart. If emphasis and proportion are deemed valuable to writers and readers of autobiography, we must consider Neider's decisions to change Clemens' emphases as unwarranted intrusions. And the intrusions occur throughout the edition.

Neider's opposition to the table-talk feature of Clemens', Paine's, and DeVoto's presentations led to his decision to run Clemens' story "in the sequence one would reasonably expect from autobiography" (ix). Neider, of course, means the sequence *he* expected of autobiography. Clemens, however, rejected that expected and conventional sequence when he drafted an introduction to one of his early attempts at autobiography: "It starts out with good confidence, but suffers the fate of its brethren—is presently abandoned for some other & newer interest. This is not to be wondered at, for its plan is an old, old, old inflexible & difficult one—the plan that starts you at the cradle & drives you straight for the grave, with no side-excursions permitted on the way. Whereas the side-excursions are the life of our life-voyage, & should be, also, of its history" (MTP‡). Clemens rejected the very form through which most of today's readers have come to know his life's story best.

What, then, should be done with Samuel Clemens' autobiography?

Editors have often lost sight of Clemens' story when they adapted it to their own image of him or when they adopted editorial strategies in reaction to a previous editor's work. At least two of the editions of the autobiography—DeVoto's and Neider's—have not agreed with Clemens' stated plans for the materials or with Clemens' own and published version of the autobiography; the third—Paine's—is suspect for its selection of materials. Each editor has given us a specific picture of the man: Paine carefully selected materials that showcase Clemens' (somewhat) reflective process and give a taste of his eccentricity and loneliness; DeVoto added to that picture by presenting samples of Clemens' wit and outrage and fondness for the past; Neider promoted the image of Clemens as consummate storyteller. All of these images are facets of Sam Clemens. Each version is part of the story. None is complete. The collected material is useful and often fascinating, but it should not be thought of as *the* autobiography. That directs attention away from and cheapens Clemens' own attempt to offer his story to the public. We must treat the autobiographical materials as Clemens' autobiography, not shape them to agree with our idea of what he wanted or how we think he should be presented.

There are, then, two different paths for Clemens' editors. Each path has explicit implications for readers and opens up a host of additional questions about Clemens and his relationship to his writing and his literary persona. One approach is to present all of the material related to the autobiography in the order in which it was composed without excising passages that may seem dull or disappointing and without unduly emphasizing passages that excite or tantalize. Such an edition will eventually be completed by the Mark Twain Project at the University of California, Berkeley, whose editors have had to contend with a host of obstacles. There are difficulties not only in editing the wealth of manuscripts that Clemens explicitly identified as autobiography but also in deciding which of his other fragments should be a part of the autobiography's manuscript (as well as deciding what other scraps—such as clippings of newspaper items that attracted Clemens' attention—should be included). There are tough editorial decisions to be made regarding the presentation of the later dictated material—along with the Grant Dictations and those composed in Florence during 1904 there are 252 dictations composed from 1906 through 1909. There are multiple typescripts, some of which have been edited several times (by Clemens and by Paine), which results in no small confusion. This project will be an important and exciting addition to the readers' bookshelves (or to their electronic bookmarks) because it will offer an opportunity not only to trace Clemens' (often failed) attempts at reflective writing but also to confront the complex wonderings and wanderings of his mind. Such an edition will create a new vantage point from which readers will be able to spy Clemens' creative processes and chart the currents, reefs, and snags that sped him along one day and held him captive the next. It will not be easy reading; nor will it always be enjoyable. But it will be instructive. The mixture of good and bad, of Clemens' brilliant insight and pedestrian comment, will deepen our understanding of Samuel Clemens and Mark Twain. It might also make us appreciate all the more his flashes of brilliance.

The second approach, and the one that I have chosen, is to treat the *North American Review* text of "Chapters from My Autobiography" as the text of Clemens' life story. There are two reasons for this decision. First, Clemens was involved in the choices for the installments, had final control over the revisions that were made to the texts, and gave his approval for their publication. Because of the depth of his involvement, it is clear that he did work to present the public with the text that he felt stood as his autobiography. Second, the twenty-five chapters compressed into a single volume present a unified tale of Clemens' life. While the chapters do not conform to any "cradle to grave" sequence, Clemens carefully mixed material from both the early written attempts and the 1904 and post-1906 dictations. He did not include all of the experiments, but he did resurrect "Early Years in Florida, Missouri," the Hannibal-based "Ancestors," "Playing 'Bear,'" "Herrings," and "Jim Wolf and the Cats," and portions of the dictations begun in Florence during 1904; he included the compelling images of the Quarles farm, as well as the masterful Hannibal tales of mesmerism and Jim Wolf and the wasps; he included tales of his household and his children and his writing. While a great deal of autobiographical material was not used in the *North American Review* chapters—some because of the subjects covered, some because it had not yet been dictated—these chapters are clearly linked to Clemens' life and his perspective on and reactions to that life.

In Clemens' introductory comments about the process and plan of the autobiography in Chapter I (7 September 1906) he states:

I intend that this autobiography shall become a model for all future autobiographies when it is published, after my death, and I also intend that it shall be read and admired a good many centuries because of its form and method—a form and method whereby the past and the present are constantly brought face to face, resulting in contrasts which newly fire up the interest all along, like the contact of flint with steel. Moreover, this autobiography of mine does not select from my life its showy episodes, but deals mainly in the common experiences which go to make up the life of the average human being, because these episodes are of a sort which he is familiar with in his own life, and in which he sees his own life reflected and set down in print. The usual, conventional autobiographer seems to particularly hunt out those occasions in his career when he came into contact with celebrated persons, whereas his contacts with the uncelebrated were just as interesting to him, and would be to his reader, and were vastly more numerous than his collisions with the famous. (321–22)

The fact that Clemens chose to emphasize his everyday friendships and acquaintances in the chapters prepared for the *North American Review* is extremely important. Clemens believed that the text should develop out of a peculiar chaos, that natural associations should lead the narrative (and the narrator) through various channels; the current of memory and the drift among characters and incidents should be enough to uncover and discover the writer's own feelings and beliefs. But Clemens hedged his bet. He scoured his manuscripts, he looked over the accumulated log of his reflections, and then offered specific highlights for publication. That is why "Chapters from My Autobiography" works as *the* autobiography of Samuel Clemens. While it is a portion of all the autobiographical manuscripts that Clemens composed between 1870 and 1910, it is also that portion ruled by Clemens' editorial decisions, his focus, emphasis, and proportion, his notion of storytelling.

Storytelling is what finally takes hold. Clemens knew his audience; his choices were aimed at satisfying and entertaining that audience. He told his story with readers in mind and with an idea of what incidents and characters should be emphasized: his family, his friends, and, sometimes, his enemies. And himself—in a variety of roles and poses. He offered a well-constructed and ultimately satisfying tale. There are clear connections among many of the chapters and a series of smooth transitions that shepherd the reader through the tale and anticipate coming episodes. During a time when many of Clemens' attempts at extended narrative remain fragmented and incomplete, these chapters stand complete as another—as the last—of Clemens' yarns.[20] This time, it is a yarn that begins with a pledge to honesty and common experience and ends with a deft wink at the reader—"Now, then, that is the tale. Some of it is true" (*NAR* 7 December 1907, 494). That comment more than any other firmly reestablishes Samuel Clemens as both the story's subject and its teller.

AUTOBIOGRAPHICAL EXPERIMENTS

We can best gain an understanding of and an appreciation for Clemens' experiments in autobiography by placing them within the context of his life's work. This is especially important for Clemens because his attempts at composing his autobiography lasted some forty years and were ultimately tied to the variety of pressures he felt in his life and to his search for the creative spark necessary for his writing. Clemens' wealth of experience provided him with a cast of characters for both his fiction and his autobiography; however, his experience not only offered the raw materials for story but also motivated the storytelling. Clemens' training as an observer and as a chronicler of events—first as a typesetter, then as a river pilot, and then as a reporter and author—helped him attract and entrance his audience.

Clemens used personal experiences as the raw material for much of his literary production. His earliest bit of reporting done for the Hannibal *Western Union* in 1851, "A Gallant Fireman" (*Early Tales and Sketches* 1:61–62), is his description of a fire in a neighboring building; a number of his letters during his trip east in 1853 were printed by Orion Clemens in the *Hannibal Journal,* and a number of his letters from the Nevada Territory were likewise published back home.[21] He carried on a particularly personal form of journalism while in Nevada and in San Francisco, using his experience as fodder for more letters and articles.[22] His Hawaiian experience gave him material for letters for the *Sacramento Union* and his first lectures throughout the West and in New York.[23] It was natural that he should use this apprenticeship to move on to become a correspondent for the New York *Tribune* and the San Francisco *Alta California* and then use his letters for them as the skeleton for *The Innocents Abroad.* It was also natural that he should rely on his experience for *Roughing It* and for sections of *The Gilded Age.* Much of this material is prelude to the vintage storytelling that flows through the pages of the Mississippi-based fiction and that has exerted so much influence on the legacy of Clemens' literary persona, Mark Twain—the rough-hewn frontier humorist who, when he turned from journalism to book writing, offered America a common and nuanced definition of childhood and established boundaries for a well-defined, if highly fictional, American (and ultimately human) character.

Clemens used his own experiences as a resource, and no experience was as visible, more useful, or more valuable to him than childhood (at first his own and, later, his son's and daughters'). Clemens' images of a bucolic and pastoral, even at times Edenic, childhood should, however, be separated from the reality of the Mississippi Valley during 1835 to 1860—life along the Mississippi was not as pleasant and affirming as it was often recalled by Clemens.[24] For while Clemens' recollection of childhood was often both muse and balm, there is an unmistakable and powerful undercurrent of danger and violence in the tales tied to his youth. Taken together, the complexity of the Hannibal frontier inspired his fiction, and it unblocked creativity. At times it offered solace and rejuvenation; more often it ignited rather than eased his guilt-stricken conscience.

Sam Clemens' descriptions of childhood adventures were important to the fiction of Mark Twain: childhood pranks and brotherly battles, the atmosphere of the frontier home, the calls to mischief. All are vivid. At first Clemens made use of many of his childhood friends and experiences as the basic material for his fiction: there are obvious connections to Clemens' past in the Mississippi trilogy—*The Adventures of Tom Sawyer, Life on the Mississippi,* and *Adventures of Huckleberry Finn.* He also invokes riverside life in *The Gilded Age, The Prince and the Pauper, A Connecticut Yankee in King Arthur's Court, Tom Sawyer Abroad, Tom Sawyer Detective, Personal Recollections of Joan of Arc,* and *Pudd'nhead Wilson,* and in each of the sections which have come to us as the *Mysterious Stranger* manuscripts (especially in the *Schoolhouse Hill* fragment).[25] So vivid are the scenes prompted by recollection and observation that we easily fall prey to the temptation to identify the Mississippi writings as the texts for Clemens' autobiography. Clemens went out of his way at times to reinforce that assumption: in an 1886 letter he pronounced, "Yes, the truth is, my books are simply autobiographies. I do not know that there is any incident in them which sets itself forth as having occurred in my personal experience which did not occur. If the incidents were dated, they could be strung together in their due order, and the result would be an autobiography" (SLC to Kate Staples, 8 October 1886; *SCH,* 65). He would later recant that claim—not with a specific statement but through his process of composition—when he looked back over the half-a-million words he gathered and began to shape and reshape his past to present those revised pictures to posterity.

An autobiography as a discrete work would not be Clemens' goal, or at least not a conscious goal, until 1906 when he leaned back comfortably and talked his thoughts and memories to his authorized biographer and newly hired stenographer.[26] But the composing and collecting, which would end in 1910, only months before his death, began as early as 1870. Early in this period, Clemens wrote about his past to rehearse for his fiction. This was especially true of his early autobiographical pieces. Perhaps the earliest of these was composed in 1870, one year after *The Innocents Abroad* was published, two years prior to *Roughing It,* and in the same year as his marriage to Olivia Langdon. In "The Tennessee Land" (1870), Clemens began to sharpen his image of the Clemens family's battle with eternally elusive riches, riches always sought but never found, the anticipation of which held the family in a firm and destructive grasp. In this piece he offered a picture of his father, John Marshall Clemens, who purchased some 75,000 acres with the hope of establishing a birthright for his children: "Whatever befalls me, my heirs are secure; I shall not live to see these acres turn to silver and gold, but my children will" (*MTA* 1:3). The elder Clemens died in 1847; the land eventually became an albatross. Clemens returned to the theme of prospective riches quite often in his fiction. It forms part of the plot of *The Adventures of Tom Sawyer*, has a role in *Huckleberry Finn*, and recurs as late as "The Man That Corrupted Hadleyburg." In "The Tennessee Land," we also have a hint of the quintessential optimism that would be the basic characteristic of Clemens' Colonel Beriah Sellers of *The Gilded Age*, which was published in 1873.

The next rehearsal comes in "Early Years in Florida, Missouri" (1877), which is the one autobiographical text most firmly rooted among the Mississippi writings. It comes after "Old Times on the Mississippi" (1874) and *The Adventures of Tom Sawyer* (1876) and before *Life on the Mississippi* (1883) and *Adventures of Huckleberry Finn* (1885). Clemens used this bit of autobiography to set up a contrast between Florida in the 1840s and Hartford in the 1870s. It is linked thematically to "The Tennessee Land" because of the preoccupation with economic concerns: land purchase and ownership tied to the cost and purchase of a variety of goods and services. "Early Years" is also important because it points to the economic conflict inherent in the transformation from a slave economy to a pay-for-service economy. Such economic topics remained important in most of Clemens' works.

Clemens spent roughly twenty-four of his seventy-four years along the river, and a good proportion of those years were spent trying to escape to the East or West. By the time he reached his fiftieth year and after the publication of *Adventures of Huckleberry Finn* in 1885, Clemens' published work also began to move further away from what Henry Nash Smith christened the Hannibal-Mississippi matrix. He did return there from time to time in his fiction, but his work took on a wider focus, less geographically specific, less concerned with the local color of the American South or West. Even *Pudd'nhead Wilson* moves away from the Mississippi matrix: it remains geographically and thematically connected to that matrix in its exploration of slavery and prejudice, but it is also separated from the earlier trilogy by its emphasis on Clemens' exploration of the processes by which external stimuli determine human development.[27] The two later attempts to bring back Tom Sawyer and Huck Finn in *Tom Sawyer Abroad* and *Tom Sawyer Detective* take one more step away from the Mississippi childhood: they resurrect the characters but place them in a balloon-travel adventure and a fairly conventional murder mystery.

Clemens moved further from Hannibal in a number of the post-1885 autobiographical experiments. A few—the Grant Dictations, "The Machine Episode," and "The Private History of a MS That Came to Grief"—focus on incidents related to his life in the East, specifically his business dealings. Others—"Old Lecture Days," "Ralph Keeler," "A Memory of John Hay," "Stevenson, Aldrich, etc.," and "Henry H. Rogers"—are brief reminiscences of well-known and well-liked friends. Still others—"Beauties of the German Language," "A Viennese Procession," "Comment on Tautology and Grammar," "Villa Quarto," and "Notes on 'Innocents Abroad'"—take their cue from contemporary incidents and experiences that were significant to Clemens and are examples of his tendency to be attracted by events at a given time, in a given place.

In spite of the changing focus of his experience or, more properly, because of the many business and personal disappointments of the 1890s, Clemens would not, or could not, divorce himself from his childhood. A significant number of the autobiographical pieces he composed after 1885 grow out of specific childhood experiences. Between 1885 and 1900, for example, Clemens composed at least five major sections of autobiography focused on Hannibal: "Jane Lampton Clemens," "Ancestors" (titled "Early Days" by Paine), "Playing 'Bear,'" "Herrings," and "Jim Wolf and the Cats." Chronologically, each of these follows a family death—Jane Lampton Clemens died in 1890, Susy Clemens in 1896. Clemens would often retreat to his past when he needed to be soothed and protected from the barbs of a hectic and sometimes tragedy-affected life. This suggests the importance of the past as a restorative, as a means of escape, and as a means of rejuvenation.

As we review the times during which Clemens composed autobiography, it becomes clear that the bulk of the material was composed during periods of creative, personal, and emotional stress. The work on "Early Years in Florida, Missouri" was done during a time ripe with thoughts of the Mississippi, and it contributed to the work that focuses on Hannibal and its environs. The Grant Dictations were composed when Clemens was beginning his stint as a publisher and provided a record of his relationship with Grant and the negotiations over Grant's memoirs in the face of rumors that called Clemens' ethics and honesty into question.[28] The work done in Vienna during 1897 and 1898 followed Susy Clemens' death and was part of Clemens' struggle to hold on to his creative energy and to salvage some hope so that he might continue to live and to write.

Written amidst the aftershock of Susy's death, "Ancestors" stands out as one of the most successful of Clemens' autobiographical experiments. Clemens himself must have thought highly of it, since he turned to the manuscript twice for the *North American Review:* sections from it appear in chapters I (7 September 1906) and XIII (1 March 1907). Those two sections present very different material. The first gives an overview of the Clemens family genealogy and offers quick sketches of a handful of ancestors; the second section—and the most important one—takes Clemens back to a childhood that revolves around the sensual atmosphere of his uncle's farm and kitchen. The first section is useful to gain a sense of the characters in Clemens' past; the second is important not as a realistic description of the past but as a deliberate attempt to gain solace and peace from memory, from a link to the joy and ease of a simpler time:

> The life which I led there with my cousins was full of charm, and so is the memory of it yet. I can call back the solemn twilight and mystery of the deep woods, the earthy smells, the faint odors of the wild flowers, the sheen of rain-washed foliage, the rattling clatter of drops when the wind shook the trees, the far-off hammering of woodpeckers and the muffled drumming of wood-pheasants in the remoteness of the forest, the snap-shot glimpses of disturbed wild creatures skurrying through the grass,—*I can call it all back and make it as real as it ever was, and as blessed. . . .* A toot on a tin horn brought twice as many dogs as were needed and in their happiness they raced and scampered about, and knocked small people down, and made no end of unnecessary noise. At the word, they vanished away toward the woods, and we drifted silently after them in the melancholy gloom. But presently the gray dawn stole over the world, the birds piped up, then the sun rose and poured light and comfort all around, everything was fresh and dewy and fragrant, and life was a boon again. After three hours of tramping we arrived back wholesomely tired, overladen with game, very hungry, and just in time for breakfast. (*NAR*, 1 March 1907; 459–63; emphasis added)

To "call it all back and make it as real as it ever was, and as blessed" is a part of the search for hope and reconnection after Susy's death. The final image points toward a refreshed and more hospitable world. The language and care in expression lead to a greater appreciation of the power of selective memory and the emotional calm that can be found in reflective writing.[29]

Clemens' two sustained efforts at dictating autobiography can be linked to that play with a selective memory and the need for calm. Both the dictations begun in Florence in 1904 and the final series of dictations begun in New York in 1906 were taken up amidst the shadows and ghosts of Clemens' past. In Florence, where the family had set up housekeeping to give a gravely ill Livy the benefits of the warm climate, Clemens took to dictating to occupy his time. It was a distraction, a way to wander through both past and present with an eye toward staying interested in the process: staying interested meant concentrating on a topic, dropping it the moment it became tiresome, and taking up any new lead that appeared. And the prospects excited Clemens. On 16 January 1904, he wrote William Dean Howells:

I've struck it! And I will give it away—to you. You will never know how much enjoyment you have lost until you get to dictating your autobiography; then you will realize, with a pang, that you might have been doing it all your life if you had only had the luck to think of it. And you will be astonished (& charmed) to see how like talk it is, & how real it sounds, & how well & compactly & sequentially it constructs itself, & what a dewy & breezy & woodsy freshness it has, & what a darling & worshipful absence of the signs of starch, & flatiron, & labor & fuss & the other artificialities. . . .

I've a good many chapters of Auto—written with a pen from time to time & laid away in envelopes—but I expect that when I come to examine them I shall throw them away & do them over again with my mouth, for I feel sure that my quondam satisfaction in them will vanish & that they will seem poor & artificial & lacking in color. (*SMTHL*, 370–72)

Clemens' dictating sessions produced a mixture of comment on the family's experience in Florence during 1904. Livy's illness remained an offstage presence throughout: the material is haunted by it. Rather than rummage through his past for events in his life, Clemens was much more focused on his present or at least on the family's connection with the villa and its surroundings. The solace and calm here come more from the work than from the images—some of which merely highlight the contrast between the family's 1892 experience and the 1904 death watch.

A death watch also plays a role in the dictations begun in 1906, the final series of dictations. These are as much an attempt to compile a record of a life in decline as they are a procession of the characters that held a prominent role in that life. The inevitable end of both story and storyteller is very much a part of the reflection. This time Clemens launches the project intent on providing material for an authorized biography. The idea of an autobiography arises after the project is begun and is more an afterthought than a part of the project's original design. The point is that Clemens begins the process entranced with the idea of exploring and logging his past and energized by the prospect of getting back into the swing of work. He is most attracted to the possibility of drifting through his past, at times tying up when a particular event or memory strikes his interest, at times floating on to other more appealing subjects, at times focusing more on the present than the past. He tells Albert Bigelow Paine: "The more I think about this [the biography], the more nearly impossible the project seems. The difficulties of it grow upon me all the time. For instance, the idea of blocking out a consecutive series of events which have happened to me, or which I imagine have happened to me—I can see that is impossible for me. The only thing possible for me is to talk about the thing that something suggests at the moment—something in the middle of my life, perhaps, or something that happened only a few months ago" (*MTA* 1:269). Clemens' talk, in fact, reveled in the chaos of associations that provided the current for his journey.

POSES, STORYTELLING, AND TRUTH

Clemens' manuscripts—the early fragments, the *North American Review* chapters, the full range of autobiographical dictations, and the pages he composed in 1909 as a letter to William Dean Howells in what has come down to us as the Ashcroft-Lyon MS[30]—cover a wide array of topics: childhood, career, family, contemporary politics, international incidents, personal affronts, personal and professional clashes, newspaper reports, and descriptions of places and journeys. All of these grow out of his attempt to follow whatever path he uncovered during this tour of the past and the present. His wanderings manage to cast light on his character, a light filtered through Clemens' own lens. Much of that light is flattering, some of it is not. But, as Clemens reassured William Dean Howells, the truth can be found out. It hides between the lines where only the reader can see.

Clemens' autobiographical manuscripts challenge editors and readers because the materials are a product of an active and curious mind. The manuscripts are open to a charge of literary chaos because of the imbalance between spoken thought, excited reaction, careful reflection, and, at times, conscious and unconscious denial and obfuscation. The material has no defined plot, no controlling theme, and no systematically drawn climactic or chronological structure. Instead, all the pieces are held together by two specific strategies. One is the use of the pose, a device that allows Clemens to establish himself as both major and supporting player in his life story. The other is Clemens' belief in the tale's ultimate truthfulness, which is based on his faith that the stories will divulge the writer's character whether or not the writer seriously tries to unburden himself to the reader.

Most discussions of Clemens' use of the pose have been aimed at clarifying characteristics of his fiction or at detailing how poses influence his style. The device can also be tied to the autobiographical manuscripts. John Gerber identified seven poses that appear in Clemens' fiction: the Gentleman, the Sentimentalist, the Instructor, the Moralist, the Sufferer, the Simpleton, and the Tenderfoot.[31] While each of these can be found in the autobiography, it is also possible to add four other primary poses: the Sage (related to the Moralist), the Diarist, the Autobiographer, and the Eulogist. Each of these plays a role in the development of the autobiographical manuscripts as a whole and of "Chapters from My Autobiography" in particular. The Eulogist becomes the most prominent in the *North American Review* chapters. It both sets Clemens' relation with his friends and frames Clemens' exploration of his domestic life, which takes on particular resonance in the published "Chapters" (more on that in the section to follow).

Clemens firmly believed that any interest readers might have in a story depended on how interested or interesting the storyteller was. He also believed that his autobiography would be successful if his audience could relate to and therefore embrace the stories told and the characters described. In the final set of dictations, his ability to interest or impress an audience was related to his longevity: his seventy years lent him the authority of a sage, and that required him to instruct his audience using the lessons he had learned and the philosophy he had acquired. This, then, meant that he needed to adopt a form, or forms, that suggested an intimacy between him and his readers and implied that he was allowing readers access to his personal thoughts even while he, at times, worked to hide those personal thoughts under the camouflage of sage-like truth telling. He could use readers' expectations to seduce them into thinking that they had access to his private thoughts. In reality, neither he nor his readers would face the deeper truths of his life and nature.[32]

As Clemens' ideas about autobiography evolved during the years 1904 to 1909, he was uncharacteristically consistent in his view that the project ought to be a hybrid—he would "make the narrative a combined Diary and Autobiography. In this way you have the vivid thing of the present to make a contrast with memories of like things in the past, and these contrasts have a charm which is all their own" (*MTA* 1:193). He adopted the poses of diarist and autobiographer intentionally, and perhaps primarily, to assure his own continued interest and to give readers a more detailed portrait than was possible from only one perspective. Resurrecting the past was not in itself enough for Clemens, but neither was reporting the present. As a diarist he had an opportunity to comment on people and contemporary events and ideas, as well as to analyze and even criticize his own autobiographical process; as an autobiographer he was able to focus on events, people, and places from his past to highlight his experiences, to trace his career, and to call attention to those people he most cared about (either loved or hated). Clemens was fascinated by the power of association, and he was anxious to see what might come to light when his interest in contemporary events sparked his memories. At one point he would comment, "Dear me, the power of association to snatch mouldy dead memories out of their graves and make them walk!" (*NAR* 16 November 1906, 964).

Neither pose, however, ensured that he would tell the truth about himself and paint an uncompromised self-portrait. He attempted to unleash his thoughts and, by issuing his directives for posthumous publication, to limit the possibility that they might cause embarrassment or litigation. While he would characterize his concern as worry over the potential discomfort others might feel over his statements, Clemens was in reality most worried about his own self-image if he somehow managed to give free rein to conscience-driven anxieties. And he was clear about the difference between the public and private self: "When people do not respect us we are sharply offended," he wrote, "yet deep down in his heart no man much respects himself" (*MTN*, 347). In the preface to the autobiography that he wrote in Florence, Clemens took on the role of a dead man, thinking he might be able to trick himself into telling the truest and frankest version of his life. Try as he might to convince himself that he could achieve the free speech of a dead man while he was still alive, Clemens realized that he was unable to speak with total freedom even "from the grave."[33] He needed yet another role to try to overcome his reluctance.

Linked to the idea of "speaking from the grave" was the image of the lover's freedom when composing a love letter: "the writer gets his limitless freedom of statement and expression from his sense that no stranger is going to see what he is writing" (*MTA* 1:xv). In fact, a large portion of the autobiographical materials—especially that portion Clemens chose for publication—does read like a love letter: the portraits of his friends and family are made more compelling by the fact of their passing and by the heart-felt emotion of his recollection. After all, Clemens composes not merely as a writer of love letters but as a eulogist: he uses the autobiography to draw portraits of those family members who were especially dear to him—Orion and Henry and Jane Clemens; Langdon, Susy, and Livy; and ultimately Jean. The episodes offer a series of contrasting characters arranged so that Clemens' tarnished, at times severely muddied and self-abused, character serves as a foil to the perfection and innocence of his brothers, children, and wife. If individual sketches are sewn together, they form Clemens' heartfelt and guilt-ridden eulogies for his family. As Sage, Autobiographer, and Diarist, Clemens was able to distance himself from an audience; as Eulogist he was able to retreat into his own, in his mind, self-inflicted grief.

Using the various poses allowed Clemens to discount the threat readers might present to his telling the truth. That strategy leads to a concern with the definition of truth as it applies to the disarray of the autobiography, especially for a writer like Clemens who was schooled in a freewheeling journalism that treasured excitement above accuracy, who relied so heavily on the facts of his life for his fiction, and who, as an accomplished lecturer, was quite aware of his audiences—in the case of the dictations, his prospective readers, his biographer, and his stenographer. Albert Bigelow Paine characterized Clemens' dictations as extraordinary performances: "We [Paine and stenographer Josephine Hobby] were watching one of the great literary creators of his time in the very process of his architecture. We constituted about the most select audience in the world, enjoying what was, likely enough, its most remarkable entertainment" (*MTB*, 1267). Paine also observed, "His gift of dramatization had been exercised too long to be discarded now" (*MTB*, 1269). Clemens' performances depended on his audience believing that he was being open and truthful with them.

Paine confronted the enigma soon after Clemens began the final series of autobiographical dictations in 1906:

It was not for several weeks that I began to realize that these marvelous reminiscences bore only an atmospheric relation to history; that they were aspects of biography rather than its veritable narrative; and built largely-sometimes wholly from an imagination that, with age, had dominated memory, creating details, even reversing them, yet with a perfect sincerity of purpose on the part of the narrator to set down the literal and unvarnished truth. . . . Those vividly real personalities that he marched and countermarched before us were the most convincing creatures in the world, the most entertaining, the most excruciatingly humorous, or wicked, or tragic; but, alas, they were not always safe to include in a record that must bear a certain semblance to history. They often disagreed in their performance, and even in their characters, with the documents in the next room, as I learned by and by when those records, disentangled, began to rebuild the structure of those years. (*MTB*, 1268–69)

Of course, Paine's presence as biographer and editor relieved Clemens from the responsibility of presenting accurate, verifiable, unblemished fact. Clemens could even treat the two projects—*his* autobiography and Paine's biography—as antithetical: his autobiography would not be structured, chronological, or troubled by inaccuracy; Paine's biography would be ordered, sequential, and correct (at least correct to a point). Paine would be responsible for "a detailed story of personality and performance, of success and failure" (*MTB*, 1263); Clemens would navigate the "storm of thoughts that is forever blowing in one's head" (*MTA* 1:283).[34] Clemens did not think it important that those thoughts be accurate; he was more concerned with being immersed in the storm.

Clemens, of course, was aware of his tendency to fictionalize the events of his own life, "events which . . . I have imagined have happened to me," and he accepted that tendency. Not only was he less serious about accuracy than conventional autobiographers but also he assumed and, perhaps, even welcomed inaccuracy. He was aware of discrepancies in the tales of his life and was ready with explanations: his own, "When I was younger I could remember anything, whether it happened or not; but I am getting old, and soon I shall remember only the latter"; and his paraphrase of Josh Billings, "It isn't so astonishing, the number of things that I can't remember, as the number of things I can remember that aren't so" (*MTB*, 1269). Paine calls this confession "quaint" (*MTB*, Preface, 1912 edition) and "lovely and whim- sical" (*MTB*, 1269). The terms leave too sweet an aftertaste. Clemens was, at this late date, simply following a life-long practice. It was a hedge against ob- scurity in the afterlife: "I have not professionally dealt in truth. Many when they come to die have spent all the truth that was in them, and enter the next world as paupers. I have saved up enough to make an astonishment there" (*MTN*, 371). Selective perjury was always Clemens' way.

After all, accurate dates and precise times held little interest for Clemens within the context of his life's story—except those of singular importance, such as the dates of Susy's and Livy's deaths. The autobiography was not a product of or a source for historical research. Though Clemens was inter- ested enough in history to develop a game so that his daughters might learn the sequence of the English monarchs (a game he would later market with some success), neatly ordered, static, and impersonal history was alien to his idea of autobiography. Autobiography allowed him to shape and personalize facts to fit his needs—whether those needs included jump-starting his cre- ative processes, restoring some level of hope, or confronting (or denying) his conflicts with conscience. Autobiography for Clemens was mythmaking.[35]

Paine again serves as a chronicler of this process. He noticed that Clem- ens' tendency to disguise the facts eased when Clemens let his guard down after the stenographer had left and they had adjourned to the billiard table:

In the talks which we usually had, when the dictations were ended and Miss Hobby had gone, I gathered much that was of still greater value. Imagination was temporar- ily dispossessed, as it were, and, whether expounding some theory or summarizing some event, he cared little for literary effect, and only for the idea and the moment immediately present.

It was at such times that he allowed me to make those inquiries we had planned in the beginning, and which apparently had little place in the dictations themselves. Sometimes I led him to speak of the genesis of his various books, how he had come to write them, and I think there was not a single case where later I did not find his memory of these matters almost exactly in accord with the letters of the moment, written to Howells or Twichell, or to some member of the family. Such reminiscence was usually followed by some vigorous burst of human philosophy, often too vigorous for print, too human, but as dazzling as a search-light in its revelation. (*MTB*, 1270)

That Clemens' memory during these private talks matched the documents suggests that his tampering with events was a carefully planned and executed strategy for telling his story, not the uncontrolled wanderings of a distracted mind.

Clemens, then, used the trappings of fiction to present himself to his audience both as a character in a sweeping and episodic (even epic) story and as a serious observer of man's intellect and emotions. His storytelling is a link to those early days when the young Sam Clemens was immersed in the storytelling of the slaves on the Quarles farm. Clemens never forgot the nights around the fires in the small kitchens; he never forgot the storytellers and the power they had over him and the other children and each other; he never forgot the response ignited by successful storytelling.[36] He loved the response and the power to incite that response. And he knew that response relied on the story's allusion to a common truth. Not accuracy. Not correctness. But a personal truth of experience and feeling. To Louis Pendleton he wrote: "a man's private thoughts can never be a lie; what he thinks, is to him the truth, always." (*MTL* 2:498). In all, Clemens was able to shape facts because the truth allowed for an array of possibilities, "truth is stranger than fiction, but it is because fiction is obliged to stick to possibilities, truth isn't" (*MTN*, 347); truth was easier to tell, "if you tell the truth you don't have to remember anything" (*MTN*, 240); and truth was available when creativity failed, "when in doubt, tell the truth" (*MTN*, 237). Truth was dynamic, harmonic, and accommodated a range of added and even fictional detail. It had meaning. It was allied to the intention to tell the truth. Clemens' subjectivity allowed him to dance around facts, perhaps even on their graves.

Clemens joined all of these facets together in the autobiographical manuscripts. His is the central consciousness, and he is dedicated to telling the truth, or at least a truth. The main characters, the characters he played, and the characters he met and invented wander around his consciousness as they are buffeted by circumstances. But they are shaped most not by the forces that play on them but by Clemens' attempt to tell the truth and by his choices of tone, style, and organization that grow out of that attempt. William Dean

Howells raised the question of truth in autobiography in a letter to Clemens dated 14 February 1904: "I'd like immensely to read your autobiography. You always bewilder me by your veracity, and I fancy you may tell the truth about yourself. But all of it? The black truth, which we all know of ourselves in our hearts, or only the whity-brown truth of the pericardium, or the nice, whitened truth of the shirtfront? Even you wont [sic] tell the black heart's truth. The man who could do it would be famed to the last day the sun shone on" (*SMTHL*, 373).

Clemens, too, was bothered by this problem. He not only admitted that it was difficult to expose the "black truth" but countered that it was only human to want to suppress it. In 1904 he thought he would be able to conquer the temptation: "Yes, I set up the safeguards, in the first day's dictating—taking this position: that an Autobiography is the truest of all books; for while it inevitably consists mainly of extinctions of the truth, shirkings of the truth, partial revealments of the truth, with hardly an instance of plain straight truth, the remorseless truth is there, between the lines, where the author-cat is raking dust upon it which hides from the disinterested spectator neither it nor its smell (though I didn't use that figure)—the result being that the reader knows the author in spite of his wily diligences" (*SMTHL*, 374).

Clemens also focused on the same question in "A Memory of John Hay," one of the autobiographical pieces composed in Florence during 1904. According to Clemens the problem with truth in autobiography arose during an 1877 conversation with Hay. Hay insisted that truth will always surface if the writer "comes as near to telling the truth about himself as he can" (*MTA* 1:235). The remarks attributed to Hay echo Clemens' response to Howells:

And he *will* tell the truth in spite of himself, for his facts and his fictions will work loyally together for the protection of the reader; each fact and each fiction will be a dab of paint, each will fall in its right place and together they will paint his portrait; not the portrait *he* thinks they are painting, but his real portrait, the inside of him, the soul of his, his character. . . . His truths will be recognizable as truths, his modifications of facts which would tell against him will go for nothing, the reader will see the fact through the film and know his man. There is subtle devilish something or other about autobiographical composition that defeats all the writers attempts to paint his portrait *his* way. (*MTA* 1:235–36)

The echo between these comments and those directed to Howells suggests that Clemens may have once again been using the manuscripts as a rehearsal, as a way to use another character (Hay) as a surrogate spokesman for his own views.

For Clemens, then, the truth of the life story is present in the consistency of the teller's perspective, the consistency of the persona—perhaps character, perhaps image—developed simultaneously with the telling. Truth hides "between the lines," a place the writer cannot touch because his control is limited to words and expressions. It shows itself through the writer's consistent, pervasive, identifiable voice. The writer's urge, even need, to suppress the truth will ultimately be defeated by the reader's ability to decipher inferences. The truth need not and perhaps cannot be explicit. And the reader should expect to have to hunt for truth and be suspicious of any writer who insists that the truth is openly, unflinchingly stated.

Clemens eventually decided that "speaking from the grave" was ineffective against the conscious or unconscious pressure of an audience, immediate or potential, exerted on his storytelling. Soon he was telling Howells that he had failed: "But one day he said that as to veracity it was a failure; he had begun to lie, and that if no man ever yet told the truth about himself it was because no man ever could" (*My Mark Twain*, 93). On 12 September 1908 Clemens wrote to Howells: "I have retired from New York for good. I have retired from labor for good. I have dismissed my stenographer and have entered upon a holiday whose other end is the cemetery" (*MTL* 2:817).

Clemens may have dismissed his stenographer, but he did not retire from the labor. He did not retire from thinking about new ways to tell his story. Writing again to Howells on 17 April 1909, he made a pitch for a new scheme: "My mind's present scheme is a good one; I could not like it better if I had invented it myself. It is this: to write letters to friends *& not send them*" (*SMTHL*, 401). After running through five complaints against the dictating process, Clemens focuses on a primary reason for the change: "the scheme furnishes a definite target for each letter, & you can choose the target that's going to be the most sympathetic for what you are hungering & thirsting to say at that particular moment. *And you can talk with a quite unallowable frankness & freedom, because you are not going to send the letter*" (*SMTHL*, 402; emphasis on the final sentence is mine). Another pose. Another attempt to trick himself. And this too failed. The one attempt—the Ashcroft-Lyon MS—quickly degenerated into a rambling indictment of his secretary and business manager.

Clemens continued to reevaluate his method and to fret over his story and whether he had found or ever would find the right way to tell it. In the end he admitted that even the right way might be wrong. But he would not begin again. Eight months later he ended his forty-year experiment with autobiography by penning "The Death of Jean" and handing it over to Albert Bigelow Paine: "It is the end of my autobiography. I shall never write any more. I can't judge it myself at all. One of you read it aloud to the other, and let me know what you think of it. If it is worthy, perhaps some day it may be published" (*MTB*, 1552).[37] That was his parting chapter, the final word on his long and complete life. There would be no more experiments. Clemens died four months later.

FAMILY, DOMESTICITY, AND AUTOBIOGRAPHY

In "The Turning Point of My Life" in 1910, Clemens wrote, "To me, the most important feature of my life is its literary feature" (*CTSSE* 2:931). It is, however, clear that the "literary feature" would have been vastly different if Clemens had not met and married Olivia Louise Langdon of Elmira, New York. Clemens' "Chapters from My Autobiography" is securely anchored in his relation to his family, to his deep emotional tie to the shared joys of home as well as to plagues of conscience as he recalls the sufferings and deaths in that family. It is shaded by Clemens' sense of guilt, a guilt that influences his interpretation of events as well as colors his contemporary situation as an aging man presiding over the dissolution of his family. While it is not unusual for Clemens to be stirred by feelings of guilt and responsibility, and for him to detail the affects of conscience and shame in his fiction,[38] it is unusual for him to make so public a display of his personal emotional response in a published work that claims so completely to be tied to his private life, the life within the Clemens home. Only "The Death of Jean," which was published posthumously, is a more poignant description of Clemens' sense of personal and emotional loss.

Clemens was always acutely aware of the power of guilt. Pondering the affect of guilt and its effects during childhood nights fresh with images of the hand of Providence, Clemens observed:

Those were awful nights, nights of despair, nights charged with the bitterness of death. After each tragedy I recognized the warning and repented; repented and begged; begged like a coward; begged like a dog; and not in the interest of the poor people who had been extinguished for my sake, but only in my own interest. . . . But in my age, as in my youth, night brings me many a deep remorse. I realize that from the cradle up I have been like the rest of my race—never quite sane in the night. (*NAR* 3 May 1907, 7)

If we keep in mind that Clemens presented these thoughts and reactions to a reading public, a public that by 1906 had cast him as the white-suited sage and national (and even international) celebrity, we can begin to see the autobiography as a project aimed at tuning Clemens' public image. For the careful reader, there is much here that argues a depth to Clemens' personality, a depth enhanced by a look behind the curtain that has separated his personal life from his professional personality. Or, more rightly perhaps, combines the private and public selves into a single unified self.

One of the most important periods for Clemens' growing awareness of the medicinal value of autobiography was during 1897 when the Clemens family was living in Austria attempting to ease their collective misery caused by the 1896 death of Susy.[39] Clemens had already outlived his brother Henry and his mother Jane Lampton Clemens. He had marked Henry's passing earlier in *Life on the Mississippi* (1883)[40] and had written a sketch of his mother soon after her death in October 1890 (incidentally, Livy's mother died one month later in November 1890; also, Theodore Crane, Olivia's and Sam's brother-in-law, died the previous year, July 1889). The Clemens family members' presence—or, rather, their absence—is most palpable in the autobiographical material Sam composed during the family's time in Austria (Orion dies in December 1897). The two bits of autobiography that he created—"Villagers of 1840–43" and "Ancestors"—look back to Hannibal and contend with Clemens' ache with the still fresh loss of Susy.

While both manuscripts are sparked by loss and seasoned with a kind of nostalgia, they are very different in tone and intent. In "Villagers" Clemens accumulates a list of individuals prominent in his memory of the home of his youth and offers sparse and sometimes stinging pocket sketches of a variety of characters. There is no idyllic intent in the collection; instead, it offers an unflinching and at times a scathing look at a community populated by personalities covering the widest spectrum from the able to the asinine. "Villagers" is much more connected to Clemens' fiction writing during the final decades of his life; for example, its characters play a role in "The Chronicle of Young Satan" (another 1897–98 composition) as well as in the later *Mysterious Stranger* manuscripts. "Ancestors," on the other hand, is more a narrative of reminiscence: it is dominated by Clemens' description of his Uncle John Quarles' farm and the intense images of family that focus Clemens' attempt to reconcile himself to Susy's loss: one of the more joyful moments is the account of the food always available (*NAR* 1 March 1907, 452); one of the more haunting is Sam's aloneness when he was left behind after the family packs and leaves Florida for Hannibal:

I remember only one circumstance connected with my life in it. I remember it very well, though I was but two and a half years old at the time. The family packed up everything and started in wagons for Hannibal, on the Mississippi, thirty miles away. Toward night, when they camped and counted the children, one was missing. I was the one. I had been left behind. *Parents ought always to count children before they start.* I was having a good time playing by myself until I found that the doors were fastened and that there was a grisly deep silence brooding over the place. I knew, then, that the family were gone, and that they had forgotten me. I was well frightened, and I made all the noise I could, but no one was near and it did no good. I spent the afternoon in captivity and was not rescued until the gloaming had fallen and the place was alive with ghosts. (*NAR* 1 March 1907, 450–51; emphasis added)

The image of the lost child and of parents who leave without thinking holds value for Clemens as he looks back to Susy's being left at home while her parents begin their world tour. That sense of aloneness is matched by the ghost image of "a cradle—out of service, but waiting, with confidence" (*NAR* 1 March 1907, 456) sitting in the midst of various suggestions of death and loss within hearing a spinning wheel, "a wheel whose rising and falling wait, heard from a distance, was the mournfulest of sounds to me, and made me homesick and low-spirited, and filled my atmosphere with the wonderings spirits of the dead" (*NAR* 1 March 1907, 455).

Mourning and reconciliation are also at the heart of many of the post-1906 dictating sessions: Clemens' self-indictment for his various failings (especially financial) and his imagined culpability for the suffering and even deaths of family members (most notably Henry, Susy, and Langdon) had no limitation. By the time he began the dictations, his loss was compounded with the loss of his wife. Clemens returned to the earlier manuscripts with the hope to spark his memory and generate talk that might help ease his conscience. That assuaging of conscience, that peace allied to domestic calm becomes doubly important in "Chapters" as Clemens struggles with the combined loss of Susy and Livy.

By 1906, when Clemens sat down to dictate his autobiography (or, most often, propped himself up in his ornately carved Venetian bed), he composes a series of tales that focus on Henry, Orion, and Jane Clemens that grow out of his interest in preserving sympathetic, if not pathetic (especially in the case of Orion), portraits of his immediate family. The tales of Henry's unrivaled goodness echo the conflict between Tom and Sid Sawyer. The tale of Henry's death, still emotional and raw after more than forty years, emphasizes Clemens' preternatural sensitivity and prompts him to revisit a dream about Henry's wake, a dream that comes to signify not only Clemens' worried conscience but also his mother's insight into his tendency to embroider when telling about the experience (*NAR* 19 April 1907, 785–93).[41] In his memorial to Orion, Clemens places his brother center stage for several tales in which Clemens points to foibles, eccentricities, and, to be kind, a portion of endearing scatterbrained demonstrations.[42] In the midst of all that, however, Clemens speaks reverently of Orion's sincerity and truthfulness, while at the same time undercutting that reverence with criticisms that may be more telling as evidence of Sam's ambivalence toward his older brother:

> He had another conspicuous characteristic, and it was the father of those which I have just spoken of. This was an intense lust for approval. He was so eager to be approved, so girlishly anxious to be approved by anybody and everybody, without discrimination, that he was commonly ready to forsake his notions, opinions, and convictions, at a moment's notice in order to get the approval of any person who disagreed with them. I wish to be understood as reserving his fundamental principles all the time. He never forsook those to please anybody. Born and raised among slaves and slaveholders, he was yet an abolitionist from his boyhood to his death. He was always truthful; he was always sincere; he was always honest and honorable. But in light matters—matters of small consequence, like religion and politics and such things—he never acquired a conviction that could survive a disapproving remark from a cat. (*NAR* 18 January 1907, 115–16)

Clemens undercuts the respect for his brother: all the compliments are called into question with the introduction of the critical cat. In an example of classic ambivalence, somewhat later Clemens offers a final comment: "He was a most strange creature—but in spite of his eccentricities he was beloved, all his life, in whatever community he lived. And he was also held in high esteem, for at bottom he was a sterling man" (*NAR* 15 February 1907, 343). Perhaps no compliment is as keen as Clemens' descriptions of Orion's veracity when he tried to write, at Sam's suggestion, an autobiography. Orion's truthfulness was so bright that Clemens could not bring himself ever to use the manuscript, which Clemens' eventually titled "An Autobiography of a Damned Fool" and which William Dean Howells found haunting and pathetic. Clemens would use the example of Orion's autobiography to introduce his own discussion of truth (*NAR* 15 February 1907, 343–46). In the end, Clemens creates sympathetic images of Henry and Orion by juxtaposing each brother to Sam's imperfection.

Similarly, Clemens' tales about Jane Clemens are meant to assure his mother's sanctification. Jane Clemens' presence hovers over large sections of the *North American Review* chapters. While several of Clemens' tales are prompted by references to his fiction (Jane is identified as one of the sources for Tom Sawyer's Aunt Polly, just as Henry is identified as the source for Sid Sawyer) or by Clemens' exploration of the likelihood of his being able to tell the truth (that is the connection to the embroidery of the dream of Henry's death), he turns to the sketch he wrote after her death and transports sections of that earlier manuscript into the later dictations. Clemens wrote his memorial "Jane Lampton Clemens" after his mother's death and as a response to Orion's attempt to eulogize their mother. In the sketch, Clemens describes Jane as a "Friend of Satan" (*HHT*, 45) and emphasizes the social setting within which Jane worked her moral lessons. Clemens writes of Jane's compassion toward those in need, especially toward those slaves within and surrounding the Clemens household.

In the *North American Review* Clemens repeats one of the tales of Jane's sympathy for a small slave child, a child who has been removed from his mother. When Sam complains of the noise and commotion that the child Sandy causes, Jane tells her son through tears: "Poor thing, when he sings, it shows that he is not remembering, and that comforts me; but when he is still, I am afraid he is thinking, and I cannot bear it. He will never see his mother again; if he can sing, I must not hinder it, but be thankful for it. If you were older, you would understand me; then that friendless child's noise would made you glad" (*NAR* 1 March 1907, 455).[43] In the original sketch, the anecdote leads to a long discussion of slavery and Hannibal; in "Chapters" the tale moves Clemens to comment, "She lived to reach the neighborhood of ninety years, and was capable with her tongue to the last—especially when a meanness of an injustice roused her spirit" (*NAR* 1 March 1907, 455). That compliment to Jane introduces a long set of memories sparked by the "Ancestors" manuscript; the compassion of Jane is prelude to the paragraphs Clemens wrote while searching for solace after the death of Susy. He has learned the lesson that Jane wished on him, the lesson of how difficult it is to lose a loved one and how necessary is compassion in the face of a broken family.

All of this is part of Clemens' immersion into the domestic sphere, an immersion that is most profoundly felt in his reminiscence of Livy, Susy, and Langdon. When invoking their memories, Clemens surrounds himself with his earlier autobiographical writings: in consort with the 1897 materials, Clemens includes anecdotes suggested by the domestic record Sam and Livy kept during their early life as parents—"A Record of the Small Foolishnesses of Susie and 'Bay' Clemens (Infants)"—and Susy's biography of her father, which she wrote during her thirteenth year (about the time Clemens was publishing Ulysses S. Grant's memoirs and *Adventures of Huckleberry Finn*).[44] The range of supplementary materials Clemens used both complicates the notion that all of the dictated material relied on Clemens' memory or storytelling ability and encourages our appreciation for Clemens' deliberate and careful approach to researching the manuscript record of his life. We also see how much of that record, from Susy's biography to Sam and Livy's day book to Sam's comments that expand on both, highlights the domestic sphere. Clemens emphasized that sphere in "Chapters" by choosing so much of this domestic material for the spine of his collection. If anything, this focus on home and hearth, and the challenges when home is lost and much sought after, is a continuation of the primary themes and motifs that run through a majority of Clemens' most successful major fiction.

When all this material is prepared for the installments in the *North American Review*, it takes Clemens very little time before he moves his story away from more-or-less conventional references to ancestors and references to his writing career and enters the intense recollections of his domestic life. Chapter III begins with his marking his wedding anniversary: "To-morrow will be the thirty-sixth anniversary of our marriage. My wife passed from this life one year and eight months ago, in Florence, Italy, after an unbroken illness of twenty-two months duration" (*NAR* 5 October 1906, 577).[45] That introduction is followed by a long paragraph that seeks to sanctify Livy: "The love which she bestowed upon those whom she loved took the form of worship, and in that form it was returned—returned by relatives, friends, and servants of her household" (*NAR* 5 October 1906, 578). To this assurance of egalitarian honor and affection is added Clemens' account of his personal salvation through Livy's affection: "It was a strange combination which wrought into one individual, so to speak, by marriage—her disposition and character and mine. She poured out her prodigal affections in kisses and caresses, and in a vocabulary of endearments whose profusion was always and astonishment to me. I was born *reserved* as to endearments of speech and caresses, and hers broke upon me as the summer waves break upon Gibraltar" (*NAR* 5 October 1906, 578). Here is set the ultimate contrast and the ultimate conflict: Livy as domestic saint is juxtaposed to Sam, her polar opposite in both outward expression of affection and, ultimately, spiritual depth.

Subsequent domestic tales reinforce this opening image of Livy as the central fixture in the Clemens family. Her temper is contrasted with Sam's. So, too, are her language, her literary sensibility, and her social grace. All are aimed at demonstrating Livy's superiority in the ways of the household and, in the role of mother. And as perfect as she is described, it is really Sam's inferiority, his restiveness, temper, and lack of good moral sense, in short his dinginess in all things family related, that brightens and purifies Livy's standing in the Clemens household. Perhaps nothing raises Livy's reputation in Sam's mind more than her understanding of the moral education of children.

That discussion takes almost the entirety of the eighteenth *North American Review* installment (*NAR* 17 May 1907, 114–22). Both Susy (from her biography) and Sam dwell on Livy's approach to punishment as a tool for moral training. In the end, however, and in what becomes a constant practice for Clemens, Susy's comments related to Livy's punishments and the small controversy stirred when Clemens took the initiative to broadcast Livy's practice to a public audience (by a letter in *The Christian Union*) becomes less a comment on Livy than a way to talk about Susy's special nature and the value of her written observations.

Family, for Samuel Clemens, was a supremely tight structure that held parents and children within its borders. As such, while a good amount of comment in "Chapters" is given over to Livy, the emphasis is on Susy and her biographical study of her father and mother and siblings. More rightly, the emphasis is placed on Clemens' reactions to Susy's comments. A large part of the *North American Review* chapters revolves around Susy's biography: Clemens introduces a section of Susy's manuscript and then cuts away from it to form his own set of recollections and observations. He, in effect, builds his story on the back of Susy's observations. He also makes clear that he is fully dependent on Susy for the direction and the emphases that his own story takes.[46]

As early as the third *North American Review* chapter, Clemens introduced Susy as a primary foil, a foil creatively, morally, and emotionally. At first, he moves through a series of connections that begin with his marriage to Olivia and then move to the family history. That history leads to a long section on Susy's death and the implications that death had for him. "It is one of the mysteries of our nature," he writes, "that a man, all unprepared, can receive a thunder-stroke like that and live" (*NAR* 5 October 1906, 580). The pathos of Susy's death is replayed for the reading public: from her early symptoms to her flaring hallucination of her mother's presence to Susy's final word—"Mamma"—Clemens reopens the wound of his daughter's death and through that process intimates publicly that he was somehow responsible for the depth of his—and perhaps more importantly his daughter's and his wife's woe. It is a very public act of contrition that reinforces (perhaps oddly since both Clara and Jean are still alive when the material is published) the pedestal on which Susy was placed: "On the 23rd, her mother and her sisters saw her laid to rest—she that had been our wonder and our worship" (*NAR* 5 October 1906, 582).

Susy remains the creative focal point for a host of installments and anecdotes; however, the pathetic nature of the opening scenes of early and profoundly affecting death lightens as Clemens builds his memories. There is a good deal of humor in the images that Clemens mines from Susy's biography, and that humor underscores the tight domestic bond that holds the family together—at least in the years that mark the childhood of Susy, Clara, and Jean. Of course, how could that be otherwise since Clemens is purposely restricting the time line by framing the domestic tales by using a thirteen-year-old's version of events. That childlike eye is important as Clemens builds his domestic scene and uses to it not only to tell charming stories of childhood experience (tethered as it is to an adult's reminiscence tinged with remorse and acute sensations of guilt) but also to demonstrate how important that small family band became to his creative work.

One of Clemens' primary goals, it seems, was to call attention to how his writing was both shaped by the sensitivities of his home-grown audience and used to reinforce the familial bond when he composed descriptions and language that he understood all along were too energetic, too strong for a reading public but that would all be part of a great and enthusiastically played domestic game. After Susy's praise of *The Prince and the Pauper*, Clemens begins a description of a family editing session. He writes:

For my own entertainment, and to enjoy the protests of the children, I often abused my editor's [Livy's] innocent confidence. I often interlarded the remarks of studied and felicitously atrocious character purposely to achieve the children's brief delight, and then see the remorseless pencil do its fatal work. I often joined my supplications to the children's for mercy, and strung the argument out and pretended to be in earnest. They were deceived, and so was their mother. It was three against one, and most unfair. But it was very delightful, and I could not resist the temptation. Now and then we gained the victory and there was much rejoicing. Then I privately struck the passage out myself. It had served its purpose. It had furnished three of us with good entertainment, and in being removed from the book by me it was only suffering the fate originally intended for it. (*NAR* 2 November 1906, 837)

The point here is clear: Mark Twain's books (at least those written during the 1870s and 1880s) would not be what they were without their review within the tight domestic sphere of the Clemens household.

While this might not be so direct a conclusion, Clemens was certainly straining to develop a public image of the intersection of his creativity and home life through telling a tale of an innocent time, of a time immersed in the calm and hope that only a firm grip on family life allowed. Clemens, however, irrevocably lost *his* innocence early with the 1872 death of his son Langdon (his loss is reminiscent of Emerson's crisis at the death of his son Waldo; and, in a different way, of Whitman's shock and reaction to the Civil

War). That loss is always in the background of his autobiography. He could bring out his grieving for Susy as a public statement and work with his dead daughter to develop the story of his life; however, Clemens was never able to tell the whole tale of Langdon's death.

In May 1872 the Clemenses returned to Hartford after spending some time in Elmira where Susy was baptized on May 26. Langdon had been ill; he was finally diagnosed with diphtheria. He died on June 2. Sam and Olivia were devastated. Lily Warner wrote to her husband: "Of course everyone thinks what a mercy that he is at rest—but his poor devoted mother is almost heart-broken. It is always so, I believe—those children that are the most delicate & need the most care—that everybody else wants to have die—are the most missed and mourned by their mothers. . . . Mr. Clemens was all tenderness but full of rejoicing for the baby—said he kept thinking it wasn't death for him but the beginning of life" (*MTLs* 5:98). Livy was too weak to travel to Elmira for the burial; Clemens could not leave Livy alone. Langdon was buried after being laid out in the parlor of the Langdon home in Elmira, the same parlor in which the Clemenses were married. Absent parents are ubiquitous throughout Clemens' major fiction. It's not unreasonable to think that that absence was driven by Clemens' sending off his first born to face the grave alone.

As he approached the mid-1870s, Clemens used domestic life as both inspiration and script for a variety of short fiction; however, he was careful to avoid a blunt biographical tie to the trauma of Langdon's death. Instead, Clemens often opted for the small inanities of family life such as scenes of the McWilliams family. Clemens published three of the McWilliams sketches between 1875 and 1882: "Experience of the McWilliamses with Membranous Croup" (1875), "Mrs. McWilliams and the Lightening" (1880), and "The McWilliamses and the Burglar Alarm" (1882). The last piece is replicated in "Chapters from My Autobiography" (*NAR* 19 October 1906, 711–15). The sketches are slight and are best in presenting the off-hand banter between an exasperated husband and his rather high-strung wife. Clemens exploits the conventional roles of husband and wife, mother and father throughout the tales. He does have an ear for the language of the domestic sphere, yet he does nothing that questions stereotypes.

Clemens turned to the theme of absent fathers (or negligent fathers) in his novels during the 1870s and 1880s and especially in those novels written during the period between 1875 and 1895: *The Adventures of Tom Sawyer, Prince and the Pauper, Adventures of Huckleberry Finn, Connecticut Yankee in King Arthur's Court,* and *Pudd'nhead Wilson.* Several of the children in these novels (Huck Finn, Tom Canty, Prince Edward, and, in a most complicated way, Valet de Chambers) all struggle after being abused or abandoned by fathers. Hank Morgan is a bit of an exception because he is the father whose actions result (or have resulted) in the death of his only child: Hank is lured back to England and away from Sandy and Hello Central by plotters who succeed in driving him into a megalomaniacal frenzy that assures the child's death.

Throughout his fiction, Sam Clemens honed the language of loss. One of the earliest expressions, however, is in a letter home recounting the death of his brother Henry. On 18 June 1858 Clemens, still a cub riverboat pilot, held vigil as his younger brother slipped into death. He wrote to Mollie Clemens: "Long before this reaches you, my poor Henry—my darling, my pride, my glory, my *all*, will have finished his blameless career, and the light of my life will have gone out in utter darkness. . . . The horrors of three days have swept over me—they have blasted my youth and left me an old man before my time" (*MTLs* 1:80–81). Like Henry's, Langdon's loss was ever a fresh wound. The loss of a child is omnipresent and never disappears; it is a wound forever raw.[47] One way to understand its importance is to recognize how often Clemens does *not* mention it. Clemens' silence marks the depth of his loss and the anxiety of his own (misplaced) culpability for that loss.

In 1906 Clemens breaks his silence in a most public way:

I was the cause of the child's illness. His mother trusted him to my care and I took him a long drive in an open barouche for an airing. It was a raw, cold morning, but he was well wrapped about with furs and, *in the hands of a careful person*, no harm would have come to him. But I soon dropped into a reverie and forgot all about my charge. The furs fell away and exposed his bare legs. By and by the coachman noticed this, and I arranged the wraps again, but it was too late. The child was almost frozen. I hurried home with him. I was aghast at what I had done, and I feared the consequences. I have always felt shame for that treacherous morning's work and have not allowed myself to think of it when I could help it. I doubt if I had the courage to make confession at that time. I think it most likely that I have never confessed until now. (*NAR* 16 November 1906, 969; emphasis added)

Thirty years earlier, in 1876 Clemens penned "The Facts Concerning the Recent Carnival of Crime in Connecticut" for the Monday Evening Club in Hartford. The tale draws on the conceit that a conscience is a man's "most pitiless enemy" (*CTSSE* 1:643).The narrator is confronted by his diminutive, vile, and mold-covered doppelganger, and their argument drives home the fact that a conscience has nothing invested in a man's moral improvement. "We do it," the conscience says, "simply because it is 'business.' It is our trade. The *purpose* of it *is* to improve the man, but *we* are merely disinterested agents" (*CTSSE* 1:652–53). In the end, the ecstatic narrator is able to kill his conscience: "I tore him to shreds and fragments. I rent the fragments to bits. I cast the bleeding rubbish into the fire, and drew into my nostrils the grateful incense of my burn offering" (*CTSSE* 1:659).

Clemens could not kill his conscience in his autobiography; he was only able to kill his conscience in the virtual world of his fiction. In 1880 Clemens captured the anxiety and trauma of conscience and its result in his description of Huck Finn's silence after the death of Buck Grangerford: "I ain't agoing to tell *all* that happened," Huck writes, "—it would make me sick again if I was to do that. I wished I hadn't ever come ashore that night, to see such things. I ain't ever going to get shut of them—lots of times I dream about them" (*Adventures of Huckleberry Finn*, 153). After the spring of 1872 Clemens' stories are shaded by the death of Langdon. By the time he turns to the public telling of his life, Clemens' autobiography pivots on that unmentionable wound.

Mark Twain's
Own Autobiography

CHAPTER I

Prefatory Note[1] — Mr. Clemens began to write his autobiography many years ago, and he continues to add to it day by day. It was his original intention to permit no publication of his memoirs until after his death; but, after leaving "Pier No. 70," he concluded that a considerable portion might now suitably be given to the public.[2] It is that portion, garnered from the quarter-million of words already written, which will appear in this *Review* during the coming year. No part of the autobiography will be published in book form during the lifetime of the author. — Editor N. A. R.

INTRODUCTION

I INTEND that this autobiography shall become a model for all future autobiographies when it is published, after my death, and I also intend that it shall be read and admired a good many centuries because of its form and method — a form and method whereby the past and the present are constantly brought face to face, resulting in contrasts which newly fire up the interest all along, like contact of flint with steel.[3] Moreover, this autobiography of mine does not select from my life its showy episodes, but deals mainly in the common experiences which go to make up the life of the average human being, because these episodes are of a sort which he is familiar with in his own life, and in which he sees his own life reflected and set down in print. The usual, conventional autobiographer seems to particularly hunt out those occasions in his career when he came into contact with celebrated persons, whereas his contacts with the uncelebrated were just as interesting to him, and would be to his reader, and were vastly more numerous than his collisions with the famous.

Howells[4] was here yesterday afternoon, and I told him the whole scheme

North American Review, vol. 183, no. 598 (September 7, 1906): 321–30.

of this autobiography and its apparently systemless system — only apparently systemless, for it is not really that. It is a deliberate system, and the law of the system is that I shall talk about the matter which for the moment interests me, and cast it aside and talk about something else the moment its interest for me is exhausted. It is a system which follows no charted course and is not going to follow any such course. It is a system which is a complete and purposed jumble — a course which begins nowhere, follows no specified route, and can never reach an end while I am alive, for the reason that, if I should talk to the stenographer two hours a day for a hundred years, I should still never be able to set down a tenth part of the things which have interested me in my lifetime. I told Howells that this autobiography of mine would live a couple of thousand years, without any effort, and would then take a fresh start and live the rest of the time.

He said he believed it would, and asked me if I meant to make a library of it.

I said that that was my design; but that, if I should live long enough, the set of volumes could not be contained merely in a city, it would require a State, and that there would not be any multi-billionaire alive, perhaps, at any time during its existence who would be able to buy a full set, except on the instalment plan.

Howells applauded, and was full of praises and endorsement, which was wise in him and judicious. If he had manifested a different spirit, I would have thrown him out of the window. I like criticism, but it must be my way.

I[5]

Back of the Virginia Clemenses is a dim procession of ancestors stretching back to Noah's time.[6] According to tradition, some of them were pirates and slavers in Elizabeth's time.[7] But this is no discredit to them, for so were Drake and Hawkins[8] and the others. It was a respectable trade, then, and monarchs were partners in it. In my time I have had desires to be a pirate myself. The reader — if he will look deep down in his secret heart, will find — but never mind what he will find there; I am not writing his Autobiography, but mine. Later, according to tradition, one of the procession was Ambassador to Spain in the time of James I, or of Charles I,[9] and married there and sent down a strain of Spanish blood to warm us up. Also, according to tradition, this one or another — Geoffrey Clement, by name — helped to sentence Charles to death.[10]

I have not examined into these traditions myself, partly because I was indolent, and partly because I was so busy polishing up this end of the line and trying to make it showy; but the other Clemenses claim that they have made the examination and that it stood the test. Therefore I have always taken for granted that I did help Charles out of his troubles, by ancestral proxy. My instincts have persuaded me, too. Whenever we have a strong and persistent and ineradicable instinct, we may be sure that it is not original with us, but inherited — inherited from away back, and hardened and perfected by the petrifying influence of time. Now I have been always and unchangingly bitter against Charles, and I am quite certain that this feeling trickled down to me through the veins of my forebears from the heart of that judge; for it is not my disposition to be bitter against people on my own personal account. I am not bitter against Jeffreys.[11] I ought to be, but I am not. It indicates that my ancestors of James II's[12] time were indifferent to him; I do not know why; I never could make it out; but that is what it indicates. And I have always felt friendly toward Satan. Of course that is ancestral; it must be in the blood, for I could not have originated it.[13]

. . . . And so, by the testimony of instinct, backed by the assertions of Clemenses who said they had examined the records, I have always been obliged to believe that Geoffrey Clement the martyr-maker was an ancestor of mine, and to regard him with favor, and in fact pride. This has not had a good effect upon me, for it has made me vain, and that is a fault. It has made me set myself above people who were less fortunate in their ancestry than I, and has moved me to take them down a peg, upon occasion, and say things to them which hurt them before company.

A case of the kind happened in Berlin several years ago. William Walter Phelps was our Minister at the Emperor's Court, then, and one evening he had me to dinner to meet Count S., a cabinet minister.[14] This nobleman was of long and illustrious descent. Of course I wanted to let out the fact that I had some ancestors, too; but I did not want to pull them out of their graves by the ears, and I never could seem to get the chance to work them in in a way that would look sufficiently casual. I suppose Phelps was in the same difficulty. In fact he looked distraught, now and then — just as a person looks who wants to uncover an ancestor purely by accident, and cannot think of a way that will seem accidental enough. But at last, after dinner, he made a try. He took us about his drawing-room, showing us the pictures, and finally stopped before a rude and ancient engraving. It was a picture of the court that tried Charles I. There was a pyramid of judges in Puritan slouch hats, and below them three bare-headed secretaries seated at a table. Mr. Phelps put his finger upon one of the three, and said with exulting indifference —

"An ancestor of mine."

I put my finger on a judge, and retorted with scathing languidness —

"Ancestor of mine. But it is a small matter. I have others."

It was not noble in me to do it. I have always regretted it since. But it landed him. I wonder how he felt? However, it made no difference in our friendship, which shows that he was fine and high, notwithstanding the humbleness of his origin. And it was also creditable in me, too, that I could overlook it. I made no change in my bearing toward him, but always treated him as an equal.

But it was a hard night for me in one way. Mr. Phelps thought I was the guest of honor, and so did Count S.; but I didn't, for there was nothing in my invitation to indicate it. It was just a friendly offhand note, on a card. By the time dinner was announced Phelps was himself in a state of doubt. Something had to be done; and it was not a handy time for explanations. He tried to get me to go out with him, but I held back; then he tried S., and he also declined. There was another guest, but there was no trouble about him. We finally went out in a pile. There was a decorous plunge for seats, and I got the one at Mr. Phelps's left, the Count captured the one facing Phelps, and the other guest had to take the place of honor, since he could not help himself. We returned to the drawing-room in the original disorder. I had new shoes on, and they were tight. At eleven I was privately crying; I couldn't help it, the pain was so cruel. Conversation had been dead for an hour. S. had been due at the bedside of a dying official ever since half past nine. At last we all rose by one blessed impulse and went down to the street door without explanations — in a pile, and no precedence; and so, parted.

The evening had its defects; still, I got my ancestor in, and was satisfied.

Among the Virginian Clemenses were Jere. (already mentioned), and Sherrard. Jere. Clemens[15] had a wide reputation as a good pistol-shot, and once it enabled him to get on the friendly side of some drummers when they wouldn't have paid any attention to mere smooth words and arguments. He was out stumping the State at the time. The drummers were grouped in front of the stand, and had been hired by the opposition to drum while he made his speech. When he was ready to begin, he got out his revolver and laid it before him, and said in his soft, silky way —

"I do not wish to hurt anybody, and shall try not to; but I have got just a bullet apiece for those six drums, and if you should want to play on them, don't stand behind them."

Sherrard Clemens[16] was a Republican Congressman from West Virginia in the war days, and then went out to St. Louis, where the James Clemens[17] branch lived, and still lives, and there he became a warm rebel. This was after the war. At the time that he was a Republican I was a rebel; but by the time he had become a rebel I was become (temporarily) a Republican. The Clemenses have always done the best they could to keep the political balances level, no matter how much it might inconvenience them. I did not know what had become of Sherrard Clemens; but once I introduced Senator Hawley[18] to a Republican mass meeting in New England, and then I got a bitter letter from Sherrard from St. Louis. He said that the Republicans of the North — no, the "mudsills of the North"— had swept away the old aristocracy of the South with fire and sword, and it ill became me, an aristocrat by blood, to train with that kind of swine. Did I forget that I was a Lambton?

That was a reference to my mother's side of the house.[19] As I have already said, she was a Lambton — Lambton with a p, for some of the American Lamptons could not spell very well in early times, and so the name suffered at their hands. She was a native of Kentucky, and married my father in Lexington in 1823, when she was twenty years old and he twenty-four.[20] Neither of them had an overplus of property. She brought him two or three negroes, but nothing else, I think. They removed to the remote and secluded village of Jamestown, in the mountain solitudes of east Tennessee. There their first crop of children was born, but as I was of a later vintage I do not remember anything about it. I was postponed — postponed to Missouri. Missouri was an unknown new State and needed attractions.

I think that my eldest brother, Orion, my sisters Pamela and Margaret, and my brother Benjamin were born in Jamestown. There may have been others, but as to that I am not sure.[21] It was a great lift for that little village to have my parents come there. It was hoped that they would stay, so that it would become a city. It was supposed that they would stay. And so there was a boom; but by and by they went away, and prices went down, and it was many years before Jamestown got another start. I have written about Jamestown in the "Gilded Age,"[22] a book of mine, but it was from hearsay, not from personal knowledge. My father left a fine estate behind him in the region round about Jamestown — 75,000 acres.* When he died in 1847 he had owned it about twenty years.[23] The taxes were almost nothing (five dollars a year for the whole), and he had always paid them regularly and kept his title perfect. He had always said that the land would not

*Correction. 1906: it was above 100,000, it appears.

become valuable in his time, but that it would be a commodious provision for his children some day. It contained coal, copper, iron and timber, and he said that in the course of time railways would pierce to that region, and then the property would be property in fact as well as in name. It also produced a wild grape of a promising sort. He had sent some samples to Nicholas Longworth, of Cincinnati, to get his judgment upon them, and Mr. Longworth had said that they would make as good wine as his Catawbas. The land contained all these riches; and also oil, but my father did not know that, and of course in those early days he would have cared nothing about it if he had known it. The oil was not discovered until about 1895. I wish I owned a couple of acres of the land now. In which case I would not be writing Autobiographies for a living. My father's dying charge was, "Cling to the land and wait; let nothing beguile it away from you." My mother's favorite cousin, James Lampton, who figures in the "Gilded Age" as "Colonel Sellers," always said of that land—and said it with blazing enthusiasm, too,—"There's millions in it—millions!" It is true that he always said that about everything—and was always mistaken, too; but this time he was right; which shows that a man who goes around with a prophecy-gun ought never to get discouraged; if he will keep up his heart and fire at everything he sees, he is bound to hit something by and by.

Many persons regarded "Colonel Sellers" as a fiction, an invention, an extravagant impossibility, and did me the honor to call him a "creation"; but they were mistaken. I merely put him on paper as he was; he was not a person who could be exaggerated. The incidents which looked most extravagant, both in the book and on the stage, were not inventions of mine but were facts of his life; and I was present when they were developed. John T. Raymond's[24] audiences used to come near to dying with laughter over the turnip-eating scene; but, extravagant as the scene was, it was faithful to the facts, in all its absurd details. The thing happened in Lampton's own house, and I was present. In fact I was myself the guest who ate the turnips. In the hands of a great actor that piteous scene would have dimmed any manly spectator's eyes with tears, and racked his ribs apart with laughter at the same time. But Raymond was great in humorous portrayal only. In that he was superb, he was wonderful—in a word, great; in all things else he was a pigmy of the pigmies.

The real Colonel Sellers, as I knew him in James Lampton, was a pathetic and beautiful spirit, a manly man, a straight and honorable man, a man with a big, foolish, unselfish heart in his bosom, a man born to be loved; and he was loved by all his friends, and by his family worshipped.

It is the right word. To them he was but little less than a god. The real Colonel Sellers was never on the stage. Only half of him was there. Raymond could not play the other half of him; it was above his level. That half was made up of qualities of which Raymond was wholly destitute. For Raymond was not a manly man, he was not an honorable man nor an honest one, he was empty and selfish and vulgar and ignorant and silly, and there was a vacancy in him where his heart should have been. There was only one man who could have played the whole of Colonel Sellers, and that was Frank Mayo.*[25]

It is a world of surprises. They fall, too, where one is least expecting them. When I introduced Sellers into the book, Charles Dudley Warner,[26] who was writing the story with me, proposed a change of Sellers's Christian name. Ten years before, in a remote corner of the West, he had come across a man named Eschol Sellers, and he thought that Eschol was just the right and fitting name for our Sellers, since it was odd and quaint and all that. I liked the idea, but I said that that man might turn up and object. But Warner said it couldn't happen; that he was doubtless dead by this time, a man with a name like that couldn't live long; and be he dead or alive we must have the name, it was exactly the right one and we couldn't do without it. So the change was made. Warner's man was a farmer in a cheap and humble way. When the book had been out a week, a college-bred gentleman of courtly manners and ducal upholstery arrived in Hartford in a sultry state of mind and with a libel suit in his eye, and *his* name was Eschol Sellers! He had never heard of the other one, and had never been within a thousand miles of him. This damaged aristocrat's programme was quite definite and businesslike: the American Publishing Company[27] must suppress the edition as far as printed, and change the name in the plates, or stand a suit for $10,000. He carried away the Company's promise and many apologies, and we changed the name back to Colonel Mulberry Sellers, in the plates. Apparently there is nothing that cannot happen. Even the existence of two unrelated men wearing the impossible name of Eschol Sellers is a possible thing.

James Lampton floated, all his days, in a tinted mist of magnificent dreams, and died at last without seeing one of them realized. I saw him last in 1884, when it had been twenty-six years since I ate the basin of raw turnips and washed them down with a bucket of water in his house. He

---

*Raymond was playing "Colonel Sellers" in 1876 and along there. About twenty years later Mayo dramatized "Pudd'nhead Wilson" and played the title rôle delightfully.

was become old and white-headed, but he entered to me in the same old breezy way of his earlier life, and he was all there, yet — not a detail wanting: the happy light in his eye, the abounding hope in his heart, the persuasive tongue, the miracle-breeding imagination — they were all there; and before I could turn around he was polishing up his Aladdin's lamp and flashing the secret riches of the world before me. I said to myself, "I did not overdraw him by a shade, I set him down as he was; and he is the same man to-day. Cable will recognize him." I asked him to excuse me a moment, and ran into the next room, which was Cable's; Cable and I were stumping the Union on a reading tour.[28] I said —

"I am going to leave your door open, so that you can listen. There is a man in there who is interesting."

I went back and asked Lampton what he was doing now. He began to tell me of a "small venture" he had begun in New Mexico through his son; "only a little thing — a mere trifle — partly to amuse my leisure, partly to keep my capital from lying idle, but mainly to develop the boy — develop the boy; fortune's wheel is ever revolving, he may have to work for his living some day — as strange things have happened in this world. But it's only a little thing — a mere trifle, as I said."

And so it was — as he began it. But under his deft hands it grew, and blossomed, and spread — oh, beyond imagination. At the end of half an hour he finished; finished with the remark, uttered in an adorably languid manner:

"Yes, it is but a trifle, as things go nowadays — a bagatelle — but amusing. It passes the time. The boy thinks great things of it, but he is young, you know, and imaginative; lacks the experience which comes of handling large affairs, and which tempers the fancy and perfects the judgment. I suppose there's a couple of millions in it, possibly three, but not more, I think; still, for a boy, you know, just starting in life, it is not bad. I should not want him to make a fortune — let that come later. It could turn his head, at his time of life, and in many ways be a damage to him."

Then he said something about his having left his pocketbook lying on the table in the main drawing-room at home, and about its being after banking hours, now, and —

I stopped him, there, and begged him to honor Cable and me by being our guest at the lecture — with as many friends as might be willing to do us the like honor. He accepted. And he thanked me as a prince might who had granted us a grace. The reason I stopped his speech about the tickets was because I saw that he was going to ask me to furnish them to him and let him pay next day; and I knew that if he made the debt he would pay it if he had to pawn his clothes. After a little further chat he shook hands heartily and affectionately, and took his leave. Cable put his head in at the door, and said—

"That was Colonel Sellers."

CHAPTER II

II

My experiences as an author began early in 1867. I came to New York from San Francisco in the first month of that year and presently Charles H. Webb,[1] whom I had known in San Francisco as a reporter on *The Bulletin*, and afterward editor of *The Californian*, suggested that I publish a volume of sketches. I had but a slender reputation to publish it on, but I was charmed and excited by the suggestion and quite willing to venture it if some industrious person would save me the trouble of gathering the sketches together. I was loath to do it myself, for from the beginning of my sojourn in this world there was a persistent vacancy in me where the industry ought to be. ("Ought to was" is better, perhaps, though the most of the authorities differ as to this.)

Webb said I had some reputation in the Atlantic States, but I knew quite well that it must be of a very attenuated sort. What there was of it rested upon the story of "The Jumping Frog."[2] When Artemus Ward[3] passed through California on a lecturing tour in 1865 or '66, I told him the "Jumping Frog" story, in San Francisco, and he asked me to write it out and send it to his publisher, Carleton, in New York, to be used in padding out a small book which Artemus had prepared for the press and which needed some more stuffing to make it big enough for the price which was to be charged for it.

It reached Carleton in time, but he didn't think much of it, and was not willing to go to the typesetting expense of adding it to the book. He did not put it in the waste-basket, but made Henry Clapp[4] a present of it, and Clapp used it to help out the funeral of his dying literary journal, *The Saturday Press*. "The Jumping Frog" appeared in the last number of that paper,

North American Review, vol. 183, no. 599 (September 21, 1906): 449–60.

was the most joyous feature of the obsequies, and was at once copied in the newspapers of America and England. It certainly had a wide celebrity, and it still had it at the time that I am speaking of — but I was aware that it was only the frog that was celebrated. It wasn't I. I was still an obscurity.

Webb undertook to collate the sketches. He performed this office, then handed the result to me, and I went to Carleton's establishment with it. I approached a clerk and he bent eagerly over the counter to inquire into my needs; but when he found that I had come to sell a book and not to buy one, his temperature fell sixty degrees, and the old-gold intrenchments in the roof of my mouth contracted three-quarters of an inch and my teeth fell out. I meekly asked the privilege of a word with Mr. Carleton, and was coldly informed that he was in his private office. Discouragements and difficulties followed, but after a while I got by the frontier and entered the holy of holies. Ah, now I remember how I managed it! Webb had made an appointment for me with Carleton; otherwise I never should have gotten over that frontier. Carleton rose and said brusquely and aggressively,

"Well, what can I do for you?"

I reminded him that I was there by appointment to offer him my book for publication. He began to swell, and went on swelling and swelling and swelling until he had reached the dimensions of a god of about the second or third degree. Then the fountains of his great deep were broken up, and for two or three minutes I couldn't see him for the rain. It was words, only words, but they fell so densely that they darkened the atmosphere. Finally he made an imposing sweep with his right hand, which comprehended the whole room and said,

"Books — look at those shelves! Every one of them is loaded with books that are waiting for publication. Do I want any more? Excuse me, I don't. Good morning."

Twenty-one years elapsed before I saw Carleton again. I was then sojourning with my family at the Schweitzerhof, in Luzerne. He called on me, shook hands cordially, and said at once, without any preliminaries,

"I am substantially an obscure person, but I have at least one distinction to my credit of such colossal dimensions that it entitles me to immortality — to wit: I refused a book of yours, and for this I stand without competitor as the prize ass of the nineteenth century."

It was a most handsome apology, and I told him so, and said it was a long-delayed revenge but was sweeter to me than any other that could be devised; that during the lapsed twenty-one years I had in fancy taken his life several times every year, and always in new and increasingly cruel and inhuman ways, but that now I was pacified, appeased, happy, even jubilant; and that thenceforth I should hold him my true and valued friend and never kill him again.

I reported my adventure to Webb, and he bravely said that not all the Carletons in the universe should defeat that book; he would publish it himself on a ten per cent. royalty. And so he did. He brought it out in blue and gold, and made a very pretty little book of it. I think he named it "The Celebrated Jumping Frog of Calaveras County, and Other Sketches," price $1.25.[5] He made the plates and printed and bound the book through a job-printing house, and published it through the American News Company.

In June I sailed in the *Quaker City* Excursion.[6] I returned in November, and in Washington found a letter from Elisha Bliss,[7] of the American Publishing Company of Hartford, offering me five per cent. royalty on a book which should recount the adventures of the Excursion. In lieu of the royalty, I was offered the alternative of ten thousand dollars cash upon delivery of the manuscript. I consulted A. D. Richardson[8] and he said "take the royalty." I followed his advice and closed with Bliss. By my contract I was to deliver the manuscript in July of 1868. I wrote the book in San Francisco and delivered the manuscript within contract time. Bliss provided a multitude of illustrations for the book, and then stopped work on it. The contract date for the issue went by, and there was no explanation of this. Time drifted along and still there was no explanation. I was lecturing all over the country; and about thirty times a day, on an average, I was trying to answer this conundrum:

"When is your book coming out?"

I got tired of inventing new answers to that question, and by and by I got horribly tired of the question itself. Whoever asked it became my enemy at once, and I was usually almost eager to make that appear.

As soon as I was free of the lecture-field I hastened to Hartford to make inquiries. Bliss said that the fault was not his; that he wanted to publish the book but the directors of his Company were staid old fossils and were afraid of it. They had examined the book, and the majority of them were of the opinion that there were places in it of a humorous character. Bliss said the house had never published a book that had a suspicion like that attaching to it, and that the directors were afraid that a departure of this kind would seriously injure the house's reputation; that he was tied hand and foot, and was not permitted to carry out his contract. One of the directors, a Mr. Drake[9] — at least he was the remains of what had once been a Mr. Drake — invited me to take a ride with him in his buggy, and I went along. He was a pathetic old relic, and his ways and his talk were also pathetic. He had a delicate purpose in view and it took him some time to hearten himself sufficiently to carry it out, but at last he accomplished it. He explained the house's difficulty and distress, as Bliss had already explained it. Then he frankly threw himself and the house upon my mercy and begged me to take away "The Innocents Abroad" and release the concern from the contract. I said I wouldn't — and so ended the interview and the buggy excursion. Then I warned Bliss that he must get to work or I should make trouble. He acted upon the warning, and set up the book and I read the proofs. Then there was another long wait and no explanation. At last toward the end of July (1869, I think), I lost patience and telegraphed Bliss that if the book was not on sale in twenty-four hours I should bring suit for damages.[10]

That ended the trouble. Half a dozen copies were bound and placed on sale within the required time. Then the canvassing began, and went briskly forward. In nine months the book took the publishing house out of debt, advanced its stock from twenty-five to two hundred, and left seventy thousand dollars profit to the good.[11] It was Bliss that told me this — but if it was true, it was the first time that he had told the truth in sixty-five years. He was born in 1804.

III

. . . This was in 1849.[12] I was fourteen years old, then. We were still living in Hannibal, Missouri, on the banks of the Mississippi, in the new "frame" house built by my father five years before. That is, some of us lived in the new part, the rest in the old part back of it — the "L." In the autumn my sister gave a party, and invited all the marriageable young people of the village. I was too young for this society, and was too bashful to mingle with young ladies, anyway, therefore I was not invited — at least not for the whole evening. Ten minutes of it was to be my whole share. I was to do the part of a bear in a small fairy play. I was to be disguised all over in a close-fitting brown hairy stuff proper for a bear. About half past ten I was told to go to my room and put on this disguise, and be ready in half an hour. I started, but changed my mind; for I wanted to practise a little, and that room was very small. I crossed over to the large unoccupied house on the corner of Main and Hill streets,* unaware that a dozen of the young people were also

*That house still stands.

going there to dress for their parts. I took the little black slave boy, Sandy, with me, and we selected a roomy and empty chamber on the second floor. We entered it talking, and this gave a couple of half-dressed young ladies an opportunity to take refuge behind a screen undiscovered. Their gowns and things were hanging on hooks behind the door, but I did not see them; it was Sandy that shut the door, but all his heart was in the theatricals, and he was as unlikely to notice them as I was myself.

That was a rickety screen, with many holes in it, but as I did not know there were girls behind it, I was not disturbed by that detail. If I had known, I could not have undressed in the flood of cruel moonlight that was pouring in at the curtainless windows; I should have died of shame. Untroubled by apprehensions, I stripped to the skin and began my practice. I was full of ambition; I was determined to make a hit; I was burning to establish a reputation as a bear and get further engagements; so I threw myself into my work with an abandon that promised great things. I capered back and forth from one end of the room to the other on all fours, Sandy applauding with enthusiasm; I walked upright and growled and snapped and snarled; I stood on my head, I flung handsprings, I danced a lubberly dance with my paws bent and my imaginary snout sniffing from side to side; I did everything a bear could do, and many things which no bear could ever do and no bear with any dignity would want to do, anyway; and of course I never suspected that I was making a spectacle of myself to any one but Sandy. At last, standing on my head, I paused in that attitude to take a minute's rest. There was a moment's silence, then Sandy spoke up with excited interest and said—

"Marse Sam, has you ever seen a smoked herring?"

"No. What is that?"

"It's a fish."

"Well, what of it? Anything peculiar about it?"

"Yes, suh, you bet you dey is. *Dey eats 'em guts and all!*"

There was a smothered burst of feminine snickers from behind the screen! All the strength went out of me and I toppled forward like an undermined tower and brought the screen down with my weight, burying the young ladies under it. In their fright they discharged a couple of piercing screams— and possibly others, but I did not wait to count. I snatched my clothes and fled to the dark hall below, Sandy following. I was dressed in half a minute, and out the back way. I swore Sandy to eternal silence, then we went away and hid until the party was over. The ambition was all out of me. I could not have faced that giddy company after my adventure, for there would be two performers there who knew my secret, and would be privately laughing at me all the time. I was searched for but not found, and the bear had to be played by a young gentleman in his civilized clothes. The house was still and everybody asleep when I finally ventured home. I was very heavy-hearted, and full of a sense of disgrace. Pinned to my pillow I found a slip of paper which bore a line that did not lighten my heart, but only made my face burn. It was written in a laboriously disguished hand, and these were its mocking terms:

"You probably couldn't have played *bear,* but you played *bare* very well — oh, very very well!"

We think boys are rude, unsensitive animals, but it is not so in all cases. Each boy has one or two sensitive spots, and if you can find out where they are located you have only to touch them and you can scorch him as with fire. I suffered miserably over that episode. I expected that the facts would be all over the village in the morning, but it was not so. The secret remained confined to the two girls and Sandy and me. That was some appeasement of my pain, but it was far from sufficient — the main trouble remained: I was under four mocking eyes, and it might as well have been a thousand, for I suspected all girls' eyes of being the ones I so dreaded. During several weeks I could not look any young lady in the face; I dropped my eyes in confusion when any one of them smiled upon me and gave me greeting; and I said to myself, "*That is one of them,*" and got quickly away. Of course I was meeting the right girls everywhere, but if they ever let slip any be-traying sign I was not bright enough to catch it. When I left Hannibal four years later, the secret was still a secret; I had never guessed those girls out, and was no longer expecting to do it. Nor wanting to, either.

One of the dearest and prettiest girls in the village at the time of my mis-hap was one whom I will call Mary Wilson, because that was not her name. She was twenty years old; she was dainty and sweet, peach-bloomy and ex-quisite, gracious and lovely in character, and I stood in awe of her, for she seemed to me to be made out of angel-clay and rightfully unapproachable by an unholy ordinary kind of a boy like me. I probably never suspected her. But —

The scene changes. To Calcutta — forty-seven years later. It was in 1896. I arrived there on my lecturing trip.[13] As I entered the hotel a divine vision passed out of it, clothed in the glory of the Indian sunshine — the Mary Wil-son of my long-vanished boyhood! It was a startling thing. Before I could recover from the bewildering shock and speak to her she was gone. I thought maybe I had seen an apparition, but it was not so, she was flesh. She was the granddaughter of the other Mary, the original Mary. That Mary, now a widow, was up-stairs, and presently sent for me. She was old and gray-haired, but she looked young and was very handsome. We sat down and talked. We steeped our thirsty souls in the reviving wine of the past, the beautiful past, the dear and lamented past; we uttered the names that had been silent upon our lips for fifty years, and it was as if they were made of music; with reverent hands we unburied our dead, the mates of our youth, and caressed them with our speech; we searched the dusty chambers of our memories and dragged forth incident after incident, episode after episode, folly after folly, and laughed such good laughs over them, with the tears running down; and finally Mary said suddenly, and without any leading up —

"Tell me! What is the special peculiarity of smoked herrings?"

It seemed a strange question at such a hallowed time as this. And so inconsequential, too. I was a little shocked. And yet I was aware of a stir of some kind away back in the deeps of my memory somewhere. It set me to musing — thinking — searching. Smoked herrings. Smoked herrings. The peculiarity of smo. . . . I glanced up. Her face was grave, but there was a dim and shadowy twinkle in her eye which — All of a sudden I knew! and far away down in the hoary past I heard a remembered voice murmur, "Dey eats 'em guts and all!"

"At — last! I've found one of you, anyway! Who was the other girl?"

But she drew the line there. She wouldn't tell me.

IV

. . . But[14] it was on a bench in Washington Square that I saw the most of Louis Stevenson.[15] It was an outing that lasted an hour or more, and was very pleasant and sociable. I had come with him from his house, where I had been paying my respects to his family. His business in the Square was to absorb the sunshine. He was most scantily furnished with flesh, his clothes seemed to fall into hollows as if there might be nothing inside but the frame for a sculptor's statue. His long face and lank hair and dark complexion and musing and melancholy expression seemed to fit these details justly and harmoniously, and the altogether of it seemed especially planned to gather the rays of your observation and focalize them upon Stevenson's special distinction and commanding feature, his splendid eyes. They burned with a smouldering rich fire under the penthouse of his brows, and they made him beautiful.

I said I thought he was right about the others, but mistaken as to Bret Harte;[16] in substance I said that Harte was good company and a thin but pleasant talker; that he was always bright, but never brilliant; that in this matter he must not be classed with Thomas Bailey Aldrich,[17] nor must any other man, ancient or modern; that Aldrich was always witty, always brilliant, if there was anybody present capable of striking his flint at the right angle; that Aldrich was as sure and prompt and unfailing as the red-hot iron on the blacksmith's anvil — you had only to hit it competently to make it deliver an explosion of sparks. I added —

"Aldrich has never had his peer for prompt and pithy and witty and humorous sayings. None has equalled him, certainly none has surpassed him, in the felicity of phrasing with which he clothed these children of his fancy. Aldrich was always brilliant, he couldn't help it, he is a fire-opal set round with rose diamonds; when he is not speaking, you know that his dainty fancies are twinkling and glimmering around in him; when he speaks the diamonds flash. Yes, he was always brilliant, he will always be brilliant; he will be brilliant in hell — you will see."

Stevenson, smiling a chuckly smile, "I hope not."

"Well, you will, and he will dim even those ruddy fires and look like a transfigured Adonis backed against a pink sunset."

.   .   .   .

There on that bench we struck out a new phrase — one or the other of us, I don't remember which — "submerged renown." Variations were discussed: "submerged fame," "submerged reputation," and so on, and a choice was made; "submerged renown" was elected, I believe. This important matter rose out of an incident which had been happening to Stevenson in Albany. While in a book-shop or book-stall there he had noticed a long rank of small books, cheaply but neatly gotten up, and bearing such titles as "Davis's Selected Speeches," "Davis's Selected Poetry," Davis's this and Davis's that and Davis's the other thing; compilations, every one of them, each with a brief, compact, intelligent and useful introductory chapter by this same Davis, whose first name I have forgotten. Stevenson had begun the matter with this question:

"Can you name the American author whose fame and acceptance stretch widest in the States?"

I thought I could, but it did not seem to me that it would be modest to speak out, in the circumstances. So I diffidently said nothing. Stevenson noticed, and said —

"Save your delicacy for another time — you are not the one. For a shilling you can't name the American author of widest note and popularity in the States. But I can."

Then he went on and told about that Albany incident. He had inquired of the shopman —

"Who is this Davis?"

The answer was —

"An author whose books have to have freight-trains to carry them, not baskets. Apparently you have not heard of him?"

Stevenson said no, this was the first time. The man said —

"Nobody has heard of Davis: you may ask all around and you will see. You never see his name mentioned in print, not even in advertisement; these things are of no use to Davis, not any more than they are to the wind and the sea. You never see one of Davis's books floating on top of the United States, but put on your diving armor and get yourself lowered away down and down and down till you strike the dense region, the sunless region of eternal drudgery and starvation wages — there you'll find them by the million. The man that gets that market, his fortune is made, his bread and butter are safe, for those people will never go back on him. An author may have a reputation which is confined to the surface, and lose it and become pitied, then despised, then forgotten, entirely forgotten — the frequent steps in a surface reputation. A surface reputation, however great, is always mortal, and always killable if you go at it right — with pins and needles, and quiet slow poison, not with the club and tomahawk. But it is a different matter with the submerged reputation — down in the deep water; once a favorite there, always a favorite; once beloved, always beloved; once respected, always respected, honored, and believed in. For, what the reviewer says never finds its way down into those placid deeps; nor the newspaper sneers, nor any breath of the winds of slander blowing above. Down there they never hear of these things. Their idol may be painted clay, up there at the surface, and fade and waste and crumble and blow away, there being much weather there; but down below he is gold and adamant and indestructible."

V

This is from this morning's paper:

MARK TWAIN LETTER SOLD.

Written to Thomas Nast,[18] it Proposed a Joint Tour.

A Mark Twain autograph letter brought $43 yesterday at the auction by the Merwin-Clayton Company of the library and correspondence of the late Thomas

Nast, cartoonist. The letter is nine pages note-paper, is dated Hartford, Nov. 12, 1877, and is addressed to Nast. It reads in part as follows:

HARTFORD, *Nov. 12.*

MY DEAR NAST: I did not think I should ever stand on a platform again until the time was come for me to say I die innocent. But the same old offers keep arriving that have arriven every year, and been every year declined — $500 for Louisville, $500 for St. Louis, $1,000 gold for two nights in Toronto, half gross proceeds for New York, Boston, Brooklyn, &c. I have declined them all just as usual, though sorely tempted as usual.

Now, I do not decline because I mind talking to an audience, but because (1) travelling alone is so heart-breakingly dreary, and (2) shouldering the whole show is such cheer-killing responsibility.

Therefore I now propose to you what you proposed to me in November, 1867 — ten years ago, (when I was unknown,) viz.; That you should stand on the platform and make pictures, and I stand by you and blackguard the audience. I should enormously enjoy meandering around (to big towns — don't want to go to little ones) with you for company.

The letter includes a schedule of cities and the number of appearances planned for each.

This is as it should be. This is worthy of all praise. I say it myself lest other competent persons should forget to do it. It appears that four of my ancient letters were sold at auction, three of them at twenty-seven dollars, twenty-eight dollars, and twenty-nine dollars respectively, and the one above mentioned at forty-three dollars. There is one very gratifying circumstance about this, to wit: that my literature has more than held its own as regards money value through this stretch of thirty-six years. I judge that the forty-three-dollar letter must have gone at about ten cents a word, whereas if I had written it to-day its market rate would be thirty cents — so I have increased in value two or three hundred per cent. I note another gratifying circumstance — that a letter of General Grant's[19] sold at something short of eighteen dollars. I can't rise to General Grant's lofty place in the estimation of this nation, but it is a deep happiness to me to know that when it comes to epistolary literature he can't sit in the front seat along with me.

This reminds me — nine years ago, when we were living in Tedworth Square, London, a report was cabled to the American journals that I was dying. I was not the one. It was another Clemens, a cousin of mine, — Dr. J. Ross Clemens, now of St. Louis — who was due to die but presently escaped, by some chicanery or other characteristic of the tribe of Clemens. The London representatives of the American papers began to flock in, with American cables in their hands, to inquire into my condition. There was nothing the matter with me, and each in his turn was astonished, and disappointed, to find me reading and smoking in my study and worth next to nothing as a text for transatlantic news. One of these men was a gentle and kindly and grave and sympathetic Irishman, who hid his sorrow the best he could, and tried to look glad, and told me that his paper, the *Evening Sun,* had cabled him that it was reported in New York that I was dead. What should he cable in reply? I said—

"Say the report is greatly exaggerated."

He never smiled, but went solemnly away and sent the cable in those words. The remark hit the world pleasantly, and to this day it keeps turning up, now and then, in the newspapers when people have occasion to discount exaggerations.

The next man was also an Irishman. He had his New York cablegram in his hand—from the New York *World*—and he was so evidently trying to get around that cable with invented softnesses and palliations that my curiosity was aroused and I wanted to see what it did really say. So when occasion offered I slipped it out of his hand. It said,

"If Mark Twain dying send five hundred words. If dead send a thousand."

Now that old letter of mine sold yesterday for forty-three dollars. When I am dead it will be worth eighty-six.

CHAPTER III

VI

To-morrow[1] will be the thirty-sixth anniversary of our marriage.[2] My wife passed from this life one year and eight months ago, in Florence, Italy, after an unbroken illness of twenty-two months' duration.[3]

I saw her first in the form of an ivory miniature in her brother Charley's[4] stateroom in the steamer "Quaker City," in the Bay of Smyrna, in the summer of 1867, when she was in her twenty-second year. I saw her in the flesh for the first time in New York in the following December.[5] She was slender and beautiful and girlish — and she was both girl and woman. She remained both girl and woman to the last day of her life. Under a grave and gentle exterior burned inextinguishable fires of sympathy, energy, devotion, enthusiasm, and absolutely limitless affection. She was *always* frail in body, and she lived upon her spirit, whose hopefulness and courage were indestructible. Perfect truth, perfect honesty, perfect candor, were qualities of her character which were born with her. Her judgments of people and things were sure and accurate. Her intuitions almost never deceived her. In her judgments of the characters and acts of both friends and strangers, there was always room for charity, and this charity never failed. I have compared and contrasted her with hundreds of persons, and my conviction remains that hers was the most perfect character I have ever met. And I may add that she was the most winningly dignified person I have ever known. Her character and disposition were of the sort that not only invites worship, but commands it. No servant ever left her service who deserved to remain in it. And, as she could choose with a glance of her eye, the servants she selected did in almost all cases deserve to remain, and they *did* remain. She

North American Review, vol. 183, no. 600 (October 5, 1906): 577–89.

was always cheerful; and she was always able to communicate her cheer-fulness to others. During the nine years that we spent in poverty and debt, she was always able to reason me out of my despairs, and find a bright side to the clouds, and make me see it. In all that time, I never knew her to utter a word of regret concerning our altered circumstances, nor did I ever know her children to do the like. For she had taught them, and they drew their fortitude from her. The love which she bestowed upon those whom she loved took the form of worship, and in that form it was returned — returned by relatives, friends and the servants of her household. It was a strange combination which wrought into one individual, so to speak, by marriage — her disposition and character and mine. She poured out her prodi-gal affections in kisses and caresses, and in a vocabulary of endearments whose profusion was always an astonishment to me. I was born *reserved* as to endearments of speech and caresses, and hers broke upon me as the summer waves break upon Gibraltar. I was reared in that atmosphere of reserve. As I have already said, in another chapter, I never knew a member of my father's family to kiss another member of it except once, and that at a death-bed.[6] And our village was not a kissing community. The kissing and caressing ended with courtship — along with the deadly piano-playing of that day.

She had the heart-free laugh of a girl. It came seldom, but when it broke upon the ear it was as inspiring as music. I heard it for the last time when she had been occupying her sick-bed for more than a year, and I made a written note of it at the time — a note not to be repeated.

To-morrow will be the thirty-sixth anniversary. We were married in her father's house in Elmira, New York, and went next day, by special train, to Buffalo, along with the whole Langdon family, and with the Beechers and the Twichells, who had solemnized the marriage.[7] We were to live in Buffalo, where I was to be one of the editors of the Buffalo "Express,"[8] and a part owner of the paper. I knew nothing about Buffalo, but I had made my household arrangements there through a friend, by letter. I had instructed him to find a boarding-house of as respectable a character as my light sal-ary as editor would command. We were received at about nine o'clock at the station in Buffalo, and were put into several sleighs and driven all over America, as it seemed to me — for, apparently, we turned all the corners in the town and followed all the streets there were — I scolding freely, and char-acterizing that friend of mine in very uncomplimentary words for securing a boarding-house that apparently had no definite locality. But there was a conspiracy — and my bride knew of it, but I was in ignorance. Her father,

Jervis Langdon,[9] had bought and furnished a new house for us in the fashionable street, Delaware Avenue, and had laid in a cook and housemaids, and a brisk and electric young coachman, an Irishman, Patrick McAleer[10] — and we were being driven all over that city in order that one sleighful of those people could have time to go to the house, and see that the gas was lighted all over it, and a hot supper prepared for the crowd. We arrived at last, and when I entered that fairy place my indignation reached high-water mark, and without any reserve I delivered my opinion to that friend of mine for being so stupid as to put us into a boarding-house whose terms would be far out of my reach. Then Mr. Langdon brought forward a very pretty box and opened it, and took from it a deed of the house. So the comedy ended very pleasantly, and we sat down to supper.

The company departed about midnight, and left us alone in our new quarters. Then Ellen, the cook, came in to get orders for the morning's marketing — and neither of us knew whether beefsteak was sold by the barrel or by the yard. We exposed our ignorance, and Ellen was full of Irish delight over it. Patrick McAleer, that brisk young Irishman, came in to get his orders for next day — and that was our first glimpse of him. . . .

Our first child, Langdon Clemens,[11] was born the 7th of November, 1870, and lived twenty-two months. Susy[12] was born the 19th of March, 1872, and passed from life in the Hartford home, the 18th of August, 1896. With her, when the end came, were Jean[13] and Katy Leary,[14] and John and Ellen (the gardener and his wife).[15] Clara[16] and her mother and I arrived in England from around the world on the 31st of July, and took a house in Guildford.[17] A week later, when Susy, Katy and Jean should have been arriving from America, we got a letter instead.

It explained that Susy was slightly ill — nothing of consequence.[18] But we were disquieted, and began to cable for later news. This was Friday. All day no answer — and the ship to leave Southampton next day, at noon. Clara and her mother began packing, to be ready in case the news should be bad. Finally came a cablegram saying, "Wait for cablegram in the morning." This was not satisfactory — not reassuring. I cabled again, asking that the answer be sent to Southampton, for the day was now closing. I waited in the post-office that night till the doors were closed, toward midnight, in the hope that good news might still come, but there was no message. We sat silent at home till one in the morning, waiting — waiting for we knew not what. Then we took the earliest morning train, and when we reached Southampton the message was there. It said the recovery would be long, but certain. This was a great relief to me, but not to my wife. She was frightened. She and Clara went aboard the steamer at once and sailed for America, to nurse Susy. I remained behind to search for a larger house in Guildford.

That was the 15th of August, 1896. Three days later, when my wife and Clara were about half-way across the ocean, I was standing in our dining-room thinking of nothing in particular, when a cablegram was put into my hand. It said, "Susy was peacefully released to-day."

It is one of the mysteries of our nature that a man, all unprepared, can receive a thunder-stroke like that and live. There is but one reasonable explanation of it. The intellect is stunned by the shock, and but gropingly gathers the meaning of the words. The power to realize their full import is mercifully wanting. The mind has a dumb sense of vast loss — that is all. It will take mind and memory months, and possibly years, to gather together the details, and thus learn and know the whole extent of the loss. A man's house burns down. The smoking wreckage represents only a ruined home that was dear through years of use and pleasant associations. By and by, as the days and weeks go on, first he misses this, then that, then the other thing. And, when he casts about for it, he finds that it was in that house. Always it is an *essential* — there was but one of its kind. It cannot be replaced. It was in that house. It is irrevocably lost. He did not realize that it was an essential when he had it; he only discovers it now when he finds himself balked, hampered, by its absence. It will be years before the tale of lost essentials is complete, and not till then can he truly know the magnitude of his disaster.

The 18th of August brought me the awful tidings. The mother and the sister were out there in mid-Atlantic, ignorant of what was happening; flying to meet this incredible calamity. All that could be done to protect them from the full force of the shock was done by relatives and good friends.[19] They went down the Bay and met the ship at night, but did not show themselves until morning, and then only to Clara. When she returned to the stateroom she did not speak, and did not need to. Her mother looked at her and said:

"Susy is dead."

At half past ten o'clock that night, Clara and her mother completed their circuit of the globe, and drew up at Elmira by the same train and in the same car which had borne them and me Westward from it one year, one month, and one week before. And again Susy was there — not waving her welcome in the glare of the lights, as she had waved her farewell to us thirteen months before, but lying white and fair in her coffin, in the house where she was born.

The last thirteen days of Susy's life were spent in our own house in Hartford, the home of her childhood, and always the dearest place in the earth to her. About her she had faithful old friends — her pastor, Mr. Twichell,[20] who had known her from the cradle, and who had come a long journey to be with her; her uncle and aunt, Mr. and Mrs. Theodore Crane;[21] Patrick, the coachman; Katy, who had begun to serve us when Susy was a child of eight years; John and Ellen, who had been with us many years. Also Jean was there.

At the hour when my wife and Clara set sail for America, Susy was in no danger. Three hours later there came a sudden change for the worse. Meningitis set in, and it was immediately apparent that she was death-struck. That was Saturday, the 15th of August.

"That evening she took food for the last time," (Jean's letter to me). The next morning the brain-fever was raging. She walked the floor a little in her pain and delirium, then succumbed to weakness and returned to her bed. Previously she had found hanging in a closet a gown which she had seen her mother wear. She thought it was her mother, dead, and she kissed it, and cried. About noon she became blind (an effect of the disease) and bewailed it to her uncle.

From Jean's letter I take this sentence, which needs no comment:

"About one in the afternoon Susy spoke for the last time."

It was only one word that she said when she spoke that last time, and it told of her longing. She groped with her hands and found Katy, and caressed her face, and said "Mamma."[22]

How gracious it was that, in that forlorn hour of wreck and ruin, with the night of death closing around her, she should have been granted that beautiful illusion — that the latest vision which rested upon the clouded mirror of her mind should have been the vision of her mother, and the latest emotion she should know in life the joy and peace of that dear imagined presence.

About two o'clock she composed herself as if for sleep, and never moved again. She fell into unconsciousness and so remained two days and five hours, until Tuesday evening at seven minutes past seven, when the release came. She was twenty-four years and five months old.

On the 23d, her mother and her sisters saw her laid to rest — she that had been our wonder and our worship.

In one of her own books I find some verses which I will copy here. Apparently, she always put borrowed matter in quotation marks. These verses lack those marks, and therefore I take them to be her own:

Love came at dawn, when all the world was fair,
  When crimson glories' bloom and sun were rife;
Love came at dawn, when hope's wings fanned the air,
  And murmured, "I am life."

Love came at eve, and when the day was done,
  When heart and brain were tired, and slumber pressed;
Love came at eve, shut out the sinking sun,
  And whispered, "I am rest."

The summer seasons of Susy's childhood were spent at Quarry Farm,[23] on the hills east of Elmira, New York; the other seasons of the year at the home in Hartford. Like other children, she was blithe and happy, fond of play; unlike the average of children, she was at times much given to retiring within herself, and trying to search out the hidden meanings of the deep things that make the puzzle and pathos of human existence, and in all the ages have baffled the inquirer and mocked him. As a little child aged seven, she was oppressed and perplexed by the maddening repetition of the stock incidents of our race's fleeting sojourn here, just as the same thing has oppressed and perplexed maturer minds from the beginning of time. A myriad of men are born; they labor and sweat and struggle for bread; they squabble and scold and fight; they scramble for little mean advantages over each other; age creeps upon them; infirmities follow; shames and humiliations bring down their prides and their vanities; those they love are taken from them, and the joy of life is turned to aching grief. The burden of pain, care, misery, grows heavier year by year; at length, ambition is dead, pride is dead; vanity is dead; longing for release is in their place. It comes at last — the only unpoisoned gift earth ever had for them — and they vanish from a world where they were of no consequence; where they achieved nothing; where they were a mistake and a failure and a foolishness; there they have left no sign that they have existed — a world which will lament them a day and forget them forever. Then another myriad takes their place, and copies all they did, and goes along the same profitless road, and vanishes as they vanished — to make room for another, and another, and a million other myriads, to follow the same arid path through the same desert, and accomplish what the first myriad, and all the myriads that came after it, accomplished — nothing!

"Mamma, what is it all for?" asked Susy, preliminarily stating the above details in her own halting language, after long brooding over them alone in the privacy of the nursery.

A year later, she was groping her way alone through another sunless bog, but this time she reached a rest for her feet. For a week, her mother had not been able to go to the nursery, evenings, at the child's prayer hour. She spoke of it — was sorry for it, and said she would come to-night, and hoped she could continue to come every night and hear Susy pray, as before. Noticing that the child wished to respond, but was evidently troubled as to how to word her answer, she asked what the difficulty was. Susy explained that Miss Foote (the governess)[24] had been teaching her about the Indians and their religious beliefs, whereby it appeared that they had not only a God, but several. This had set Susy to thinking. As a result of this thinking, she had stopped praying. She qualified this statement — that is, she modified it — saying she did not now pray "in the same way" as she had formerly done. Her mother said:

"Tell me about it, dear."

"Well, mamma, the Indians believed they knew, but now we know they were wrong. By and by, it can turn out that we are wrong. So now I only pray that there may be a God and a Heaven — or something better."

I wrote down this pathetic prayer in its precise wording, at the time, in a record which we kept of the children's sayings, and my reverence for it has grown with the years that have passed over my head since then.[25] Its untaught grace and simplicity are a child's, but the wisdom and the pathos of it are of all the ages that have come and gone since the race of man has lived, and longed, and hoped, and feared, and doubted.

To go back a year — Susy aged seven. Several times her mother said to her: "There, there, Susy, you mustn't cry over little things."

This furnished Susy a text for thought. She had been breaking her heart over what had seemed vast disasters — a broken toy; a picnic cancelled by thunder and lightning and rain; the mouse that was growing tame and friendly in the nursery caught and killed by the cat — and now came this strange revelation. For some unaccountable reason, these were not vast calamities. Why? How is the size of calamities measured? What is the rule? There must be some way to tell the great ones from the small ones; what is the law of these proportions? She examined the problem earnestly and long. She gave it her best thought from time to time, for two or three days — but it baffled her — defeated her. And at last she gave up and went to her mother for help.

"Mamma, what is 'little things'?"

It seemed a simple question — at first. And yet, before the answer could be put into words, unsuspected and unforeseen difficulties began to appear. They increased; they multiplied; they brought about another defeat. The effort to explain came to a standstill. Then Susy tried to help her mother out — with an instance, an example, an illustration. The mother was getting ready to go down-town, and one of her errands was to buy a long-promised toy-watch for Susy.

"If you forgot the watch, mamma, would that be a little thing?"

She was not concerned about the watch, for she knew it would not be forgotten. What she was hoping for was that the answer would unriddle the riddle, and bring rest and peace to her perplexed little mind.

The hope was disappointed, of course — for the reason that the size of a misfortune is not determinable by an outsider's measurement of it, but only by the measurements applied to it by the person specially affected by it. The king's lost crown is a vast matter to the king, but of no consequence to the child. The lost toy is a great matter to the child, but in the king's eyes it is not a thing to break the heart about. A verdict was reached, but it was based upon the above model, and Susy was granted leave to measure her disasters thereafter with her own tape-line.

As a child,[26] Susy had a passionate temper; and it cost her much remorse and many tears before she learned to govern it, but after that it was a wholesome salt, and her character was the stronger and healthier for its presence. It enabled her to be good with dignity; it preserved her not only from being good for vanity's sake, but from even the appearance of it. In looking back over the long vanished years, it seems but natural and excusable that I should dwell with longing affection and preference upon incidents of her young life which made it beautiful to us, and that I should let its few small offences go unsummoned and unreproached.

In the summer of 1880, when Susy was just eight years of age, the family were at Quarry Farm, as usual at that season of the year. Hay-cutting time was approaching, and Susy and Clara were counting the hours, for the time was big with a great event for them; they had been promised that they might mount the wagon and ride home from the fields on the summit of the hay mountain. This perilous privilege, so dear to their age and species, had never been granted them before. Their excitement had no bounds. They could talk of nothing but this epoch-making adventure, now. But misfortune overtook Susy on the very morning of the important day. In a sudden outbreak of passion, she corrected Clara — with a shovel, or stick, or something of the sort. At any rate, the offence committed was of a gravity clearly beyond the limit allowed in the nursery. In accordance with the rule and custom of the house, Susy went to her mother to confess, and to help decide upon the size and character of the punishment due. It was quite understood that, as a punishment could have but one rational object and function — to act as a reminder, and warn the transgressor against transgressing in the same way again — the children would know about as well as any how to choose a penalty which would be rememberable and effective. Susy and her mother discussed various punishments, but none of them seemed adequate. This fault was an unusually serious one, and required the setting up of a danger-signal in the memory that would not blow out nor burn out, but remain a fixture there and furnish its saving warning indefinitely. Among the punishments mentioned was deprivation of the hay-wagon ride. It was noticeable that this one hit Susy hard. Finally, in the summing up, the mother named over the list and asked:

"Which one do you think it ought to be, Susy?"

Susy studied, shrank from her duty, and asked:

"Which do you think, mamma?"

"Well, Susy, I would rather leave it to you. *You* make the choice yourself."

It cost Susy a struggle, and much and deep thinking and weighing — but she came out where any one who knew her could have foretold she would.

"Well, mamma, I'll make it the hay-wagon, because you know the other things might not make me remember not to do it again, but if I don't get to ride on the hay-wagon I can remember it easily."

In this world the real penalty, the sharp one, the lasting one, never falls otherwise than on the wrong person. It was not *I* that corrected Clara, but the remembrance of poor Susy's lost hay-ride still brings *me* a pang — after twenty-six years.

Apparently, Susy was born with humane feelings for the animals, and compassion for their troubles. This enabled her to see a new point in an old story, once, when she was only six years old — a point which had been overlooked by older, and perhaps duller, people for many ages. Her mother told her the moving story of the sale of Joseph by his brethren, the staining of his coat with the blood of the slaughtered kid, and the rest of it.[27] She dwelt upon the inhumanity of the brothers; their cruelty toward their helpless young brother; and the unbrotherly treachery which they practised upon him; for she hoped to teach the child a lesson in gentle pity and mercifulness which she would remember. Apparently, her desire was accomplished, for the tears came into Susy's eyes and she was deeply moved. Then she said:

"Poor little kid!"

A child's frank envy of the privileges and distinctions of its elders is often a delicately flattering attention and the reverse of unwelcome, but sometimes the envy is not placed where the beneficiary is expecting it to be placed.

Once, when Susy was seven, she sat breathlessly absorbed in watching a guest of ours adorn herself for a ball. The lady was charmed by this homage; this mute and gentle admiration; and was happy in it. And when her pretty labors were finished, and she stood at last perfect, unimprovable, clothed like Solomon[28] in all his glory, she paused, confident and expectant, to receive from Susy's tongue the tribute that was burning in her eyes. Susy drew an envious little sigh and said:

"I wish *I* could have crooked teeth and spectacles!"

Once, when Susy was six months along in her eighth year, she did something one day in the presence of company, which subjected her to criticism and reproof. Afterward, when she was alone with her mother, as was her custom she reflected a little while over the matter. Then she set up what I think — and what the shade of Burns would think — was a quite good philosophical defence.

"Well, mamma, you know I didn't see myself, and so I couldn't know how it looked."

In homes where the near friends and visitors are mainly literary people — lawyers, judges, professors and clergymen — the children's ears become early familiarized with wide vocabularies. It is natural for them to pick up any words that fall in their way; it is natural for them to pick up big and little ones indiscriminately; it is natural for them to use without fear any word that comes to their net, no matter how formidable it may be as to size. As a result, their talk is a curious and funny musketry clatter of little words, interrupted at intervals by the heavy artillery crash of a word of such imposing sound and size that it seems to shake the ground and rattle the windows. Sometimes the child gets a wrong idea of a word which it has picked up by chance, and attaches to it a meaning which impairs its usefulness — but this does not happen as often as one might expect it would. Indeed, it happens with an infrequency which may be regarded as remarkable. As a child, Susy had good fortune with her large words, and she employed many of them. She made no more than her fair share of mistakes. Once when she thought something very funny was going to happen (but it didn't), she was racked and torn with laughter, by anticipation. But, apparently, she still felt sure of her position, for she said, "If it had happened, I should have been transformed [transported] with glee."

And earlier, when she was a little maid of five years, she informed a visitor that she had been in a church only once, and that was the time when Clara was "crucified" [christened]. . . .

In Heidelberg, when Susy was six, she noticed that the Schloss gardens were populous with snails creeping all about everywhere. One day she found a new dish on her table and inquired concerning it, and learned that it was made of snails. She was awed and impressed, and said:

"Wild ones, mamma?"

She was thoughtful and considerate of others—an acquired quality, no doubt. No one seems to be born with it. One hot day, at home in Hartford, when she was a little child, her mother borrowed her fan several times (a Japanese one, value five cents), refreshed herself with it a moment or two, then handed it back with a word of thanks. Susy knew her mother would use the fan all the time if she could do it without putting a deprivation upon its owner. She also knew that her mother could not be persuaded to do that. A relief must be devised somehow; Susy devised it. She got five cents out of her money-box and carried it to Patrick, and asked him to take it down-town (a mile and a half) and buy a Japanese fan and bring it home. He did it—and thus thoughtfully and delicately was the exigency met and the mother's comfort secured. It is to the child's credit that she did not save herself expense by bringing down another and more costly kind of fan from up-stairs, but was content to act upon the impression that her mother desired the Japanese kind—content to accomplish the desire and stop with that, without troubling about the wisdom or unwisdom of it.

Sometimes, while she was still a child, her speech fell into quaint and strikingly expressive forms. Once—aged nine or ten—she came to her mother's room, when her sister Jean was a baby, and said Jean was crying in the nursery, and asked if she might ring for the nurse. Her mother asked:

"Is she crying hard?"—meaning cross, ugly.

"Well, no, mamma. It is a weary, lonesome cry."

It is a pleasure to me to recall various incidents which reveal the delicacies of feeling that were so considerable a part of her budding character. Such a revelation came once in a way which, while creditable to her heart, was defective in another direction. She was in her eleventh year then. Her mother had been making the Christmas purchases, and she allowed Susy to see the presents which were for Patrick's children. Among these was a handsome sled for Jimmy, on which a stag was painted; also, in gilt capitals, the word "Deer." Susy was excited and joyous over everything, until she came to this sled. Then she became sober and silent—yet the sled was the choicest of all the gifts. Her mother was surprised, and also disappointed, and said:

"Why, Susy, doesn't it please you? Isn't it fine?"

Susy hesitated, and it was plain that she did not want to say the thing that was in her mind. However, being urged, she brought it haltingly out:

"Well, mamma, it *is* fine, and of course it *did* cost a good deal — but — but — why should that be mentioned?"

Seeing that she was not understood, she reluctantly pointed to that word "Deer." It was her orthography that was at fault, not her heart. She had inherited both from her mother.

CHAPTER IV

WHEN Susy was thirteen,[1] and was a slender little maid with plaited tails of copper-tinged brown hair down her back, and was perhaps the busiest bee in the household hive, by reason of the manifold studies, health exercises and recreations she had to attend to, she secretly, and of her own motion, and out of love, added another task to her labors — the writing of a biography of me. She did this work in her bedroom at night, and kept her record hidden. After a little, the mother discovered it and filched it, and let me see it; then told Susy what she had done, and how pleased I was, and how proud. I remember that time with a deep pleasure. I had had compliments before, but none that touched me like this; none that could approach it for value in my eyes. It has kept that place always since. I have had no compliment, no praise, no tribute from any source, that was so precious to me as this one was and still is. As I read it *now*, after all these many years, it is still a king's message to me, and brings me the same dear surprise it brought me then — with the pathos added, of the thought that the eager and hasty hand that sketched it and scrawled it will not touch mine again — and I feel as the humble and unexpectant must feel when their eyes fall upon the edict that raises them to the ranks of the noble.

Yesterday while I was rummaging in a pile of ancient notebooks of mine which I had not seen for years, I came across a reference to that biography. It is quite evident that several times, at breakfast and dinner, in those long-past days, I was posing for the biography. In fact, I clearly remember that I *was* doing that — and I also remember that Susy detected it. I remember saying a very smart thing, with a good deal of an air, at the breakfast-table

North American Review, vol. 183, no. 601 (October 19, 1906): 705–16.

one morning, and that Susy observed to her mother privately, a little later, that papa was doing that for the biography.

I cannot bring myself to change any line or word in Susy's sketch of me, but will introduce passages from it now and then just as they came in their quaint simplicity out of her honest heart, which was the beautiful heart of a child. What comes from that source has a charm and grace of its own which may transgress all the recognized laws of literature, if it choose, and yet be literature still, and worthy of hospitality. I shall print the whole of this little biography, before I have done with it — every word, every sentence.

The spelling is frequently desperate, but it was Susy's, and it shall stand. I love it, and cannot profane it. To me, it is gold. To correct it would alloy it, not refine it. It would spoil it. It would take from it its freedom and flexibility and make it stiff and formal. Even when it is most extravagant I am not shocked. It is Susy's spelling, and she was doing the best she could — and nothing could better it for me. . . .

Susy began the biography in 1885, when I was in the fiftieth year of my age, and she just entering the fourteenth of hers. She begins in this way:

We are a very happy family. We consist of Papa, Mamma, Jean, Clara and me. It is papa I am writing about, and I shall have no trouble in not knowing what to say about him, as he is a very striking character.

But wait a minute — I will return to Susy presently.

In the matter of slavish imitation, man is the monkey's superior all the time. The average man is destitute of independence of opinion. He is not interested in contriving an opinion of his own, by study and reflection, but is only anxious to find out what his neighbor's opinion is and slavishly adopt it.[2] A generation ago, I found out that the latest review of a book was pretty sure to be just a reflection of the *earliest* review of it; that whatever the first reviewer found to praise or censure in the book would be repeated in the latest reviewer's report, with nothing fresh added. Therefore more than once I took the precaution of sending my book, in manuscript, to Mr. Howells, when he was editor of the "Atlantic Monthly," so that he could prepare a review of it at leisure. I knew he would say the truth about the book — I also knew that he would find more merit than demerit in it, because I already knew that that was the condition of the book. I allowed no copy of it to go out to the press until after Mr. Howells's notice of it had appeared. That book was always safe. There wasn't a man behind a pen in all America that had the courage to find anything in the book which Mr. Howells had not found — there wasn't a man behind a pen in America that had spirit enough to say a brave and original thing about the book on his own responsibility.

I believe that the trade of critic, in literature, music, and the drama, is the most degraded of all trades, and that it has no real value—certainly no large value. When Charles Dudley Warner and I were about to bring out "The Gilded Age," the editor of the "Daily Graphic" persuaded me to let him have an advance copy, he giving me his word of honor that no notice of it would appear in his paper until after the "Atlantic Monthly" notice should have appeared. This reptile published a review of the book within three days afterward. I could not really complain, because he had only given me his word of honor as security; I ought to have required of him something substantial. I believe his notice did not deal mainly with the merit of the book, or the lack of it, but with my moral attitude toward the public. It was charged that I had used my reputation to play a swindle upon the public; that Mr. Warner had written as much as half of the book, and that I had used my name to float it and give it currency; a currency—so the critic averred—which it could not have acquired without my name, and that this conduct of mine was a grave fraud upon the people.[3] The "Graphic" was not an authority upon any subject whatever. It had a sort of distinction, in that it was the first and only illustrated daily newspaper that the world had seen; but it was without character; it was poorly and cheaply edited; its opinion of a book or of any other work of art was of no consequence. Everybody knew this, yet all the critics in America, one after the other, copied the "Graphic's" criticism, merely changing the phraseology, and left me under that charge of dishonest conduct. Even the great Chicago "Tribune," the most important journal in the Middle West, was not able to invent anything fresh, but adopted the view of the humble "Daily Graphic," dishonesty-charge and all.

However, let it go. It is the will of God that we must have critics, and missionaries, and Congressmen, and humorists, and we must bear the burden. Meantime, I seem to have been drifting into criticism myself. But that is nothing. At the worst, criticism is nothing more than a crime, and I am not unused to that.

What I have been travelling toward all this time is this: the first critic that ever had occasion to describe my personal appearance littered his description with foolish and inexcusable errors whose aggregate furnished the result that I was distinctly and distressingly unhandsome. That description floated around the country in the papers, and was in constant use and wear for a quarter of a century. It seems strange to me that apparently no critic in the country could be found who could look at me and have the courage to take up his pen and destroy that lie. That lie began its course on the Pacific coast, in 1864, and it likened me in personal appearance to Petroleum V. Nasby,[4] who had been out there lecturing. For twenty-five years afterward, no critic could furnish a description of me without fetching in Nasby to help out my portrait. I knew Nasby well, and he was a good fellow, but in my life I have not felt malignant enough about any more than three persons to charge those persons with resembling Nasby. It hurts me to the heart. I was always handsome. Anybody but a critic could have seen it. And it had long been a distress to my family — including Susy — that the critics should go on making this wearisome mistake, year after year, when there was no foundation for it. Even when a critic wanted to be particularly friendly and complimentary to me, he didn't dare to go beyond my clothes. He never ventured beyond that old safe frontier. When he had finished with my clothes he had said all the kind things, the pleasant things, the complimentary things he could risk. Then he dropped back on Nasby.

Yesterday I found this clipping in the pocket of one of those ancient memorandum-books of mine. It is of the date of thirty-nine years ago, and both the paper and the ink are yellow with the bitterness that I felt in that old day when I clipped it out to preserve it and brood over it, and grieve about it. I will copy it here, to wit:

A correspondent of the Philadelphia "Press," writing of one of Schuyler Colfax's receptions, says of our Washington correspondent: "Mark Twain, the delicate humorist, was present; quite a lion, as he deserves to be. Mark is a bachelor, faultless in taste, whose snowy vest is suggestive of endless quarrels with Washington washerwomen; but the heroism of Mark is settled for all time, for such purity and smoothness were never seen before. His lavender gloves might have been stolen from some Turkish harem, so delicate were they in size; but more likely — anything else were more likely than that. In form and feature he bears some resemblance to the immortal Nasby; but whilst Petroleum is brunette to the core, Twain is golden, amber-hued, melting, blonde."

Let us return to Susy's biography now, and get the opinion of one who is unbiassed:

From Susy's Biography

Papa's appearance has been described many times, but very incorrectly. He has beautiful gray hair, not any too thick or any too long, but just right; a Roman nose, which greatly improves the beauty of his features; kind blue eyes and a small mustache. He has a wonderfully shaped head and profile. He has a very good figure — in short, he is an extrodinarily fine looking man. All his features are perfect, except that he hasn't extrodinary teeth. His complexion is very fair, and he doesn't ware a beard. He is a very good man and a very funny one. He *has* got a temper, but we all of us have in this family. He is the loveliest man I ever saw or ever hope to see — and oh, so absent-minded. He does tell perfectly delightful stories. Clara and I used to sit on each arm of his chair and listen while he told us stories about the pictures on the wall.

I remember the story-telling days vividly. They were a difficult and exacting audience — those little creatures.

Along one side of the library, in the Hartford home, the bookshelves joined the mantelpiece — in fact there were shelves on both sides of the mantelpiece.[5] On these shelves, and on the mantelpiece, stood various ornaments. At one end of the procession was a framed oil-painting of a cat's head, at the other end was a head of a beautiful young girl, life-size — called Emmeline, because she looked just about like that — an impressionist water-color. Between the one picture and the other there were twelve or fifteen of the bric-à-brac things already mentioned; also an oil-painting by Elihu Vedder,[6] "The Young Medusa." Every now and then the children required me to construct a romance — always impromptu — not a moment's preparation permitted — and into that romance I had to get all that bric-à-brac and the three pictures. I had to start always with the cat and finish with Emmeline. I was never allowed the refreshment of a change, end-for-end. It was not permissible to introduce a bric-à-brac ornament into the story out of its place in the procession.

These bric-à-bracs were never allowed a peaceful day, a reposeful day, a restful Sabbath. In their lives there was no Sabbath, in their lives there was no peace; they knew no existence but a monotonous career of violence and bloodshed. In the course of time, the bric-à-brac and the pictures showed wear. It was because they had had so many and such tumultuous adventures in their romantic careers.

As romancer to the children I had a hard time, even from the beginning. If they brought me a picture, in a magazine, and required me to build a story to it, they would cover the rest of the page with their pudgy hands to keep me from stealing an idea from it. The stories had to come hot from the bat, always. They had to be absolutely original and fresh. Sometimes the children furnished me simply a character or two, or a dozen, and required me to start out at once on that slim basis and deliver those characters up to a vigorous and entertaining life of crime. If they heard of a new trade, or an unfamiliar animal, or anything like that, I was pretty sure to have to deal with those things in the next romance. Once Clara required me to build a sudden tale out of a plumber and a "bawgunstrictor," and I had to do it. She didn't know what a boa-constrictor was, until he developed in the tale—then she was better satisfied with it than ever.

From Susy's Biography

Papa's favorite game is billiards, and when he is tired and wishes to rest himself he stays up all night and plays billiards, it seems to rest his head. He smokes a great deal almost incessantly. He has the mind of an author exactly, some of the simplest things he cant understand. Our burglar-alarm is often out of order, and papa had been obliged to take the mahogany-room off from the alarm altogether for a time, because the burglar-alarm had been in the habit of ringing even when the mahogany-room was closed. At length he thought that perhaps the burglar-alarm might be in order, and he decided to try and see; accordingly he put it on and then went down and opened the window; consequently the alarm bell rang, it would even if the alarm had been in order. Papa went despairingly upstairs and said to mamma, "Livy the mahogany-room won't go on. I have just opened the window to see."

"Why, Youth," mamma replied, "if you've opened the window, why of course the alarm will ring!"

"That's what I've opened it for, why I just went down to see if it would ring!"

Mamma tried to explain to papa that when he wanted to go and see whether the alarm would ring while the window was closed he *mustn't* go and open the window—but in vain, papa couldn't understand, and got very impatient with mamma for trying to make him believe an impossible thing true.

This is a frank biographer, and an honest one; she uses no sandpaper on me. I have, to this day, the same dull head in the matter of conundrums and perplexities which Susy had discovered in those long-gone days. Complexities annoy me; they irritate me; then this progressive feeling presently warms into anger. I cannot get far in the reading of the commonest and simplest contract—with its "parties of the first part," and "parties of the second part," and "parties of the third part,"—before my temper is all gone. Ashcroft[7] comes up here every day and pathetically tries to make me understand the points of the lawsuit which we are conducting against Henry Butters, Harold Wheeler, and the rest of those Plasmon buccaneers, but daily he has to give it up.[8] It is pitiful to see, when he bends his earnest and appealing eyes upon me and says, after one of his efforts, "Now you *do* understand *that*, don't you?"

I am always obliged to say, "I *don't*, Ashcroft. I wish I could understand it, but I don't. Send for the cat."

In the days which Susy is talking about, a perplexity fell to my lot one day. F. G. Whitmore was my business agent, and he brought me out from town in his buggy.[9] We drove by the *porte-cochère* and toward the stable. Now this was a *single* road, and was like a spoon whose handle stretched from the gate to a great round flower-bed in the neighborhood of the stable. At the approach to the flower-bed the road divided and circumnavigated it, making a loop, which I have likened to the bowl of the spoon. As we neared the loop, I saw that Whitmore was laying his course to port, (I was sitting on the starboard side — the side the house was on), and was going to start around that spoon-bowl on that left-hand side. I said,

"Don't do that, Whitmore; take the right-hand side. Then I shall be next to the house when we get to the door."

He said, "*That* will not happen in *any case*, it doesn't make any difference which way I go around this flower-bed."

I explained to him that he was an ass, but he stuck to his proposition, and I said,

"Go on and try it, and see."

He went on and tried it, and sure enough he fetched me up at the door on the very side that he had said I would be. I was not able to believe it then, and I don't believe it yet.

I said, "Whitmore, that is merely an accident. You can't do it again."

He said he could — and he drove down into the street, fetched around, came back, and actually did it again. I was stupefied, paralyzed, petrified, with these strange results, but they did not convince me. I didn't believe he could do it another time, but he did. He said he could do it all day, and fetch up the same way every time. By that time my temper was gone, and I asked him to go home and apply to the Asylum and I would pay the expenses; I didn't want to see him any more for a week.

I went up-stairs in a rage and started to tell Livy about it, expecting to get her sympathy for me and to breed aversion in her for Whitmore; but she merely burst into peal after peal of laughter, as the tale of my adventure went on, for her head was like Susy's: riddles and complexities had no terrors for it. Her mind and Susy's were analytical; I have tried to make it appear that mine was different. Many and many a time I have told that buggy experiment, hoping against hope that I would some time or other find somebody who would be on my side, but it has never happened. And I am never able to go glibly forward and state the circumstances of that buggy's progress without having to halt and consider, and call up in my mind the spoon-handle, the bowl of the spoon, the buggy and the horse, and my position in the buggy: and the minute I have got that far and try to turn it to the left it goes to ruin; I can't see how it is ever going to fetch me out right when we get to the door. Susy is right in her estimate. I can't understand things.

That burglar-alarm which Susy mentions led a gay and careless life, and had no principles. It was generally out of order at one point or another; and there was plenty of opportunity, because all the windows and doors in the house, from the cellar up to the top floor, were connected with it. However, in its seasons of being out of order it could trouble us for only a very little while: we quickly found out that it was fooling us, and that it was buzzing its blood-curdling alarm merely for its own amusement. Then we would shut it off, and send to New York for the electrician — there not being one in all Hartford in those days. When the repairs were finished we would set the alarm again and reestablish our confidence in it. It never did any real business except upon one single occasion. All the rest of its expensive career was frivolous and without purpose. Just that one time it performed its duty, and its whole duty — gravely, seriously, admirably. It let fly about two o'clock one black and dreary March morning, and I turned out promptly, because I knew that it was not fooling, this time.[10] The bathroom door was on my side of the bed. I stepped in there, turned up the gas, looked at the annunciator, and turned off the alarm — so far as the door indicated was concerned — thus stopping the racket. Then I came back to bed. Mrs. Clemens opened the debate:

"What was it?"

"It was the cellar door."

"Was it a burglar, do you think?"

"Yes," I said, "of course it was. Did you suppose it was a Sunday-school superintendent?"

"No. What do you suppose he wants?"

"I suppose he wants jewelry, but he is not acquainted with the house and he thinks it is in the cellar. I don't like to disappoint a burglar whom I am not acquainted with, and who has done me no harm, but if he had had common sagacity enough to inquire, I could have told him we kept nothing down there but coal and vegetables. Still it may be that he *is* acquainted with the place, and that what he really wants is coal and vegetables. On the whole, I think it is vegetables he is after."

"Are you going down to see?"

"No; I could not be of any assistance. Let him select for himself; I don't know where the things are."

Then she said, "But suppose he comes up to the ground floor!"

"That's all right. We shall know it the minute he opens a door on that floor. It will set off the alarm."

Just then the terrific buzzing broke out again. I said,

"He has arrived. I told you he would. I know all about burglars and their ways. They are systematic people."

I went into the bath-room to see if I was right, and I was. I shut off the dining-room and stopped the buzzing, and came back to bed. My wife said,

"What do you suppose he is after now?"

I said, "I think he has got all the vegetables he wants and is coming up for napkin-rings and odds and ends for the wife and children. They all have families — burglars have — and they are always thoughtful of them, always take a few necessaries of life for themselves, and fill out with tokens of remembrance for the family. In taking them they do not forget us: those very things represent tokens of his remembrance of us, and also of our remembrance of him. We never get them again; the memory of the attention remains embalmed in our hearts."

"Are you going down to see what it is he wants now?"

"No," I said, "I am no more interested than I was before. They are experienced people,— burglars; *they* know what they want; I should be no help to him. I *think* he is after ceramics and bric-à-brac and such things. If he knows the house he knows that that is all that he can find on the dining-room floor."

She said, with a strong interest perceptible in her tone, "Suppose he comes up here!"

I said, "It is all right. He will give us notice."

"What shall we do then?"

"Climb out of the window."

She said, a little restively, "Well, what is the use of a burglar-alarm for us?"

"You have seen, dear heart, that it has been useful up to the present moment, and I have explained to you how it will be continuously useful after he gets up here."

That was the end of it. He didn't ring any more alarms. Presently I said,

"He is disappointed, I think. He has gone off with the vegetables and the bric-à-brac, and I think he is dissatisfied."

We went to sleep, and at a quarter before eight in the morning I was out, and hurrying, for I was to take the 8.29 train for New York. I found the gas burning brightly — full head — all over the first floor. My new overcoat was gone; my old umbrella was gone; my new patent-leather shoes, which I had never worn, were gone. The large window which opened into the *ombra* at the rear of the house was standing wide. I passed out through it and tracked the burglar down the hill through the trees; tracked him without difficulty, because he had blazed his progress with imitation silver napkin-rings, and my umbrella, and various other things which he had disapproved of; and I went back in triumph and proved to my wife that he *was* a disappointed burglar. I had suspected he would be, from the start, and from his not coming up to our floor to get human beings.

Things happened to me that day in New York. I will tell about them another time.

From Susy's Biography

Papa has a peculiar gait we like, it seems just to sute him, but most people do not; he always walks up and down the room while thinking and between each coarse at meals.

A lady distantly related to us came to visit us once in those days. She came to stay a week, but all our efforts to make her happy failed, we could not imagine why, and she got up her anchor and sailed the next morning. We did much guessing, but could not solve the mystery. Later we found out what the trouble was. It was my tramping up and down between the courses. She conceived the idea that I could not stand her society.

That word "Youth," as the reader has perhaps already guessed, was my wife's pet name for me. It was gently satirical, but also affectionate. I had certain mental and material peculiarities and customs proper to a much younger person than I was.

From Susy's Biography

Papa is very fond of animals particularly of cats, we had a dear little gray kitten once that he named "Lazy" (papa always wears gray to match his hair and eyes) and he would carry him around on his shoulder, it was a mighty pretty sight! the gray cat sound asleep against papa's gray coat and hair. The names that he has given our different cats, are realy remarkably funny, they are namely Stray Kit, Abner, Motley, Fraeulein, Lazy, Bufalo Bill, Cleveland, Sour Mash, and Pestilence and Famine.

At one time when the children were small, we had a very black mother-cat named Satan, and Satan had a small black offspring named Sin. Pronouns were a difficulty for the children. Little Clara came in one day, her black eyes snapping with indignation, and said,

"Papa, Satan ought to be punished. She is out there at the greenhouse and there she stays and stays, and his kitten is down-stairs crying."

From Susy's Biography

Papa uses very strong language, but I have an idea not nearly so strong as when he first maried mamma. A lady acquaintance of his is rather apt to interupt what one is saying, and papa told mamma that he thought he should say to the lady's husband "I am glad your wife wasn't present when the Deity said 'Let there be light.'"

It is as I have said before. This is a frank historian. She doesn't cover up one's deficiencies, but gives them an equal showing with one's handsomer qualities. Of course I made the remark which she has quoted — and even at this distant day I am still as much as half persuaded that if that lady had been present when the Creator said, "Let there be light," she would have interrupted Him and we shouldn't ever have got it.

From Susy's Biography

Papa said the other day, "I am a mugwump and a mugwump is pure from the marrow out. (Papa knows that I am writing this biography of him, and he said this for it.) He doesn't like to go to church at all, why I never understood, until just now, he told us the other day that he couldn't bear to hear any one talk but himself, but that he could listen to himself talk for hours without getting tired, of course he said this in joke, but I've no dought it was founded on truth.

CHAPTER V

Susy's remark about my strong language troubles me, and I must go back to it.[1] All through the first ten years of my married life I kept a constant and discreet watch upon my tongue while in the house, and went outside and to a distance when circumstances were too much for me and I was obliged to seek relief. I prized my wife's respect and approval above all the rest of the human race's respect and approval. I dreaded the day when she should discover that I was but a whited sepulchre partly freighted with suppressed language. I was so careful, during ten years, that I had not a doubt that my suppressions had been successful. Therefore I was quite as happy in my guilt as I could have been if I had been innocent.

But at last an accident exposed me. I went into the bath-room one morning to make my toilet, and carelessly left the door two or three inches ajar. It was the first time that I had ever failed to take the precaution of closing it tightly. I knew the necessity of being particular about this, because shaving was always a trying ordeal for me, and I could seldom carry it through to a finish without verbal helps. Now this time I was unprotected, but did not suspect it. I had no extraordinary trouble with my razor on this occasion, and was able to worry through with mere mutterings and growlings of an improper sort, but with nothing noisy or emphatic about them — no snapping and barking. Then I put on a shirt. My shirts are an invention of my own. They open in the back, and are buttoned there — when there are buttons. This time the button was missing. My temper jumped up several degrees in a moment, and my remarks rose accordingly, both in loudness and vigor of expression. But I was not troubled, for the bath-room door was a solid one and I supposed it was firmly closed. I flung up the window

North American Review, vol. 183, no. 602 (November 2, 1906): 833–44.

46

and threw the shirt out. It fell upon the shrubbery where the people on their way to church could admire it if they wanted to; there was merely fifty feet of grass between the shirt and the passer-by. Still rumbling and thundering distantly, I put on another shirt. Again the button was absent. I augmented my language to meet the emergency, and threw that shirt out of the window. I was too angry — too insane — to examine the third shirt, but put it furiously on. Again the button was absent, and that shirt followed its comrades out of the window. Then I straightened up, gathered my reserves, and let myself go like a cavalry charge. In the midst of that great assault, my eye fell upon that gaping door, and I was paralyzed.

It took me a good while to finish my toilet. I extended the time unnecessarily in trying to make up my mind as to what I would best do in the circumstances. I tried to hope that Mrs. Clemens was asleep, but I knew better. I could not escape by the window. It was narrow, and suited only to shirts. At last I made up my mind to boldly loaf through the bedroom with the air of a person who had not been doing anything. I made half the journey successfully. I did not turn my eyes in her direction, because that would not be safe. It is very difficult to look as if you have not been doing anything when the facts are the other way, and my confidence in my performance oozed steadily out of me as I went along. I was aiming for the left-hand door because it was furthest from my wife. It had never been opened from the day that the house was built, but it seemed a blessed refuge for me now. The bed was this one, wherein I am lying now, and dictating these histories morning after morning with so much serenity. It was this same old elaborately carved black Venetian bedstead — the most comfortable bedstead that ever was, with space enough in it for a family, and carved angels enough surmounting its twisted columns and its headboard and footboard to bring peace to the sleepers, and pleasant dreams. I had to stop in the middle of the room. I hadn't the strength to go on. I believed that I was under accusing eyes — that even the carved angels were inspecting me with an unfriendly gaze. You know how it is when you are convinced that somebody behind you is looking steadily at you. You *have* to turn your face — you can't help it. I turned mine. The bed was placed as it is now, with the foot where the head ought to be. If it had been placed as it should have been, the high headboard would have sheltered me. But the footboard was no sufficient protection, for I could be seen over it. I was exposed. I was wholly without protection. I turned, because I couldn't help it — and my memory of what I saw is still vivid, after all these years.

Against the white pillows I saw the black head — I saw that young and beautiful face; and I saw the gracious eyes with a something in them which I had never seen there before. They were snapping and flashing with indignation. I felt myself crumbling; I felt myself shrinking away to nothing under that accusing gaze. I stood silent under that desolating fire for as much as a minute, I should say — it seemed a very, very long time. Then my wife's lips parted, and from them issued — *my latest bath-room remark.* The language perfect, but the expression velvety, unpractical, apprenticelike, ignorant, inexperienced, comically inadequate, absurdly weak and unsuited to the great language. In my lifetime I had never heard anything so out of tune, so inharmonious, so incongruous, so ill-suited to each other as were those mighty words set to that feeble music. I tried to keep from laughing, for I was a guilty person in deep need of charity and mercy. I tried to keep from bursting, and I succeeded — until she gravely said, "There, now you know how it sounds."

Then I exploded; the air was filled with my fragments, and you could hear them whiz. I said, "Oh Livy, if it sounds like *that* I will never do it again!"

Then she had to laugh herself. Both of us broke into convulsions, and went on laughing until we were physically exhausted and spiritually reconciled.

The children were present at breakfast — Clara aged six and Susy eight — and the mother made a guarded remark about strong language; guarded because she did not wish the children to suspect anything — a guarded remark which censured strong language. Both children broke out in one voice with this comment, "Why, mamma, papa uses it!"

I was astonished. I had supposed that that secret was safe in my own breast, and that its presence had never been suspected. I asked,

"How did you know, you little rascals?"

"Oh," they said, "we often listen over the balusters when you are in the hall explaining things to George."[2]

From Susy's Biography

One of papa's latest books is "The Prince and the Pauper"[3] and it is unquestionably the best book he has ever written, some people want him to keep to his old style, some gentleman wrote him, "I enjoyed Huckleberry Finn[4] immensely and am glad to see that you have returned to your old style." That enoyed me that enoyed me greatly, because it trobles me [Susy was troubled by that word, and uncertain; she wrote a *u* above it in the proper place, but reconsidered the matter and struck it out] to have so few people know papa, I mean realy know him, they think of

Mark Twain as a humorist joking at everything; "And with a mop of reddish brown hair which sorely needs the barbars brush a roman nose, short stubby mustache, a sad care-worn face, with maney crow's feet" etc. That is the way people picture papa, I have wanted papa to write a book that would reveal something of his kind sympathetic nature, and "The Prince and the Pauper" partly does it. The book is full of lovely charming ideas, and oh the language! It is *perfect*. I think that one of the most touching scenes in it, is where the pauper is riding on horseback with his nobles in the "recognition procession" and he sees his mother oh and then what followed! How she runs to his side, when she sees him throw up his hand palm outward, and is rudely pushed off by one of the King's officers, and then how the little pauper's consceince troubles him when he remembers the shameful words that were falling from his lips, when she was turned from his side "I know you not woman" and how his grandeurs were stricken valueless, and his pride consumed to ashes. It is a wonderfully beautiful and touching little scene, and papa has described it so wonderfully. I never saw a man with so much variety of feeling as papa has; now the "Prince and the Pauper" is full of touching places; but there is most always a streak of humor in them somewhere. Now in the coronation—in the stirring coronation, just after the little king has got his crown back again papa brings that in about the Seal, where the pauper says he used the Seal "to crack nuts with." Oh it is so funny and nice! Papa very seldom writes a passage without some humor in it somewhere, and I dont think he ever will.

The children always helped their mother to edit my books in manuscript. She would sit on the porch at the farm and read aloud, with her pencil in her hand, and the children would keep an alert and suspicious eye upon her right along, for the belief was well grounded in them that whenever she came across a particularly satisfactory passage she would strike it out. Their suspicions were well founded. The passages which were so satisfactory to them always had an element of strength in them which sorely needed modification or expurgation, and were always sure to get it at their mother's hand. For my own entertainment, and to enjoy the protests of the children, I often abused my editor's innocent confidence. I often interlarded remarks of a studied and felicitously atrocious character purposely to achieve the children's brief delight, and then see the remorseless pencil do its fatal work. I often joined my supplications to the children's for mercy, and strung the argument out and pretended to be in earnest. They were deceived, and so was their mother. It was three against one, and most unfair. But it was very delightful, and I could not resist the temptation. Now and then we gained the victory and there was much rejoicing. Then I privately struck the passage out myself. It had served its purpose. It had furnished three of us with good entertainment, and in being removed from the book by me it was only suffering the fate originally intended for it.

From Susy's Biography

Papa was born in Missouri. His mother is Grandma Clemens (Jane Lampton Clemens) of Kentucky. Grandpa Clemens was of the F.F.V.'s of Virginia.[5]

Without doubt it was I that gave Susy that impression. I cannot imagine why, because I was never in my life much impressed by grandeurs which proceed from the accident of birth. I did not get this indifference from my mother. She was always strongly interested in the ancestry of the house. She traced her own line back to the Lambtons of Durham, England — a family which had been occupying broad lands there since Saxon times. I am not sure, but I think that those Lambtons got along without titles of nobility for eight or nine hundred years, then produced a great man, three-quarters of a century ago, and broke into the peerage. My mother knew all about the Clemenses of Virginia, and loved to aggrandize them to me, but she has long been dead. There has been no one to keep those details fresh in my memory, and they have grown dim.

There was a Jere. Clemens who was a United States Senator, and in his day enjoyed the usual Senatorial fame — a fame which perishes whether it spring from four years' service or forty. After Jere. Clemens's fame as a Senator passed away, he was still remembered for many years on account of another service which he performed. He shot old John Brown's Governor Wise in the hind leg in a duel. However, I am not very clear about this. It may be that Governor Wise shot *him* in the hind leg.[6] However, I don't think it is important. I think that the only thing that is really important is that one of them got shot in the hind leg. It would have been better and nobler and more historical and satisfactory if both of them had got shot in the hind leg — but it is of no use for me to try to recollect history. I never had a historical mind. Let it go. Whichever way it happened I am glad of it, and that is as much enthusiasm as I can get up for a person bearing my name. But I am forgetting the first Clemens — the one that stands furthest back toward the really original *first* Clemens, which was Adam.[7]

From Susy's Biography[8]

Clara and I are sure that papa played the trick on Grandma, about the whipping, that is related in "The Adventures of Tom Sayer";[9] "Hand me that switch." The switch hovered in the air, the peril was desperate — "My, look behind you Aunt!" The old lady whirled around and snatched her skirts out of danger. The lad fled on the instant, scrambling up the high board fence and dissapeared over it.

Susy and Clara were quite right about that.
Then Susy says:

And we know papa played "Hookey" all the time. And how readily would papa pretend to be dying so as not to have to go to school!

These revelations and exposures are searching, but they are just. If I am as transparent to other people as I was to Susy, I have wasted much effort in this life.

Grandma couldn't make papa go to school, so she let him go into a printing-office to learn the trade. He did so, and gradually picked up enough education to enable him to do about as well as those who were more studious in early life.

It is noticeable that Susy does not get overheated when she is complimenting me, but maintains a proper judicial and biographical calm. It is noticeable, also, and it is to her credit as a biographer, that she distributes compliment and criticism with a fair and even hand.

My mother had a good deal of trouble with me, but I think she enjoyed it. She had none at all with my brother Henry, who was two years younger than I, and I think that the unbroken monotony of his goodness and truthfulness and obedience would have been a burden to her but for the relief and variety which I furnished in the other direction. I was a tonic. I was valuable to her. I never thought of it before, but now I see it. I never knew Henry to do a vicious thing toward me, or toward any one else — but he frequently did righteous ones that cost me as heavily. It was his duty to report me, when I needed reporting and neglected to do it myself, and he was very faithful in discharging that duty. He is "Sid" in "Tom Sawyer." But Sid was not Henry. Henry was a very much finer and better boy than ever Sid was.

It was Henry who called my mother's attention to the fact that the thread with which she had sewed my collar together to keep me from going in swimming, had changed color. My mother would not have discovered it but for that, and she was manifestly piqued when she recognized that that prominent bit of circumstantial evidence had escaped her sharp eye. That detail probably added a detail to my punishment. It is human. We generally visit our shortcomings on somebody else when there is a possible excuse for it — but no matter, I took it out of Henry. There is always compensation for such as are unjustly used. I often took it out of him — sometimes as an advance payment for something which I hadn't yet done. These were occasions when the opportunity was too strong a temptation, and I had to draw on the future. I did not need to copy this idea from my mother, and probably didn't. Still she wrought upon that principle upon occasion.

If the incident of the broken sugar-bowl is in "Tom Sawyer"— I don't re-

member whether it is or not — that is an example of it. Henry never stole
sugar. He took it openly from the bowl. His mother knew he wouldn't take
sugar when she wasn't looking, but she had her doubts about me. Not exactly doubts, either. She knew very well I *would*. One day when she was
not present, Henry took sugar from her prized and precious old English sugar-
bowl, which was an heirloom in the family — and he managed to break the
bowl. It was the first time I had ever had a chance to tell anything on him,
and I was inexpressibly glad. I told him I was going to tell on him, but he
was not disturbed. When my mother came in and saw the bowl lying on
the floor in fragments, she was speechless for a minute. I allowed that silence to work; I judged it would increase the effect. I was waiting for her
to ask "Who did that?"— so that I could fetch out my news. But it was an
error of calculation. When she got through with her silence she didn't ask
anything about it — she merely gave me a crack on the skull with her thim-
ble that I felt all the way down to my heels. Then I broke out with my injured innocence, expecting to make her very sorry that she had punished
the wrong one. I expected her to do something remorseful and pathetic.
I told her that I was not the one — it was Henry. But there was no upheaval.
She said, without emotion, "It's all right. It isn't any matter. You deserve
it for something you've done that I didn't know about; and if you haven't
done it, why then you deserve it for something that you are going to do,
that I sha'n't hear about."

There was a stairway outside the house, which led up to the rear part
of the second story. One day Henry was sent on an errand, and he took a
tin bucket along. I knew he would have to ascend those stairs, so I went
up and locked the door on the inside, and came down into the garden, which
had been newly ploughed and was rich in choice firm clods of black mold.
I gathered a generous equipment of these, and ambushed him. I waited till
he had climbed the stairs and was near the landing and couldn't escape.
Then I bombarded him with clods, which he warded off with his tin bucket
the best he could, but without much success, for I was a good marksman.
The clods smashing against the weather-boarding fetched my mother out
to see what was the matter, and I tried to explain that I was amusing Henry.
Both of them were after me in a minute, but I knew the way over that high
board fence and escaped for that time. After an hour or two, when I ventured back, there was no one around and I thought the incident was closed.
But it was not. Henry was ambushing me. With an unusually competent
aim for him, he landed a stone on the side of my head which raised a bump
there that felt like the Matterhorn. I carried it to my mother straightway

for sympathy, but she was not strongly moved. It seemed to be her idea that incidents like this would eventually reform me if I harvested enough of them. So the matter was only educational. I had had a sterner view of it than that, before.

It was not right to give the cat the "Pain-Killer"; I realize it now. I would not repeat it in these days. But in those "Tom Sawyer" days it was a great and sincere satisfaction to me to see Peter perform under its influence — and if actions *do* speak as loud as words, he took as much interest in it as I did. It was a most detestable medicine, Perry Davis's Pain-Killer. Mr. Pavey's negro man, who was a person of good judgment and considerable curiosity, wanted to sample it, and I let him. It was his opinion that it was made of hell-fire.

Those were the cholera days of '49. The people along the Mississippi were paralyzed with fright. Those who could run away, did it. And many died of fright in the flight. Fright killed three persons where the cholera killed one. Those who couldn't flee kept themselves drenched with cholera preventives, and my mother chose Perry Davis's Pain-Killer for me. She was not distressed about herself. She avoided that kind of preventive. But she made me promise to take a teaspoonful of Pain-Killer every day. Originally it was my intention to keep the promise, but at that time I didn't know as much about Pain-Killer as I knew after my first experiment with it. She didn't watch Henry's bottle — she could trust Henry. But she marked my bottle with a pencil, on the label, every day, and examined it to see if the teaspoonful had been removed. The floor was not carpeted. It had cracks in it, and I fed the Pain-Killer to the cracks with very good results — no cholera occurred down below.

It was upon one of these occasions that that friendly cat came waving his tail and supplicating for Pain-Killer — which he got — and then went into those hysterics which ended with his colliding with all the furniture in the room and finally going out of the open window and carrying the flower-pots with him, just in time for my mother to arrive and look over her glasses in petrified astonishment and say, "What in the world is the matter with Peter?"

I don't remember what my explanation was, but if it is recorded in that book it may not be the right one.

Whenever my conduct was of such exaggerated impropriety that my mother's extempory punishments were inadequate, she saved the matter up for Sunday, and made me go to church Sunday night — which was a penalty sometimes bearable, perhaps, but as a rule it was not, and I avoided it for the sake of my constitution. She would never believe that I had been to church until she had applied her test: she made me tell her what the text was. That was a simple matter, and caused me no trouble. I didn't have to go to church to get a text. I selected one for myself. This worked very well until one time when my text and the one furnished by a neighbor, who had been to church, didn't tally. After that my mother took other methods. I don't know what they were now.

In those days men and boys wore rather long cloaks in the winter-time. They were black, and were lined with very bright and showy Scotch plaids. One winter's night when I was starting to church to square a crime of some kind committed during the week, I hid my cloak near the gate and went off and played with the other boys until church was over. Then I returned home. But in the dark I put the cloak on wrong side out, entered the room, threw the cloak aside, and then stood the usual examination. I got along very well until the temperature of the church was mentioned. My mother said,

"It must have been impossible to keep warm there on such a night."

I didn't see the art of that remark, and was foolish enough to explain that I wore my cloak all the time that I was in church. She asked if I kept it on from church home, too. I didn't see the bearing of that remark. I said that that was what I had done. She said,

"You wore it in church with that red Scotch plaid outside and glaring? Didn't that attract any attention?"

Of course to continue such a dialogue would have been tedious and un-profitable, and I let it go, and took the consequences.

That was about 1849. Tom Nash was a boy of my own age — the post-master's son. The Mississippi was frozen across, and he and I went skating one night, probably without permission. I cannot see why we should go skating in the night unless without permission, for there could be no con-siderable amusement to be gotten out of skating at night if nobody was go-ing to object to it. About midnight, when we were more than half a mile out toward the Illinois shore, we heard some ominous rumbling and grind-ing and crashing going on between us and the home side of the river, and we knew what it meant — the ice was breaking up. We started for home, pretty badly scared. We flew along at full speed whenever the moonlight sifting down between the clouds enabled us to tell which was ice and which was water. In the pauses we waited; started again whenever there was a good bridge of ice; paused again when we came to naked water and waited in distress until a floating vast cake should bridge that place. It took us an hour to make the trip—a trip which we made in a misery of apprehension all the time. But at last we arrived within a very brief distance of the shore. We waited again; there was another place that needed bridging. All about us the ice was plunging and grinding along and piling itself up in mountains on the shore, and the dangers were increasing, not diminishing. We grew very impatient to get to solid ground, so we started too early and went springing from cake to cake. Tom made a miscalculation, and fell short. He got a bitter bath, but he was so close to shore that he only had to swim a stroke or two—then his feet struck hard bottom and he crawled out. I arrived a little later, without accident. We had been in a drenching perspiration, and Tom's bath was a disaster for him. He took to his bed sick, and had a procession of diseases. The closing one was scarlet-fever, and he came out of it stone deaf. Within a year or two speech departed, of course. But some years later he was taught to talk, after a fashion—one couldn't always make out what it was he was trying to say. Of course he could not modulate his voice, since he couldn't hear himself talk. When he supposed he was talking low and confidentially, you could hear him in Illinois.

Four years ago (1902) I was invited by the University of Missouri to come out there and receive the honorary degree of LL.D. I took that opportunity to spend a week in Hannibal—a city now, a village in my day. It had been fifty-three years since Tom Nash and I had had that adventure. When I was at the railway station ready to leave Hannibal, there was a crowd of citizens there. I saw Tom Nash approaching me across a vacant space, and I walked toward him, for I recognized him at once. He was old and white-headed, but the boy of fifteen was still visible in him. He came up to me, made a trumpet of his hands at my ear, nodded his head toward the citizens and said confidentially—in a yell like a fog-horn—

"Same damned fools, Sam!"

From Susy's Biography

Papa was about twenty years old when he went on the Mississippi as a pilot. Just before he started on his tripp Grandma Clemens asked him to promise her on the Bible not to touch intoxicating liquors or swear, and he said "Yes, mother, I will," and he kept that promise seven years when Grandma released him from it.[10]

Under the inspiring influence of that remark, what a garden of forgotten reforms rises upon my sight!

CHAPTER VI

From Susy's Biography

Papa[1] made arrangements to read at Vassar College the 1st of May, and I went with him.[2] We went by way of New York City. Mamma went with us to New York and stayed two days to do some shopping. We started Tuesday, at ½ past two o'clock in the afternoon, and reached New York about ¼ past six. Papa went right up to General Grants from the station and mamma and I went to the Everett House. Aunt Clara[3] came to supper with us up in our room. . . .

We and Aunt Clara were going to the theatre right after supper, and we expected papa to take us there and to come home as early as he could. But we got through dinner and he didn't come, and didn't come, and mamma got more perplexed and worried, but at last we thought we would have to go without him. So we put on our things and started down stairs but before we'd goten half down we met papa coming up with a great bunch of roses in his hand. He explained that the reason he was so late was that his watch stopped and he didn't notice and kept thinking it an hour earlier than it really was. The roses he carried were some Col. Fred Grant[4] sent to mamma. We went to the theatre and enjoyed "Adonis" [word illegible] acted very much. We reached home about ½ past eleven o'clock and went right to bed. Wednesday morning we got up rather late and had breakfast about ½ past nine o'clock. After breakfast mamma went out shopping and papa and I went to see papa's agent about some business matters. After papa had gotten through talking to Cousin Charlie, [Webster][5] papa's agent, we went to get a friend of papa's, Major Pond,[6] to go and see a Dog Show with us. Then we went to see the dogs with Major Pond and we had a delightful time seeing so many dogs together; when we got through seeing the dogs papa thought he would go and see General Grant and I went with him—this was April 29, 1885. Papa went up into General Grant's room and he took me with him, I felt greatly honored and delighted when papa took me into General Grant's room and let me see the General and Col. Grant, for General Grant is a man I shall be glad all my life that I have seen. Papa and General Grant had a long talk together and papa has written an account of his talk and visit with General Grant for me to put into this biography.

North American Review, vol. 183, no. 603 (November 16, 1906): 961–70.

Susy has inserted in this place that account of mine—as follows:

April 29, 1885.

I called on General Grant and took Susy with me. The General was looking and feeling far better than he had looked or felt for some months. He had ventured to work again on his book that morning—the first time he had done any work for perhaps a month. This morning's work was his first attempt at dictating,[7] and it was a thorough success, to his great delight. He had always said that it would be impossible for him to dictate anything, but I had said that he was noted for clearness of statement, and as a narrative was simply a statement of consecutive facts, he was consequently peculiarly qualified and equipped for dictation. This turned out to be true. For he had dictated two hours that morning to a shorthand writer, had never hesitated for words, had not repeated himself, and the manuscript when finished needed no revision. The two hours' work was an account of Appomattox[8]—and this was such an extremely important feature that his book would necessarily have been severely lame without it. Therefore I had taken a shorthand writer there before, to see if I could not get him to write at least a few lines about Appomattox.* But he was at that time not well enough to undertake it. I was aware that of all the hundred versions of Appomattox, not one was really correct. Therefore I was extremely anxious that he should leave behind him the truth. His throat was not distressing him, and his voice was much better and stronger than usual. He was so delighted to have gotten Appomattox accomplished once more in his life—to have gotten the matter off his mind—that he was as talkative as his old self. He received Susy very pleasantly, and then fell to talking about certain matters which he hoped to be able to dictate next day; and he said in substance that, among other things, he wanted to settle once for all a question that had been bandied about from mouth to mouth and from newspaper to newspaper. That question was, "With whom originated the idea of the march to the sea?[9] Was it Grant's, or was it Sherman's idea?" Whether I, or some one else (being anxious to get the important fact settled) asked him with whom the idea originated, I don't remember. But I remember his answer. I shall always remember his answer. General Grant said:

"Neither of us originated the idea of Sherman's march to the sea. The enemy did it."

He went on to say that the enemy, however, necessarily originated a great many of the plans that the general on the opposite side gets the credit for; at the same time that the enemy is doing that, he is laying open other moves which the opposing general sees and takes advantage of. In this case, Sherman had a plan all thought out, of course. He meant to destroy the two remaining railroads in that part of the country, and that would finish up that region. But General Hood[10] did not play the military part that he was expected to play. On the contrary, General Hood made a dive at Chattanooga. This left the march to the sea open to Sherman, and so after sending part of his army to defend and hold what he had acquired in the Chattanooga region, he was perfectly free to proceed, with the rest of it,

*I was his publisher. I was putting his "Personal Memoirs" to press at the time.—S. L. C.

through Georgia. He saw the opportunity, and he would not have been fit for his place if he had not seized it.

"He wrote me" (the General is speaking) "what his plan was, and I sent him word to go ahead. My staff were opposed to the movement." (I think the General said they tried to persuade him to stop Sherman. The chief of his staff, the General said, even went so far as to go to Washington without the General's knowledge and get the ear of the authorities, and he succeeded in arousing their fears to such an extent that they telegraphed General Grant to stop Sherman.)

Then General Grant said, "Out of deference to the Government, I telegraphed Sherman and stopped him twenty-four hours; and then considering that that was deference enough to the Government, I telegraphed him to go ahead again."

I have not tried to give the General's language, but only the general idea of what he said. The thing that mainly struck me was his terse remark that the enemy originated the idea of the march to the sea. It struck me because it was so suggestive of the General's epigrammatic fashion — saying a great deal in a single crisp sentence. (This is my account, and signed "Mark Twain.")

Susy Resumes

After papa and General Grant had had their talk, we went back to the hotel where mamma was, and papa told mamma all about his interview with General Grant. Mamma and I had a nice quiet afternoon together.

That pair of devoted comrades were always shutting themselves up together when there was opportunity to have what Susy called "a cozy time." From Susy's nursery days to the end of her life, she and her mother were close friends; intimate friends, passionate adorers of each other. Susy's was a beautiful mind, and it made her an interesting comrade. And with the fine mind she had a heart like her mother's. Susy never had an interest or an occupation which she was not glad to put aside for that something which was in all cases more precious to her — a visit with her mother. Susy died at the right time, the fortunate time of life; the happy age — twenty-four years. At twenty-four, such a girl has seen the best of life — life as a happy dream. After that age the risks begin; responsibility comes, and with it the cares, the sorrows, and the inevitable tragedy. For her mother's sake I would have brought her back from the grave if I could, but I would not have done it for my own.[11]

From Susy's Biography

Then papa went to read in public; there were a great many authors that read, that Thursday afternoon, beside papa; I would have liked to have gone and heard papa read, but papa said he was going to read in Vassar just what he was planning to read in New York, so I stayed at home with mamma.

The next day mamma planned to take the four o'clock car back to Hartford.[12]

We rose quite early that morning and went to the Vienna Bakery and took breakfast there. From there we went to a German bookstore and bought some German
books for Clara's birthday.

Dear me, the power of association to snatch mouldy dead memories out
of their graves and make them walk! That remark about buying foreign
books throws a sudden white glare upon the distant past; and I see the long
stretch of a New York street with an unearthly vividness, and John Hay[13]
walking down it, grave and remorseful. I was walking down it too, that
morning, and I overtook Hay and asked him what the trouble was. He
turned a lustreless eye upon me and said:

"My case is beyond cure. In the most innocent way in the world I have
committed a crime which will never be forgiven by the sufferers, for they
will never believe — oh, well, no, I was going to say they would never believe that I did the thing innocently. The truth is they will know that I acted
innocently, because they are rational people; but what of that? I never can
look them in the face again — nor they me, perhaps."

Hay was a young bachelor, and at that time was on the "Tribune" staff.
He explained his trouble in these words, substantially:

"When I was passing along here yesterday morning on my way down-
town to the office, I stepped into a bookstore where I am acquainted, and
asked if they had anything new from the other side. They handed me a
French novel, in the usual yellow paper cover, and I carried it away. I didn't
even look at the title of it. It was for recreation reading, and I was on my
way to my work. I went mooning and dreaming along, and I think I hadn't
gone more than fifty yards when I heard my name called. I stopped, and
a private carriage drew up at the sidewalk and I shook hands with the in-
mates — mother and young daughter, excellent people. They were on their
way to the steamer to sail for Paris. The mother said,

"'I saw that book in your hand and I judged by the look of it that it was
a French novel. Is it?'"

"I said it was.

"She said, 'Do let me have it, so that my daughter can practise her French
on it on the way over.'

"Of course I handed her the book, and we parted. Ten minutes ago I was
passing that bookstore again, and I stepped in and fetched away another
copy of that book. Here it is. Read the first page of it. That is enough. You
will know what the rest is like. I think it must be the foulest book in the
French language — one of the foulest, anyway. I would be ashamed to offer

it to a harlot — but, oh dear, I gave it to that sweet young girl without shame. Take my advice; don't give away a book until you have examined it."

From Susy's Biography

Then mamma and I went to do some shopping and papa went to see General Grant. After we had finished doing our shopping we went home to the hotel together. When we entered our rooms in the hotel we saw on the table a vase full of exquisett red roses. Mamma who is very fond of flowers exclaimed "Oh I wonder who could have sent them." We both looked at the card in the midst of the roses and saw that it was written on in papa's handwriting, it was written in German. 'Liebes Geshchenk on die mamma.'[14] [I am sure I didn't say "on" — that is Susy's spelling, not mine; also I am sure I didn't spell Geschenk so liberally as all that. — S. L. C.] Mamma was delighted. Papa came home and gave mamma her ticket; and after visiting a while with her went to see Major Pond and mamma and I sat down to our lunch. After lunch most of our time was taken up with packing, and at about three o'clock we went to escort mamma to the train. We got on board the train with her and stayed with her about five minutes and then we said good-bye to her and the train started for Hartford. It was the first time I had ever beene away from home without mamma in my life, although I was 13 yrs. old. Papa and I drove back to the hotel and got Major Pond and then went to see the Brooklyn Bridge we went across it to Brooklyn on the cars and then walked back across it from Brooklyn to New York. We enjoyed looking at the beautiful scenery and we could see the bridge moove under the intense heat of the sun. We had a perfectly delightful time, but weer pretty tired when we got back to the hotel.

The next morning we rose early, took our breakfast and took an early train to Poughkeepsie. We had a very pleasant journey to Poughkeepsie. The Hudson was magnificent — shrouded with beautiful mist. When we arived at Poughkeepsie it was raining quite hard; which fact greatly dissapointed me because I very much wanted to see the outside of the buildings of Vassar College and as it rained that would be impossible. It was quite a long drive from the station to Vasser College and papa and I had a nice long time to discuss and laugh over German profanity. One of the German phrases papa particularly enjoys is "O heilige maria Mutter Jesus!"[15] Jean has a German nurse, and this was one of her phrases, there was a time when Jean exclaimed, "Ach Gott!"[16] to every trifle, but when mamma found it out she was shocked and instantly put a stop to it.

It brings that pretty little German girl vividly before me — a sweet and innocent and plump little creature with peachy cheeks; a clear-souled little maiden and without offence, notwithstanding her profanities, and she was loaded to the eyebrows with them. She was a mere child. She was not fifteen yet. She was just from Germany, and knew no English. She was always scattering her profanities around, and they were such a satisfaction to me that I never dreamed of such a thing as modifying her. For my own sake, I had no disposition to tell on her. Indeed I took pains to keep her from being

found out. I told her to confine her religious exercises to the children's quarters, and urged her to remember that Mrs. Clemens was prejudiced against
pieties on week-days. To the children, the little maid's profanities sounded
natural and proper and right, because they had been used to that kind of
talk in Germany, and they attached no evil importance to it. It grieves me
that I have forgotten those vigorous remarks. I long hoarded them in my
memory as a treasure. But I remember one of them still, because I heard
it so many times. The trial of that little creature's life was the children's
hair. She would tug and strain with her comb, accompanying her work with
her misplaced pieties. And when finally she was through with her triple
job she always fired up and exploded her thanks toward the sky, where they
belonged, in this form: *"Gott sei Dank ich bin fertig mit'm Gott verdammtes
Haar!"* (I believe I am not quite brave enough to translate it.)[17]

From Susy's Biography

We at length reached Vassar College and she looked very finely, her buildings
and her grounds being very beautiful. We went to the front doore and range the
bell. The young girl who came to the doore wished to know who we wanted to
see. Evidently we were not expected. Papa told her who we wanted to see and she
showed us to the parlor. We waited, no one came; and waited, no one came, still
no one came. It was beginning to seem pretty awkward, "Oh well this is a pretty
piece of business," papa exclaimed. At length we heard footsteps coming down the
long corridor and Miss C, (the lady who had invited papa) came into the room.
She greeted papa very pleasantly and they had a nice little chatt together. Soon the
lady principal also entered and she was very pleasant and agreable. She showed
us to our rooms and said she would send for us when dinner was ready. We went
into our rooms, but we had nothing to do for half an hour exept to watch the rain
drops as they fell upon the window panes. At last we were called to dinner, and
I went down without papa as he never eats anything in the middle of the day. I
sat at the table with the lady principal and enjoyed very much seeing all the young
girls trooping into the dining-room. After dinner I went around the College with
the young ladies and papa stayed in his room and smoked. When it was supper time
papa went down and ate supper with us and we had a very delightful supper. After
supper the young ladies went to their rooms to dress for the evening. Papa went
to his room and I went with the lady principal. At length the guests began to arive,
but papa still remained in his room until called for. Papa read in the chapell. It
was the first time I had ever heard him read in my life—that is in public. When
he came out on to the stage I remember the people behind me exclaimed "Oh how
queer he is! Isn't he funny!" I thought papa was very funny, although I did not think
him queer. He read "A Trying Situation" and "The Golden Arm," a ghost story that
he heard down South when he was a little boy. "The Golden Arm" papa had told
me before, but he had startled me so that I did not much wish to hear it again.
But I had resolved this time to be prepared and not to let myself be startled, but

still papa did, and very very much; he startled the whole roomful of people and they jumped as one man. The other story was also very funny and interesting and I enjoyed the evening inexpressibly much. After papa had finished reading we all went down to the collation in the dining-room and after that there was dancing and singing. Then the guests went away and papa and I went to bed. The next morning we rose early, took an early train for Hartford and reached Hartford at ½ past 2 o'clock. We were very glad to get back.

How charitably she treats that ghastly experience! It is a dear and lovely disposition, and a most valuable one, that can brush away indignities and discourtesies and seek and find the pleasanter features of an experience. Susy had that disposition, and it was one of the jewels of her character that had come to her straight from her mother. It is a feature that was left out of me at birth. And, at seventy, I have not yet acquired it. I did not go to Vassar College professionally, but as a guest — as a guest, and gratis. Aunt Clara (now Mrs. John B. Stanchfield) was a graduate of Vassar and it was to please her that I inflicted that journey upon Susy and myself. The invitation had come to me from both the lady mentioned by Susy and the President of the College — a sour old saint who has probably been gathered to his fathers long ago; and I hope they enjoy him; I hope they value his society. I think I can get along without it, in either end of the next world.

We arrived at the College in that soaking rain, and Susy has described, with just a suggestion of dissatisfaction, the sort of reception we got. Susy had to sit in her damp clothes half an hour while we waited in the parlor; then she was taken to a fireless room and left to wait there again, as she has stated. I do not remember that President's name, and I am sorry. He did not put in an appearance until it was time for me to step upon the platform in front of that great garden of young and lovely blossoms. He caught up with me and advanced upon the platform with me and was going to introduce me. I said in substance:

"You have allowed me to get along without your help thus far, and if you will retire from the platform I will try to do the rest without it."

I did not see him any more, but I detest his memory. Of course my resentment did not extend to the students, and so I had an unforgettable good time talking to them. And I think they had a good time too, for they responded "as one man," to use Susy's unimprovable phrase.

Girls are charming creatures. I shall have to be twice seventy years old before I change my mind as to that. I am to talk to a crowd of them this afternoon, students of Barnard College (the sex's annex to Columbia University), and I think I shall have as pleasant a time with those lasses as I had with the Vassar girls twenty-one years ago.

From Susy's Biography

I stopped in the middle of mamma's early history to tell about our tripp to Vassar because I was afraid I would forget about it, now I will go on where I left off.[18] Some time after Miss Emma Nigh[19] died papa took mamma and little Langdon to Elmira for the summer. When in Elmira Langdon began to fail but I think mamma did not know just what was the matter with him.

I was the cause of the child's illness. His mother trusted him to my care and I took him a long drive in an open barouche for an airing. It was a raw, cold morning, but he was well wrapped about with furs and, in the hands of a careful person, no harm would have come to him. But I soon dropped into a reverie and forgot all about my charge. The furs fell away and exposed his bare legs. By and by the coachman noticed this, and I arranged the wraps again, but it was too late. The child was almost frozen. I hurried home with him. I was aghast at what I had done, and I feared the consequences. I have always felt shame for that treacherous morning's work and have not allowed myself to think of it when I could help it. I doubt if I had the courage to make confession at that time. I think it most likely that I have never confessed until now.[20]

From Susy's Biography

At last it was time for papa to return to Hartford, and Langdon was real sick at that time, but still mamma decided to go with him, thinking the journey might do him good. But after they reached Hartford he became very sick, and his trouble prooved to be diptheeria. He died about a week after mamma and papa reached Hartford. He was burried by the side of grandpa at Elmira, New York. [Susy rests there with them.—S. L. C.] After that, mamma became very very ill, so ill that there seemed great danger of death, but with a great deal of good care she recovered. Some months afterward mamma and papa [and Susy, who was perhaps fourteen or fifteen months old at the time.—S. L. C.] went to Europe and stayed for a time in Scotland and England. In Scotland mamma and papa became very well equanted with Dr. John Brown, the author of "Rab and His Friends," and he mett, but was not so well equanted with, Mr. Charles Kingsley, Mr. Henry M. Stanley, Sir Thomas Hardy grandson of the Captain Hardy to whom Nellson said "Kiss me Hardy," when dying on shipboard, Mr. Henry Irving, Robert Browning, Sir Charles Dilke, Mr. Charles Reade, Mr. William Black, Lord Houghton, Frank Buckland, Mr. Tom Hughes, Anthony Trollope, Tom Hood, son of the poet—and mamma and papa were quite well equanted with Dr. Macdonald and family, and papa met Harrison Ainsworth.

I remember all these men very well indeed, except the last one. I do not recall Ainsworth. By my count, Susy mentions fourteen men. They are all dead except Sir Charles Dilke.[21]

We met a great many other interesting people, among them Lewis

Carroll,[22] author of the immortal "Alice"— but he was only interesting to look at, for he was the stillest and shyest full-grown man I have ever met except "Uncle Remus."[23] Dr. Macdonald and several other lively talkers were present, and the talk went briskly on for a couple of hours, but Carroll sat still all the while except that now and then he answered a question. His answers were brief. I do not remember that he elaborated any of them.

At a dinner at Smalley's[24] we met Herbert Spencer.[25] At a large luncheon party at Lord Houghton's we met Sir Arthur Helps,[26] who was a celebrity of world-wide fame at the time, but is quite forgotten now. Lord Elcho,[27] a large vigorous man, sat at some distance down the table. He was talking earnestly about Godalming. It was a deep and flowing and unarticulated rumble, but I got the Godalming pretty clearly every time it broke free of the rumble, and as all the strength was on the first end of the word it startled me every time, because it sounded so like swearing. In the middle of the luncheon Lady Houghton rose, remarked to the guests on her right and on her left in a matter-of-fact way, "Excuse me, I have an engagement," and without further ceremony she went off to meet it. This would have been doubtful etiquette in America. Lord Houghton told a number of delightful stories. He told them in French, and I lost nothing of them but the nubs.

CHAPTER VII

I was always heedless.[1] I was born heedless; and therefore I was constantly, and quite unconsciously, committing breaches of the minor proprieties, which brought upon me humiliations which ought to have humiliated me but didn't, because I didn't know anything had happened. But Livy knew; and so the humiliations fell to her share, poor child, who had not earned them and did not deserve them. She always said I was the most difficult child she had. She was very sensitive about me. It distressed her to see me do heedless things which could bring me under criticism, and so she was always watchful and alert to protect me from the kind of transgressions which I have been speaking of.

When I was leaving Hartford for Washington, upon the occasion referred to, she said: "I have written a small warning and put it in a pocket of your dress-vest. When you are dressing to go to the Authors' Reception at the White House[2] you will naturally put your fingers in your vest pockets, according to your custom, and you will find that little note there. Read it carefully, and do as it tells you. I cannot be with you, and so I delegate my sentry duties to this little note. If I should give you the warning by word of mouth, now, it would pass from your head and be forgotten in a few minutes."

It was President Cleveland's first term.[3] I had never seen his wife — the young, the beautiful, the good-hearted, the sympathetic, the fascinating.[4] Sure enough, just as I had finished dressing to go to the White House I found that little note, which I had long ago forgotten. It was a grave little note, a serious little note, like its writer, but it made me laugh. Livy's gentle gravi-

North American Review, vol. 183, no. 604 (December 7, 1906): 1089–95.

ties often produced that effect upon me, where the expert humorist's best joke would have failed, and I do not laugh easily.

When we reached the White House and I was shaking hands with the President, he started to say something, but I interrupted him and said:

"If your Excellency will excuse me, I will come back in a moment; but now I have a very important matter to attend to, and it must be attended to at once."

I turned to Mrs. Cleveland, the young, the beautiful, the fascinating, and gave her my card, on the back of which I had written *"He didn't"*—and I asked her to sign her name below those words.

She said: "He didn't? He didn't what?"

"Oh," I said, "never mind. We cannot stop to discuss that now. This is urgent. Won't you please sign your name?" (I handed her a fountain-pen.)

"Why," she said, "I cannot commit myself in that way. Who is it that didn't?—and what is it that he didn't?"

"Oh," I said, "time is flying, flying, flying. Won't you take me out of my distress and sign your name to it? It's all right. I give you my word it's all right."

She looked nonplussed; but hesitatingly and mechanically she took the pen and said:

"I will sign it. I will take the risk. But you must tell me all about it, right afterward, so that you can be arrested before you get out of the house in case there should be anything criminal about this."

Then she signed; and I handed her Mrs. Clemens's note, which was very brief, very simple, and to the point. It said: *"Don't wear your arctics in the White House."* It made her shout; and at my request she summoned a messenger and we sent that card at once to the mail on its way to Mrs. Clemens in Hartford.

When the little Ruth[5] was about a year or a year and a half old, Mason, an old and valued friend of mine, was consul-general at Frankfort-on-the-Main. I had known him well in 1867, '68 and '69, in America, and I and mine had spent a good deal of time with him and his family in Frankfort in '78. He was a thoroughly competent, diligent, and conscientious official. Indeed he possessed these qualities in so large a degree that among American consuls he might fairly be said to be monumental, for at that time our consular service was largely—and I think I may say mainly—in the hands of ignorant, vulgar, and incapable men who had been political heelers in America, and had been taken care of by transference to consulates where they could be supported at the Government's expense instead of being transferred to the poor house, which would have been cheaper and more patriotic. Mason, in '78, had been consul-general in Frankfort several years — four, I think. He had come from Marseilles with a great record. He had been consul there during thirteen years, and one part of his record was heroic. There had been a desolating cholera epidemic, and Mason was the only representative of any foreign country who stayed at his post and saw it through. And during that time he not only represented his own country, but he represented all the other countries in Christendom and did their work, and did it well and was praised for it by them in words of no uncertain sound. This great record of Mason's had saved him from official decapitation straight along while Republican Presidents occupied the chair, but now it was occupied by a Democrat. Mr. Cleveland was not seated in it — he was not yet inaugurated — before he was deluged with applications from Democratic politicians desiring the appointment of a thousand or so politically useful Democrats to Mason's place. A year or two later Mason wrote me and asked me if I couldn't do something to save him from destruction.

I was very anxious to keep him in his place,[6] but at first I could not think of any way to help him, for I was a mugwump.[7] We, the mugwumps, a little company made up of the unenslaved of both parties, the very best men to be found in the two great parties — that was our idea of it — voted sixty thousand strong for Mr. Cleveland in New York and elected him. Our principles were high, and very definite. We were not a party; we had no candidates; we had no axes to grind. Our vote laid upon the man we cast it for no obligation of any kind. By our rule we could not ask for office; we could not accept office. When voting, it was our duty to vote for the best man, regardless of his party name. We had no other creed. Vote for the best man — that was creed enough.

Such being my situation, I was puzzled to know how to try to help Mason, and, at the same time, save my mugwump purity undefiled. It was a delicate place. But presently, out of the ruck of confusions in my mind, rose a sane thought, clear and bright — to wit: since it was a mugwump's duty to do his best to put the best man in office, necessarily it must be a mugwump's duty to try to *keep* the best man in when he was already there. My course was easy now. It might not be quite delicate for a mugwump to approach the President directly, but I could approach him indirectly, with all delicacy, since in that case not even courtesy would require him to take notice of an application which no one could prove had ever reached him.

Yes, it was easy and simple sailing now. I could lay the matter before Ruth, in her cradle, and wait for results. I wrote the little child, and said to her all that I have just been saying about mugwump principles and the limitations which they put upon me. I explained that it would not be proper for me to apply to her father in Mr. Mason's behalf, but I detailed to her Mr. Mason's high and honorable record and suggested that she take the matter in her own hands and do a patriotic work which I felt some delicacy about venturing upon myself. I asked her to forget that her father was only President of the United States, and her subject and servant; I asked her not to put her application in the form of a command, but to modify it, and give it the fictitious and pleasanter form of a mere request — that it would be no harm to let him gratify himself with the superstition that he was independent and could do as he pleased in the matter. I begged her to put stress, and plenty of it, upon the proposition that to keep Mason in his place would be a benefaction to the nation; to enlarge upon that, and keep still about all other considerations.

In due time I received a letter from the President, written with his own hand, signed by his own hand, acknowledging Ruth's intervention and thanking me for enabling him to save to the country the services of so good and well-tried a servant as Mason, and thanking me, also, for the detailed fulness of Mason's record, which could leave no doubt in any one's mind that Mason was in his right place and ought to be kept there. Mason has remained in the service ever since, and is now consul-general at Paris.

During the time that we were living in Buffalo in '70–'71, Mr. Cleveland was sheriff, but I never happened to make his acquaintance, or even see him. In fact, I suppose I was not even aware of his existence. Fourteen years later, he was become the greatest man in the State. I was not living in the State at the time. He was Governor, and was about to step into the post of President of the United States. At that time I was on the public highway in company with another bandit, George W. Cable. We were robbing the public with readings from our works during four months — and in the course of time we went to Albany to levy tribute, and I said, "We ought to go and pay our respects to the Governor."

So Cable and I went to that majestic Capitol building and stated our errand. We were shown into the Governor's private office, and I saw Mr. Cleveland for the first time. We three stood chatting together. I was born lazy, and I comforted myself by turning the corner of a table into a sort of seat. Presently the Governor said:

"Mr. Clemens, I was a fellow citizen of yours in Buffalo a good many months, a good while ago, and during those months you burst suddenly into a mighty fame, out of a previous long-continued and no doubt proper obscurity — but I was a nobody, and you wouldn't notice me nor have anything to do with me. But now that I have become somebody, you have changed your style, and you come here to shake hands with me and be sociable. How do you explain this kind of conduct?"

"Oh," I said, "it is very simple, your Excellency. In Buffalo you were nothing but a sheriff. I was in society. I couldn't afford to associate with sheriffs. But you are a Governor now, and you are on your way to the Presidency. It is a great difference, and it makes you worth while."

There appeared to be about sixteen doors to that spacious room. From each door a young man now emerged, and the sixteen lined up and moved forward and stood in front of the Governor with an aspect of respectful expectancy in their attitude. No one spoke for a moment. Then the Governor said:

"You are dismissed, gentlemen. Your services are not required. Mr. Clemens is sitting on the bells."

There was a cluster of sixteen bell buttons on the corner of the table; my proportions at that end of me were just right to enable me to cover the whole of that nest, and that is how I came to hatch out those sixteen clerks.

In accordance with the suggestion made in Gilder's letter recently received I have written the following note to ex-President Cleveland upon his sixty-ninth birthday:

HONORED SIR: —
Your patriotic virtues have won for you the homage of half the nation and the enmity of the other half. This places your character as a citizen upon a summit as high as Washington's. The verdict is unanimous and unassailable. The votes of both sides are necessary in cases like these, and the votes of the one side are quite as valuable as are the votes of the other. Where the votes are all in a man's favor the verdict is against him. It is sand, and history will wash it away. But the verdict for you is rock, and will stand.

S. L. CLEMENS.

As of date March 18, 1906. . . .

In a diary which Mrs. Clemens kept for a little while,[8] a great many years ago, I find various mentions of Mrs. Harriet Beecher Stowe,[9] who was a near neighbor of ours in Hartford, with no fences between. And in those days she made as much use of our grounds as of her own, in pleasant weather. Her mind had decayed, and she was a pathetic figure. She wandered about all the day long in the care of a muscular Irishwoman. Among the colonists of our neighborhood the doors always stood open in pleasant weather. Mrs. Stowe entered them at her own free will, and as she was always softly slippered and generally full of animal spirits, she was able to deal in surprises, and she liked to do it. She would slip up behind a person who was deep in dreams and musings and fetch a war-whoop that would jump that person out of his clothes. And she had other moods. Sometimes we would hear gentle music in the drawing-room and would find her there at the piano singing ancient and melancholy songs with infinitely touching effect.

Her husband, old Professor Stowe,[10] was a picturesque figure. He wore a broad slouch hat. He was a large man, and solemn. His beard was white and thick and hung far down on his breast. The first time our little Susy ever saw him she encountered him on the street near our house and came flying wide-eyed to her mother and said, "Santa Claus has got loose!"

Which reminds me of Rev. Charley Stowe's[11] little boy — a little boy of seven years. I met Rev. Charley crossing his mother's grounds one morning and he told me this little tale. He had been out to Chicago to attend a Convention of Congregational clergymen, and had taken his little boy with him. During the trip he reminded the little chap, every now and then, that he must be on his very best behavior there in Chicago. He said: "We shall be the guests of a clergyman, there will be other guests — clergymen and their wives — and you must be careful to let those people see by your walk and conversation that you are of a godly household. Be very careful about this." The admonition bore fruit. At the first breakfast which they ate in the Chicago clergyman's house he heard his little son say in the meekest and most reverent way to the lady opposite him,

"Please, won't you, for Christ's sake, pass the butter?"

CHAPTER VIII

[*Dictated in 1906*][1] In those early days duelling suddenly became a fashion in the New Territory of Nevada, and by 1864 everybody was anxious to (1864) have a chance in the new sport, mainly for the reason that he was not able to thoroughly respect himself so long as he had not killed or crippled somebody in a duel or been killed or crippled in one himself.

At that time I had been serving as city editor on Mr. Goodman's Virginia City "Enterprise"[2] for a matter of two years. I was twenty-nine years old. I was ambitious in several ways, but I had entirely escaped the seductions of that particular craze. I had had no desire to fight a duel; I had no intention of provoking one. I did not feel respectable, but I got a certain amount of satisfaction out of feeling safe. I was ashamed of myself; the rest of the staff were ashamed of me — but I got along well enough. I had always been accustomed to feeling ashamed of myself, for one thing or another, so there was no novelty for me in the situation. I bore it very well. Plunkett was on the staff; R. M. Daggett[3] was on the staff. These had tried to get into duels, but for the present had failed, and were waiting. Goodman was the only one of us who had done anything to shed credit upon the paper. The rival paper was the Virginia "Union."[4] Its editor for a little while was Tom Fitch,[5] called the "silver-tongued orator of Wisconsin"— that was where he came from. He tuned up his oratory in the editorial columns of the "Union," and Mr. Goodman invited him out and modified him with a bullet.[6] I remember the joy of the staff when Goodman's challenge was accepted by Fitch. We ran late that night, and made much of Joe Goodman. He was only twenty-four years old; he lacked the wisdom which a person has at twenty-nine, and he was as glad of being *it* as I was that I wasn't. He chose

North American Review, vol. 183, no. 605 (December 21, 1906): 1217–24.

Major Graves for his second (that name is not right, but it's close enough; I don't remember the Major's name). Graves came over to instruct Joe in the duelling art. He had been a Major under Walker,[7] the "gray-eyed man of destiny," and had fought all through that remarkable man's filibustering campaign in Central America. That fact gauges the Major. To say that a man was a Major under Walker, and came out of that struggle ennobled by Walker's praise, is to say that the Major was not merely a brave man but that he was brave to the very utmost limit of that word. All of Walker's men were like that. I knew the Gillis family intimately. The father made the campaign under Walker, and with him one son.[8] They were in the memorable Plaza fight, and stood it out to the last against overwhelming odds, as did also all of the Walker men. The son was killed at the father's side. The father received a bullet through the eye. The old man — for he was an old man at the time — wore spectacles, and the bullet and one of the glasses went into his skull and remained there. There were some other sons: Steve, George, and Jim,[9] very young chaps — the merest lads — who wanted to be in the Walker expedition, for they had their father's dauntless spirit. But Walker wouldn't have them; he said it was a serious expedition, and no place for children.

The Major was a majestic creature, with a most stately and dignified and impressive military bearing, and he was by nature and training courteous, polite, graceful, winning; and he had that quality which I think I have encountered in only one other man — Bob Howland[10] — a mysterious quality which resides in the eye; and when that eye is turned upon an individual or a squad, in warning, that is enough. The man that has that eye doesn't need to go armed; he can move upon an armed desperado and quell him and take him prisoner without saying a single word. I saw Bob Howland do that, once — a slender, good-natured, amiable, gentle, kindly little skeleton of a man, with a sweet blue eye that would win your heart when it smiled upon you, or turn cold and freeze it, according to the nature of the occasion.

The Major stood Joe up straight; stood Steve Gillis up fifteen paces away; made Joe turn right side towards Steve, cock his navy six-shooter — that prodigious weapon — and hold it straight down against his leg; told him that *that* was the correct position for the gun — that the position ordinarily in use at Virginia City (that is to say, the gun straight up in the air, then brought slowly down to your man) was all wrong. At the word *"One,"* you must raise the gun slowly and steadily to the place on the other man's body that you desire to convince. Then, after a pause, *"two, three — fire — Stop!"* At the word "stop," you may fire—but not earlier. You may give yourself as much time as you please *after* that word. Then, when you fire, you may advance and go on firing at your leisure and pleasure, if you can get any pleasure out of it. And, in the meantime, the other man, if he has been properly instructed and is alive to his privileges, is advancing on *you*, and firing—and it is always likely that more or less trouble will result.

Naturally, when Joe's revolver had risen to a level it was pointing at Steve's breast, but the Major said "No, that is not wise. Take all the risks of getting murdered yourself, but don't run any risk of murdering the other man. If you survive a duel you want to survive it in such a way that the memory of it will not linger along with you through the rest of your life and interfere with your sleep. Aim at your man's leg; not at the knee, not above the knee; for those are dangerous spots. Aim below the knee; cripple him, but leave the rest of him to his mother."

By grace of these truly wise and excellent instructions, Joe tumbled Fitch down next morning with a bullet through his lower leg, which furnished him a permanent limp. And Joe lost nothing but a lock of hair, which he could spare better then than he could now. For when I saw him here in New York a year ago, his crop was gone; he had nothing much left but a fringe, with a dome rising above.

About a year later I got *my* chance. But I was not hunting for it. Goodman went off to San Francisco for a week's holiday, and left me to be chief editor. I had supposed that that was an easy berth, there being nothing to do but write one editorial per day; but I was disappointed in that superstition. I couldn't find anything to write an article about, the first day. Then it occurred to me that inasmuch as it was the 22nd of April, 1864, the next

(1864) morning would be the three-hundredth anniversary of Shakespeare's birthday—and what better theme could I want than that? I got the Cyclopaedia and examined it, and found out who Shakespeare was and what he had done, and I borrowed all that and laid it before a community that couldn't have been better prepared for instruction about Shakespeare than if they had been prepared by art. There wasn't enough of what Shakespeare had done to make an editorial of the necessary length, but I filled it out with what he hadn't done—which in many respects was more important and striking and readable than the handsomest things he had really accomplished. But next day I was in trouble again. There were no more Shakespeares to work up. There was nothing in past history, or in the world's future possibilities, to make an editorial out of, suitable to that community; so there was but one theme left. That theme was Mr. Laird,[11] proprietor of the Virginia "Union." *His* editor had gone off to San Francisco too, and Laird was trying his hand at editing. I woke up Mr. Laird with some courtesies of the kind that were fashionable among newspaper editors in that region, and he came back at me the next day in a most vitriolic way. He was hurt by something I had said about him — some little thing — I don't remember what it was now — probably called him a horse-thief, or one of those little phrases customarily used to describe another editor. They were no doubt just, and accurate, but Laird was a very sensitive creature, and he didn't like it. So we expected a challenge from Mr. Laird, because according to the rules — according to the etiquette of duelling as reconstructed and reorganized and improved by the duellists of that region — whenever you said a thing about another person that he didn't like, it wasn't sufficient for him to talk back in the same offensive spirit: etiquette required him to send a challenge; so we waited for a challenge — waited all day. It didn't come. And as the day wore along, hour after hour, and no challenge came, the boys grew depressed. They lost heart. But I was cheerful; I felt better and better all the time. They couldn't understand it, but *I* could understand it. It was my *make* that enabled me to be cheerful when other people were despondent. So then it became necessary for us to waive etiquette and challenge Mr. Laird. When we reached that decision, they began to cheer up, but I began to lose some of my animation. However, in enterprises of this kind you are in the hands of your friends; there is nothing for you to do but to abide by what they consider to be the best course. Daggett wrote a challenge for me, for Daggett had the language — the right language — the convincing language — and I lacked it. Daggett poured out a stream of unsavory epithets upon Mr. Laird, charged with a vigor and venom of a strength calculated to persuade him; and Steve Gillis, my second, carried the challenge and came back to wait for the return. It didn't come. The boys were exasperated, but I kept my temper. Steve carried another challenge, hotter than the other, and we waited again. Nothing came of it. I began to feel quite comfortable. I began to take an interest in the challenges myself. I had not felt any before; but it seemed to me that I was accumulating a great and valuable reputation at no expense, and my delight in this grew and grew, as challenge after challenge was declined, until by midnight I was beginning to think that there was nothing in the world so much to be desired as a chance to fight a duel. So I hurried Daggett up; made him keep on sending challenge after challenge. Oh, well, I overdid it; Laird accepted. I might have known that that would happen — Laird was a man you couldn't depend on.

The boys were jubilant beyond expression. They helped me make my will, which was another discomfort — and I already had enough. Then they took me home. I didn't sleep any — didn't want to sleep. I had plenty of things to think about, and less than four hours to do it in — because five o'clock was the hour appointed for the tragedy, and I should have to use up one hour — beginning at four — in practising with the revolver and finding out which end of it to level at the adversary. At four we went down into a little gorge, about a mile from town, and borrowed a barn door for a mark — borrowed it of a man who was over in California on a visit — and we set the barn door up and stood a fence-rail up against the middle of it, to represent Mr. Laird. But the rail was no proper representative of him, for he was longer than a rail and thinner. Nothing would ever fetch him but a line shot, and then as like as not he would split the bullet — the worst material for duelling purposes that could be imagined. I began on the rail. I couldn't hit the rail; then I tried the barn door; but I couldn't hit the barn door. There was nobody in danger except stragglers around on the flanks of that mark. I was thoroughly discouraged, and I didn't cheer up any when we presently heard pistol-shots over in the next little ravine. I knew what that was — that was Laird's gang out practising him. They would hear my shots, and of course they would come up over the ridge to see what kind of a record I was making — see what their chances were against me. Well, I hadn't any record; and I knew that if Laird came over that ridge and saw my barn door without a scratch on it, he would be as anxious to fight as I was — or as I had been at midnight, before that disastrous acceptance came.

Now just at this moment, a little bird, no bigger than a sparrow, flew along by and lit on a sage-bush about thirty yards away. Steve whipped out his revolver and shot its head off. Oh, he was a marksman — much better than I was. We ran down there to pick up the bird, and just then, sure enough, Mr. Laird and his people came over the ridge, and they joined us. And when Laird's second saw that bird, with its head shot off, he lost color, he faded, and you could see that he was interested. He said:

"Who did that?"

Before I could answer, Steve spoke up and said quite calmly, and in a matter-of-fact way,

"Clemens did it."

The second said, "Why, that is wonderful. How far off was that bird?"

Steve said, "Oh, not far — about thirty yards."

The second said, "Well, that is astonishing shooting. How often can he do that?"

Steve said languidly, "Oh, about four times out of five."

I knew the little rascal was lying, but I didn't say anything. The second said, "Why, that is *amazing* shooting; I supposed he couldn't hit a church."

He was supposing very sagaciously, but I didn't say anything. Well, they said good morning. The second took Mr. Laird home, a little tottery on his legs, and Laird sent back a note in his own hand declining to fight a duel with me on any terms whatever.

Well, my life was saved — saved by that accident. I don't know what the bird thought about that interposition of Providence, but I felt very, very comfortable over it — satisfied and content. Now, we found out, later, that Laird had *hit* his mark four times out of six, right along. If the duel had come off, he would have so filled my skin with bullet-holes that it wouldn't have held my principles.

By breakfast-time the news was all over town that I had sent a challenge and Steve Gillis had carried it. Now that would entitle us to two years apiece in the penitentiary, according to the brand-new law.[12] Judge North[13] sent us no message as coming from himself, but a message *came* from a close friend of his. He said it would be a good idea for us to leave the territory by the first stage-coach. This would sail next morning, at four o'clock — and in the meantime we would be searched for, but not with avidity; and if we were in the Territory after that stage-coach left, we would be the first victims of the new law.[14] Judge North was anxious to have some object-lessons for that law, and he would absolutely keep us in the prison the full two years.

Well, it seemed to me that our society was no longer desirable in Nevada; so we stayed in our quarters and observed proper caution all day — except that once Steve went over to the hotel to attend to another customer of mine. That was a Mr. Cutler.[15] You see Laird was not the only person whom I had tried to reform during my occupancy of the editorial chair. I had looked around and selected several other people, and delivered a new zest of life into them through warm criticism and disapproval — so that when I laid down my editorial pen I had four horse-whippings and two duels owing to me. We didn't care for the horse-whippings; there was no glory in them; they were not worth the trouble of collecting. But honor required that some notice should be taken of that other duel. Mr. Cutler had come up from Carson City, and had sent a man over with a challenge from the hotel. Steve went over to pacify him. Steve weighed only ninety-five pounds, but it was well known throughout the territory that with his fists he could whip anybody that walked on two legs, let his weight and science be what they might. Steve was a Gillis, and when a Gillis confronted a man and had a proposition to make, the proposition always contained business. When Cutler found that Steve was my second he cooled down; he became calm and rational, and was ready to listen. Steve gave him fifteen minutes to get out of the hotel, and half an hour to get out of town or there would be results. So *that* duel went off successfully, because Mr. Cutler immediately left for Carson a convinced and reformed man.

I have never had anything to do with duels since. I thoroughly disapprove of duels. I consider them unwise, and I know they are dangerous. Also, sinful. If a man should challenge me now, I would go to that man and take him kindly and forgivingly by the hand and lead him to a quiet retired spot, and *kill* him.

CHAPTER IX

[*Dictated December 13, 1906*][1] As regards the coming American monarchy. It was before the Secretary of State had been heard from that the chairman of the banquet said:

"In this time of unrest it is of great satisfaction that such a man as you, Mr. Root, is chief adviser of the President."[2]

Mr. Root then got up and in the most quiet and orderly manner touched off the successor to the San Francisco earthquake. As a result, the several State governments were well shaken up and considerably weakened. Mr. Root was prophesying. He was prophesying, and it seems to me that no shrewder and surer forecasting has been done in this country for a good many years.

He did not say, in so many words, that we are proceeding, in a steady march, toward eventual and unavoidable replacement of the republic by monarchy; but I suppose he was aware that that is the case. He notes the several steps, the customary steps, which in all the ages have led to the consolidation of loose and scattered governmental forces into formidable centralizations of authority; but he stops there, and doesn't add up the sum. He is not unaware that heretofore the sum has been ultimate monarchy, and that the same figures can fairly be depended upon to furnish the same sum whenever and wherever they can be produced, so long as human nature shall remain as it is; but it was not needful that he do the adding, since any one can do it; neither would it have been gracious in him to do it.

In observing the changed conditions which in the course of time have made certain and sure the eventual seizure by the Washington government of a number of State duties and prerogatives which have been betrayed and

North American Review, vol. 184, no. 606 (January 4, 1907): 1–14.

neglected by the several States, he does not attribute those changes and the vast results which are to flow from them to any thought-out policy of any party or of any body of dreamers or schemers, but properly and rightly attributes them to that stupendous power — *Circumstance* — which moves by laws of its own, regardless of parties and policies, and whose decrees are final, and must be obeyed by all — and will be. The railway is a Circumstance, the steamship is a Circumstance, the telegraph is a Circumstance. They were mere happenings; and to the whole world, the wise and the foolish alike, they were entirely trivial, wholly inconsequential; indeed silly, comical, grotesque. No man, and no party, and no thought-out policy said, "Behold, we will build railways and steamships and telegraphs, and presently you will see the condition and way of life of every man and woman and child in the nation totally changed; unimaginable changes of law and custom will follow, in spite of anything that anybody can do to prevent it."

The changed conditions have come, and Circumstance knows what is following, and will follow. So does Mr. Root. His language is not unclear, it is crystal:

"Our whole life has swung away from the old State centres, and is crystallizing about national centres."

" . . . . The old barriers which kept the States as separate communities are completely lost from sight."

" . . . . That [State] power of regulation and control is gradually passing into the hands of the national government."

"Sometimes by an assertion of the inter-State commerce power, sometimes by an assertion of the taxing power, the national government is taking up the performance of duties which under the changed conditions the separate States are no longer capable of adequately performing."

"We are urging forward in a development of business and social life which tends more and more to the obliteration of State lines and the decrease of State power as compared with national power."

"It is useless for the advocates of State rights to inveigh against . . . the extension of national authority in the fields of necessary control where the States themselves fail in the performance of their duty."

He is not announcing a policy; he is not forecasting what a party of planners will bring about; he is merely telling what the people will require and compel. And he could have added — which would be perfectly true — that the people will not be moved to it by speculation and cogitation and planning, but by *Circumstance* — that power which arbitrarily compels all their actions, and over which they have not the slightest control.

"The end is not yet."

It is a true word. We are on the march, but at present we are only just getting started.

If the States continue to fail to do their duty as required by the people —

". . . *constructions of the Constitution will be found* to vest the power where it will be exercised — in the national government."

I do not know whether that has a sinister meaning or not, and so I will not enlarge upon it lest I should chance to be in the wrong. It sounds like ship-money come again, but it may not be so intended.[3]

Human nature being what it is, I suppose we must expect to drift into monarchy by and by. It is a saddening thought, but we cannot change our nature: we are all alike, we human beings; and in our blood and bone, and ineradicable, we carry the seeds out of which monarchies and aristocracies are grown: worship of gauds, titles, distinctions, power. We have to worship these things and their possessors, we are all born so, and we cannot help it. We have to be despised by somebody whom we regard as above us, or we are not happy; we have to have somebody to worship and envy, or we cannot be content. In America we manifest this in all the ancient and customary ways. In public we scoff at titles and hereditary privilege, but privately we hanker after them, and when we get a chance we buy them for cash and a daughter. Sometimes we get a good man and worth the price, but we are ready to take him anyway, whether he be ripe or rotten, whether he be clean and decent, or merely a basket of noble and sacred and long-descended offal. And when we get him the whole nation publicly chaffs and scoffs — and privately envies; and also is proud of the honor which has been conferred upon us. We run over our list of titled purchases every now and then, in the newspapers, and discuss them and caress them, and are thankful and happy.

Like all the other nations, we worship money and the possessors of it — they being our aristocracy, and we have to have one. We like to read about rich people in the papers; the papers know it, and they do their best to keep this appetite liberally fed. They even leave out a football bull-fight now and then to get room for all the particulars of how — according to the display heading — "Rich Woman Fell Down Cellar — Not Hurt." The falling down the cellar is of no interest to us when the woman is not rich, but no rich woman can fall down cellar and we not yearn to know all about it and wish it was us.

In a monarchy the people willingly and rejoicingly revere and take pride in their nobilities, and are not humiliated by the reflection that this humble and hearty homage gets no return but contempt. Contempt does not shame them, they are used to it, and they recognize that it is their proper due. We are all made like that. In Europe we easily and quickly learn to take that attitude toward the sovereigns and the aristocracies; moreover, it has been observed that when we get the attitude we go on and exaggerate it, presently becoming more servile than the natives, and vainer of it. The next step is to rail and scoff at republics and democracies. All of which is natural, for we have not ceased to be human beings by becoming Americans, and the human race was always intended to be governed by kingship, not by popular vote.

I suppose we must expect that unavoidable and irresistible Circumstances will gradually take away the powers of the States and concentrate them in the central government, and that the republic will then repeat the history of all time and become a monarchy; but I believe that if we obstruct these encroachments and steadily resist them the monarchy can be postponed for a good while yet.

[*Dictated December 1, 1906*] An exciting event in our village (Hannibal) was the arrival of the mesmerizer. I think the year was 1850. As to that I am not sure, but I know the month — it was May; that detail (1849–'51) has survived the wear of fifty-five years. A pair of connected little incidents of that month have served to keep the memory of it green for me all this time; incidents of no consequence, and not worth embalming, yet my memory has preserved them carefully and flung away things of real value to give them space and make them comfortable. The truth is, a person's memory has no more sense than his conscience, and no appreciation whatever of values and proportions. However, never mind those trifling incidents; my subject is the mesmerizer, now.

He advertised his show, and promised marvels. Admission as usual: 25 cents, children and negroes half price. The village had heard of mesmerism, in a general way, but had not encountered it yet. Not many people attended, the first night, but next day they had so many wonders to tell that everybody's curiosity was fired, and after that for a fortnight the magician had prosperous times. I was fourteen or fifteen years old — the age at which a boy is willing to endure all things, suffer all things, short of death by fire, if thereby he may be conspicuous and show off before the public; and so, when I saw the "subjects" perform their foolish antics on the platform and make the people laugh and shout and admire, I had a burning desire to be a subject myself. Every night, for three nights, I sat in the row of candidates on the platform, and held the magic disk in the palm of my hand, and gazed at it and tried to get sleepy, but it was a failure; I remained wide awake, and had to retire defeated, like the majority. Also, I had to sit there and be gnawed with envy of Hicks,[4] our journeyman; I had to sit there and see him scamper and jump when Simmons the enchanter exclaimed, "See the snake! see the snake!" and hear him say, "My, how beautiful!" in response to the suggestion that he was observing a splendid sunset; and so on — the whole insane business. I couldn't laugh, I couldn't applaud; it filled me with bitterness to have others do it, and to have people make a hero of Hicks, and crowd around him when the show was over, and ask him for more and more particulars of the wonders he had seen in his visions, and manifest in many ways that they were proud to be acquainted with him. Hicks — the idea! I couldn't stand it; I was getting boiled to death in my own bile.

On the fourth night temptation came, and I was not strong enough to resist. When I had gazed at the disk awhile I pretended to be sleepy, and began to nod. Straightway came the professor and made passes over my head and down my body and legs and arms, finishing each pass with a snap of his fingers in the air, to discharge the surplus electricity; then he began to "draw" me with the disk, holding it in his fingers and telling me I could not take my eyes off it, try as I might; so I rose slowly, bent and gazing, and followed that disk all over the place, just as I had seen the others do. Then I was put through the other paces. Upon suggestion I fled from snakes; passed buckets at a fire; became excited over hot steamboat-races; made love to imaginary girls and kissed them; fished from the platform and landed mud-cats that outweighed me — and so on, all the customary marvels. But not in the customary way. I was cautious at first, and watchful, being afraid the professor would discover that I was an impostor and drive me from the platform in disgrace; but as soon as I realized that I was not in danger, I set myself the task of terminating Hicks's usefulness as a subject, and of usurping his place.

It was a sufficiently easy task. Hicks was born honest; I, without that incumbrance — so some people said. Hicks saw what he saw, and reported accordingly; I saw more than was visible, and added to it such details as could help. Hicks had no imagination, I had a double supply. He was born calm, I was born excited. No vision could start a rapture in him, and he was constipated as to language, anyway; but if I saw a vision I emptied the dictionary onto it and lost the remnant of my mind into the bargain.

At the end of my first half-hour Hicks was a thing of the past, a fallen hero, a broken idol, and I knew it and was glad, and said in my heart, Success to crime! Hicks could never have been mesmerized to the point where he could kiss an imaginary girl in public, or a real one either, but I was competent. Whatever Hicks had failed in, I made it a point to succeed in, let the cost be what it might, physically or morally. He had shown several bad defects, and I had made a note of them. For instance, if the magician asked, "What do you see?" and left him to invent a vision for himself, Hicks was dumb and blind, he couldn't see a thing nor say a word, whereas the magician soon found that when it came to seeing visions of a stunning and marketable sort I could get along better without his help than with it. Then there was another thing: Hicks wasn't worth a tallow dip on mute mental suggestion. Whenever Simmons stood behind him and gazed at the back of his skull and tried to drive a mental suggestion into it, Hicks sat with vacant face, and never suspected. If he had been noticing, he could have seen by the rapt faces of the audience that something was going on behind his back that required a response. Inasmuch as I was an impostor I dreaded to have this test put upon me, for I knew the professor would be "willing" me to do something, and as I couldn't know what it was, I should be exposed and denounced. However, when my time came, I took my chance. I perceived by the tense and expectant faces of the people that Simmons was behind me willing me with all his might. I tried my best to imagine what he wanted, but nothing suggested itself. I felt ashamed and miserable, then. I believed that the hour of my disgrace was come, and that in another moment I should go out of that place disgraced. I ought to be ashamed to confess it, but my next thought was, not how I could win the compassion of kindly hearts by going out humbly and in sorrow for my misdoings, but how I could go out most sensationally and spectacularly.

There was a rusty and empty old revolver lying on the table, among the "properties" employed in the performances. On May-day, two or three weeks before, there had been a celebration by the schools, and I had had a quarrel with a big boy who was the school-bully, and I had not come out of it with credit. That boy was now seated in the middle of the house, halfway down the main aisle. I crept stealthily and impressively toward the table, with a dark and murderous scowl on my face, copied from a popular romance, seized the revolver suddenly, flourished it, shouted the bully's name, jumped off the platform, and made a rush for him and chased him out of the house before the paralyzed people could interfere to save him. There was a storm of applause, and the magician, addressing the house, said, most impressively—

"That you may know how really remarkable this is, and how wonderfully developed a subject we have in this boy, I assure you that without a single spoken word to guide him he has carried out what I mentally commanded him to do, to the minutest detail. I could have stopped him at a moment in his vengeful career by a mere exertion of my will, therefore the poor fellow who has escaped was at no time in danger."

So I was not in disgrace. I returned to the platform a hero, and happier than I have ever been in this world since. As regards mental suggestion, my fears of it were gone. I judged that in case I failed to guess what the professor might be willing me to do, I could count on putting up something that would answer just as well. I was right, and exhibitions of unspoken suggestion became a favorite with the public. Whenever I perceived that I was being willed to do something I got up and did something — anything that occurred to me — and the magician, not being a fool, always ratified it. When people asked me, "How *can* you tell what he is willing you to do?" I said, "It's just as easy," and they always said, admiringly, "Well it beats *me* how you can do it."

Hicks was weak in another detail. When the professor made passes over him and said "his whole body is without sensation now — come forward and test him, ladies and gentlemen," the ladies and gentlemen always complied eagerly, and stuck pins into Hicks, and if they went deep Hicks was sure to wince, then that poor professor would have to explain that Hicks "wasn't sufficiently under the influence." But I didn't wince; I only suffered, and shed tears on the inside. The miseries that a conceited boy will endure to keep up his "reputation"! And so will a conceited man; I know it in my own person, and have seen it in a hundred thousand others. That professor ought to have protected me, and I often hoped he would, when the tests were unusually severe, but he didn't. It may be that he was deceived as well as the others, though I did not believe it nor think it possible. Those were dear good people, but they must have carried simplicity and credulity to the limit. They would stick a pin in my arm and bear on it until they drove it a third of its length in, and then be lost in wonder that by a mere exercise of will-power the professor could turn my arm to iron and make it insensible to pain. Whereas it was not insensible at all; I was suffering agonies of pain.

After that fourth night, that proud night, that triumphant night, I was the only subject. Simmons invited no more candidates to the platform. I performed alone, every night, the rest of the fortnight. In the beginning of the second week I conquered the last doubters. Up to that time a dozen wise old heads, the intellectual aristocracy of the town, had held out, as implacable unbelievers. I was as hurt by this as if I were engaged in some honest occupation. There is nothing surprising about this. Human beings feel dishonor the most, sometimes, when they most deserve it. That handful of overwise old gentlemen kept on shaking their heads all the first week, and saying they had seen no marvels there that could not have been produced by collusion; and they were pretty vain of their unbelief, too, and liked to show it and air it, and be superior to the ignorant and the gullible. Particularly old Dr. Peake,[5] who was the ringleader of the irreconcilables, and very formidable; for he was an F.F.V., he was learned, white-haired and venerable, nobly and richly clad in the fashions of an earlier and a courtlier day, he was large and stately, and he not only seemed wise, but was what he seemed, in that regard. He had great influence, and his opinion upon any matter was worth much more than that of any other person in the community. When I conquered him, at last, I knew I was undisputed master of the field; and now, after more than fifty years, I acknowledge, with a few dry old tears, that I rejoiced without shame.

[*Dictated December 2, 1906*] In 1847 we were living in a large white house on the corner of Hill and Main Streets — a house that still stands, but (1847) isn't large now, although it hasn't lost a plank; I saw it a year ago and noticed that shrinkage.[6] My father died in it in March of the year mentioned, but our family did not move out of it until some months afterward. Ours was not the only family in the house, there was another — Dr. Grant's.[7] One day Dr. Grant and Dr. Reyburn argued a matter on the street with sword-canes, and Grant was brought home multifariously punctured. Old Dr. Peake calked the leaks, and came every day for a while, to look after him. The Grants were Virginians, like Peake, and one day when Grant was getting well enough to be on his feet and sit around in the parlor and talk, the conversation fell upon Virginia and old times. I was present, but the group were probably quite unconscious of me, I being only a lad and a negligible quantity. Two of the group — Dr. Peake and Mrs. Crawford, Mrs. Grant's mother — had been of the audience when the Richmond theatre burned down, thirty-six years before, and they talked over the frightful details of that memorable tragedy. These were eyewitnesses, and with their eyes I saw it all with an intolerable vividness: I saw the black smoke rolling and tumbling toward the sky, I saw the flames burst through it and turn red, I heard the shrieks of the despairing, I glimpsed their faces at the windows, caught fitfully through the veiling smoke, I saw them jump to their death, or to mutilation worse than death. The picture is before me yet, and can never fade.

In due course they talked of the colonial mansion of the Peakes, with its stately columns and its spacious grounds, and by odds and ends I picked up a clearly defined idea of the place. I was strongly interested, for I had not before heard of such palatial things from the lips of people who had seen them with their own eyes. One detail, casually dropped, hit my imagination hard. In the wall, by the great front door, there was a round hole as big as a saucer — a British cannon-ball had made it, in the war of the Revolution. It was breath-taking; it made history real; history had never been real to me before.

Very well, three or four years later, as already mentioned, I was king-bee and sole "subject" in the mesmeric show; it was the beginning of the second week; the performance was half over; just then the majestic Dr. Peake, with his ruffled bosom and wristbands and his gold-headed cane, entered, and a deferential citizen vacated his seat beside the Grants and made the great chief take it. This happened while I was trying to invent something fresh in the way of a vision, in response to the professor's remark —

"Concentrate your powers. Look — look attentively. There — don't you see something? Concentrate — concentrate. Now then — describe it."

Without suspecting it, Dr. Peake, by entering the place, had reminded me of the talk of three years before. He had also furnished me capital and was become my confederate, an accomplice in my frauds. I began on a vision, a vague and dim one (that was part of the game at the beginning of a vision; it isn't best to see it too clearly at first, it might look as if you had come loaded with it). The vision developed, by degrees, gathered swing, momentum, energy. It was the Richmond fire. Dr. Peake was cold, at first, and his fine face had a trace of polite scorn in it; but when he began to recognize that fire, that expression changed, and his eyes began to light up. As soon as I saw that, I threw the valves wide open and turned on all the steam, and gave those people a supper of fire and horrors that was calculated to last them one while! They couldn't gasp, when I got through — they were petrified. Dr. Peake had risen, and was standing, — and breathing hard. He said, in a great voice —

"My doubts are ended. No collusion could produce that miracle. It was totally impossible for him to know those details, yet he has described them with the clarity of an eye-witness — and with what unassailable truthfulness God knows I know!"

I saved the colonial mansion for the last night, and solidified and perpetuated Dr. Peake's conversion with the cannon-ball hole. He explained to the house that I could never have heard of that small detail, which differentiated this mansion from all other Virginian mansions and perfectly identified it, therefore the fact stood proven that I had *seen* it in my vision. Lawks!

It is curious. When the magician's engagement closed there was but one person in the village who did not believe in mesmerism, and I was the one. All the others were converted, but I was to remain an implacable and unpersuadable disbeliever in mesmerism and hypnotism for close upon fifty years. This was because I never would examine them, in after life. I couldn't. The subject revolted me. Perhaps because it brought back to me a passage in my life which for pride's sake I wished to forget; though I thought — or persuaded myself I thought — I should never come across a "proof" which wasn't thin and cheap, and probably had a fraud like me behind it.

The truth is, I did not have to wait long to get tired of my triumphs. Not thirty days, I think. The glory which is built upon a lie soon becomes a most unpleasant incumbrance. No doubt for a while I enjoyed having my exploits told and retold and told again in my presence and wondered over and exclaimed about, but I quite distinctly remember that there presently came a time when the subject was wearisome and odious to me and I could not endure the disgusting discomfort of it. I am well aware that the world-glorified doer of a deed of great and real splendor has just my experience; I know that he deliciously enjoys hearing about it for three or four weeks, and that pretty soon after that he begins to dread the mention of it, and by and by wishes he had been with the damned before he ever thought of doing that deed; I remember how General Sherman used to rage and swear over "When we were Marching through Georgia," which was played at him and sung at him everywhere he went; still, I think I suffered a shade more than the legitimate hero does, he being privileged to soften his misery with the reflection that his glory was at any rate golden and reproachless in its origin, whereas I had no such privilege, there being no possible way to make mine respectable.

How easy it is to make people believe a lie, and how hard it is to undo that work again! Thirty-five years after those evil exploits of mine I visited my old mother, whom I had not seen for ten years; and being moved by what seemed to me a rather noble and perhaps heroic impulse, I thought I would humble myself and confess my ancient fault. It cost me a great effort to make up my mind; I dreaded the sorrow that would rise in her face, and the shame that would look out of her eyes; but after long and troubled reflection, the sacrifice seemed due and right, and I gathered my resolution together and made the confession.

To my astonishment there were no sentimentalities, no dramatics, no George Washington effects; she was not moved in the least degree; she simply did not believe me, and said so! I was not merely disappointed, I was nettled, to have my costly truthfulness flung out of the market in this placid and confident way when I was expecting to get a profit out of it. I asserted, and reasserted, with rising heat, my statement that every single thing I had done on those long-vanished nights was a lie and a swindle; and when she shook her head tranquilly and said she knew better, I put up my hand and *swore* to it — adding a triumphant "*Now* what do you say?"

It did not affect her at all; it did not budge her the fraction of an inch from her position. If this was hard for me to endure, it did not begin with the blister she put upon the raw when she began to put my sworn oath out of court with *arguments* to prove that I was under a delusion and did not know what I was talking about. Arguments! Arguments to show that a person on a man's outside can know better what is on his inside than he does himself! I had cherished some contempt for arguments before, I have not enlarged my respect for them since. She refused to believe that I had invented my visions myself; she said it was folly: that I was only a child at the time and could not have done it. She cited the Richmond fire and the colonial mansion and said they were quite beyond my capacities. Then I saw my chance! I said she was right — I didn't invent those, I got them from Dr. Peake. Even this great shot did no damage. She said Dr. Peake's evidence was better than mine, and he had said in plain words that it was impossible for me to have heard about those things. Dear, dear, what a grotesque and unthinkable situation: a confessed swindler convicted of honesty and condemned to acquittal by circumstantial evidence furnished by the swindled!

I realized, with shame and with impotent vexation, that I was defeated all along the line. I had but one card left, but it was a formidable one. I played it — and stood from under. It seemed ignoble to demolish her fortress, after she had defended it so valiantly; but the defeated know not mercy. I played that master card. It was the pin-sticking. I said, solemnly —

"I give you my honor, a pin was never stuck into me without causing me cruel pain."

She only said —

"It is thirty-five years. I believe you do think that, *now*, but I was there, and I know better. You never winced."

She was so calm! and I was so far from it, so nearly frantic.

"Oh, my goodness!" I said, "let me *show* you that I am speaking the truth. Here is my arm; drive a pin into it — drive it to the head — I shall not wince."

She only shook her gray head and said, with simplicity and conviction —

"You are a man, now, and could dissemble the hurt; but you were only a child then, and could not have done it."

And so the lie which I played upon her in my youth remained with her as an unchallengeable truth to the day of her death. Carlyle[8] said "a lie cannot live." It shows that he did not know how to tell them. If I had taken out a life policy on this one the premiums would have bankrupted me ages ago.

CHAPTER X

[*Dictated March 28, 1906*] Orion Clemens[1] was born in Jamestown, Fentress County, Tennessee, in 1825. He was the family's first-born, and ante-
(1825) dated me ten years. Between him and me came a sister, Margaret, who died, aged ten, in 1837, in that village of Florida, Missouri, where I was born; and Pamela, mother of Samuel E. Moffett, who was an
(1837) invalid all her life and died in the neighborhood of New York a year ago, aged about seventy-five. Her character was without blemish, and she was of a most kindly and gentle disposition. Also there was a
(1843) brother, Benjamin, who died in 1843 aged ten or twelve.
Orion's boyhood was spent in that wee little log hamlet of Jamestown up there among the "knobs"— so called — of East Tennessee. The family migrated to Florida, Missouri, then moved to Hannibal, Missouri, when Orion was twelve and a half years old. When he was fifteen or sixteen he was sent to St. Louis and there he learned the printer's trade. One of his characteristics was eagerness. He woke with an eagerness about some matter or other every morning; it consumed him all day; it perished in the night and he was on fire with a fresh new interest next morning before he could get his clothes on. He exploited in this way three hundred and sixty-five red-hot new eagernesses every year of his life. But I am forgetting another characteristic, a very pronounced one. That was his deep glooms, his despondencies, his despairs; these had their place in each and every day along with the eagernesses. Thus his day was divided — no, not divided, mottled — from sunrise to midnight with alternating brilliant sunshine and black cloud. Every day he was the most joyous and hopeful man that ever was, I think, and also every day he was the most miserable man that ever was.

North American Review, vol. 184, no. 607 (January 18, 1907): 113–19.

While he was in his apprenticeship in St. Louis, he got well acquainted with Edward Bates, who was afterwards in Mr. Lincoln's first cabinet.[2] Bates was a very fine man, an honorable and upright man, and a distinguished lawyer. He patiently allowed Orion to bring to him each new project; he discussed it with him and extinguished it by argument and irresistible logic — at first. But after a few weeks he found that this labor was not necessary; that he could leave the new project alone and it would extinguish itself the same night. Orion thought he would like to become a lawyer. Mr. Bates encouraged him, and he studied law nearly a week, then of course laid it aside to try something new. He wanted to become an orator. Mr. Bates gave him lessons. Mr. Bates walked the floor reading from an English book aloud and rapidly turning the English into French, and he recommended this exercise to Orion. But as Orion knew no French, he took up that study and wrought at it like a volcano for two or three days; then gave it up. During his apprenticeship in St. Louis he joined a number of churches, one after another, and taught in their Sunday-schools — changing his Sunday-school every time he changed his religion. He was correspondingly erratic in his politics — Whig to-day, Democrat next week, and anything fresh that he could find in the political market the week after.[3] I may remark here that throughout his long life he was always trading religions and enjoying the change of scenery. I will also remark that his sincerity was never doubted; his truthfulness was never doubted; and in matters of business and money his honesty was never questioned. Notwithstanding his forever-recurring caprices and changes, his principles were high, always high, and absolutely unshakable. He was the strangest compound that ever got mixed in a human mould. Such a person as that is given to acting upon impulse and without reflection; that was Orion's way. Everything he did he did with conviction and enthusiasm and with a vainglorious pride in the thing he was doing — and no matter what that thing was, whether good, bad or indifferent, he repented of it every time in sackcloth and ashes before twenty-four hours had sped. Pessimists are born, not made. Optimists are born, not made. But I think he was the only person I have ever known in whom pessimism and optimism were lodged in exactly equal proportions. Except in the matter of grounded principle, he was as unstable as water. You could dash his spirits with a single word; you could raise them into the sky again with another one. You could break his heart with a word of disapproval; you could make him as happy as an angel with a word of approval. And there was no occasion to put any sense or any vestige of mentality of any kind into these miracles; anything you might say would answer.

He had another conspicuous characteristic, and it was the father of those which I have just spoken of. This was an intense lust for approval. He was so eager to be approved, so girlishly anxious to be approved by anybody and everybody, without discrimination, that he was commonly ready to forsake his notions, opinions and convictions at a moment's notice in order to get the approval of any person who disagreed with them. I wish to be understood as reserving his fundamental principles all the time. He never forsook those to please anybody. Born and reared among slaves and slaveholders, he was yet an abolitionist from his boyhood to his death. He was always truthful; he was always sincere; he was always honest and honorable. But in light matters — matters of small consequence, like religion and politics and such things — he never acquired a conviction that could survive a disapproving remark from a cat.

He was always dreaming; he was a dreamer from birth, and this characteristic got him into trouble now and then.

Once when he was twenty-three or twenty-four years old, and was become a journeyman, he conceived the romantic idea of coming to Hannibal without giving us notice, in order that he might furnish to the family a pleasant surprise. If he had given notice, he would have been informed that we had changed our residence and that that gruff old bass-voiced sailorman, Dr. G.,[4] our family physician, was living in the house which we had formerly occupied and that Orion's former room in that house was now occupied by Dr. G.'s two middle-aged maiden sisters. Orion arrived at Hannibal per steamboat in the middle of the night, and started with his customary eagerness on his excursion, his mind all on fire with his romantic project and building and enjoying his surprise in advance. He was always enjoying things in advance; it was the make of him. He never could wait for the event, but must build it out of dream-stuff and enjoy it beforehand — consequently sometimes when the event happened he saw that it was not as good as the one he had invented in his imagination, and so he had lost profit by not keeping the imaginary one and letting the reality go.

When he arrived at the house he went around to the back door and slipped off his boots and crept up-stairs and arrived at the room of those elderly ladies without having wakened any sleepers. He undressed in the dark and got into bed and snuggled up against somebody. He was a little surprised, but not much — for he thought it was our brother Ben. It was winter, and the bed was comfortable, and the supposed Ben added to the comfort — and so he was dropping off to sleep very well satisfied with his progress so far and full of happy dreams of what was going to happen in the morning. But something else was going to happen sooner than that, and it happened now. The maid that was being crowded fumed and fretted and struggled and presently came to a half-waking condition and protested against the crowding. That voice paralyzed Orion. He couldn't move a limb; he couldn't get his breath; and the crowded one discovered his new whiskers and began to scream. This removed the paralysis, and Orion was out of bed and clawing round in the dark for his clothes in a fraction of a second. Both maids began to scream, then, so Orion did not wait to get his whole wardrobe. He started with such parts of it as he could grab. He flew to the head of the stairs and started down, and was paralyzed again at that point, because he saw the faint yellow flame of a candle soaring up the stairs from below and he judged that Dr. G. was behind it, and he was. He had no clothes on to speak of, but no matter, he was well enough fixed for an occasion like this, because he had a butcher-knife in his hand. Orion shouted to him, and this saved his life, for the Doctor recognized his voice. Then in those deep-sea-going bass tones of his that I used to admire so much when I was a little boy, he explained to Orion the change that had been made, told him where to find the Clemens family, and closed with some quite unnecessary advice about posting himself before he undertook another adventure like that — advice which Orion probably never needed again as long as he lived.

One bitter December night, Orion sat up reading until three o'clock in the morning and then, without looking at a clock, sallied forth to call on a young lady. He hammered and hammered at the door; couldn't get any response; didn't understand it. Anybody else would have regarded that as an indication of some kind or other and would have drawn inferences and gone home. But Orion didn't draw inferences, he merely hammered and hammered, and finally the father of the girl appeared at the door in a dressing-gown. He had a candle in his hand and the dressing-gown was all the clothing he had on — except an expression of unwelcome which was so thick and so large that it extended all down his front to his instep and nearly obliterated the dressing-gown. But Orion didn't notice that this was an unpleasant expression. He merely walked in. The old gentleman took him into the parlor, set the candle on a table, and stood. Orion made the usual remarks about the weather, and sat down — sat down and talked and talked and went on talking — that old man looking at him vindictively and waiting for his chance — waiting treacherously and malignantly for his chance. Orion had not asked for the young lady. It was not customary. It was understood that a young fellow came to see the girl of the house, not the founder of it. At last Orion got up and made some remark to the effect that probably the young lady was busy and he would go now and call again. That was the old man's chance, and he said with fervency "Why good land, aren't you going to stop to breakfast?"

Orion did not come to Hannibal until two or three years after my father's death.[5] Meantime he remained in St. Louis. He was a journeyman printer and earning wages. Out of his wage he supported my mother and my brother Henry, who was two years younger than I. My sister Pamela helped in this support by taking piano pupils. Thus we got along, but it was pretty hard sledding. I was not one of the burdens, because I was taken from school at once, upon my father's death, and placed in the office of the Hannibal "Courier," as printer's apprentice, and Mr. S., the editor and proprietor of the paper, allowed me the usual emolument of the office of apprentice — that is to say board and clothes, but no money.[6] The clothes consisted of two suits a year, but one of the suits always failed to materialize and the other suit was not purchased so long as Mr. S.'s old clothes held out. I was only about half as big as Mr. S., consequently his shirts gave me the uncomfortable sense of living in a circus tent, and I had to turn up his pants to my ears to make them short enough.

There were two other apprentices. One was Steve Wilkins,[7] seventeen or eighteen years old and a giant. When he was in Mr. S.'s clothes they fitted him as the candle-mould fits the candle — thus he was generally in a suffocated condition, particularly in the summer-time. He was a reckless, hilarious, admirable creature; he had no principles, and was delightful company. At first we three apprentices had to feed in the kitchen with the old slave cook and her very handsome and bright and well-behaved young mulatto daughter. For his own amusement — for he was not generally laboring for other people's amusement — Steve was constantly and persistently and loudly and elaborately making love to that mulatto girl and distressing the life out of her and worrying the old mother to death. She would say, "Now, Marse Steve, Marse Steve, can't you behave yourself?" With encouragement like that, Steve would naturally renew his attentions and emphasize them. It was killingly funny to Ralph and me. And, to speak truly, the old mother's distress about it was merely a pretence. She quite well understood that by the customs of slaveholding communities it was Steve's right to make love to that girl if he wanted to. But the girl's distress was very real. She had a refined nature, and she took all Steve's extravagant love-making in resentful earnest.

We got but little variety in the way of food at that kitchen table, and there wasn't enough of it anyway. So we apprentices used to keep alive by arts of our own — that is to say, we crept into the cellar nearly every night, by a private entrance which we had discovered, and we robbed the cellar of potatoes and onions and such things, and carried them down-town to the printing-office, where we slept on pallets on the floor, and cooked them at the stove and had very good times.

As I have indicated, Mr. S.'s economies were of a pretty close and rigid kind. By and by, when we apprentices were promoted from the basement to the ground floor and allowed to sit at the family table, along with the one journeyman, Harry H.,[8] the economies continued. Mrs. S. was a bride.[9] She had attained to that distinction very recently, after waiting a good part of a lifetime for it, and she was the right woman in the right place, according to the economics of the place, for she did not trust the sugar-bowl to us, but sweetened our coffee herself. That is, she went through the motions. She didn't really sweeten it. She seemed to put one heaping teaspoonful of brown sugar into each cup, but, according to Steve, that was a deceit. He said she dipped the spoon in the coffee first to make the sugar stick, and then scooped the sugar out of the bowl with the spoon upside down, so that the effect to the eye was a heaped-up spoon, whereas the sugar on it was nothing but a layer. This all seems perfectly true to me, and yet that thing would be so difficult to perform that I suppose it really didn't happen, but was one of Steve's lies.

CHAPTER XI

[*Dictated March 28th, 1906*][1] About 1849 or 1850 Orion severed his connection with the printing-house in St. Louis and came up to Hannibal, and (1850) bought a weekly paper called the Hannibal "Journal," together with its plant and its good-will, for the sum of five hundred dollars cash.[2] He borrowed the cash at ten per cent. interest, from an old farmer named Johnson who lived five miles out of town. Then he reduced the subscription price of the paper from two dollars to one dollar. He reduced the rates for advertising in about the same proportion, and thus he created one absolute and unassailable certainty — to wit: that the business would never pay him a single cent of profit. He took me out of the "Courier" office and engaged my services in his own at three dollars and a half a week, which was an extravagant wage, but Orion was always generous, always liberal with everybody except himself. It cost him nothing in my case, for he never was able to pay me a penny as long as I was with him. By the end of the first year he found he must make some economies. The office rent was cheap, but it was not cheap enough. He could not afford to pay rent of any kind, so he moved the whole plant into the house we lived in, and it cramped the dwelling-place cruelly. He kept that paper alive during four years, but I have at this time no idea how he accomplished it. Toward the end of each year he had to turn out and scrape and scratch for the fifty dollars of interest due Mr. Johnson, and that fifty dollars was about the only cash he ever received or paid out, I suppose, while he was proprietor of that newspaper, except for ink and printing-paper. The paper was a dead failure. It had to be that from the start. Finally he handed it over to Mr. Johnson,

North American Review, vol. 184, no. 608 (February 1, 1907): 225–32.

and went up to Muscatine, Iowa, and acquired a small interest in a weekly newspaper there.[3] It was not a sort of property to marry on — but no matter. He came across a winning and pretty girl who lived in Quincy, Illinois, a few miles below Keokuk, and they became engaged. He was always falling in love with girls, but by some accident or other he had never gone so far as engagement before. And now he achieved nothing but misfortune by it, because he straightway fell in love with a Keokuk girl. He married the Keokuk girl and they began a struggle for life which turned out to be a difficult enterprise, and very unpromising.[4]

To gain a living in Muscatine was plainly impossible, so Orion and his new wife went to Keokuk to live, for she wanted to be near her relatives.[5] He bought a little bit of a job-printing plant — on credit, of course — and at once put prices down to where not even the apprentices could get a living out of it, and this sort of thing went on.

I had not joined the Muscatine migration. Just before that happened (1853) (which I think was in 1853) I disappeared one night and fled to St. Louis. There I worked in the composing-room of the "Evening News" for a time, and then started on my travels to see the world. The world was New York City, and there was a little World's Fair there.[6] It had just been opened where the great reservoir afterward was, and where the sumptuous public library is now being built — Fifth Avenue and Forty-second Street. I arrived in New York with two or three dollars in pocket change and a ten-dollar bank-bill concealed in the lining of my coat. I got work at villainous wages in the establishment of John A. Gray and Green in Cliff Street, and I found board in a sufficiently villainous mechanics' boarding-house in Duane Street. The firm paid my wages in wildcat money at its face value, and my week's wage merely sufficed to pay board and lodging.[7] By and by I went to Philadelphia and worked there some months as a "sub" on the "Inquirer" and the "Public Ledger."[8] Finally I made a flying trip to Washington to see (1854) the sights there, and in 1854 I went back to the Mississippi Valley, sitting upright in the smoking-car two or three days and nights. When I reached St. Louis I was exhausted. I went to bed on board a steamboat that was bound for Muscatine. I fell asleep at once, with my clothes on, and didn't wake again for thirty-six hours.[9]

. . . I worked in that little job-office in Keokuk as much as two years, I should say, without ever collecting a cent of wages, for Orion was never able to pay anything — but Dick Higham[10] and I had good times. I don't know what Dick got, but it was probably only uncashable promises.

One day in the midwinter of 1856 or 1857 — I think it was 1856 — I was
coming along the main street of Keokuk in the middle of the forenoon. It
(1856)   was bitter weather — so bitter that that street was deserted, almost.
         A light dry snow was blowing here and there on the ground and on
the pavement, swirling this way and that way and making all sorts of beautiful figures, but very chilly to look at. The wind blew a piece of paper past
me and it lodged against a wall of a house. Something about the look of
it attracted my attention and I gathered it in. It was a fifty-dollar bill, the
only one I had ever seen, and the largest assemblage of money I had ever
encountered in one spot. I advertised it in the papers and suffered more
than a thousand dollars' worth of solicitude and fear and distress during
the next few days lest the owner should see the advertisement and come
and take my fortune away. As many as four days went by without an applicant; then I could endure this kind of misery no longer. I felt sure that another four could not go by in this safe and secure way. I felt that I must
take that money out of danger. So I bought a ticket for Cincinnati and went
to that city. I worked there several months in the printing-office of Wrightson and Company.[11] I had been reading Lieutenant Herndon's account of
his explorations of the Amazon[12] and had been mightily attracted by what
he said of coca. I made up my mind that I would go to the head waters
of the Amazon and collect coca and trade in it and make a fortune.[13] I left
for New Orleans in the steamer "Paul Jones" with this great idea filling my
mind. One of the pilots of that boat was Horace Bixby. Little by little I got
acquainted with him, and pretty soon I was doing a lot of steering for him
in his daylight watches. When I got to New Orleans I inquired about ships
leaving for Pará and discovered that there weren't any, and learned that there
probably wouldn't be any during that century. It had not occurred to me
to inquire about these particulars before leaving Cincinnati, so there I was.
I couldn't get to the Amazon. I had no friends in New Orleans and no
money to speak of. I went to Horace Bixby and asked him to make a pilot
out of me. He said he would do it for a hundred dollars cash in advance.
So I steered for him up to St. Louis, borrowed the money from my brother-
in-law and closed the bargain. I had acquired this brother-in-law several
years before. This was Mr. William A. Moffett, a merchant, a Virginian —
a fine man in every way. He had married my sister Pamela, and the Samuel E. Moffett of whom I have been speaking was their son.[14] Within eighteen months I became a competent pilot, and I served that office until the
Mississippi River traffic was brought to a standstill by the breaking out of
the civil war.[15]

. . . Meantime Orion had gone down the river and established his little job-printing-office in Keokuk. On account of charging next to nothing for the work done in his job-office, he had almost nothing to do there. He was never able to comprehend that work done on a profitless basis deteriorates and is presently not worth anything, and that customers are then obliged to go where they can get better work, even if they must pay better prices for it. He had plenty of time, and he took up Blackstone again. He also put up a sign which offered his services to the public as a lawyer. He never got a case, in those days, nor even an applicant, although he was quite willing to transact law business for nothing and furnish the stationery himself. He was always liberal that way.

Presently he moved to a wee little hamlet called Alexandria, two or three miles down the river, and he put up that sign there. He got no custom. He was by this time very hard aground. But by this time I was beginning to earn a wage of two hundred and fifty dollars a month as pilot, and (1861) so I supported him thenceforth until 1861, when his ancient friend, Edward Bates, then a member of Mr. Lincoln's first cabinet, got him the place of Secretary of the new Territory of Nevada, and Orion and I cleared for that country in the overland stage-coach, I paying the fares, which were pretty heavy, and carrying with me what money I had been able to save—this was eight hundred dollars, I should say—and it was all in silver coin and a good deal of a nuisance because of its weight. And we had another nuisance, which was an Unabridged Dictionary. It weighed about a thousand pounds, and was a ruinous expense, because the stage-coach Company charged for extra baggage by the ounce. We could have kept a family for a time on what that dictionary cost in the way of extra freight—and it wasn't a good dictionary anyway—didn't have any modern words in it—only had obsolete ones that they used to use when Noah Webster was a child.[16]

The Government of the new Territory of Nevada was an interesting menagerie.[17] Governor Nye was an old and seasoned politician from New York—politician, not statesman.[18] He had white hair; he was in fine physical condition; he had a winningly friendly face and deep lustrous brown eyes that could talk as a native language the tongue of every feeling, every passion, every emotion. His eyes could outtalk his tongue, and this is saying a good deal, for he was a very remarkable talker, both in private and on the stump. He was a shrewd man; he generally saw through surfaces and perceived what was going on inside without being suspected of having an eye on the matter.

When grown-up persons indulge in practical jokes, the fact gauges them. They have lived narrow, obscure, and ignorant lives, and at full manhood they still retain and cherish a job-lot of left-over standards and ideals that would have been discarded with their boyhood if they had then moved out into the world and a broader life. There were many practical jokers in the new Territory. I do not take pleasure in exposing this fact, for I liked those people; but what I am saying is true. I wish I could say a kindlier thing about them instead — that they were burglars, or hat-rack thieves, or something like that, that wouldn't be utterly uncomplimentary. I would prefer it, but I can't say those things, they would not be true. These people were practical jokers, and I will not try to disguise it. In other respects they were plenty good-enough people; honest people; reputable and likable. They played practical jokes upon each other with success, and got the admiration and applause and also the envy of the rest of the community. Naturally they were eager to try their arts on big game, and that was what the Governor was. But they were not able to score. They made several efforts, but the Governor defeated these efforts without any trouble and went on smiling his pleasant smile as if nothing had happened. Finally the joker chiefs of Carson City and Virginia City conspired together to see if their combined talent couldn't win a victory, for the jokers were getting into a very uncomfortable place: the people were laughing at them, instead of at their proposed victim. They banded themselves together to the number of ten and invited the Governor to what was a most extraordinary attention in those days — pickled oyster stew and champagne — luxuries very seldom seen in that region, and existing rather as fabrics of the imagination than as facts.

The Governor took me with him. He said disparagingly,

"It's a poor invention. It doesn't deceive. Their idea is to get me drunk and leave me under the table, and from their standpoint this will be very funny. But they don't know me. I am familiar with champagne and have no prejudices against it."

The fate of the joke was not decided until two o'clock in the morning. At that hour the Governor was serene, genial, comfortable, contented, happy and sober, although he was so full that he couldn't laugh without shedding champagne tears. Also, at that hour the last joker joined his comrades under the table, drunk to the last perfection. The Governor remarked,

"This is a dry place, Sam, let's go and get something to drink and go to bed."

The Governor's official menagerie had been drawn from the humblest

ranks of his constituents at home — harmless good fellows who had helped
in his campaigns, and now they had their reward in petty salaries payable
in greenbacks that were worth next to nothing. Those boys had a hard time
to make both ends meet. Orion's salary was eighteen hundred dollars a year,
and he couldn't even support his dictionary on it. But the Irishwoman who
had come out on the Governor's staff charged the menagerie only ten dollars a week apiece for board and lodging. Orion and I were of her boarders
and lodgers; and so, on these cheap terms the silver I had brought from
home held out very well.

At first I roamed about the country seeking silver, but at the end of '62
or the beginning of '63 when I came up from Aurora to begin a journalistic
('62 or '63) life on the Virginia City "Enterprise," I was presently sent down
to Carson City to report the legislative session. Orion was soon
very popular with the members of the legislature, because they found that
whereas they couldn't usually trust each other, nor anybody else, they could
trust him. He easily held the belt for honesty in that country, but it didn't
do him any good in a pecuniary way, because he had no talent for either
persuading or scaring legislators. But I was differently situated. I was there
every day in the legislature to distribute compliment and censure with evenly
balanced justice and spread the same over half a page of the "Enterprise"
every morning, consequently I was an influence. I got the legislature to pass
a wise and very necessary law requiring every corporation doing business
in the Territory to record its charter in full, without skipping a word, in
a record to be kept by the Secretary of the Territory — my brother. All the
charters were framed in exactly the same words. For this record-service
he was authorized to charge forty cents a folio of one hundred words for
making the record; also five dollars for furnishing a certificate of each record, and so on. Everybody had a toll-road franchise but no toll-road. But
the franchise had to be recorded and paid for. Everybody was a mining
corporation, and had to have himself recorded and pay for it. Very well,
we prospered. The record-service paid an average of a thousand dollars a
month, in gold.

Governor Nye was often absent from the Territory. He liked to run down
to San Francisco every little while and enjoy a rest from Territorial civiliza-
tion. Nobody complained, for he was prodigiously popular. He had been
a stage-driver in his early days in New York or New England, and had acquired the habit of remembering names and faces, and of making himself
agreeable to his passengers. As a politician this had been valuable to him,
and he kept his arts in good condition by practice. By the time he had been

Governor a year, he had shaken hands with every human being in the Territory of Nevada, and after that he always knew these people instantly at sight and could call them by name. The whole population, of 20,000 persons, were his personal friends, and he could do anything he chose to do and count upon their being contented with it. Whenever he was absent from the Territory—which was generally—Orion served his office in his place, as Acting Governor, a title which was soon and easily shortened to "Governor."[19] He recklessly built and furnished a house at a cost of twelve thousand dollars, and there was no other house in the sage-brush capital that could approach this property for style and cost.

When Governor Nye's four-year term was drawing to a close, the mystery of why he had ever consented to leave the great State of New York and help inhabit that jack-rabbit desert was solved: he had gone out there in order to become a United States Senator. All that was now necessary was to turn the Territory into a State. He did it without any difficulty.[20] That undeveloped country and that sparse population were not well fitted for the heavy burden of a State Government, but no matter, the people were willing to have the change, and so the Governor's game was made.

Orion's game was made too, apparently, for he was as popular because of his honesty as the Governor was for more substantial reasons; but at the critical moment the inborn capriciousness of his character rose up without warning, and disaster followed.[21]

CHAPTER XII

Orion Clemens — resumed

[*Dictated April 5, 1906*][1] There were several candidates for all the offices in the gift of the new State of Nevada save two — United States Senator, and (1864–5) Secretary of State. Nye was certain to get a Senatorship, and Orion was so sure to get the Secretaryship that no one but him was named for that office. But he was hit with one of his spasms of virtue on the very day that the Republican party was to make its nominations in the Convention, and refused to go near the Convention. He was urged, but all persuasions failed. He said his presence there would be an unfair and improper influence and that if he was to be nominated the compliment must come to him as a free and unspotted gift. This attitude would have settled his case for him without further effort, but he had another attack of virtue on the same day, that made it absolutely sure. It had been his habit for a great many years to change his religion with his shirt, and his ideas about temperance at the same time. He would be a teetotaler for a while and the champion of the cause; then he would change to the other side for a time. On nomination day he suddenly changed from a friendly attitude toward whiskey — which was the popular attitude — to uncompromising teetotalism, and went absolutely dry. His friends besought and implored, but all in vain. He could not be persuaded to cross the threshold of a saloon. The paper next morning contained the list of chosen nominees. His name was not in it. He had not received a vote.[2]

His rich income ceased when the State government came into power. He was without an occupation. Something had to be done. He put up his sign as attorney-at-law, but he got no clients. It was strange. It was difficult to

North American Review, vol. 184, no. 609 (February 15, 1907): 337–46.

account for. I cannot account for it — but if I were going to guess at a solution I should guess that by the make of him he would examine both sides of a case so diligently and so conscientiously that when he got through with his argument neither he nor a jury would know which side he was on. I think that his client would find out his make in laying his case before him, and would take warning and withdraw it in time to save himself from probable disaster.

I had taken up my residence in San Francisco about a year before the time I have just been speaking of.[3] One day I got a tip from Mr. Camp,[4] a bold man who was always making big fortunes in ingenious speculations and losing them again in the course of six months by other speculative ingenuities. Camp told me to buy some shares in the Hale and Norcross.[5] I bought fifty shares at three hundred dollars a share. I bought on a margin, and put up twenty per cent. It exhausted my funds. I wrote Orion and offered him half, and asked him to send his share of the money. I waited and waited. He wrote and said he was going to attend to it. The stock went along up pretty briskly. It went higher and higher. It reached a thousand dollars a share. It climbed to two thousand, then to three thousand; then to twice that figure. The money did not come, but I was not disturbed. By and by that stock took a turn and began to gallop down. Then I wrote urgently. Orion answered that he had sent the money long ago — said he had sent it to the Occidental Hotel. I inquired for it. They said it was not there. To cut a long story short, that stock went on down until it fell below the price I had paid for it. Then it began to eat up the margin, and when at last I got out I was very badly crippled.

When it was too late, I found out what had become of Orion's money. Any other human being would have sent a check, but he sent gold. The hotel clerk put it in the safe and went on vacation, and there it had reposed all this time enjoying its fatal work, no doubt. Another man might have thought to tell me that the money was not in a letter, but was in an express package, but it never occurred to Orion to do that.

Later, Mr. Camp gave me another chance. He agreed to buy our Tennessee land for two hundred thousand dollars, pay a part of the amount in cash and give long notes for the rest.[6] His scheme was to import foreigners from grape-growing and wine-making districts in Europe, settle them on the land, and turn it into a wine-growing country. He knew what Mr. Longworth thought of those Tennessee grapes, and was satisfied. I sent the contracts and things to Orion for his signature, he being one of the three heirs. But they arrived at a bad time — in a doubly bad time, in fact. The temperance virtue was temporarily upon him in strong force, and he wrote and said that he would not be a party to debauching the country with wine. Also he said how could he know whether Mr. Camp was going to deal fairly and honestly with those poor people from Europe or not?— and so, without waiting to find out, he quashed the whole trade, and there it fell, never to be brought to life again. The land, from being suddenly worth two hundred thousand dollars, became as suddenly worth what it was before— nothing, and taxes to pay. I had paid the taxes and the other expenses for some years, but I dropped the Tennessee land there, and have never taken any interest in it since, pecuniarily or otherwise, until yesterday.

I had supposed, until yesterday, that Orion had frittered away the last acre, and indeed that was his own impression. But a gentleman arrived yesterday from Tennessee and brought a map showing that by a correction of the ancient surveys we still own a thousand acres, in a coal district, out of the hundred thousand acres which my father left us when he died in 1847. The gentleman brought a proposition; also he brought a reputable and well-to-do citizen of New York. The proposition was that the Tennesseean gentleman should sell that land; that the New York gentleman should pay all the expenses and fight all the lawsuits, in case any should turn up, and that of such profit as might eventuate the Tennesseean gentleman should take a third, the New-Yorker a third, and Sam Moffett and his sister and I—who are surviving heirs—the remaining third.

This time I hope we shall get rid of the Tennessee land for good and all and never hear of it again.

I came East in January, 1867.[7] Orion remained in Carson City perhaps a year longer. Then he sold his twelve-thousand-dollar house and its furniture for thirty-five hundred in greenbacks at about sixty per cent.
(1867) discount. He and his wife took passage in the steamer for home in Keokuk.[8] About 1871 or '72 they came to New York. Orion had been trying to make a living in the law ever since he had arrived from the Pacific
(1871) Coast, but he had secured only two cases. Those he was to try free of charge—but the possible result will never be known, because the parties settled the cases out of court without his help.

Orion got a job as proof-reader on the New York "Evening Post" at ten dollars a week. By and by he came to Hartford and wanted me to get him a place as reporter on a Hartford paper.[9] Here was a chance to try my scheme again, and I did it. I made him go to the Hartford "Evening Post," without any letter of introduction, and propose to scrub and sweep and do all sorts of things for nothing, on the plea that he didn't need money but only needed work, and that that was what he was pining for. Within six weeks he was on the editorial staff of that paper at twenty dollars a week, and he was worth the money. He was presently called for by some other paper at better wages, but I made him go to the "Post" people and tell them about it. They stood the raise and kept him. It was the pleasantest berth he had ever had in his life. It was an easy berth. He was in every way comfortable. But ill-luck came. It was bound to come.

A new Republican daily was to be started in a New England city[10] by a stock company of well-to-do politicians, and they offered him the chief editorship at three thousand a year. He was eager to accept. My beseechings and reasonings went for nothing. I said,

"You are as weak as water. Those people will find it out right away. They will easily see that you have no backbone; that they can deal with you as they would deal with a slave. You may last six months, but not longer. Then they will not dismiss you as they would dismiss a gentleman: they will fling you out as they would fling out an intruding tramp."

It happened just so. Then he and his wife migrated to Keokuk once more.[11] Orion wrote from there that he was not resuming the law; that he thought that what his health needed was the open air, in some sort of outdoor occupation; that his father-in-law[12] had a strip of ground on the river border a mile above Keokuk with some sort of a house on it, and his idea was to buy that place and start a chicken-farm and provide Keokuk with chickens and eggs, and perhaps butter — but I don't know whether you can raise butter on a chicken-farm or not. He said the place could be had for three thousand dollars cash, and I sent the money. He began to raise chickens, and he made a detailed monthly report to me, whereby it appeared that he was able to work off his chickens on the Keokuk people at a dollar and a quarter a pair. But it also appeared that it cost a dollar and sixty cents to raise the pair. This did not seem to discourage Orion, and so I let it go. Meantime he was borrowing a hundred dollars per month of me regularly, month by month. Now to show Orion's stern and rigid business ways — and he really prided himself on his large business capacities — the moment he received the advance of a hundred dollars at the beginning of each month, he always sent me his note for the amount, and with it he sent, *out of that money, three months' interest* on the hundred dollars at six per cent. per annum, these notes being always for three months.

As I say, he always sent a detailed statement of the month's profit and loss on the chickens — at least the month's loss on the chickens — and this detailed statement included the various items of expense — corn for the

chickens, boots for himself, and so on; even car fares, and the weekly contribution of ten cents to help out the missionaries who were trying to damn
the Chinese after a plan not satisfactory to those people.

I think the poultry experiment lasted about a year, possibly two years.[13]
It had then cost me six thousand dollars.

Orion returned to the law business, and I suppose he remained in that
harness off and on for the succeeding quarter of a century, but so far as
my knowledge goes he was only a lawyer in name, and had no clients.

My mother died, in her eighty-eighth year, in the summer of 1890.[14] She
had saved some money, and she left it to me, because it had come from me.
(1890) I gave it to Orion and he said, with thanks, that I had supported
him long enough and now he was going to relieve me of that burden,
and would also hope to pay back some of that expense, and maybe the
whole of it. Accordingly, he proceeded to use up that money in building a
considerable addition to the house, with the idea of taking boarders and
getting rich. We need not dwell upon this venture. It was another of his
failures. His wife tried hard to make the scheme succeed, and if anybody
could have made it succeed she would have done it. She was a good woman,
and was greatly liked. She had a practical side, and she would have made
that boarding-house lucrative if circumstances had not been against her.

Orion had other projects for recouping me, but as they always required
capital I stayed out of them, and they did not materialize. Once he wanted
to start a newspaper. It was a ghastly idea, and I squelched it with a prompt-
ness that was almost rude. Then he invented a wood-sawing machine and
patched it together himself, and he really sawed wood with it. It was ingenious; it was capable; and it would have made a comfortable little fortune for him; but just at the wrong time Providence interfered again. Orion
applied for a patent and found that the same machine had already been
patented and had gone into business and was thriving.

Presently the State of New York offered a fifty-thousand-dollar prize for
a practical method of navigating the Erie Canal with steam canal-boats.
Orion worked at that thing for two or three years, invented and completed
a method, and was once more ready to reach out and seize upon imminent
wealth when somebody pointed out a defect: his steam canal-boat could
not be used in the winter-time; and in the summer-time the commotion
its wheels would make in the water would wash away the State of New York
on both sides.

Innumerable were Orion's projects for acquiring the means to pay off the
debt to me. These projects extended straight through the succeeding thirty

years, but in every case they failed. During all those thirty years his well-established honesty kept him in offices of trust where other people's money had to be taken care of, but where no salary was paid. He was treasurer of all the benevolent institutions; he took care of the money and other property of widows and orphans; he never lost a cent for anybody, and never made one for himself. Every time he changed his religion the church of his new faith was glad to get him; made him treasurer at once, and at once he stopped the graft and the leaks in that church. He exhibited a facility in changing his political complexion that was a marvel to the whole community. Once the following curious thing happened, and he wrote me all about it himself.

One morning he was a Republican, and upon invitation he agreed to make a campaign speech at the Republican mass-meeting that night. He prepared the speech. After luncheon he became a Democrat and agreed to write a score of exciting mottoes to be painted upon the transparencies which the Democrats would carry in their torchlight procession that night. He wrote these shouting Democratic mottoes during the afternoon, and they occupied so much of his time that it was night before he had a chance to change his politics again; so he actually made a rousing Republican campaign speech in the open air while his Democratic transparencies passed by in front of him, to the joy of every witness present.

He was a most strange creature — but in spite of his eccentricities he was beloved, all his life, in whatsoever community he lived. And he was also held in high esteem, for at bottom he was a sterling man.

About twenty-five years ago — along there somewhere — I suggested to Orion that he write an autobiography.[15] I asked him to try to tell the straight truth in it; to refrain from exhibiting himself in creditable attitudes exclusively, and to honorably set down all the incidents of his life which he had found interesting to him, including those which were burned into his memory because he was ashamed of them. I said that this had never been done, and that if he could do it his autobiography would be a most valuable piece of literature. I said I was offering him a job which I could not duplicate in my own case, but I would cherish the hope that he might succeed with it. I recognize now that I was trying to saddle upon him an impossibility. I have been dictating this autobiography of mine daily for three months; I have thought of fifteen hundred or two thousand incidents in my life which I am ashamed of, but I have not gotten one of them to consent to go on paper yet. I think that that stock will still be complete and unimpaired when I finish these memoirs, if I ever finish them. I believe that if

I should put in all or any of those incidents I should be sure to strike them out when I came to revise this book.

Orion wrote his autobiography and sent it to me. But great was my disappointment; and my vexation, too. In it he was constantly making a hero of himself, exactly as I should have done and am doing now, and he was constantly forgetting to put in the episodes which placed him in an unheroic light. I knew several incidents of his life which were distinctly and painfully unheroic, but when I came across them in his autobiography they had changed color. They had turned themselves inside out, and were things to be intemperately proud of.[16] In my dissatisfaction I destroyed a considerable part of that autobiography. But in what remains there are passages which are interesting, and I shall quote from them here and there and now and then, as I go along.[17]

While we were living in Vienna in 1898 a cablegram came from Keokuk announcing Orion's death.[18] He was seventy-two years old. He had gone (1898) down to the kitchen in the early hours of a bitter December morning; he had built the fire, and had then sat down at a table to write something; and there he died, with the pencil in his hand and resting against the paper in the middle of an unfinished word — an indication that his release from the captivity of a long and troubled and pathetic and unprofitable life was mercifully swift and painless.

[*Dictated in 1904*][19] A quarter of a century ago I was visiting John Hay at Whitelaw Reid's[20] house in New York, which Hay was occupying for a few months while Reid was absent on a holiday in Europe. Temporarily also, Hay was editing Reid's paper, the New York "Tribune." I remember two incidents of that Sunday visit particularly well. I had known John Hay a good many years, I had known him when he was an obscure young editorial writer on the "Tribune" in Horace Greeley's[21] time, earning three or four times the salary he got, considering the high character of the work which came from his pen. In those earlier days he was a picture to look at, for beauty of feature, perfection of form and grace of carriage and movement. He had a charm about him of a sort quite unusual to my Western ignorance and inexperience — a charm of manner, intonation, apparently native and unstudied elocution, and all that — the groundwork of it native, the ease of it, the polish of it, the winning naturalness of it, acquired in Europe where he had been Chargé d'Affaires some time at the Court of Vienna. He was joyous and cordial, a most pleasant comrade. One of the two incidents above referred to as marking that visit was this:

In trading remarks concerning our ages I confessed to forty-two and Hay to forty. Then he asked if I had begun to write my autobiography, and I said I hadn't. He said that I ought to begin at once, and that I had already lost two years. Then he said in substance this:

"At forty a man reaches the top of the hill of life and starts down on the sunset side. The ordinary man, the average man, not to particularize too closely and say the commonplace man, has at that age succeeded or failed; in either case he has lived all of his life that is likely to be worth recording; also in either case the life lived is worth setting down, and cannot fail to be interesting if he comes as near to telling the truth about himself as he can. And he *will* tell the truth in spite of himself, for his facts and his fictions will work loyally together for the protection of the reader; each fact and each fiction will be a dab of paint, each will fall in its right place, and together they will paint his portrait; not the portrait *he* thinks they are painting, but his real portrait, the inside of him, the soul of him, his character. Without intending to lie he will lie all the time; not bluntly, consciously, not dully unconsciously, but half-consciously — consciousness in twilight; a soft and gentle and merciful twilight which makes his general form comely, with his virtuous prominences and projections discernible and his ungracious ones in shadow. His truths will be recognizable as truths, his modifications of facts which would tell against him will go for nothing, the reader will see the fact through the film and know his man.

"There is a subtle devilish something or other about autobiographical composition that defeats all the writer's attempts to paint his portrait *his* way."

Hay meant that he and I were ordinary average commonplace people, and I did not resent my share of the verdict, but nursed my wound in silence. His idea that we had finished our work in life, passed the summit and were westward bound down-hill, with me two years ahead of him and neither of us with anything further to do as benefactors to mankind, was all a mistake. I had written four books then, possibly five.[22] I have been drowning the world in literary wisdom ever since, volume after volume; since that day's sun went down he has been the historian of Mr. Lincoln, and his book will never perish; he has been ambassador, brilliant orator, competent and admirable Secretary of State.

CHAPTER XIII

... As I have said, that vast plot of Tennessee land* was held by my father twenty years—intact.[1] When he died in 1847, we began to manage it (1847) ourselves. Forty years afterward, we had managed it all away except 10,000 acres, and gotten nothing to remember the sales by. About 1887—possibly it was earlier—the 10,000 went. My brother found a chance to trade it for a house and lot in the town of Corry, in the oil regions of Pennsylvania. About 1894 he sold this property for $250. That ended the Tennessee Land.[2]

If any penny of cash ever came out of my father's wise investment but that, I have no recollection of it. No, I am overlooking a detail. It furnished me a field for Sellers and a book.[3] Out of my half of the book I got $15,000 or $20,000; out of the play I got $75,000 or $80,000—just about a dollar an acre.[4] It is curious: I was not alive when my father made the investment, therefore he was not intending any partiality; yet I was the only member of the family that ever profited by it. I shall have occasion to mention this land again, now and then, as I go along, for it influenced our life in one way or another during more than a generation. Whenever things grew dark it rose and put out its hopeful Sellers hand and cheered us up, and said "Do not be afraid—trust in me—wait." It kept us hoping and hoping, during forty years, and forsook us at last. It put our energies to sleep and made visionaries of us—dreamers and indolent. We were always going to be rich next year—no occasion to work. It is good to begin life poor; it is good to begin life rich—these are wholesome; but to begin it *prospectively* rich! The man who has not experienced it cannot imagine the curse of it.

*100,000 acres.

North American Review, vol. 184, no. 610 (March 1, 1907): 449–63.

My parents removed to Missouri in the early thirties; I do not remember just when, for I was not born then, and cared nothing for such things.[5] It was a long journey in those days, and must have been a rough and tiresome one. The home was made in the wee village of Florida, in Monroe county, and I was born there in 1835.[6] The village contained a hundred people and I increased the population by one per cent. It is more than the best man in history ever did for any other town. It may not be modest in me to refer to this, but it is true. There is no record of a person doing as much — not even Shakespeare. But I did it for Florida, and it shows that I could have done it for any place — even London, I suppose.

Recently some one in Missouri has sent me a picture of the house I was born in. Heretofore I have always stated that it was a palace, but I shall be more guarded, now.

I remember only one circumstance connected with my life in it. I remember it very well, though I was but two and a half years old at the time. The family packed up everything and started in wagons for Hannibal, on the Mississippi, thirty miles away. Toward night, when they camped and counted up the children, one was missing. I was the one. I had been left behind. Parents ought always to count the children before they start. I was having a good enough time playing by myself until I found that the doors were fastened and that there was a grisly deep silence brooding over the place. I knew, then, that the family were gone, and that they had forgotten me. I was well frightened, and I made all the noise I could, but no one was near and it did no good. I spent the afternoon in captivity and was not rescued until the gloaming had fallen and the place was alive with ghosts.

My brother Henry was six months old at that time. I used to remember his walking into a fire outdoors when he was a week old. It was remarkable in me to remember a thing like that, which occurred when I was so young. And it was still more remarkable that I should cling to the delusion, for thirty years, that I *did* remember it — for of course it never happened; he would not have been able to walk at that age.[7] If I had stopped to reflect, I should not have burdened my memory with that impossible rubbish so long. It is believed by many people that an impression deposited in a child's memory within the first two years of its life cannot remain there five years, but that is an error. The incident of Benvenuto Cellini and the salamander must be accepted as authentic and trustworthy;[8] and then that remarkable and indisputable instance in the experience of Helen Keller[9] — however, I will speak of that at another time. For many years I believed that I remembered helping my grandfather drink his whiskey toddy when I was six weeks old, but I do not tell about that any more, now; I am grown old, and my memory is not as active as it used to be. When I was younger I could remember anything, whether it had happened or not; but my faculties are decaying, now, and soon I shall be so I cannot remember any but the things that happened.[10] It is sad to go to pieces like this, but we all have to do it.

My uncle, John A. Quarles, was a farmer, and his place was in the country four miles from Florida.[11] He had eight children, and fifteen or twenty negroes, and was also fortunate in other ways. Particularly in his character. I have not come across a better man than he was. I was his guest for two or three months every year, from the fourth year after we removed to Hannibal till I was eleven or twelve years old. I have never consciously used him or his wife in a book, but his farm has come very handy to me in literature, once or twice. In "Huck Finn" and in "Tom Sawyer Detective" I moved it down to Arkansas.[12] It was all of six hundred miles, but it was no trouble, it was not a very large farm; five hundred acres, perhaps, but I could have done it if it had been twice as large. And as for the morality of it, I cared nothing for that; I would move a State if the exigencies of literature required it.

It was a heavenly place for a boy, that farm of my uncle John's. The house was a double log one, with a spacious floor (roofed in) connecting it with the kitchen. In the summer the table was set in the middle of that shady and breezy floor, and the sumptuous meals — well, it makes me cry to think of them. Fried chicken, roast pig, wild and tame turkeys, ducks and geese; venison just killed; squirrels, rabbits, pheasants, partridges, prairie-chickens; biscuits, hot batter cakes, hot buckwheat cakes, hot "wheat bread," hot rolls, hot corn pone; fresh corn boiled on the ear, succotash, butter-beans, string-beans, tomatoes, pease, Irish potatoes, sweet-potatoes; butter-milk, sweet milk, "clabber"; watermelons, muskmelons, cantaloups — all fresh from the garden — apple pie, peach pie, pumpkin pie, apple dumplings, peach cobbler — I can't remember the rest. The way that the things were cooked was perhaps the main splendor — particularly a certain few of the dishes. For instance, the corn bread, the hot biscuits and wheat bread, and the fried chicken. These things have never been properly cooked in the North — in fact, no one there is able to learn the art, so far as my experience goes. The North thinks it knows how to make corn bread, but this is gross superstition. Perhaps no bread in the world is quite as good as Southern corn bread, and perhaps no bread in the world is quite so bad as the Northern imitation of it. The North seldom tries to fry chicken, and this is well; the art cannot be learned north of the line of Mason and Dixon, nor anywhere in Europe. This is not hearsay; it is experience that is speaking. In Europe it is imagined that the custom of serving various kinds of bread blazing hot is "American," but that is too broad a spread; it is custom in the South, but is much less than that in the North. In the North and in Europe hot bread is considered unhealthy. This is probably another fussy superstition, like the European superstition that ice-water is unhealthy. Europe does not need ice-water, and does not drink it; and yet, notwithstanding this, its word for it is better than ours, because it describes it, whereas ours doesn't. Europe calls it "iced" water. Our word describes water made from melted ice— a drink which we have but little acquaintance with.

It seems a pity that the world should throw away so many good things merely because they are unwholesome. I doubt if God has given us any refreshment which, taken in moderation, is unwholesome, except microbes. Yet there are people who strictly deprive themselves of each and every eatable, drinkable and smokable which has in any way acquired a shady reputation. They pay this price for health. And health is all they get for it. How strange it is; it is like paying out your whole fortune for a cow that has gone dry.

The farmhouse stood in the middle of a very large yard, and the yard was fenced on three sides with rails and on the rear side with high palings; against these stood the smokehouse; beyond the palings was the orchard; beyond the orchard were the negro quarter and the tobacco-fields. The front yard was entered over a stile, made of sawed-off logs of graduated heights; I do not remember any gate. In a corner of the front yard were a dozen lofty hickory-trees and a dozen black-walnuts, and in the nutting season riches were to be gathered there.

Down a piece, abreast the house, stood a little log cabin against the rail fence; and there the woody hill fell sharply away, past the barns, the corn-crib, the stables and the tobacco-curing house, to a limpid brook which sang along over its gravelly bed and curved and frisked in and out and here and there and yonder in the deep shade of overhanging foliage and vines — a divine place for wading, and it had swimming-pools, too, which were forbidden to us and therefore much frequented by us. For we were little Christian children, and had early been taught the value of forbidden fruit.

In the little log cabin lived a bedridden white-headed slave woman whom we visited daily, and looked upon with awe, for we believed she was upwards of a thousand years old and had talked with Moses. The younger negroes credited these statistics, and had furnished them to us in good faith.

We accommodated all the details which came to us about her; and so we believed that she had lost her health in the long desert trip coming out of Egypt, and had never been able to get it back again. She had a round bald place on the crown of her head, and we used to creep around and gaze at it in reverent silence, and reflect that it was caused by fright through seeing Pharaoh drowned. We called her "Aunt" Hannah, Southern fashion. She was superstitious like the other negroes; also, like them, she was deeply religious. Like them, she had great faith in prayer, and employed it in all ordinary exigencies, but not in cases where a dead certainty of result was urgent. Whenever witches were around she tied up the remnant of her wool in little tufts, with white thread, and this promptly made the witches impotent.

All the negroes were friends of ours, and with those of our own age we were in effect comrades. I say in effect, using the phrase as a modification. We were comrades, and yet not comrades; color and condition interposed a subtle line which both parties were conscious of, and which rendered complete fusion impossible. We had a faithful and affectionate good friend, ally and adviser in "Uncle Dan'l," a middle-aged slave whose head was the best one in the negro quarter, whose sympathies were wide and warm, and whose heart was honest and simple and knew no guile. He has served me well, these many, many years. I have not seen him for more than half a century, and yet spiritually I have had his welcome company a good part of that time, and have staged him in books under his own name and as "Jim," and carted him all around—to Hannibal, down the Mississippi on a raft, and even across the Desert of Sahara in a balloon[13]—and he has endured it all with the patience and friendliness and loyalty which were his birthright. It was on the farm that I got my strong liking for his race and my appreciation of certain of its fine qualities. This feeling and this estimate have stood the test of sixty years and more and have suffered no impairment. The black face is as welcome to me now as it was then.

In my schoolboy days I had no aversion to slavery. I was not aware that there was anything wrong about it. No one arraigned it in my hearing; the local papers said nothing against it; the local pulpit taught us that God approved it, that it was a holy thing, and that the doubter need only look in the Bible if he wished to settle his mind—and then the texts were read aloud to us to make the matter sure; if the slaves themselves had an aversion to slavery they were wise and said nothing. In Hannibal we seldom saw a slave misused; on the farm, never.

There was, however, one small incident of my boyhood days which touched this matter, and it must have meant a good deal to me or it would not have stayed in my memory, clear and sharp, vivid and shadowless, all these slow-drifting years. We had a little slave boy whom we had hired from some one, there in Hannibal. He was from the Eastern Shore of Maryland, and had been brought away from his family and his friends, half-way across the American continent, and sold. He was a cheery spirit, innocent and gentle, and the noisiest creature that ever was, perhaps. All day long he was singing, whistling, yelling, whooping, laughing—it was maddening, devastating, unendurable. At last, one day, I lost all my temper, and went raging to my mother, and said Sandy had been singing for an hour without a single break, and I couldn't stand it, and *wouldn't* she please shut him up. The tears came into her eyes, and her lip trembled, and she said something like this—

"Poor thing, when he sings, it shows that he is not remembering, and that comforts me; but when he is still, I am afraid he is thinking, and I cannot bear it. He will never see his mother again; if he can sing, I must not hinder it, but be thankful for it. If you were older, you would understand me; then that friendless child's noise would make you glad."

It was a simple speech, and made up of small words, but it went home, and Sandy's noise was not a trouble to me any more. She never used large words, but she had a natural gift for making small ones do effective work. She lived to reach the neighborhood of ninety years, and was capable with her tongue to the last—especially when a meanness or an injustice roused her spirit. She has come handy to me several times in my books, where she figures as Tom Sawyer's "Aunt Polly." I fitted her out with a dialect, and tried to think up other improvements for her, but did not find any. I used Sandy once, also; it was in "Tom Sawyer"; I tried to get him to whitewash the fence, but it did not work. I do not remember what name I called him by in the book.[14]

I can see the farm yet, with perfect clearness. I can see all its belongings, all its details; the family room of the house, with a "trundle" bed in one corner and a spinning-wheel in another—a wheel whose rising and falling wail, heard from a distance, was the mournfulest of all sounds to me, and made me homesick and low-spirited, and filled my atmosphere with the wandering spirits of the dead; the vast fireplace, piled high, on winter nights, with flaming hickory logs from whose ends a sugary sap bubbled out but did not go to waste, for we scraped it off and ate it; the lazy cat spread out on the rough hearthstones, the drowsy dogs braced against the jambs and blinking; my aunt in one chimney-corner knitting, my uncle in the other smoking his corn-cob pipe; the slick and carpetless oak floor faintly mirroring the dancing flame-tongues and freckled with black indentations where fire-coals had popped out and died a leisurely death; half a dozen children romping in the background twilight; "split"-bottomed chairs here and there, some with rockers; a cradle—out of service, but waiting, with confidence; in the early cold mornings a snuggle of children, in shirts and chemises, occupying the hearthstone and procrastinating—they could not bear to leave that comfortable place and go out on the wind-swept floor-space between the house and kitchen where the general tin basin stood, and wash.

Along outside of the front fence ran the country road; dusty in the summer-time, and a good place for snakes — they liked to lie in it and sun themselves; when they were rattlesnakes or puff adders, we killed them; when they were black snakes, or racers, or belonged to the fabled "hoop" breed, we fled, without shame; when they were "house snakes" or "garters" we carried them home and put them in Aunt Patsy's work-basket for a surprise; for she was prejudiced against snakes, and always when she took the basket in her lap and they began to climb out of it it disordered her mind. She never could seem to get used to them; her opportunities went for nothing. And she was always cold toward bats, too, and could not bear them; and yet I think a bat is as friendly a bird as there is. My mother was Aunt Patsy's sister, and had the same wild superstitions. A bat is beautifully soft and silky; I do not know any creature that is pleasanter to the touch, or is more grateful for caressings, if offered in the right spirit. I know all about these coleoptera, because our great cave, three miles below Hannibal, was multitudi-nously stocked with them, and often I brought them home to amuse my mother with. It was easy to manage if it was a school day, because then I had ostensibly been to school and hadn't any bats. She was not a suspicious person, but full of trust and confidence; and when I said "There's something in my coat pocket for you," she would put her hand in. But she always took it out again, herself; I didn't have to tell her. It was remarkable, the way she couldn't learn to like private bats.

I think she was never in the cave in her life; but everybody else went there. Many excursion parties came from considerable distances up and down the river to visit the cave. It was miles in extent, and was a tangled wilderness of narrow and lofty clefts and passages. It was an easy place to get lost in; anybody could do it—including the bats. I got lost in it myself, along with a lady, and our last candle burned down to almost nothing be-fore we glimpsed the search-party's lights winding about in the distance.

"Injun Joe" the half-breed got lost in there once, and would have starved to death if the bats had run short. But there was no chance of that; there were myriads of them. He told me all his story. In the book called "Tom Sawyer" I starved him entirely to death in the cave, but that was in the interest of art; it never happened. "General" Gaines, who was our first town drunkard before Jimmy Finn got the place, was lost in there for the space of a week, and finally pushed his handkerchief out of a hole in a hilltop near Saverton, several miles down the river from the cave's mouth, and somebody saw it and dug him out. There is nothing the matter with his statistics except the handkerchief. I knew him for years, and he hadn't any. But it could have been his nose. That would attract attention.

Beyond the road where the snakes sunned themselves was a dense young thicket, and through it a dim-lighted path led a quarter of a mile; then out of the dimness one emerged abruptly upon a level great prairie which was covered with wild strawberry-plants, vividly starred with prairie pinks, and walled in on all sides by forests. The strawberries were fragrant and fine, and in the season we were generally there in the crisp freshness of the early morning, while the dew-beads still sparkled upon the grass and the woods were ringing with the first songs of the birds.

Down the forest slopes to the left were the swings. They were made of bark stripped from hickory saplings. When they became dry they were dangerous. They usually broke when a child was forty feet in the air, and this was why so many bones had to be mended every year. I had no ill-luck myself, but none of my cousins escaped. There were eight of them, and at one time and another they broke fourteen arms among them. But it cost next to nothing, for the doctor worked by the year — $25 for the whole family. I remember two of the Florida doctors, Chowning and Meredith. They not only tended an entire family for $25 a year, but furnished the medicines themselves. Good measure, too. Only the largest persons could hold a whole dose. Castor-oil was the principal beverage. The dose was half a dipperful, with half a dipperful of New Orleans molasses added to help it down and make it taste good, which it never did. The next standby was calomel; the next, rhubarb; and the next, jalap. Then they bled the patient, and put mustard-plasters on him. It was a dreadful system, and yet the death-rate was not heavy. The calomel was nearly sure to salivate the patient and cost him some of his teeth. There were no dentists. When teeth became touched with decay or were otherwise ailing, the doctor knew of but one thing to do: he fetched his tongs and dragged them out. If the jaw remained, it was not his fault.

Doctors were not called, in cases of ordinary illness; the family's grand-mother attended to those. Every old woman was a doctor, and gathered her own medicines in the woods, and knew how to compound doses that would stir the vitals of a cast-iron dog. And then there was the "Indian doctor"; a grave savage, remnant of his tribe, deeply read in the mysteries of nature and the secret properties of herbs; and most backwoodsmen had high faith in his powers and could tell of wonderful cures achieved by him. In Mauritius, away off yonder in the solitudes of the Indian Ocean, there is a person who answers to our Indian doctor of the old times. He is a negro, and has had no teaching as a doctor, yet there is one disease which he is master of and can cure, and the doctors can't. They send for him when they have a case. It is a child's disease of a strange and deadly sort, and the negro cures it with a herb medicine which he makes, himself, from a prescription which has come down to him from his father and grandfather. He will not let any one see it. He keeps the secret of its components to himself, and it is feared that he will die without divulging it; then there will be consternation in Mauritius. I was told these things by the people there, in 1896.

We had the "faith doctor," too, in those early days — a woman. Her specialty was toothache. She was a farmer's old wife, and lived five miles from Hannibal. She would lay her hand on the patient's jaw and say "Believe!" and the cure was prompt. Mrs. Utterback. I remember her very well. Twice I rode out there behind my mother, horseback, and saw the cure performed. My mother was the patient.

Dr. Meredith removed to Hannibal, by and by, and was our family physician there, and saved my life several times. Still, he was a good man and meant well. Let it go.

I was always told that I was a sickly and precarious and tiresome and uncertain child, and lived mainly on allopathic medicines during the first seven years of my life. I asked my mother about this, in her old age — she was in her 88th year — and said:

"I suppose that during all that time you were uneasy about me?"

"Yes, the whole time."

"Afraid I wouldn't live?"

After a reflective pause — ostensibly to think out the facts —

"No — afraid you would."

It sounds like a plagiarism, but it probably wasn't. The country school-house was three miles from my uncle's farm. It stood in a clearing in the woods, and would hold about twenty-five boys and girls. We attended the school with more or less regularity once or twice a week, in summer, walking to it in the cool of the morning by the forest paths, and back in the gloaming at the end of the day. All the pupils brought their dinners in baskets — corn-dodger, buttermilk and other good things — and sat in the shade of the trees at noon and ate them. It is the part of my education which I look back upon with the most satisfaction. My first visit to the school was when I was seven. A strapping girl of fifteen, in the customary sunbonnet and calico dress, asked me if I "used tobacco"— meaning did I chew it. I said, no. It roused her scorn. She reported me to all the crowd, and said —

"Here is a boy seven years old who can't chaw tobacco."

By the looks and comments which this produced, I realized that I was a degraded object; I was cruelly ashamed of myself. I determined to reform. But I only made myself sick; I was not able to learn to chew tobacco. I learned to smoke fairly well, but that did not conciliate anybody, and I remained a poor thing, and characterless. I longed to be respected, but I never was able to rise. Children have but little charity for each other's defects.

As I have said, I spent some part of every year at the farm until I was twelve or thirteen years old.[15] The life which I led there with my cousins was full of charm, and so is the memory of it yet. I can call back the solemn twilight and mystery of the deep woods, the earthy smells, the faint odors of the wild flowers, the sheen of rain-washed foliage, the rattling clatter of drops when the wind shook the trees, the far-off hammering of woodpeckers and the muffled drumming of wood-pheasants in the remoteness of the forest, the snap-shot glimpses of disturbed wild creatures skurrying through the grass,— I can call it all back and make it as real as it ever was, and as blessed. I can call back the prairie, and its loneliness and peace, and a vast hawk hanging motionless in the sky, with his wings spread wide and the blue of the vault showing through the fringe of their end-feathers. I can see the woods in their autumn dress, the oaks purple, the hickories washed with gold, the maples and the sumacs luminous with crimson fires, and I can hear the rustle made by the fallen leaves as we ploughed through them. I can see the blue clusters of wild grapes hanging amongst the foliage of the saplings, and I remember the taste of them and the smell. I know how the wild blackberries looked, and how they tasted; and the same with the pawpaws, the hazelnuts and the persimmons; and I can feel the thumping rain, upon my head, of hickory-nuts and walnuts when we were out in the frosty dawn to scramble for them with the pigs, and the gusts of wind loosed them and sent them down. I know the stain of blackberries, and how pretty it is; and I know the stain of walnut hulls, and how little it minds soap and water; also what grudged experience it had of either of them. I know the taste of maple sap, and when to gather it, and how to arrange the troughs and the delivery tubes, and how to boil down the juice, and how to hook the sugar after it is made; also how much better hooked sugar tastes than any that is honestly come by, let bigots say what they will. I know how a prize watermelon looks when it is sunning its fat rotundity among pumpkin-vines and "simblins"; I know how to tell when it is ripe without "plugging" it; I know how inviting it looks when it is cooling itself in a tub of water under the bed, waiting; I know how it looks when it lies on the table in the sheltered great floor-space between house and kitchen, and the children gathered for the sacrifice and their mouths watering; I know the crackling sound it makes when the carving-knife enters its end, and I can see the split fly along in front of the blade as the knife cleaves its way to the other end; I can see its halves fall apart and display the rich red meat and the black seeds, and the heart standing up, a luxury fit for the elect; I know how a boy looks, behind a yard-long slice of that melon, and I know how he feels; for I have been there. I know the taste of the watermelon which has been honestly come by, and I know the taste of the watermelon which has been acquired by art. Both taste good, but the experienced know which tastes best. I know the look of green apples and peaches and pears on the trees, and I know how entertaining they are when they are inside of a person. I know how ripe ones look when they are piled in pyramids under the trees, and how pretty they are and how vivid their colors. I know how a frozen apple looks, in a barrel down cellar in the winter-time, and how hard it is to bite, and how the frost makes the teeth ache, and yet how good it is, notwithstanding. I know the disposition of elderly people to select the specked apples for the children, and I once knew ways to beat the game. I know the look of an apple that is roasting and sizzling on a hearth on a winter's evening, and I know the comfort that comes of eating it hot, along with some sugar and a drench of cream. I know the delicate art and mystery of so cracking hickory-nuts and walnuts on a flatiron with a hammer that the kernels will be delivered whole, and I know how the nuts, taken in conjunction with winter apples, cider and doughnuts, make old people's tales and old jokes sound fresh and crisp and enchanting, and juggle an evening away before you know what went with the time. I know the look of Uncle Dan'l's kitchen as it was on privileged nights when I was a child, and I can see the white and black children grouped on the hearth, with the firelight playing on their faces and the shadows flickering upon the walls, clear back toward the cavernous gloom of the rear, and I can hear Uncle Dan'l telling the immortal tales which Uncle Remus Harris was to gather into his books and charm the world with, by and by; and I can feel again the creepy joy which quivered through me when the time for the ghost-story of the "Golden Arm" was reached — and the sense of regret, too, which came over me, for it was always the last story of the evening, and there was nothing between it and the unwelcome bed.

I can remember the bare wooden stairway in my uncle's house, and the turn to the left above the landing, and the rafters and the slanting roof over my bed, and the squares of moonlight on the floor, and the white cold world of snow outside, seen through the curtainless window. I can remember the howling of the wind and the quaking of the house on stormy nights, and how snug and cozy one felt, under the blankets, listening, and how the powdery snow used to sift in, around the sashes, and lie in little ridges on the floor, and make the place look chilly in the morning, and curb the wild desire to get up — in case there was any. I can remember how very dark that room was, in the dark of the moon, and how packed it was with ghostly stillness when one woke up by accident away in the night, and forgotten sins came flocking out of the secret chambers of the memory and wanted a hearing; and how ill chosen the time seemed for this kind of business; and how dismal was the hoo-hooing of the owl and the wailing of the wolf, sent mourning by on the night wind.

I remember the raging of the rain on that roof, summer nights, and how pleasant it was to lie and listen to it, and enjoy the white splendor of the lightning and the majestic booming and crashing of the thunder. It was a very satisfactory room; and there was a lightning-rod which was reachable from the window, an adorable and skittish thing to climb up and down, summer nights, when there were duties on hand of a sort to make privacy desirable.

I remember the 'coon and 'possum hunts, nights, with the negroes, and the long marches through the black gloom of the woods, and the excitement which fired everybody when the distant bay of an experienced dog announced that the game was treed; then the wild scramblings and stumblings through briars and bushes and over roots to get to the spot; then the lighting of a fire and the felling of the tree, the joyful frenzy of the dogs and the negroes, and the weird picture it all made in the red glare — I remember it all well, and the delight that every one got out of it, except the 'coon.

I remember the pigeon seasons, when the birds would come in millions, and cover the trees, and by their weight break down the branches. They were clubbed to death with sticks; guns were not necessary, and were not used. I remember the squirrel hunts, and the prairie-chicken hunts, and the wild-turkey hunts, and all that; and how we turned out, mornings, while it was still dark, to go on these expeditions, and how chilly and dismal it was, and how often I regretted that I was well enough to go. A toot on a tin horn brought twice as many dogs as were needed, and in their happiness they raced and scampered about, and knocked small people down, and made no end of unnecessary noise. At the word, they vanished away toward the woods, and we drifted silently after them in the melancholy gloom. But presently the gray dawn stole over the world, the birds piped up, then the sun rose and poured light and comfort all around, everything was fresh and dewy and fragrant, and life was a boon again. After three hours of tramping we arrived back wholesomely tired, overladen with game, very hungry, and just in time for breakfast.

CHAPTER XIV

[Dictated Thursday, December 6, 1906]

From Susy's Biography of Me

Feb. 27, Sunday.

Clara's reputation as a baby was always a fine one, mine exactly the contrary. One often related story concerning her braveness as a baby and her own opinion of this quality of hers is this. Clara and I often got slivers in our hands and when mama took them out with a much dreaded needle, Clara was always very brave, and I very cowardly. One day Clara got one of these slivers in her hand, a very bad one, and while mama was taking it out, Clara stood perfectly still without even wincing; I saw how brave she was and turning to mamma said "Mamma isn't she a brave little thing! presently mamma had to give the little hand quite a dig with the needle and noticing how perfectly quiet Clara was about it she exclaimed, Why Clara! you *are* a brave little thing! Clara responded "No bodys braver but God!"—

Clara's pious remark is the main detail, and Susy has accurately remembered its phrasing. The three-year-older's wound was of a formidable sort, and not one which the mother's surgery would have been equal to. The flesh of the finger had been burst by a cruel accident. It was the doctor that sewed it up, and to all appearances it was he, and the other independent witnesses, that did the main part of the suffering; each stitch that he took made Clara wince slightly, but it shrivelled the others.

I take pride in Clara's remark, because it shows that although she was only three years old, her fireside teachings were already making her a thinker—a thinker and also an observer of proportions. I am not claiming any credit for this. I furnished to the children worldly knowledge and wisdom, but was not competent to go higher, and so I left their spiritual edu-

North American Review, vol. 184, no. 611 (March 15, 1907): 561–71.

cation in the hands of the mother. A result of this modesty of mine was made manifest to me in a very striking way, some years afterward, when Jean was nine years old.[1] We had recently arrived in Berlin, at the time, and had begun housekeeping in a furnished apartment. One morning at breakfast a vast card arrived — an invitation. To be precise, it was a command from the Emperor of Germany to come to dinner.[2] During several months I had encountered socially, on the Continent, men bearing lofty titles; and all this while Jean was becoming more and more impressed, and awed, and subdued, by these imposing events, for she had not been abroad before, and they were new to her — wonders out of dreamland turned into realities. The imperial card was passed from hand to hand, around the table, and examined with interest; when it reached Jean she exhibited excitement and emotion, but for a time was quite speechless; then she said,

"Why, papa, if it keeps going on like this, pretty soon there won't be anybody left for you to get acquainted with but God."

It was not complimentary to think I was not acquainted in that quarter, but she was young, and the young jump to conclusions without reflection.

Necessarily, I did myself the honor to obey the command of the Emperor Wilhelm II. Prince Heinrich,[3] and six or eight other guests were present. The Emperor did most of the talking, and he talked well, and in faultless English. In both of these conspicuousnesses I was gratified to recognize a resemblance to myself — a very exact resemblance; no, almost exact, but not quite that — a modified exactness, with the advantage in favor of the Emperor. My English, like his, is nearly faultless; like him I talk well; and when I have guests at dinner I prefer to do all the talking myself. It is the best way, and the pleasantest. Also the most profitable for the others.

I was greatly pleased to perceive that his Majesty was familiar with my books, and that his attitude toward them was not uncomplimentary. In the course of his talk he said that my best and most valuable book was "Old Times on the Mississippi."[4] I will refer to that remark again, presently.

An official who was well up in the Foreign Office at that time, and had served under Bismarck[5] for fourteen years, was still occupying his old place under Chancellor Caprivi.[6] Smith, I will call him of whom I am speaking, though that is not his name.[7] He was a special friend of mine, and I greatly enjoyed his society, although in order to have it it was necessary for me to seek it as late as midnight, and not earlier. This was because Government officials of his rank had to work all day, after nine in the morning, and then attend official banquets in the evening; wherefore they were usually unable to get life-restoring fresh air and exercise for their jaded minds and bodies earlier than midnight; then they turned out, in groups of two or three, and gratefully and violently tramped the deserted streets until two in the morning. Smith had been in the Government service, at home and abroad, for more than thirty years, and he was now sixty years old, or close upon it. He could not remember a year in which he had had a vacation of more than a fortnight's length; he was weary all through to the bones and the marrow, now, and was yearning for a holiday of a whole three months — yearning so longingly and so poignantly that he had at last made up his mind to make a desperate cast for it and stand the consequences, whatever they might be. It was against all rules to *ask* for a vacation — quite against all etiquette; the shock of it would paralyze the Chancellery; stern etiquette and usage required another form: the applicant was not privileged to ask for a vacation, he must send in his *resignation.* The chancellor would know that the applicant was not really trying to resign, and didn't want to resign, but was merely trying in this left-handed way to get a vacation.

The night before the Emperor's dinner I helped Smith take his exercise, after midnight, and he was full of his project. He had sent in his resignation that day, and was trembling for the result; and naturally, because it might possibly be that the chancellor would be happy to fill his place with somebody else, in which case he could accept the resignation without comment and without offence. Smith was in a very anxious frame of mind; not that he feared that Caprivi was dissatisfied with him, for he had no such fear; it was the Emperor that he was afraid of; he did not know how he stood with the Emperor. He said that while apparently it was Caprivi who would decide his case, it was in reality the Emperor who would perform that service; that the Emperor kept personal watch upon everything, and that no official sparrow could fall to the ground without his privity and consent; that the resignation would be laid before his Majesty, who would accept it or decline to accept it, according to his pleasure, and that then his pleasure in the matter would be communicated by Caprivi. Smith said he would know his fate the next evening, after the imperial dinner; that when I should escort his Majesty into the large salon contiguous to the dining-room, I would find there about thirty men — Cabinet ministers, admirals, generals and other great officials of the Empire — and that these men would be standing talking together in little separate groups of two or three persons; that the Emperor would move from group to group and say a word to each, sometimes two words, sometimes ten words; and that the length of his speech, whether brief or not so brief, would indicate the exact standing in the Emperor's regard, of the man accosted; and that by observing this thermometer an expert could tell, to half a degree, the state of the imperial weather in each case; that in Berlin, as in the imperial days of Rome, the Emperor was the sun, and that his smile or his frown meant good fortune or disaster to the man upon whom it should fall. Smith suggested that I watch the thermometer while the Emperor went his rounds of the groups; and added that if his Majesty talked four minutes with any person there present, it meant high favor, and that the sun was in the zenith, and cloudless, for that man.

I mentally recorded that four-minute altitude, and resolved to see if any man there on that night stood in sufficient favor to achieve it.

Very well. After the dinner I watched the Emperor while he passed from group to group, and privately I timed him with a watch. Two or three times he came near to reaching the four-minute altitude, but always he fell short a little. The last man he came to was Smith. He put his hand on Smith's shoulder and began to talk to him; and when he finished, the thermometer had scored seven minutes! The company then moved toward the smoking-room, where cigars, beer and anecdotes would be in brisk service until midnight, and as Smith passed me he whispered,

"That settles it. The chancellor will ask me how much of a vacation I want, and I sha'n't be afraid to raise the limit. I shall call for six months."

Smith's dream had been to spend his three months' vacation — in case he got a vacation instead of the other thing — in one of the great capitals of the Continent — a capital whose name I shall suppress, at present. The next day the chancellor asked him how much of a vacation he wanted, and where he desired to spend it. Smith told him. His prayer was granted, and rather more than granted. The chancellor augmented his salary and attached him to the German Embassy of that selected capital, giving him a place of high dignity bearing an imposing title, and with nothing to do except attend banquets of an extraordinary character at the Embassy, once or twice a year. The term of his vacation was not specified; he was to continue it until requested to come back to his work in the Foreign Office. This was in 1891.[8] Eight years later Smith was passing through Vienna, and he called upon me. There had been no interruption of his vacation, as yet, and there was no likelihood that an interruption of it would occur while he should still be among the living.

(1891)

(1899)

[*Dictated Monday, December 17, 1906*] As I have already remarked, "Old Times on the Mississippi" got the Kaiser's best praise. It was after midnight when I reached home; I was usually out until toward midnight, and the pleasure of being out late was poisoned, every night, by the dread of what I must meet at my front door — an indignant face, a resentful face, the face of the *portier.* The *portier* was a tow-headed young German, twenty-two or three years old; and it had been for some time apparent to me that he did not enjoy being hammered out of his sleep, nights, to let me in. He never had a kind word for me, nor a pleasant look. I couldn't understand it, since it was his business to be on watch and let the occupants of the several flats in at any and all hours of the night. I could not see why he so distinctly failed to get reconciled to it.

The fact is, I was ignorantly violating, every night, a custom in which he was commercially interested. I did not suspect this. No one had told me of the custom, and if I had been left to guess it, it would have taken me a very long time to make a success of it. It was a custom which was so well established and so universally recognized, that it had all the force and dignity of law. By authority of this custom, whosoever entered a Berlin house after ten at night must pay a trifling toll to the *portier* for breaking his sleep to let him in. This tax was either two and a half cents or five cents, I don't remember which; but I had never paid it, and didn't know I owed it, and as I had been residing in Berlin several weeks, I was so far in arrears that my presence in the German capital was getting to be a serious disaster to that young fellow.

I arrived from the imperial dinner sorrowful and anxious, made my presence known and prepared myself to wait in patience the tedious minute or two which the *portier* usually allowed himself to keep me tarrying — as a punishment. But this time there was no stage-wait; the door was instantly unlocked, unbolted, unchained and flung wide; and in it appeared the strange and welcome apparition of the *portier*'s round face all sunshine and smiles and welcome, in place of the black frowns and hostility that I was expecting. Plainly he had not come out of his bed: he had been waiting for me, watching for me. He began to pour out upon me in the most enthusiastic and energetic way a generous stream of German welcome and homage, meanwhile dragging me excitedly to his small bedroom beside the front door; there he made me bend down over a row of German translations of my books and said,

"There — you wrote them! I have found it out! By God, I did not know it before, and I ask a million pardons! That one there, the 'Old Times on the Mississippi,' is the best book you ever wrote!"

The usual number of those curious accidents which we call coincidences have fallen to my share in this life, but for picturesqueness this one puts all the others in the shade: that a crowned head and a *portier,* the very top of an empire and the very bottom of it, should pass the very same criticism and deliver the very same verdict upon a book of mine — and almost in the same hour and the same breath — is a coincidence which out-coincidences any coincidence which I could have imagined with such powers of imagination as I have been favored with; and I have not been accustomed to regard them as being small or of an inferior quality. It is always a satisfaction to me to remember that whereas I do not know, for sure, what any other nation thinks of any one of my twenty-three volumes, I do at least know for a certainty what one nation of fifty millions thinks of one of them, at any rate; for if the mutual verdict of the top of an empire and the bottom of it does not establish for good and all the judgment of the entire nation concerning that book, then the axiom that we can get a sure estimate of a thing by arriving at a general average of all the opinions involved, is a fallacy.

[*Dictated Monday, February 10, 1907*] Two months ago (December 6) I was dictating a brief account of a private dinner in Berlin, where the Emperor of Germany was host and I the chief guest. Something happened day before yesterday which moves me to take up that matter again.

At the dinner his Majesty chatted briskly and entertainingly along in easy and flowing English, and now and then he interrupted himself to address a remark to me, or to some other individual of the guests. When the reply had been delivered, he resumed his talk. I noticed that the table etiquette tallied with that which was the law of my house at home when we had guests: that is to say, the guests answered when the host favored them with a remark, and then quieted down and behaved themselves until they got another chance. If I had been in the Emperor's chair and he in mine, I should have felt infinitely comfortable and at home, and should have done a world of talking, and done it well; but I was guest now, and consequently I felt less at home. From old experience, I was familiar with the rules of the game, and familiar with their exercise from the high place of host; but I was not familiar with the trammelled and less satisfactory position of guest, therefore I felt a little strange and out of place. But there was no animosity — no, the Emperor was host, therefore according to my own rule he had a right to do the talking, and it was my honorable duty to intrude no interruptions or other improvements, except upon invitation; and of course it could be *my* turn some day: some day, on some friendly visit of inspection to America, it might be my pleasure and distinction to have him as guest at my table; then I would give him a rest, and a remarkably quiet time.

In one way there was a difference between his table and mine — for instance, atmosphere; the guests stood in awe of him, and naturally they conferred that feeling upon me, for, after all, I am only human, although I regret it. When a guest answered a question he did it with deferential voice and manner; he did not put any emotion into it, and he did not spin it out, but got it out of his system as quickly as he could, and then looked relieved. The Emperor was used to this atmosphere, and it did not chill his blood; maybe it was an inspiration to him, for he was alert, brilliant and full of animation; also he was most gracefully and felicitously complimentary to my books,—and I will remark here that the happy phrasing of a compliment is one of the rarest of human gifts, and the happy delivery of it another. In that other chapter I mentioned the high compliment which he paid to the book, "Old Times on the Mississippi," but there were others; among them some gratifying praise of my description in "A Tramp Abroad"[9] of certain striking phases of German student life. I mention these things here because I shall have occasion to hark back to them presently.

[*Dictated Tuesday, February 12, 1907*]

   .   .   .   .

Those stars indicate the long chapter which I dictated yesterday, a chapter which is much too long for magazine purposes, and therefore must wait until this Autobiography shall appear in book form, five years hence, when I am dead:[10] five years according to my calculation, twenty-seven years according to the prediction furnished me a week ago by the latest and most confident of all the palmists who have ever read my future in my hand. The Emperor's dinner, and its beer-and-anecdote appendix, covered six hours of diligent industry, and this accounts for the extraordinary length of that chapter.

A couple of days ago a gentleman called upon me with a message. He had just arrived from Berlin, where he had been acting for our Government in a matter concerning tariff revision, he being a member of the commission appointed by our Government to conduct our share of the affair. Upon the completion of the commission's labors, the Emperor invited the members of it to an audience, and in the course of the conversation he made a reference to me; continuing, he spoke of my chapter on the German language in "A Tramp Abroad,"[11] and characterized it by an adjective which is too complimentary for me to repeat here without bringing my modesty under suspicion. Then he paid some compliments to "The Innocents Abroad,"[12] and followed these with the remark that my account in one of my books of certain striking phases of German student life was the best and truest that had ever been written. By this I perceive that he remembers that dinner of sixteen years ago, for he said the same thing to me about the student-chapter at that time. Next he said he wished this gentleman to convey two messages to America from him and deliver them — one to the President, the other to me. The wording of the message to me was:

"Convey to Mr. Clemens my kindest regards. Ask him if he remembers that dinner, and ask him why he didn't do any talking."

Why, how could I talk when he was talking? He "held the age," as the poker-clergy say, and two can't talk at the same time with good effect. It reminds me of the man who was reproached by a friend, who said,

"I think it a shame that you have not spoken to your wife for fifteen years. How do you explain it? How do you justify it?"

That poor man said,

"I didn't want to interrupt her."

If the Emperor had been at my table, he would not have suffered from my silence, he would only have suffered from the sorrows of his own solitude. If I were not too old to travel I would go to Berlin and introduce the etiquette of my own table, which tallies with the etiquette observable at other royal tables. I would say, "Invite me again, your Majesty, and give me a chance"; then I would courteously waive rank and do all the talking myself. I thank his Majesty for his kind message, and am proud to have it and glad to express my sincere reciprocation of its sentiments.

[*Dictated January 17, 1906*] . . . Rev. Joseph T. Harris and I have been visiting General Sickles.[13] Once, twenty or twenty-five years ago, just as Harris was coming out of his gate Sunday morning to walk to his church and preach, a telegram was put into his hand. He read it immediately, and then, in a manner, collapsed. It said: "General Sickles died last night at midnight." [He had been a chaplain under Sickles through the war.]

It wasn't so. But no matter — it was so to Harris at the time. He walked along — walked to the church — but his mind was far away. All his affection (1880) and homage and worship of his General had come to the fore. His heart was full of these emotions. He hardly knew where he was. In his pulpit, he stood up and began the service, but with a voice over which he had almost no command. The congregation had never seen him thus moved, before, in his pulpit. They sat there and gazed at him and wondered what was the matter; because he was now reading, in this broken voice and with occasional tears trickling down his face, what to them seemed a quite unemotional chapter — that one about Moses begat Aaron, and Aaron begat Deuteronomy, and Deuteronomy begat St. Peter, and St. Peter begat Cain, and Cain begat Abel[14] — and he was going along with this, and half crying — his voice continually breaking. The congregation left the church that morning without being able to account for this most extraordinary

thing—as it seemed to them. That a man who had been a soldier for more
than four years, and who had preached in that pulpit so many, many times
on really moving subjects, without even the quiver of a lip, should break
all down over the Begats, they couldn't understand. But there it is—any one
can see how such a mystery as that would arouse the curiosity of those people to the boiling-point.

Harris has had many adventures. He has more adventures in a year than
anybody else has in five. One Saturday night he noticed a bottle on his uncle's dressing-bureau. He thought the label said "Hair Restorer," and he took
it in his room and gave his head a good drenching and sousing with it and
carried it back and thought no more about it. Next morning when he got
up his head was a bright green! He sent around everywhere and couldn't
get a substitute preacher, so he had to go to his church himself and preach
—and he did it. He hadn't a sermon in his barrel—as it happened—of any
lightsome character, so he had to preach a very grave one—a very serious
one—and it made the matter worse. The gravity of the sermon did not har-
monize with the gayety of his head, and the people sat all through it with
handkerchiefs stuffed in their mouths to try to keep down their joy. And
Harris told me that he was sure he never had seen his congregation—the
whole body of his congregation—the *entire* body of his congregation—
absorbed in interest in his sermon, from beginning to end, before. Always
there had been an aspect of indifference, here and there, or wandering,
somewhere; but this time there was nothing of the kind. Those people sat
there as if they thought, "Good for this day and train only: we must have
all there is of this show, not waste any of it." And he said that when he came
down out of the pulpit more people waited to shake him by the hand and
tell him what a good sermon it was, than ever before. And it seemed a pity
that these people should do these fictions in such a place—right in the
church—when it was quite plain they were not interested in the sermon
at all; they only wanted to get a near view of his head.

Well, Harris said—no, Harris didn't say, *I* say, that as the days went on
and Sunday followed Sunday, the interest in Harris's hair grew and grew;
because it didn't stay merely and monotonously green, it took on deeper
and deeper shades of green; and then it would change and become reddish,
and would go from that to some other color—purplish, yellowish, bluish,
and so on—but it was never a solid color. It was always mottled. And each
Sunday it was a little more interesting than it was the Sunday before—and
Harris's head became famous, and people came from New York, and Boston,
and South Carolina, and Japan, and so on, to look. There wasn't seating-

capacity for all the people that came while his head was undergoing these various and fascinating mottlings. And it was a good thing in several ways, because the business had been languishing a little, and now a lot of people joined the church so that they could have the show, and it was the beginning of a prosperity for that church which has never diminished in all these years.

CHAPTER XV

[*Dictated October 8, 1906*]

From Susy's Biography of Me

Papa says that if the collera comes here he will take Sour Mash to the mountains.

This remark about the cat is followed by various entries, covering a month, in which Jean, General Grant, the sculptor Gerhardt, Mrs. Candace Wheeler, (1885) Miss Dora Wheeler, Mr. Frank Stockton, Mrs. Mary Mapes Dodge, and the widow of General Custer[1] appear and drift in procession across the page, then vanish forever from the Biography; then Susy drops this remark in the wake of the vanished procession:

Sour Mash is a constant source of anxiety, care, and pleasure to papa.

I did, in truth, think a great deal of that old tortoise-shell harlot; but I haven't a doubt that in order to impress Susy I was pretending agonies of solicitude which I didn't honestly feel. Sour Mash never gave me any real anxiety; she was always able to take care of herself, and she was ostentatiously vain of the fact; vain of it to a degree which often made me ashamed of her, much as I esteemed her.

Many persons would like to have the society of cats during the summer vacation in the country, but they deny themselves this pleasure because they think they must either take the cats along when they return to the city, where they would be a trouble and an encumbrance, or leave them in the country, houseless and homeless. These people have no ingenuity, no invention, no wisdom; or it would occur to them to do as I do: rent cats by the month

North American Review, vol. 184, no. 612 (April 5, 1907): 673–82.

134

for the summer and return them to their good homes at the end of it. Early last May I rented a kitten of a farmer's wife, by the month; then I got a discount by taking three. They have been good company for about five months now, and are still kittens — at least they have not grown much, and to all intents and purposes are still kittens, and as full of romping energy and enthusiasm as they were in the beginning. This is remarkable. I am an expert in cats, but I have not seen a kitten keep its kittenhood nearly so long before.

These are beautiful creatures — these triplets. Two of them wear the blackest and shiniest and thickest of sealskin vestments all over their bodies except the lower half of their faces and the terminations of their paws. The black masks reach down below the eyes, therefore when the eyes are closed they are not visible; the rest of the face, and the gloves and stockings, are snow white. These markings are just the same on both cats — so exactly the same that when you call one the other is likely to answer, because they cannot tell each other apart. Since the cats are precisely alike, and can't be told apart by any of us, they do not need two names, so they have but one between them. We call both of them Sackcloth, and we call the gray one Ashes. I believe I have never seen such intelligent cats as these before. They are full of the nicest discriminations. When I read German aloud they weep; you can see the tears run down. It shows what pathos there is in the German tongue. I had not noticed before that all German is pathetic, no matter what the subject is nor how it is treated. It was these humble observers that brought the knowledge to me. I have tried all kinds of German on these cats; romance, poetry, philosophy, theology, market reports; and the result has always been the same — the cats sob, and let the tears run down, which shows that all German is pathetic. French is not a familiar tongue to me, and the pronunciation is difficult, and comes out of me encumbered with a Missouri accent; but the cats like it, and when I make impassioned speeches in that language they sit in a row and put up their paws, palm to palm, and frantically give thanks. Hardly any cats are affected by music, but these are; when I sing they go reverently away, showing how deeply they feel it. Sour Mash never cared for these things. She had many noble qualities, but at bottom she was not refined, and cared little or nothing for theology and the arts.

It is a pity to say it, but these cats are not above the grade of human beings, for I know by certain signs that they are not sincere in their exhibitions of emotion, but exhibit them merely to show off and attract attention — conduct which is distinctly human, yet with a difference: they do not know enough to conceal their desire to show off, but the grown human being does. What is ambition? It is only the desire to be conspicuous. The desire for fame is only the desire to be continuously conspicuous and attract attention and be talked about.

These cats are like human beings in another way: when Ashes began to work his fictitious emotions, and show off, the other members of the firm followed suit, in order to be in the fashion. That is the way with human beings; they are afraid to be outside; whatever the fashion happens to be, they conform to it, whether it be a pleasant fashion or the reverse, they lacking the courage to ignore it and go their own way. All human beings would like to dress in loose and comfortable and highly colored and showy garments, and they had their desire until a century ago, when a king, or some other influential ass, introduced sombre hues and discomfort and ugly designs into masculine clothing. The meek public surrendered to the outrage, and by consequence we are in that odious captivity to-day, and are likely to remain in it for a long time to come.

Fortunately the women were not included in the disaster, and so their graces and their beauty still have the enhancing help of delicate fabrics and varied and beautiful colors. Their clothing makes a great opera audience an enchanting spectacle, a delight to the eye and the spirit, a Garden of Eden for charm and color. The men, clothed in dismal black, are scattered here and there and everywhere over the Garden, like so many charred stumps, and they damage the effect, but cannot annihilate it.

In summer we poor creatures have a respite, and may clothe ourselves in white garments; loose, soft, and in some degree shapely; but in the winter — the sombre winter, the depressing winter, the cheerless winter, when white clothes and bright colors are especially needed to brighten our spirits and lift them up — we all conform to the prevailing insanity, and go about in dreary black, each man doing it because the others do it, and not because he wants to. They are really no sincerer than Sackcloth and Ashes. At bottom the Sackcloths do not care to exhibit their emotions when I am performing before them, they only do it because Ashes started it.

I would like to dress in a loose and flowing costume made all of silks and velvets, resplendent with all the stunning dyes of the rainbow, and so would every sane man I have ever known; but none of us dares to venture it. There is such a thing as carrying conspicuousness to the point of discomfort; and if I should appear on Fifth Avenue on a Sunday morning, at church-time, clothed as I would like to be clothed, the churches would be vacant, and I should have all the congregations tagging after me, to look, and secretly

envy, and publicly scoff. It is the way human beings are made; they are always keeping their real feelings shut up inside, and publicly exploiting their
fictitious ones.

Next after fine colors, I like plain white. One of my sorrows, when the
summer ends, is that I must put off my cheery and comfortable white clothes
and enter for the winter into the depressing captivity of the shapeless and
degrading black ones. It is mid-October now, and the weather is growing
cold up here in the New Hampshire hills,[2] but it will not succeed in freez-
ing me out of these white garments, for here the neighbors are few, and
it is only of crowds that I am afraid. I made a brave experiment, the other
night, to see how it would feel to shock a crowd with these unseasonable
clothes, and also to see how long it might take the crowd to reconcile itself
to them and stop looking astonished and outraged. On a stormy evening
I made a talk before a full house, in the village, clothed like a ghost, and
looking as conspicuously, all solitary and alone on that platform, as any
ghost could have looked; and I found, to my gratification, that it took the
house less than ten minutes to forget about the ghost and give its attention
to the tidings I had brought.

I am nearly seventy-one, and I recognize that my age has given me a
good many privileges; valuable privileges; privileges which are not granted
to younger persons. Little by little I hope to get together courage enough
to wear white clothes all through the winter, in New York. It will be a great
satisfaction to me to show off in this way; and perhaps the largest of all
the satisfactions will be the knowledge that every scoffer, of my sex, will
secretly envy me and wish he dared to follow my lead.

That mention that I have acquired new and great privileges by grace of
my age, is not an uncalculated remark. When I passed the seventieth mile-
stone, ten months ago, I instantly realized that I had entered a new country and a new atmosphere. To all the public I was become recognizably
old, undeniably old; and from that moment everybody assumed a new attitude toward me — the reverent attitude granted by custom to age — and
straightway the stream of generous new privileges began to flow in upon
me and refresh my life. Since then, I have lived an ideal existence; and I
now believe what Choate[3] said last March, and which at the time I didn't
credit: that the best of life begins at seventy; for then your work is done;
you know that you have done your best, let the quality of the work be what
it may; that you have earned your holiday — a holiday of peace and contentment — and that thenceforth, to the setting of your sun, nothing will
break it, nothing interrupt it.

[*Dictated January 22, 1907*] In an earlier chapter I inserted some verses beginning "Love Came at Dawn" which had been found among Susy's papers after her death. I was not able to say that they were hers, but I judged that they might be, for the reason that she had not enclosed them in quotation marks according to her habit when storing up treasures gathered from other people. Stedman[4] was not able to determine the authorship for me, as the verses were new to him, but the authorship has now been traced. The verses were written by William Wilfred Campbell, a Canadian poet, and they form a part of the contents of his book called "Beyond the Hills of Dream."[5]

The authorship of the beautiful lines which my wife and I inscribed upon Susy's gravestone was untraceable for a time. We had found them in a book in India, but had lost the book and with it the author's name. But in time an application to the editor of "Notes and Queries" furnished me the author's name,* and it has been added to the verses upon the gravestone.[6]

Last night, at a dinner-party where I was present, Mr. Peter Dunne Dooley[7] handed to the host several dollars, in satisfaction of a lost bet. I seemed to see an opportunity to better my condition, and I invited Dooley, apparently disinterestedly, to come to my house Friday and play billiards. He accepted, and I judge that there is going to be a deficit in the Dooley treasury as a result. In great qualities of the heart and brain, Dooley is gifted beyond all propriety. He is brilliant; he is an expert with his pen, and he easily stands at the head of all the satirists of this generation — but he is going to walk in darkness Friday afternoon. It will be a fraternal kindness to teach him that with all his light and culture, he does not know all the valuable things; and it will also be a fraternal kindness to him to complete his education for him — and I shall do this on Friday, and send him home in that perfected condition.

I possess a billiard secret which can be valuable to the Dooley sept, after I shall have conferred it upon Dooley — for a consideration. It is a discovery which I made by accident, thirty-eight years ago, in my father-in-law's house in Elmira. There was a scarred and battered and ancient billiard-table in the garret, and along with it a peck of checked and chipped balls, and a rackful of crooked and headless cues. I played solitaire up there every day with that difficult outfit. The table was not level, but slanted sharply to the southeast; there wasn't a ball that was round, or would complete the

---

*Robert Richardson, deceased, of Australia.

journey you started it on, but would always get tired and stop half-way and settle, with a jolty wabble, to a standstill on its chipped side. I tried making counts with four balls, but found it difficult and discouraging, so I added a fifth ball, then a sixth, then a seventh, and kept on adding until at last I had twelve balls on the table and a thirteenth to play with. My game was caroms — caroms solely — caroms plain, or caroms with cushion to help — anything that could furnish a count. In the course of time I found to my astonishment that I was never able to run fifteen, under any circumstances. By huddling the balls advantageously in the beginning, I could now and then coax fourteen out of them, but I couldn't reach fifteen by either luck or skill. Sometimes the balls would get scattered into difficult positions and defeat me in that way; sometimes if I managed to keep them together, I would freeze; and always when I froze, and had to play away from the contact, there was sure to be nothing to play at but a wide and uninhabited vacancy.

One day Mr. Dalton called on my brother-in-law, on a matter of business, and I was asked if I could entertain him awhile, until my brother-in-law should finish an engagement with another gentleman. I said I could, and took him up to the billiard-table. I had played with him many times at the club, and knew that he could play billiards tolerably well — only tolerably well — but not any better than I could. He and I were just a match. He didn't know our table; he didn't know those balls; he didn't know those warped and headless cues; he didn't know the southeastern slant of the table, and how to allow for it. I judged it would be safe and profitable to offer him a bet on my scheme. I emptied the avalanche of thirteen balls on the table and said:

"Take a ball and begin, Mr. Dalton. How many can you run with an outlay like that?"

He said, with the half-affronted air of a mathematician who has been asked how much of the multiplication table he can recite without a break:

"I suppose a million — eight hundred thousand, anyway."

I said "You shall have the privilege of placing the balls to suit yourself, and I want to bet you a dollar that you can't run fifteen."

I will not dwell upon the sequel. At the end of an hour his face was red, and wet with perspiration; his outer garments lay scattered here and there over the place; he was the angriest man in the State, and there wasn't a rag or remnant of an injurious adjective left in him anywhere — and I had all his small change.

When the summer was over, we went home to Hartford, and one day

Mr. George Robertson arrived from Boston with two or three hours to spare between then and the return train, and as he was a young gentleman to whom we were in debt for much social pleasure, it was my duty, and a welcome duty, to make his two or three hours interesting for him. So I took him up-stairs and set up my billard scheme for his comfort. Mine was a good table, in perfect repair; the cues were in perfect condition; the balls were ivory, and flawless — but I knew that Mr. Robertson was my prey, just the same, for by exhaustive tests with this outfit I had found that my limit was thirty-one. I had proved to my satisfaction that whereas I could not fairly expect to get more than six or eight or a dozen caroms out of a run, I could now and then reach twenty and twenty-five, and after a long procession of failures finally achieve a run of thirty-one; but in no case had I ever got beyond thirty-one. Robertson's game, as I knew, was a little better than mine, so I resolved to require him to make thirty-two. I believed it would entertain him. He was one of these brisk and hearty and cheery and self-satisfied young fellows who are brimful of confidence, and who plunge with grateful eagerness into any enterprise that offers a showy test of their abilities. I emptied the balls on the table and said,

"Take a cue and a ball, George, and begin. How many caroms do you think you can make out of that layout?"

He laughed the laugh of the gay and the care-free, as became his youth and inexperience, and said,

"I can punch caroms out of that bunch a week without a break."

I said "Place the balls to suit yourself, and begin."

Confidence is a necessary thing in billiards, but overconfidence is bad. George went at his task with much too much lightsomeness of spirit and disrespect for the situation. On his first shot he scored three caroms; on his second shot he scored four caroms; and on his third shot he missed as simple a carom as could be devised. He was very much astonished, and said he would not have supposed that careful play could be needed with an acre of bunched balls in front of a person.

He began again, and played more carefully, but still with too much lightsomeness; he couldn't seem to learn to take the situation seriously. He made about a dozen caroms and broke down. He was irritated with himself now, and he thought he caught me laughing. He didn't. I do not laugh publicly at my client when this game is going on; I only do it inside — or save it for after the exhibition is over. But he thought he had caught me laughing, and it increased his irritation. Of course I knew he thought I was laughing privately — for I was experienced; they all think that, and it has a good effect; it sharpens their annoyance and debilitates their play.

He made another trial and failed. Once more he was astonished; once more he was humiliated — and as for his anger, it rose to summer-heat. He arranged the balls again, grouping them carefully, and said he would win this time, or die. When a client reaches this condition, it is a good time to damage his nerve further, and this can always be done by saying some little mocking thing or other that has the outside appearance of a friendly remark — so I employed this art. I suggested that a bet might tauten his nerves, and that I would offer one, but that as I did not want it to be an expense to him, but only a help, I would make it small — a cigar, if he were willing — a cigar that he would fail again; not an expensive one, but a cheap native one, of the Crown Jewel breed, such as is manufactured in Hartford for the clergy. It set him afire all over! I could see the blue flame issue from his eyes. He said,

"Make it a hundred! — and no Connecticut cabbage-leaf product, but Havana, $25 the box!"

I took him up, but said I was sorry to see him do this, because it did not seem to me right or fair for me to rob him under our own roof, when he had been so kind to us. He said, with energy and acrimony:

"You take care of your own pocket, if you'll be so good, and leave me to take care of mine."

And he plunged at the congress of balls with a vindictiveness which was infinitely contenting to me. He scored a failure — and began to undress. I knew it would come to that, for he was in the condition now that Mr. Dooley will be in at about that stage of the contest on Friday afternoon. A clothes-rack will be provided for Mr. Dooley to hang his things on as fast as he shall from time to time shed them. George raised his voice four degrees and flung out the challenge —

"Double or quits!"

"Done," I responded, in the gentle and compassionate voice of one who is apparently getting sorrier and sorrier.

There was an hour and a half of straight disaster after that, and if it was a sin to enjoy it, it is no matter — I did enjoy it. It is half a lifetime ago, but I enjoy it yet, every time I think of it. George made failure after failure. His fury increased with each failure as he scored it. With each defeat he flung off one or another rag of his raiment, and every time he started on a fresh inning he made it "double or quits" once more. Twice he reached thirty and broke down; once he reached thirty-one and broke down. These "nears" made him frantic, and I believe I was never so happy in my life, except the time, a few years later, when the Rev. J. H. Twichell and I walked to Boston and he had the celebrated conversation with the hostler at the Inn at Ashford, Connecticut.[8]

At last, when we were notified that Patrick was at the door to drive him to his train, George owed me five thousand cigars at twenty-five cents apiece, and I was so sorry I could have hugged him. But he shouted,

"Give me ten minutes more!" and added stormily, "it's double or quits again, and I'll win out free of debt or owe you ten thousand cigars, and you'll pay the funeral expenses."

He began on his final effort, and I believe that in all my experience among both amateurs and experts, I have never seen a cue so carefully handled in my lifetime as George handled his upon this intensely interesting occasion. He got safely up to twenty-five, and then ceased to breathe. So did I. He labored along, and added a point, another point, still another point, and finally reached thirty-one. He stopped there, and we took a breath. By this time the balls were scattered all down the cushions, about a foot or two apart, and there wasn't a shot in sight anywhere that any man might hope to make. In a burst of anger and confessed defeat, he sent his ball flying around the table at random, and it crotched a ball that was packed against the cushion and sprang across to a ball against the bank on the opposite side, and counted!

His luck had set him free, and he didn't owe me anything. He had used up all his spare time, but we carried his clothes to the carriage, and he dressed on his way to the station, greatly wondered at and admired by the ladies, as he drove along—but he got his train.

I am very fond of Mr. Dooley, and shall await his coming with affectionate and pecuniary interest.

P.S. Saturday. He has been here. Let us not talk about it.

CHAPTER XVI

[*Dictated January 12th, 1905*][1] . . . But I am used to having my statements discounted. My mother began it before I was seven years old. Yet all through my life my facts have had a substratum of truth, and therefore they were not without preciousness. Any person who is familiar with me knows how to strike my average, and therefore knows how to get at the jewel of any fact of mine and dig it out of its blue-clay matrix. My mother knew that art. When I was seven or eight, or ten, or twelve years old — along there — a neighbor said to her,

"Do you ever believe anything that that boy says?"

My mother said,

"He is the well-spring of truth, but you can't bring up the whole well with one bucket"— and she added, "I know his average, therefore he never deceives me. I discount him thirty per cent. for embroidery, and what is left is perfect and priceless truth, without a flaw in it anywhere."

Now to make a jump of forty years, without breaking the connection: that word "embroidery" was used again in my presence and concerning me, when I was fifty years old, one night at Rev. Frank Goodwin's[2] house in Hartford, at a meeting of the Monday Evening Club.[3] The Monday Evening Club still exists. It was founded about forty-five years ago by that theological giant, Rev. Dr. Bushnell,[4] and some comrades of his, men of large intellectual calibre and more or less distinction, local or national. I was admitted to membership in it in the fall of 1871 and was an active member thenceforth until I left Hartford in the summer of 1891.[5] The membership was restricted, in those days, to eighteen — possibly twenty. The meetings began about the 1st of October and were held in the private houses of the

North American Review, vol. 184, no. 613 (April 19, 1907): 785–93.

members every fortnight thereafter throughout the cold months until the 1st of May. Usually there were a dozen members present — sometimes as many as fifteen. There was an essay and a discussion. The essayists followed each other in alphabetical order through the season. The essayist could choose his own subject and talk twenty minutes on it, from MS. or orally, according to his preference. Then the discussion followed, and each member present was allowed ten minutes in which to express his views. The wives of these people were always present. It was their privilege. It was also their privilege to keep still; they were not allowed to throw any light upon the discussion. After the discussion there was a supper, and talk, and cigars. This supper began at ten o'clock promptly, and the company broke up and went away at midnight. At least they did except upon one occasion. In my recent Birthday speech, I remarked upon the fact that I have always bought cheap cigars, and that is true. I have never bought costly ones.[6]

Well, that night at the Club meeting — as I was saying — George, our colored butler, came to me when the supper was nearly over, and I noticed that he was pale. Normally his complexion was a clear black, and very handsome, but now it had modified to old amber. He said:

"Mr. Clemens, what are we going to do? There is not a cigar in the house but those old Wheeling long nines. Can't nobody smoke them but you. They kill at thirty yards. It is too late to telephone — we couldn't get any cigars out from town — what can we do? Ain't it best to say nothing, and let on that we didn't think?"

"No," I said, "that would not be honest. Fetch out the long nines"— which he did.

I had just come across those "long nines" a few days or a week before. I hadn't seen a long nine for years. When I was a cub pilot on the Mississippi in the late '50's, I had had a great affection for them, because they were not only — to my mind — perfect, but you could get a basketful of them for a cent — or a dime, they didn't use cents out there in those days. So when I saw them advertised in Hartford I sent for a thousand at once. They came out to me in badly battered and disreputable-looking old square pasteboard boxes, two hundred in a box. George brought a box, which was caved in on all sides, looking the worst it could, and began to pass them around. The conversation had been brilliantly animated up to that moment — but now a frost fell upon the company. That is to say, not all of a sudden, but the frost fell upon each man as he took up a cigar and held it poised in the air — and there, in the middle, his sentence broke off. That kind of thing went on all around the table, until when George had completed his crime the whole place was full of a thick solemnity and silence.

Those men began to light the cigars. Rev. Dr. Parker[7] was the first man to light. He took three or four heroic whiffs — then gave it up. He got up with the remark that he had to go to the bedside of a sick parishioner. He started out. Rev. Dr. Burton[8] was the next man. He took only one whiff, and followed Parker. He furnished a pretext, and you could see by the sound of his voice that he didn't think much of the pretext, and was vexed with Parker for getting in ahead with a fictitious ailing client. Rev. Mr. Twichell followed, and said he had to go now because he must take the midnight train for Boston. Boston was the first place that occurred to him, I suppose.

It was only a quarter to eleven when they began to distribute pretexts. At ten minutes to eleven all those people were out of the house. When nobody was left but George and me I was cheerful — I had no compunctions of conscience, no griefs of any kind. But George was beyond speech, because he held the honor and credit of the family above his own, and he was ashamed that this smirch had been put upon it. I told him to go to bed and try to sleep it off. I went to bed myself. At breakfast in the morning when George was passing a cup of coffee, I saw it tremble in his hand. I knew by that sign that there was something on his mind. He brought the cup to me and asked impressively,

"Mr. Clemens, how far is it from the front door to the upper gate?"

I said, "It is a hundred and twenty-five steps."

He said, "Mr. Clemens, you can start at the front door and you can go plumb to the upper gate and tread on one of them cigars every time."

It wasn't true in detail, but in essentials it was.

The subject under discussion on the night in question was Dreams. The talk passed from mouth to mouth in the usual serene way.

I do not now remember what form my views concerning dreams took at the time.[9] I don't remember now what my notion about dreams was then, but I do remember telling a dream by way of illustrating some detail of my speech, and I also remember that when I had finished it Rev. Dr. Burton made that doubting remark which contained that word I have already spoken of as having been uttered by my mother, in some such connection, forty or fifty years before. I was probably engaged in trying to make those people believe that now and then, by some accident, or otherwise, a dream which was prophetic turned up in the dreamer's mind. The date of my memorable dream was about the beginning of May, 1858. It was a remarkable dream, and I had been telling it several times every year for more than fifteen years — and now I was telling it again, here in the club.

In 1858 I was a steersman on board the swift and popular New Orleans and St. Louis packet, "Pennsylvania," Captain Kleinfelter.[10] I had been lent to Mr. Brown,[11] one of the pilots of the "Pennsylvania," by my owner, Mr. Horace E. Bixby, and I had been steering for Brown about eighteen months, I think.[12] Then in the early days of May, 1858, came a tragic trip — the last trip of that fleet and famous steamboat. I have told all about it in one of my books called "Old Times on the Mississippi."[13] But it is not likely that I told the dream in that book. It is impossible that I can ever have published it, I think, because I never wanted my mother to know about the dream, and she lived several years after I published that volume.[14]

I had found a place on the "Pennsylvania" for my brother Henry, who was two years my junior. It was not a place of profit, it was only a place of promise. He was "mud" clerk. Mud clerks received no salary, but they were in the line of promotion. They could become, presently, third clerk and second clerk, then chief clerk — that is to say, purser. The dream begins when Henry had been mud clerk about three months. We were lying in port at St. Louis. Pilots and steersmen had nothing to do during the three days that the boat lay in port in St. Louis and New Orleans, but the mud clerk had to begin his labors at dawn and continue them into the night, by the light of pine-knot torches. Henry and I, moneyless and unsalaried, had billeted ourselves upon our brother-in-law, Mr. Moffet, as night lodgers while in port. We took our meals on board the boat. No, I mean *I* lodged at the house, not Henry. He spent the *evenings* at the house, from nine until eleven, then went to the boat to be ready for his early duties. On the night of the dream he started away at eleven, shaking hands with the family, and said good-by according to custom. I may mention that hand-shaking as a good-by was not merely the custom of that family, but the custom of the region — the custom of Missouri, I may say. In all my life, up to that time, I had never seen one member of the Clemens family kiss another one — except once. When my father lay dying in our home in Hannibal — the 24th of March, 1847 — he put his arm around my sister's neck and drew her down and kissed her, saying "Let me die."[15] I remember that, and I remember the death rattle which swiftly followed those words, which were his last. These good-bys of Henry's were always executed in the family sitting-room on the second floor, and Henry went from that room and down-stairs without further ceremony. But this time my mother went with him to the head of the stairs and said good-by *again*. As I remember it she was moved to this by something in Henry's manner, and she remained at the head of the stairs while he descended. When he reached the door he hesitated, and climbed the stairs and shook hands good-by once more.

In the morning, when I awoke I had been dreaming, and the dream was so vivid, so like reality, that it deceived me, and I thought it *was* real. In the dream I had seen Henry a corpse. He lay in a metallic burial-case. He was dressed in a suit of my clothing, and on his breast lay a great bouquet of flowers, mainly white roses, with a red rose in the centre. The casket stood upon a couple of chairs. I dressed, and moved toward that door, thinking I would go in there and look at it, but I changed my mind. I thought I could not yet bear to meet my mother. I thought I would wait awhile and make some preparation for that ordeal. The house was in Locust Street, a little above 13th, and I walked to 14th, and to the middle of the block beyond, before it suddenly flashed upon me that there was nothing real about this — it was only a dream. I can still feel something of the grateful upheaval of joy of that moment, and I can also still feel the remnant of doubt, the suspicion that maybe it *was* real, after all. I returned to the house almost on a run, flew up the stairs two or three steps at a jump, and rushed into that sitting-room — and was made glad again, for there was no casket there.

We made the usual eventless trip to New Orleans — no, it was not eventless, for it was on the way down that I had the fight with Mr. Brown* which resulted in his requiring that I be left ashore at New Orleans.[16] In New Orleans I always had a job. It was my privilege to watch the freight-piles from seven in the evening until seven in the morning, and get three dollars for it. It was a three-night job and occurred every thirty-five days. Henry always joined my watch about nine in the evening, when his own duties were ended, and we often walked my rounds and chatted together until midnight. This time we were to part, and so the night before the boat sailed I gave Henry some advice. I said, "In case of disaster to the boat, don't lose your head — leave that unwisdom to the passengers — they are competent — they'll attend to it. But you rush for the hurricane-deck, and astern to one of the life-boats lashed aft the wheel-house, and obey the mate's orders — thus you will be useful. When the boat is launched, give such help as you can in getting the women and children into it, and be sure you don't try to get into it yourself. It is summer weather, the river is only a mile wide, as a rule, and you can swim that without any trouble." Two or three days afterward the boat's boilers exploded at Ship Island, below Memphis, early one morning — and what happened afterward I have already told in "Old Times on the Mississippi." As related there, I followed the "Pennsylvania" about a day later, on another boat, and we began to

*See "Old Times on the Mississippi."

get news of the disaster at every port we touched at, and so by the time we reached Memphis we knew all about it.[17]

I found Henry stretched upon a mattress on the floor of a great building, along with thirty or forty other scalded and wounded persons, and was promptly informed, by some indiscreet person, that he had inhaled steam; that his body was badly scalded, and that he would live but a little while; also, I was told that the physicians and nurses were giving their whole attention to persons who had a chance of being saved. They were short-handed in the matter of physicians and nurses; and Henry and such others as were considered to be fatally hurt were receiving only such attention as could be spared, from time to time, from the more urgent cases. But Dr. Peyton,[18] a fine and large-hearted old physician of great reputation in the community, gave me his sympathy and took vigorous hold of the case, and in about a week he had brought Henry around. Dr. Peyton never committed himself with prognostications which might not materialize, but at eleven o'clock one night he told me that Henry was out of danger, and would get well. Then he said, "At midnight these poor fellows lying here and there all over this place will begin to mourn and mutter and lament and make outcries, and if this commotion should disturb Henry it will be bad for him; therefore ask the physician on watch to give him an eighth of a grain of morphine, but this is not to be done unless Henry shall show signs that he is being disturbed."

Oh well, never mind the rest of it. The physicians on watch were young fellows hardly out of the medical college, and they made a mistake — they had no way of measuring the eighth of a grain of morphine, so they guessed at it and gave him a vast quantity heaped on the end of a knife-blade, and the fatal effects were soon apparent.[19] I think he died about dawn, I don't remember as to that. He was carried to the dead-room and I went away for a while to a citizen's house and slept off some of my accumulated fatigue — and meantime something was happening. The coffins provided for the dead were of unpainted white pine, but in this instance some of the ladies of Memphis had made up a fund of sixty dollars and bought a metallic case, and when I came back and entered the dead-room Henry lay in that open case, and he was dressed in a suit of my clothing. He had borrowed it without my knowledge during our last sojourn in St. Louis; and I recognized instantly that my dream of several weeks before was here exactly reproduced, so far as these details went — and I think I missed one detail; but that one was immediately supplied, for just then an elderly lady entered the place with a large bouquet consisting mainly of white roses, and in the centre of it was a red rose, and she laid it on his breast.

I told the dream there in the Club that night just as I have told it here.

Rev. Dr. Burton swung his leonine head around, focussed me with his eye, and said:[20]

"When was it that this happened?"

"In June, '58."

"It is a good many years ago. Have you told it several times since?"

"Yes, I have, a good many times."

"How many?"

"Why, I don't know how many."

"Well, strike an average. How many times a year do you think you have told it?"

"Well, I have told it as many as six times a year, possibly oftener."

"Very well, then you've told it, we'll say, seventy or eighty times since it happened?"

"Yes," I said, "that's a conservative estimate."

"Now then, Mark, a very extraordinary thing happened to me a great many years ago, and I used to tell it a number of times — a good many times — every year, for it was so wonderful that it always astonished the hearer, and that astonishment gave me a distinct pleasure every time. I never suspected that that tale was acquiring any auxiliary advantages through repetition until one day after I had been telling it ten or fifteen years it struck me that either I was getting old, and slow in delivery, or that the tale was longer than it was when it was born. Mark, I diligently and prayerfully examined that tale with this result: that I found that its proportions were now, as nearly as I could make out, one part fact, straight fact, fact pure and undiluted, golden fact, and twenty-four parts embroidery. I never told that tale afterwards — I was never able to tell it again, for I had lost confidence in it, and so the pleasure of telling it was gone, and gone permanently. How much of this tale of yours is embroidery?"

"Well," I said, "I don't know. I don't think any of it is embroidery. I think it is all just as I have stated it, detail by detail."

"Very well," he said, "then it is all right, but I wouldn't tell it any more; because if you keep on, it will begin to collect embroidery sure. The safest thing is to stop now."

That was a great many years ago. And to-day is the first time that I have told that dream since Dr. Burton scared me into fatal doubts about it. No, I don't believe I can say that. I don't believe that I ever really had any doubts whatever concerning the salient points of the dream, for those points are of such a nature that they are *pictures,* and pictures can be remembered, when they are vivid, much better than one can remember remarks and un-concreted facts. Although it has been so many years since I have told that dream, I can see those pictures now just as clearly defined as if they were before me in this room. I have not told the entire dream. There was a good deal more of it. I mean I have not told all that happened in the dream's fulfilment. After the incident in the death-room I may mention one detail, and that is this. When I arrived in St. Louis with the casket it was about eight o'clock in the morning, and I ran to my brother-in-law's place of business, hoping to find him there, but I missed him, for while I was on the way to his office he was on his way from the house to the boat. When I got back to the boat the casket was gone. He had conveyed it out to his house. I hastened thither, and when I arrived the men were just removing the casket from the vehicle to carry it up-stairs. I stopped that procedure, for I did not want my mother to see the dead face, because one side of it was drawn and distorted by the effects of the opium. When I went up-stairs, there stood the two chairs — placed to receive the coffin — just as I had seen them in my dream; and if I had arrived two or three minutes later, the casket would have been resting upon them, precisely as in my dream of several weeks before.[21]

CHAPTER XVII

From Susy's Biography of Me

Sept. 9, '85. — Mamma is teaching Jean a little natural history and is making a little collection of insects for her. But mamma does not allow Jean to kill any insects she only collects those insects that are found dead. Mamma has told us all, perticularly Jean, to bring her all the little dead insects that she finds. The other day as we were all sitting at supper Jean broke into the room and ran triumfantly up to Mamma and presented her with a plate full of dead flies. Mamma thanked Jean very enthusiastically although she with difficulty concealed her amusement. Just then Sour Mash entered the room and Jean believing her hungry asked Mamma for permission to give her the flies. Mamma laughingly consented and the flies almost immediately dissapeared.

[*Monday, October 15, 1906.*] Sour Mash's presence indicates that this adventure occurred at Quarry Farm. Susy's Biography interests itself pretty exclusively with historical facts; where they happen is not a matter of much concern to her. When other historians refer to the Bunker Hill Monument they know it is not necessary to mention that that monument is in Boston. Susy recognizes that when she mentions Sour Mash it is not necessary to localize her. To Susy, Sour Mash is the Bunker Hill Monument of Quarry Farm.

Ordinary cats have some partiality for living flies, but none for dead ones; but Susy does not trouble herself to apologize for Sour Mash's eccentricities of taste. This Biography was for *us*, and Susy knew that nothing that Sour Mash might do could startle us or need explanation, we being aware that she was not an ordinary cat, but moving upon a plane far above the prejudices and superstitions which are law to common catdom.

Once in Hartford the flies were so numerous for a time, and so trouble-

North American Review, vol. 185, no. 614 (May 3, 1907): 1–12.

some, that Mrs. Clemens conceived the idea of paying George* a bounty on all the flies he might kill. The children saw an opportunity here for the acquisition of sudden wealth. They supposed that their mother merely wanted to accumulate dead flies, for some aesthetic or scientific reason or other, and they judged that the more flies she could get the happier she would be; so they went into business with George on a commission. Straightway the dead flies began to arrive in such quantities that Mrs. Clemens was pleased beyond words with the success of her idea. Next, she was astonished that one house could furnish so many. She was paying an extravagantly high bounty, and it presently began to look as if by this addition to our expenses we were now probably living beyond our income. After a few days there was peace and comfort; not a fly was discoverable in the house; there wasn't a straggler left. Still, to Mrs. Clemens's surprise, the dead flies continued to arrive by the plateful, and the bounty expense was as crushing as ever. Then she made inquiry, and found that our innocent little rascals had established a Fly Trust, and had hired all the children in the neighborhood to collect flies on a cheap and unburdensome commission.

Mrs. Clemens's experience in this matter was a new one for her, but the governments of the world had tried it, and wept over it, and discarded it, every half-century since man was created. Any Government could have told her that the best way to increase wolves in America, rabbits in Australia, and snakes in India, is to pay a bounty on their scalps. Then every patriot goes to raising them.

From Susy's Biography of Me

Sept. 10, '85. —The other evening Clara and I brought down our new soap bubble water and we all blew soap bubles. Papa blew his soap bubles and filled them with tobacco smoke and as the light shone on them they took very beautiful opaline colors. Papa would hold them and then let us catch them in our hand and they felt delightful to the touch the mixture of the smoke and water had a singularly pleasant effect.

It is human life. We are blown upon the world; we float buoyantly upon the summer air a little while, complacently showing off our grace of form and our dainty iridescent colors; then we vanish with a little puff, leaving nothing behind but a memory — and sometimes not even that. I suppose that at those solemn times when we wake in the deeps of the night and reflect,

*The colored butler.

there is not one of us who is not willing to confess that he is really only a soap-bubble, and as little worth the making.

I remember those days of twenty-one years ago, and a certain pathos clings about them. Susy, with her manifold young charms and her iridescent mind, was as lovely a bubble as any we made that day — and as transitory. She passed, as they passed, in her youth and beauty, and nothing of her is left but a heartbreak and a memory. That long-vanished day came vividly back to me a few weeks ago when, for the first time in twenty-one years, I found myself again amusing a child with smoke-charged soap-bubbles.

Susy's next date is November 29th, 1885, the eve of my fiftieth birthday. It seems a good while ago. I must have been rather young for my age then, (1885) for I was trying to tame an old-fashioned bicycle nine feet high.[1] It is to me almost unbelievable, at my present stage of life, that there have really been people willing to trust themselves upon a dizzy and unstable altitude like that, and that I was one of them. Twichell and I took lessons every day. He succeeded, and became a master of the art of riding that wild vehicle, but I had no gift in that direction and was never able to stay on mine long enough to get any satisfactory view of the planet. Every time I tried to steal a look at a pretty girl, or any other kind of scenery, that single moment of inattention gave the bicycle the chance it had been waiting for, and I went over the front of it and struck the ground on my head or my back before I had time to realize that something was happening. I didn't always go over the front way; I had other ways, and practised them all; but no matter which way was chosen for me there was always one monotonous result — the bicycle skinned my leg and leaped up into the air and came down on top of me. Sometimes its wires were so sprung by this violent performance that it had the collapsed look of an umbrella that had had a misunderstanding with a cyclone. After each day's practice I arrived at home with my skin hanging in ribbons, from my knees down. I plastered the ribbons on where they belonged, and bound them there with handkerchiefs steeped in Pond's Extract, and was ready for more adventures next day. It was always a surprise to me that I had so much skin, and that it held out so well. There was always plenty, and I soon came to understand that the supply was going to remain sufficient for all my needs. It turned out that I had nine skins, in layers, one on top of the other like the leaves of a book, and some of the doctors said it was quite remarkable.

I was full of enthusiasm over this insane amusement. My teacher was a young German from the bicycle factory, a gentle, kindly, patient creature, with a pathetically grave face. He never smiled; he never made a remark; he always gathered me tenderly up when I plunged off, and helped me on again without a word. When he had been teaching me twice a day for three weeks I introduced a new gymnastic — one that he had never seen before — and so at last a compliment was wrung from him, a thing which I had been risking my life for days to achieve. He gathered me up and said mournfully: "Mr. Clemens, you can fall off a bicycle in more different ways than any person I ever saw before."

A boy's life is not all comedy; much of the tragic enters into it.[2] The drunken tramp — mentioned in "Tom Sawyer" or "Huck Finn" — who was (1849) burned up in the village jail,[3] lay upon my conscience a hundred nights afterward and filled them with hideous dreams — dreams in which I saw his appealing face as I had seen it in the pathetic reality, pressed against the window-bars, with the red hell glowing behind him — a face which seemed to say to me, "If you had not give me the matches, this would not have happened; you are responsible for my death." I was *not* responsible for it, for I had meant him no harm, but only good, when I let him have the matches; but no matter, mine was a trained Presbyterian conscience, and knew but the one duty — to hunt and harry its slave upon all pretexts and on all occasions; particularly when there was no sense or reason in it. The tramp — who was to blame — suffered ten minutes; I, who was not to blame, suffered three months.

The shooting down of poor old Smarr in the main street* at noonday supplied me with some more dreams[4]; and in them I always saw again the grotesque closing picture — the great family Bible spread open on the profane old man's breast by some thoughtful idiot, and rising and sinking to the labored breathings, and adding the torture of its leaden weight to the dying struggles. We are curiously made. In all the throng of gaping and sympathetic onlookers there was not one with common sense enough to perceive that an anvil would have been in better taste there than the Bible, less open to sarcastic criticism, and swifter in its atrocious work. In my nightmares I gasped and struggled for breath under the crush of that vast book for many a night.

All within the space of a couple of years we had two or three other tragedies, and I had the ill-luck to be too near by on each occasion. There was the slave man who was struck down with a chunk of slag for some small

*See "Adventures of Huckleberry Finn."

offence; I saw him die. And the young California emigrant who was stabbed with a bowie knife by a drunken comrade: I saw the red life gush from his breast. And the case of the rowdy young Hyde brothers and their harmless old uncle: one of them held the old man down with his knees on his breast while the other one tried repeatedly to kill him with an Allen revolver which wouldn't go off.[5] I happened along just then, of course.

Then there was the case of the young California emigrant who got drunk and proposed to raid the "Welshman's house" all alone one dark and threatening night.* This house stood half-way up Holliday's Hill ("Cardiff" Hill), and its sole occupants were a poor but quite respectable widow and her young and blameless daughter. The invading ruffian woke the whole village with his ribald yells and coarse challenges and obscenities. I went up there with a comrade — John Briggs, I think — to look and listen. The figure of the man was dimly visible; the women were on their porch, but not visible in the deep shadow of its roof, but we heard the elder woman's voice. She had loaded an old musket with slugs, and she warned the man that if he stayed where he was while she counted ten it would cost him his life. She began to count, slowly: he began to laugh. He stopped laughing at "six"; then through the deep stillness, in a steady voice, followed the rest of the tale: "seven . . . eight . . . nine"— a long pause, we holding our breath — "ten!" A red spout of flame gushed out into the night, and the man dropped, with his breast riddled to rags. Then the rain and the thunder burst loose and the waiting town swarmed up the hill in the glare of the lightning like an invasion of ants. Those people saw the rest; I had had my share and was satisfied. I went home to dream, and was not disappointed.

My teaching and training enabled me to see deeper into these tragedies than an ignorant person could have done. I knew what they were for. I tried to disguise it from myself, but down in the secret deeps of my heart I knew — and I *knew* that I knew. They were inventions of Providence to beguile me to a better life. It sounds curiously innocent and conceited, now, but to me there was nothing strange about it; it was quite in accordance with the thoughtful and judicious ways of Providence as I understood them. It would not have surprised me, nor even over-flattered me, if Providence had killed off that whole community in trying to save an asset like me. Educated as I had been, it would have seemed just the thing, and well worth the expense. *Why* Providence should take such an anxious interest in such a

---

*Used in "Huck Finn," I think.[6]

property — that idea never entered my head, and there was no one in that simple hamlet who would have dreamed of putting it there. For one thing, no one was equipped with it.

It is quite true I took all the tragedies to myself; and tallied them off, in turn as they happened, saying to myself in each case, with a sigh, "Another one gone — and on my account; this ought to bring me to repentance; His patience will not always endure." And yet privately I believed it would. That is, I believed it in the daytime; but not in the night. With the going down of the sun my faith failed, and the clammy fears gathered about my heart. It was then that I repented. Those were awful nights, nights of despair, nights charged with the bitterness of death. After each tragedy I recognized the warning and repented; repented and begged; begged like a coward, begged like a dog; and not in the interest of those poor people who had been extinguished for my sake, but only in my own interest. It seems selfish, when I look back on it now.

My repentances were very real, very earnest; and after each tragedy they happened every night for a long time. But as a rule they could not stand the daylight. They faded out and shredded away and disappeared in the glad splendor of the sun. They were the creatures of fear and darkness, and they could not live out of their own place. The day gave me cheer and peace, and at night I repented again. In all my boyhood life I am not sure that I ever tried to lead a better life in the daytime — or wanted to. In my age I should never think of wishing to do such a thing. But in my age, as in my youth, night brings me many a deep remorse. I realize that from the cradle up I have been like the rest of the race — never quite sane in the night. When "Injun Joe" died.*[7] . . . But never mind: in another chapter I have already described what a raging hell of repentance I passed through then. I believe that for months I was as pure as the driven snow. After dark.

It was back in those far-distant days — 1848 or '9 — that Jim Wolf came to us.[8] He was from Shelbyville, a hamlet thirty or forty miles back in the country, and he brought all his native sweetnesses and gentlenesses and simplicities with him. He was approaching seventeen, a grave and slender lad, trustful, honest, a creature to love and cling to. And he was incredibly bashful.

It is to this kind that untoward things happen. My sister gave a "candy-pull" on a winter's night. I was too young to be of the company, and Jim was too diffident. I was sent up to bed early, and Jim followed of his own

*Used in "Tom Sawyer."

motion. His room was in the new part of the house, and his window looked out on the roof of the L annex. That roof was six inches deep in snow, and the snow had an ice-crust upon it which was as slick as glass. Out of the comb of the roof projected a short chimney, a common resort for sentimental cats on moonlight nights — and this was a moonlight night. Down at the eaves, below the chimney, a canopy of dead vines spread away to some posts, making a cozy shelter, and after an hour or two the rollicking crowd of young ladies and gentlemen grouped themselves in its shade, with their saucers of liquid and piping-hot candy disposed about them on the frozen ground to cool. There was joyous chaffing and joking and laughter — peal upon peal of it.

About this time a couple of old disreputable tom-cats got up on the chimney and started a heated argument about something; also about this time I gave up trying to get to sleep, and went visiting to Jim's room. He was awake and fuming about the cats and their intolerable yowling. I asked him, mockingly, why he didn't climb out and drive them away. He was nettled, and said over-boldly that for two cents he *would*.

It was a rash remark, and was probably repented of before it was fairly out of his mouth. But it was too late — he was committed. I knew him; and I knew he would rather break his neck than back down, if I egged him on judiciously.

"Oh, of course you would! Who's doubting it?"

It galled him, and he burst out, with sharp irritation —

"Maybe *you* doubt it!"

"I? Oh no, I shouldn't think of such a thing. You are always doing wonderful things. With your mouth."

He was in a passion, now. He snatched on his yarn socks and began to raise the window, saying in a voice unsteady with anger —

"*You* think I dasn't — *you* do! Think what you blame please — *I* don't care what you think. I'll show you!"

The window made him rage; it wouldn't stay up. I said —

"Never mind, I'll hold it."

Indeed, I would have done anything to help. I was only a boy, and was already in a radiant heaven of anticipation. He climbed carefully out, clung to the window-sill until his feet were safely placed, then began to pick his perilous way on all fours along the glassy comb, a foot and a hand on each side of it. I believe I enjoy it now as much as I did then: yet it is a good deal over fifty years ago. The frosty breeze flapped his short shirt about his lean legs; the crystal roof shone like polished marble in the intense glory of the moon; the unconscious cats sat erect upon the chimney, alertly watching each other, lashing their tails and pouring out their hollow grievances; and slowly and cautiously Jim crept on, flapping as he went, the gay and frolicsome young creatures under the vine-canopy unaware, and outraging these solemnities with their misplaced laughter. Every time Jim slipped I had a hope; but always on he crept and disappointed it. At last he was within reaching distance. He paused, raised himself carefully up, measured his distance deliberately, then made a frantic grab at the nearest cat — and missed. Of course he lost his balance. His heels flew up, he struck on his back, and like a rocket he darted down the roof feet first, crashed through the dead vines and landed in a sitting posture in fourteen saucers of red-hot candy, in the midst of all that party — and dressed as *he* was: this lad who could not look a girl in the face with his clothes on. There was a wild scramble and a storm of shrieks, and Jim fled up the stairs, dripping broken crockery all the way.

The incident was ended. But I was not done with it yet, though I supposed I was. Eighteen or twenty years later I arrived in New York from California, and by that time I had failed in all my other undertakings and had stumbled into literature without intending it. This was early in 1867. (1867)   I was offered a large sum to write something for the "Sunday Mercury," and I answered with the tale of "Jim Wolf and the Cats."[9] I also collected the money for it — twenty-five dollars. It seemed over-pay, but I did not say anything about that, for I was not so scrupulous then as I am now.

A year or two later "Jim Wolf and the Cats" appeared in a Tennessee paper in a new dress — as to spelling; spelling borrowed from Artemus Ward.[10] The appropriator of the tale had a wide reputation in the West, and was exceedingly popular. Deservedly so, I think. He wrote some of the breeziest and funniest things I have ever read, and did his work with distinguished ease and fluency. His name has passed out of my memory.

A couple of years went by; then the original story — my own version — cropped up again and went floating around in the original spelling, and with my name to it. Soon first one paper and then another fell upon me vigorously for "stealing" Jim Wolf and the Cats from the Tennessee man. I got a merciless basting, but I did not mind it. It's all in the game. Besides, I had learned, a good while before that, that it is not wise to keep the fire going under a slander unless you can get some large advantage out of keeping it alive. Few slanders can stand the wear of silence.

But I was not done with Jim and the Cats yet. In 1873 I was lecturing

in London, in the Queen's Concert Rooms, Hanover Square, and was living
(1873) at the Langham Hotel, Portland Place.[11] I had no domestic household, and no official household except George Dolby,[12] lecture-agent,
and Charles Warren Stoddard,[13] the California poet, now (1900) Professor
(1900) of English Literature in the Roman Catholic University, Washington. Ostensibly Stoddard was my private secretary; in reality he was
merely my comrade — I hired him in order to have his company. As secretary there was nothing for him to do except to scrap-book the daily reports
of the great trial of the Tichborne Claimant for perjury.[14] But he made a
sufficient job out of that, for the reports filled six columns a day and he
usually postponed the scrap-booking until Sunday; then he had 36 columns
to cut out and paste in — a proper labor for Hercules. He did his work well,
but if he had been older and feebler it would have killed him once a week.
Without doubt he does his literary lectures well, but also without doubt
he prepares them fifteen minutes before he is due on his platform and thus
gets into them a freshness and sparkle which they might lack if they under-
went the staling process of overstudy.

He was good company when he was awake. He was refined, sensitive,
charming, gentle, generous, honest himself and unsuspicious of other people's honesty, and I think he was the purest male I have known, in mind
and speech. George Dolby was something of a contrast to him, but the two
were very friendly and sociable together, nevertheless. Dolby was large and
ruddy, full of life and strength and spirits, a tireless and energetic talker,
and always overflowing with good-nature and bursting with jollity. It was
a choice and satisfactory menagerie, this pensive poet and this gladsome
gorilla. An indelicate story was a sharp distress to Stoddard; Dolby told him
twenty-five a day. Dolby always came home with us after the lecture, and
entertained Stoddard till midnight. Me too. After he left, I walked the floor
and talked, and Stoddard went to sleep on the sofa. I hired him for company.

Dolby had been agent for concerts, and theatres, and Charles Dickens
and all sorts of shows and "attractions" for many years; he had known the
human being in many aspects, and he didn't much believe in him. But the
poet did. The waifs and estrays found a friend in Stoddard: Dolby tried
to persuade him that he was dispensing his charities unworthily, but he was
never able to succeed.

One night a young American got access to Stoddard at the Concert Rooms
and told him a moving tale. He said he was living on the Surrey side, and
for some strange reason his remittances had failed to arrive from home; he
had no money, he was out of employment, and friendless; his girl-wife and

his new baby were actually suffering for food; for the love of heaven could he lend him a sovereign until his remittances should resume? Stoddard was deeply touched, and gave him a sovereign on my account. Dolby scoffed, but Stoddard stood his ground. Each told me his story later in the evening, and I backed Stoddard's judgment. Dolby said we were women in disguise, and not a sane kind of women, either.

The next week the young man came again. His wife was ill with the pleurisy, the baby had the bots, or something, I am not sure of the name of the disease; the doctor and the drugs had eaten up the money, the poor little family was starving. If Stoddard "in the kindness of his heart could only spare him another sovereign," etc., etc. Stoddard was much moved, and spared him a sovereign for me. Dolby was outraged. He spoke up and said to the customer —

"Now, young man, you are going to the hotel with us and state your case to the other member of the family. If you don't make him believe in you I sha'n't honor this poet's drafts in your interest any longer, for I don't believe in you myself."

The young man was quite willing. I found no fault in him. On the contrary, I believed in him at once, and was solicitous to heal the wounds inflicted by Dolby's too frank incredulity; therefore I did everything I could think of to cheer him up and entertain him and make him feel at home and comfortable. I spun many yarns; among others the tale of Jim Wolf and the Cats. Learning that he had done something in a small way in literature, I offered to try to find a market for him in that line. His face lighted joyfully at that, and he said that if I could only sell a small manuscript to Tom Hood's Annual[15] for him it would be the happiest event of his sad life and he would hold me in grateful remembrance always. That was a most pleasant night for three of us, but Dolby was disgusted and sarcastic.

Next week the baby died. Meantime I had spoken to Tom Hood and gained his sympathy. The young man had sent his manuscript to him, and the very day the child died the money for the MS. came — three guineas. The young man came with a poor little strip of crape around his arm and thanked me, and said that nothing could have been more timely than that money, and that his poor little wife was grateful beyond words for the service I had rendered. He wept, and in fact Stoddard and I wept with him, which was but natural. Also Dolby wept. At least he wiped his eyes and wrung out his handkerchief, and sobbed stertorously and made other exaggerated shows of grief. Stoddard and I were ashamed of Dolby, and tried to make the young man understand that he meant no harm, it was only his way. The young man said sadly that he was not minding it, his grief was too deep for other hurts; that he was only thinking of the funeral, and the heavy expenses which —

We cut that short and told him not to trouble about it, leave it all to us; send the bills to Mr. Dolby and —

"Yes," said Dolby, with a mock tremor in his voice, "send them to me, and I will pay them. What, are you going? You must not go alone in your worn and broken condition; Mr. Stoddard and I will go with you. Come, Stoddard. We will comfort the bereaved mamma and get a lock of the baby's hair."

It was shocking. We were ashamed of him again, and said so. But he was not disturbed. He said —

"Oh, I know this kind, the woods are full of them. I'll make this offer: if he will show me his family I will give him twenty pounds. Come!" The young man said he would not remain to be insulted; and he said good-night and took his hat. But Dolby said he would go with him, and stay by him until he found the family. Stoddard went along to soothe the young man and modify Dolby. They drove across the river and all over Southwark, but did not find the family. At last the young man confessed there wasn't any.

The thing he sold to Tom Hood's Annual was "Jim and the Cats." And he did not put my name to it.

So that small tale was sold three times. I am selling it again, now. It is one of the best properties I have come across.

CHAPTER XVIII

[*Dictated December 21, 1906*] I wish to insert here some pages of Susy's Biography of me in which the biographer does not scatter, according to her custom, but sticks pretty steadily to a single subject until she has fought it to a finish:

Feb. 27, '86. — Last summer while we were in Elmira an article came out in the "Christian Union"[1] by name "What ought he to have done" treating of the government of children, or rather giving an account of a fathers battle with his little baby boy, by the mother of the child and put in the form of a question as to whether the father disciplined the child corectly or not, different people wrote their opinions of the fathers behavior, and told what they thought he should have done. Mamma had long known how to disciplin children, for in fact the bringing up of children had been one of her specialties for many years. She had a great many theories, but one of them was, that if a child was big enough to be nauty, it was big enough to be whipped and here we all agreed with her. I remember one morning when Dr. ____ came up to the farm he had a long discussion with mamma, upon the following topic. Mamma gave *this* as illustrative of one important rule for punishing a child. She said we will suppose the boy has thrown a handkerchief onto the floor, I tell him to pick it up, he refuses. I tell him again, he refuses. Then I say you must either pick up the handkerchief or have a whipping. My theory is never to make a child have a whipping and pick up the handkerchief too. I say "If you do not pick it up, I must punish you," if he doesn't he gets the whipping, but *I* pick up the handkerchief, if he does he gets no punishment. I tell him to do a thing if he disobeys me he is punished for so doing, but not forced to obey me afterwards.

When Clara and I had been very nauty or were being very nauty, the nurse would go and call Mamma and she would appear suddenly and look at us (she had a way of looking at us when she was displeased as if she could see right through us) till we were ready to sink through the floor from embarasment, and total absence of

---

North American Review, vol. 186, no. 615 (May 17, 1907): 114–22.

knowing what to say. This look was usually followed with "Clara" or "Susy what do you mean by this? do you want to come to the bath-room with me?" Then followed the climax for Clara and I both new only too well what going to the bath-room meant.

But mamma's first and foremost object was to make the child understand that he is being punished for *his* sake, and because the mother so loves him that she cannot allow him to do wrong; also that it is as hard for her to punish him as for him to be punished and even harder. Mamma never allowed herself to punish us when she was angry with us she never struck us because she was enoyed at us and felt like striking us if we had been nauty and had enoyed her, so that she thought she felt or would show the least bit of temper toward us while punishing us, she always postponed the punishment until *she* was no more chafed by our behavior. She never humored herself by striking or punishing us because or while she was the least bit enoyed with us.

Our very worst nautinesses were punished by being taken to the bath-room and being whipped by the paper cutter. But after the whipping was over, mamma did not allow us to leave her until we were perfectly happy, and perfectly understood why we had been whipped. I never remember having felt the least bit bitterly toward mamma for punishing me. I always felt I had deserved my punishment, and was much happier for having received it. For after mamma had punished us and shown her displeasure, she showed no signs of further displeasure, but acted as if we had not displeased her in any way.

Ordinary punishments answered very well for Susy. She was a thinker, and would reason out the purpose of them, apply the lesson, and achieve the reform required. But it was much less easy to devise punishments that would reform Clara. This was because she was a philosopher who was always turning her attention to finding something good and satisfactory and entertaining in everything that came her way; consequently it was sometimes pretty discouraging to the troubled mother to find that after all her pains and thought in inventing what she meant to be a severe and reform-compelling punishment, the child had entirely missed the severities through her native disposition to get interest and pleasure out of them as novelties. The mother, in her anxiety to find a penalty that would take sharp hold and do its work effectively, at last resorted, with a sore heart, and with a reproachful conscience, to that punishment which the incorrigible criminal in the penitentiary dreads above all the other punitive miseries which the warden inflicts upon him for his good — solitary confinement in the dark chamber. The grieved and worried mother shut Clara up in a very small clothes-closet and went away and left her there — for fifteen minutes — it was all that the mother-heart could endure. Then she came softly back and listened — listened for the sobs, but there weren't any; there were muffled and inarticulate sounds, but they could not be construed into sobs. The mother waited half an hour longer; by that time she was suffering so intensely with sorrow and compassion for the little prisoner that she was not able to wait any longer for the distressed sounds which she had counted upon to inform her when there had been punishment enough and the reform accomplished. She opened the closet to set the prisoner free and take her back into her loving favor and forgiveness, but the result was not the one expected. The captive had manufactured a fairy cavern out of the closet, and friendly fairies out of the clothes hanging from the hooks, and was having a most sinful and unrepentant good time, and requested permission to spend the rest of the day there!

From Susy's Biography of Me

But Mamma's oppinions and ideas upon the subject of bringing up children has always been more or less of a joke in our family, perticularly since Papa's article in the "Christian Union,"[2] and I am sure Clara and I have related the history of our old family paper-cutter, our punishments and privations with rather more pride and triumph than any other sentiment; because of Mamma's way of rearing us.

When the article "What ought he to have done?" came out Mamma read it, and was very much interested in it. And when papa heard that she had read it he went to work and secretly wrote his opinion of what the father ought to have done. He told Aunt Susy, Clara and I, about it but mamma was not to see it or hear any thing about it till it came out. He gave it to Aunt Susy to read, and after Clara and I had gone up to get ready for bed he brought it up for us to read. He told what he thought the father ought to have done by telling what mamma would have done. The article was a beautiful tribute to mamma and every word in it true. But still in writing about mamma he partly forgot that the article was going to be published, I think, and expressed himself more fully than he would do the second time he wrote it; I think the article has done and will do a great deal of good, and I think it would have been perfect for the family and friend's enjoyment, but a little bit too private to have been published as it was. And Papa felt so too, because the very next day or a few days after, he went down to New York to see if he couldn't get it back before it was published but it was too late, and he had to return without it. When the Christian Union reached the farm and papa's article in it all ready and waiting to be read to mamma papa hadn't the courage to show it to her (for he knew she wouldn't like it at all) at first, and he didn't but he might have let it go and never let her see it, but finally he gave his consent to her seeing it, and told Clara and I we could take it to her, which we did, with tardiness, and we all stood around mamma while she read it, all wondering what she would say and think about it.

She was too much surprised, (and pleased privately, too) to say much at first, but as we all expected publicly, (or rather when she remembered that this article was to be read by every one that took the Christian Union) she was rather shocked and a little displeased.

Clara and I had great fun the night papa gave it to us to read and then hide, so mamma couldn't see it, for just as we were in the midst of reading it mamma appeared papa following anxiously and asked why we were not in bed? then a scuffle ensued for we told her it was a secret and tried to hide it; but she chased us wherever we went, till she thought it was time for us to go to bed, then she surendered and left us to tuck it under Clara's matress.

A little while after the article was published letters began to come in to papa crittisizing it, there were some very pleasant ones but a few very disagreable. One of these, the very worst, mamma got hold of and read, to papa's great regret, it was full of the most disagreble things, and so very enoying to papa that he for a time felt he must do something to show the author of it his great displeasure at being so insulted. But he finally decided not to, because he felt the man had some cause for feeling enoyed at, for papa had spoken of him, (he was the baby's father) rather slightingly in his Christian Union Article.[3]

After all this, papa and mamma both wished I think they might never hear or be spoken to on the subject of the Christian Union article, and whenever any has spoken to me and told me "How much they did enjoy my father's article in the Christian Union" I almost laughed in their faces when I remembered what a great variety of oppinions had been expressed upon the subject of the Christian Union article of papa's.

The article was written in July or August and just the other day papa received quite a bright letter from a gentleman who has read the C. U. article and gave his opinion of it in these words.

It is missing. She probably put the letter between the leaves of the Biography and it got lost out. She threw away the hostile letters, but tried to keep the pleasantest one for her book; surely there has been no kindlier biographer than this one. Yet to a quite creditable degree she is loyal to the responsibilities of her position as historian — not eulogist — and honorably gives me a quiet prod now and then. But how many, many, many she has withheld that I deserved! I could prize them now; there would be no acid in her words, and it is loss to me that she did not set them all down. Oh, Susy, you sweet little biographer, you break my old heart with your gentle charities!

I think a great deal of her work. Her canvases are on their easels, and her brush flies about in a care-free and random way, delivering a dash here, a dash there and another yonder, and one might suppose that there would be no definite result; on the contrary I think that an intelligent reader of her little book must find that by the time he has finished it he has somehow accumulated a pretty clear and nicely shaded idea of the several members of this family — including Susy herself — and that the random dashes on the canvases have developed into portraits. I feel that my own portrait, with some of the defects fined down and others left out, is here; and I am sure that any who knew the mother will recognize her without difficulty, and will say that the lines are drawn with a just judgment and a sure hand. Little creature though Susy was, the penetration which was born in her finds its way to the surface more than once in these pages.

Before Susy began the Biography she let fall a remark now and then concerning my character which showed that she had it under observation. In the Record which we kept of the children's sayings there is an instance of this. She was twelve years old at the time. We had established a rule that each member of the family must bring a fact to breakfast — a fact drawn from a book or from any other source; any fact would answer. Susy's first contribution was in substance as follows. Two great exiles and former opponents in war met in Ephesus — Scipio and Hannibal.[4] Scipio asked Hannibal to name the greatest general the world had produced.

"Alexander"[5] — and he explained why.

"And the next greatest?"

"Pyrrhus"[6] — and he explained why.

"But where do you place yourself, then?"

"If I had conquered you I would place myself before the others."

Susy's grave comment was —

"That *attracted* me, it was just like papa — he is so frank about his books."

So frank in admiring them, she meant.

[*Thursday, March 28, 1907*] Some months ago I commented upon a chapter of Susy's Biography wherein she very elaborately discussed an article about the training and disciplining of children, which I had published in the "Christian Union" (this was twenty-one years ago), an article which was full of worshipful praises of Mrs. Clemens as a mother, and which little Clara, and Susy, and I had been hiding from this lovely and admirable mother because we knew she would disapprove of public and printed praises of herself. At the time that I was dictating these comments, several months ago, I was trying to call back to my memory some of the details of that article, but I was not able to do it, and I wished I had a copy of the article so that I could see what there was about it which gave it such large interest for Susy.

Yesterday afternoon I elected to walk home from the luncheon at the St. Regis, which is in 55th Street and Fifth Avenue, for it was a fine spring day and I hadn't had a walk for a year or two, and felt the need of exercise. As I walked along down Fifth Avenue the desire to see that "Christian Union" article came into my head again. I had just reached the corner of 42nd

Street then, and there was the usual jam of wagons, carriages, and auto-mobiles there. I stopped to let it thin out before trying to cross the street, but a stranger, who didn't require as much room as I do, came racing by and darted into a crack among the vehicles and made the crossing. But on his way past me he thrust a couple of ancient newspaper clippings into my hand, and said,

"There, you don't know me, but I have saved them in my scrap-book for twenty years, and it occurred to me this morning that perhaps you would like to see them, so I was carrying them down-town to mail them, I not expecting to run across you in this accidental way, of course; but I will give them into your own hands now. Good-by!"— and he disappeared among the wagons.

Those scraps which he had put into my hand were ancient newspaper copies of that "Christian Union" article! It is a handsome instance of men-tal telegraphy—or if it isn't that, it is a handsome case of coincidence.

From the Biography

March 14th, '86. — Mr. Laurence Barrette[7] and Mr. and Mrs. Hutton[8] were here a little while ago, and we had a very interesting visit from them. Papa said Mr. Barette never had acted so well before when he had seen him, as he did the first night he was staying with us. And Mrs. _____ said she never had seen an actor on the stage, whom she more wanted to speak with.

Papa has been very much interested of late, in the "Mind Cure" theory. And in fact so have we all. A young lady in town has worked wonders, by using the "Mind Cure" upon people; she is constantly busy now curing peoples deseases in this way — and curing her own even, which to me seems the most remarkable of all.

A little while past, papa was delighted with the knowledge of what he thought the best way of curing a cold, which was by starving it. This starving did work beautifully, and freed him from a great many severe colds. Now he says it wasn't the starving that helped his colds, but the trust in the starving, the mind cure con-nected with the starving.

I shouldn't wonder if we finally became firm believers in Mind Cure. The next time papa has a cold, I haven't a doubt, he will send for Miss H____ the young lady who is doctoring in the "Mind Cure" theory, to cure him of it.

Mamma was over at Mrs. George Warners[9] to lunch the other day, and Miss H____ was there too. Mamma asked if anything as natural as near sightedness could be cured she said oh yes just as well as other deseases.

When mamma came home, she took me into her room, and told me that perhaps my near-sightedness could be cured by the "Mind Cure" and that she was going to have me try the treatment any way, there could be no harm in it, and there might be great good. If her plan succeeds there certainly will be a great deal in "Mind Cure" to my oppinion, for I am *very* near sighted and so is mamma, and I never expected there could be any more cure for it than for blindness, but now I dont know but what there is a cure for *that*.

It was a disappointment; her near-sightedness remained with her to the end. She was born with it, no doubt; yet, strangely enough, she must have been four years old, and possibly five, before we knew of its existence. It is not easy to understand how that could have happened. I discovered the defect by accident. I was half-way up the hall stairs one day at home, and was leading her by the hand, when I glanced back through the open door of the dining-room and saw what I thought she would recognize as a pretty picture. It was "Stray Kit," the slender, the graceful, the sociable, the beautiful, the incomparable, the cat of cats, the tortoise-shell, curled up as round as a wheel and sound asleep on the fire-red cover of the dining-table, with a brilliant stream of sunlight falling across her. I exclaimed about it, but Susy said she could see nothing there, neither cat nor table-cloth. The distance was so slight — not more than twenty feet perhaps — that if it had been any other child I should not have credited the statement.

From the Biography

March 14th, '86. — Clara sprained her ankle, a little while ago, by running into a tree, when coasting, and while she was unable to walk with it she played solotaire with cards a great deal. While Clara was sick and papa saw her play solotaire so much, he got very much interested in the game, and finally began to play it himself a little, then Jean took it up, and at last *mamma*, even played it ocasionally; Jean's and papa's love for it rapidly increased, and now Jean brings the cards every night to the table and papa and mamma help her play, and before dinner is at an end, papa has gotten a separate pack of cards, and is playing alone, with great interest. Mamma and Clara next are made subject to the contagious solatair, and there are four solotaireans at the table; while you hear nothing but "Fill up the place" etc. It is dreadful! after supper Clara goes into the library, and gets a little red mahogany table, and placing it under the gas fixture seats herself and begins to play again, then papa follows with another table of the same discription, and they play solotair till bed-time.

We have just had our Prince and Pauper pictures taken; two groups and some little single ones. The groups (the Interview and Lady Jane Grey scene) were pretty good, the lady Jane scene was perfect, just as pretty as it could be, the Interview was not so good; and two of the little single pictures were very good indeed, but one was very bad. Yet on the whole we think they were a success.

Papa has done a great deal in his life I think, that is good, and very remarkable, but I think if he had had the advantages with which he could have developed the gifts which he has made no use of in writing his books, or in any other way for other peoples pleasure and benefit outside of his own family and intimate friends, he could have done *more* than he has and a great deal more even. He is known to the public as a humorist, but he has much more in him that is earnest than that is humorous. He has a keen sense of the ludicrous, notices funny stories and incidents knows how to tell them, to improve upon them, and does not forget them. He has been through a great many of the funny adventures related in "Tom Sayer" and in "Huckleberry Finn," *himself* and he lived among just such boys, and in just such villages all the days of his early life. His "Prince and Pauper[10] is his most orriginal, and best production; it shows the most of any of his books what kind of pictures are in his mind, usually. Not that the pictures of England in the 16th Century and the adventures of a little prince and pauper are the kind of things he mainly thinks about; but that *that* book, and those pictures represent the train of thought and imagination he would be likely to be thinking of to-day, to-morrow, or next day, more nearly than those given in "Tom Sawyer or "Huckleberry Finn."*

Papa can make exceedingly bright jokes, and he enjoys funny things, and when he is with people he jokes and laughs a great deal, but still he is more interested in earnest books and earnest subjects to talk upon, than in humorous ones.†

When we are all alone at home, nine times out of ten, he talks about some very earnest subjects, (with an ocasional joke thrown in) and he a good deal more often talks upon such subjects than upon the other kind.

He is as much of a Phoosopher as anything I think. I think he could have done a great deal in this direction if he had studied while young, for he seems to enjoy reasoning out things, no matter what; in a great many such directions he has greater ability than in the gifts which have made him famous.

Thus at fourteen she had made up her mind about me, and in no timorous or uncertain terms had set down her reasons for her opinion. Fifteen years were to pass before any other critic — except Mr. Howells, I think — was to reutter that daring opinion and print it. Right or wrong, it was a brave position for that little analyzer to take. She never withdrew it afterward, nor modified it. She has spoken of herself as lacking physical courage, and has evinced her admiration of Clara's; but she had moral courage, which is the rarest of human qualities, and she kept it functionable by exercising it. I think that in questions of morals and politics she was usually on my side; but when she was not she had her reasons and maintained her ground. Two years after she passed out of my life I wrote a Philosophy.[12] Of the three persons who have seen the manuscript only one understood it, and all three condemned it. If she could have read it, she also would have condemned it, possibly,— probably, in fact — but she would have understood it. It would have had no difficulties for her on that score; also she would have found a tireless pleasure in analyzing and discussing its problems.

---

*It is so yet.— M. T.

†She has said it well and correctly. Humor is a subject which has never had much interest for me. This is why I have never examined it, nor written about it nor used it as a topic for a speech. A hundred times it has been offered me as a topic in these past forty years, but in no case has it attracted me.— M. T.[11]

CHAPTER XIX

From Susy's Biography of Me

March 23, '86. —The other day was my birthday, and I had a little birthday party in the evening and papa acted some very funny charades with Mr. Gherhardt, Mr. Jesse Grant[1] (who had come up from New York and was spending the evening with us) and Mr. Frank Warner. One of them was "on his knees" honys-sneeze. There were a good many other funny ones, all of which I dont remember. Mr. Grant was very pleasant, and began playing the charades in the most delightful way.

Susy's spelling has defeated me, this time. I cannot make out what "honys-sneeze" stands for. Impromptu charades were almost a nightly pastime of ours, from the children's earliest days — they played in them with me when they were only five or six years old. As they increased in years and practice their love for the sport almost amounted to a passion, and they acted their parts with a steadily increasing ability. At first they required much drilling; but later they were generally ready as soon as the parts were assigned, and they acted them according to their own devices. Their stage facility and absence of constraint and self-consciousness in the "Prince and Pauper" was a result of their charading practice.[2]

At ten and twelve Susy wrote plays, and she and Daisy Warner[3] and Clara played them in the library or up-stairs in the school-room, with only themselves and the servants for audience. They were of a tragic and tremendous sort, and were performed with great energy and earnestness. They were dramatized (freely) from English history, and in them Mary Queen of Scots[4] and Elizabeth had few holidays. The clothes were borrowed from the mother's wardrobe and the gowns were longer than necessary, but that was not regarded as a defect. In one of these plays Jean (three years old,

North American Review, vol. 186, no. 616 (June 7, 1907): 241–51.

perhaps) was Sir Francis Bacon.[5] She was not dressed for the part, and did not have to say anything, but sat silent and decorous at a tiny table and was kept busy signing death-warrants. It was a really important office, for few entered those plays and got out of them alive.

March 26. — Mamma and Papa have been in New York for two or three days, and Miss Corey has been staying with us. They are coming home to-day at two o'clock.

Papa has just begun to play chess, and he is very fond of it, so he has engaged to play with Mrs. Charles Warner[6] every morning from 10 to 12, he came down to supper last night, full of this pleasant prospect, but evidently with something on his mind. Finally he said to mamma in an appologetical tone, Susy Warner and I have a plan.

"Well" mamma said "what now, I wonder?"

Papa said that Susy Warner and he were going to name the chess men after some of the old bible heroes, and then play chess on Sunday.

April 18, '86. — Mamma and papa Clara and Daisy have gone to New York to see the "Mikado." They are coming home to-night at half past seven.

Last winter when Mr. Cable was lecturing with papa, he wrote this letter to him just before he came to visit us.

DEAR UNCLE,— That's one nice thing about me, I never bother any one, to offer me a good thing twice. You dont ask me to stay over Sunday, but then you dont ask me to leave Saturday night, and knowing the nobility of your nature as I do — thank you, I'll stay till Monday morning.*

Your's and the dear familie's

GEORGE W. CABLE.

[*December 22, 1906*] It seems a prodigious while ago! Two or three nights ago I dined at a friend's house with a score of other men, and at my side was Cable — actually almost an old man, really almost an old man, that once so young chap! 62 years old, frost on his head, seven grandchildren in stock, and a brand-new wife to re-begin life with!

[*Dictated Nov. 19, 1906*]

Ever since papa and mamma were married, papa has written his books and then taken them to mamma in manuscript and she has expergated them.[7] Papa read "Huckleberry Finn" to us in manuscript just before it came out, and then he would leave parts of it with mamma to expergate, while he went off up to the study to work, and sometimes Clara and I would be sitting with mamma while she was looking the manuscript over, and I remember so well, with what pangs of regret we used to see her turn down the leaves of the pages, which meant that some delightfully dreadful part must be scratched out. And I remember one part pertickularly

---

*Cable never travelled Sundays.

which was perfectly fascinating it was dreadful, that Clara and I used to delight in, and oh with what dispair we saw mamma turn down the leaf on which it was written, we thought the book would be almost ruined without it. But we gradually came to feel as mamma did.

It would be a pity to replace the vivacity and quaintness and felicity of Susy's innocent free spelling with the dull and petrified uniformities of the spelling-book. Nearly all the grimness is taken out of the "expergating" of my books by the subtle mollification accidentally infused into the word by Susy's modification of the spelling of it.

I remember the special case mentioned by Susy, and can see the group yet — two-thirds of it pleading for the life of the culprit sentence that was so fascinatingly dreadful and the other third of it patiently explaining why the court could not grant the prayer of the pleaders; but I do not remember what the condemned phrase was. It had much company, and they all went to the gallows; but it is possible that that specially dreadful one which gave those little people so much delight was cunningly devised and put into the book for just that function, and not with any hope or expectation that it would get by the "expergator" alive. It is possible, for I had that custom.

Susy's quaint and effective spelling falls quite opportunely into to-day's atmosphere, which is heavy with the rumblings and grumblings and mutterings of the Simplified Spelling Reform. Andrew Carnegie[8] started this storm, a couple of years ago, by moving a simplifying of English orthography, and establishing a fund for the prosecution and maintenance of the crusade. He began gently. He addressed a circular to some hundreds of his friends, asking them to simplify the spelling of a dozen of our badly spelt words — I think they were only words which end with the superfluous *ugh*. He asked that these friends use the suggested spellings in their private correspondence.

By this, one perceives that the beginning was sufficiently quiet and unaggressive.

Next stage: a small committee was appointed, with Brander Matthews[9] for managing director and spokesman. It issued a list of three hundred words, of average silliness as to spelling, and proposed new and sane spellings for these words. The President of the United States, unsolicited, adopted these simplified three hundred officially, and ordered that they be used in the official documents of the Government. It was now remarked, by all the educated and the thoughtful except the clergy that Sheol was to pay. This was most justly and comprehensively descriptive. The indignant British lion rose, with a roar that was heard across the Atlantic, and stood there on his little isle, gazing, red-eyed, out over the glooming seas, snow-flecked with driving spindrift, and lashing his tail — a most scary spectacle to see.

The lion was outraged because we, a nation of children, without any grown-up people among us, with no property in the language, but using it merely by courtesy of its owner the English nation, were trying to defile the sacredness of it by removing from it peculiarities which had been its ornament and which had made it holy and beautiful for ages.

In truth there is a certain sardonic propriety in preserving our orthography, since ours is a mongrel language which started with a child's vocabulary of three hundred words, and now consists of two hundred and twenty-five thousand; the whole lot, with the exception of the original and legitimate three hundred, borrowed, stolen, smouched from every unwatched language under the sun, the spelling of each individual word of the lot locating the source of the theft and preserving the memory of the revered crime.

Why is it that I have intruded into this turmoil and manifested a desire to get our orthography purged of its asininities? Indeed I do not know why I should manifest any interest in the matter, for at bottom I disrespect our orthography most heartily, and as heartily disrespect everything that has been said by anybody in defence of it. Nothing professing to be a defence of our ludicrous spellings has had any basis, so far as my observation goes, except sentimentality. In these "arguments" the term venerable is used instead of mouldy, and hallowed instead of devilish; whereas there is nothing properly venerable or antique about a language which is not yet four hundred years old, and about a jumble of imbecile spellings which were grotesque in the beginning, and which grow more and more grotesque with the flight of the years.

[*Dictated Monday, November 30, 1906*]

Jean and Papa were walking out past the barn the other day when Jean saw some little newly born baby ducks, she exclaimed as she perceived them "I dont see why God gives us so much ducks when Patrick kills them so."

Susy is mistaken as to the origin of the ducks. They were not a gift, I bought them. I am not finding fault with her, for that would be most unfair. She is remarkably accurate in her statements as a historian, as a rule, and it would not be just to make much of this small slip of hers; besides I think it was a quite natural slip, for by heredity and habit ours was a religious household, and it was a common thing with us whenever anybody did a handsome thing, to give the credit of it to Providence, without examining into the matter. This may be called automatic religion—in fact that is what it is; it is so used to its work that it can do it without your help or even your privity; out of all the facts and statistics that may be placed before it, it will always get the one result, since it has never been taught to seek any other. It is thus the unreflecting cause of much injustice. As we have seen, it betrayed Susy into an injustice toward me. It had to be automatic, for she would have been far from doing me an injustice when in her right mind. It was a dear little biographer, and she meant me no harm, and I am not censuring her now, but am only desirous of correcting in advance an erroneous impression which her words would be sure to convey to a reader's mind. No elaboration of this matter is necessary; it is sufficient to say *I* provided the ducks.

It was in Hartford. The greensward sloped down-hill from the house to the sluggish little river that flowed through the grounds, and Patrick, who was fertile in good ideas, had early conceived the idea of having home-made ducks for our table. Every morning he drove them from the stable down to the river, and the children were always there to see and admire the waddling white procession; they were there again at sunset to see Patrick conduct the procession back to its lodgings in the stable. But this was not always a gay and happy holiday show, with joy in it for the witnesses; no, too frequently there was a tragedy connected with it, and then there were tears and pain for the children. There was a stranded log or two in the river, and on these certain families of snapping-turtles used to congregate and drowse in the sun and give thanks, in their dumb way, to Providence for benevolence extended to them. It was but another instance of misplaced credit; it was the young ducks that those pious reptiles were so thankful for —whereas they were *my* ducks. I bought the ducks.

When a crop of young ducks, not yet quite old enough for the table but approaching that age, began to join the procession, and paddle around in the sluggish water, and give thanks—not to me—for that privilege, the snapping-turtles would suspend their songs of praise and slide off the logs and paddle along under the water and chew the feet of the young ducks. Presently Patrick would notice that two or three of those little creatures were not moving about, but were apparently at anchor, and were not looking as thankful as they had been looking a short time before. He early found out what that sign meant—a submerged snapping-turtle was taking his breakfast, and silently singing his gratitude. Every day or two Patrick would rescue and fetch up a little duck with incomplete legs to stand upon—

nothing left of their extremities but gnawed and bleeding stumps. Then the children said pitying things and wept — and at dinner we finished the tragedy which the turtles had begun. Thus, as will be seen — out of season, at least — it was really the turtles that gave us so much ducks. At my expense.

Papa has written a new version of "There is a happy land" it is—

> "There is a boarding-house
> Far, far away,
> Where they have ham and eggs,
> Three times a day,
> Oh dont those boarders yell
> When they hear the dinner-bell,
> They give that land-lord rats
> Three times a day."

Again Susy has made a small error. It was not I that wrote the song. I heard Billy Rice sing it in the negro minstrel show, and I brought it home and sang it — with great spirit — for the elevation of the household. The children admired it to the limit, and made me sing it with burdensome frequency. To their minds it was superior to the Battle Hymn of the Republic.

How many years ago that was! Where now is Billy Rice? He was a joy to me, and so were the other stars of the nigger-show — Billy Birch, David Wambold, Backus, and a delightful dozen of their brethren, who made life a pleasure to me forty years ago, and later.[10] Birch, Wambold, and Backus are gone years ago; and with them departed to return no more forever, I suppose, the real nigger-show — the genuine nigger-show, the extravagant nigger-show,— the show which to me had no peer and whose peer has not yet arrived, in my experience. We have the grand opera; and I have witnessed, and greatly enjoyed, the first act of everything which Wagner created, but the effect on me has always been so powerful that one act was quite sufficient; whenever I have witnessed two acts I have gone away physically exhausted; and whenever I have ventured an entire opera the result has been the next thing to suicide. But if I could have the nigger-show back again, in its pristine purity and perfection, I should have but little further use for opera. It seems to me that to the elevated mind and the sensitive spirit the hand-organ and the nigger-show are a standard and a summit to whose rarefied altitude the other forms of musical art may not hope to reach.

[*Dictated September 5, 1906*] It is years since I have examined "The Children's Record."[11] I have turned over a few of its pages this morning. This book is a record in which Mrs. Clemens and I registered some of the sayings and doings of the children, in the long ago, when they were little chaps. Of course, we wrote these things down at the time because they were of momentary interest — things of the passing hour, and of no permanent value — but at this distant day I find that they still possess an interest for me and also a value, because it turns out that they were *registrations of character*. The qualities then revealed by fitful glimpses, in childish acts and speeches, remained as a permanency in the children's characters in the drift of the years, and were always afterwards clearly and definitely recognizable.

There is a masterful streak in Jean that now and then moves her to set my authority aside for a moment and end a losing argument in that prompt and effective fashion. And here in this old book I find evidence that she was just like that before she was quite four years old.

From The Children's Record. Quarry Farm, July 7, 1884. —Yesterday evening our cows (after being inspected and worshipped by Jean from the shed for an hour,) wandered off down into the pasture, and left her bereft. I thought I was going to get back home, now, but that was an error. Jean knew of some more cows, in a field somewhere, and took my hand and led me thitherward. When we turned the corner and took the right-hand road, I saw that we should presently be out of range of call and sight; so I began to argue against continuing the expedition, and Jean began to argue in favor of it — she using English for light skirmishing, and German for "business." I kept up my end with vigor, and demolished her arguments in detail, one after the other, till I judged I had her about cornered. She hesitated a moment, then answered up sharply:

"*Wir werden nichts mehr darüber sprechen!*" (We won't talk any more about it!)

It nearly took my breath away; though I thought I might possibly have misunderstood. I said:

"Why, you little rascal! *Was hast du gesagt?*"[12]

But she said the same words again, and in the same decided way. I suppose I ought to have been outraged; but I wasn't, I was charmed. And I suppose I ought to have spanked her; but I didn't. I fraternized with the enemy, and we went on and spent half an hour with the cows.

That incident is followed in the "Record" by the following paragraph, which is another instance of a juvenile characteristic maintaining itself into mature age. Susy was persistently and conscientiously truthful throughout her life with the exception of one interruption covering several months, and perhaps a year. This was while she was still a little child. Suddenly — not gradually — she began to lie; not furtively, but frankly, openly, and on a scale quite disproportioned to her size. Her mother was so stunned, so nearly paralyzed for a day or two, that she did not know what to do with the emergency. Reasonings, persuasions, beseechings, all went for nothing; they produced no effect; the lying went tranquilly on. Other remedies were tried, but they failed. There is a tradition that success was finally accomplished by whipping. I think the Record says so, but if it does it is because the Record is incomplete. Whipping was indeed tried, and was faithfully kept up during two or three weeks, but the results were merely temporary; the reforms achieved were discouragingly brief.

Fortunately for Susy, an incident presently occurred which put a complete stop to all the mother's efforts in the direction of reform. This incident was the chance discovery in Darwin of a passage which said that when a child exhibits a sudden and unaccountable disposition to forsake the truth and restrict itself to lying, the explanation must be sought away back in the past; that an ancestor of the child had had the same disease, at the same tender age; that it was irremovable by persuasion or punishment, and that it had ceased as suddenly and as mysteriously as it had come, when it had run its appointed course. I think Mr. Darwin said that nothing was necessary but to leave the matter alone and let the malady have its way and perish by the statute of limitations.

We had confidence in Darwin, and after that day Susy was relieved of our reformatory persecutions. She went on lying without let or hindrance during several months, or a year; then the lying suddenly ceased, and she became as conscientiously and exactingly truthful as she had been before the attack, and she remained so to the end of her life.

The paragraph in the Record to which I have been leading up is in my handwriting, and is of a date so long posterior to the time of the lying malady that she had evidently forgotten that truth-speaking had ever had any difficulties for her.

Mama was speaking of a servant who had been pretty unveracious, but was now "trying to tell the truth." Susy was a good deal surprised, and said she shouldn't think anybody would have to *try* to tell the truth.

In the Record the children's acts and speeches quite definitely define their characters. Susy's indicated the presence of mentality — thought — and they were generally marked by gravity. She was timid, on her physical side, but had an abundance of moral courage. Clara was sturdy, independent, orderly, practical, persistent, plucky — just a little animal, and very satisfactory. Charles Dudley Warner said Susy was made of mind, and Clara of matter.

When Motley, the kitten, died, some one said that the thoughts of the two children need not be inquired into, they could be divined: that Susy was wondering if this was the *end* of Motley, and had his life been worth while; whereas Clara was merely interested in seeing to it that there should be a creditable funeral.

In those days Susy was a dreamer, a thinker, a poet and philosopher, and Clara — well, Clara wasn't. In after-years a passion for music developed the latent spirituality and intellectuality in Clara, and her practicality took second and, in fact, even third place. Jean was from the beginning orderly, steady, diligent, persistent; and remains so. She picked up languages easily, and kept them.

Susy aged eleven, Jean three. — Susy said the other day when she saw Jean bringing a cat to me of her own motion, "Jean has found out already that mamma loves morals and papa loves cats."

It is another of Susy's remorselessly sound verdicts.

As a child, Jean neglected my books. When she was nine years old Will Gillette[13] invited her and the rest of us to a dinner at the Murray Hill Hotel in New York, in order that we might get acquainted with Mrs. Leslie and her daughters. Elsie Leslie[14] was nine years old, and was a great celebrity on the stage. Jean was astonished and awed to see that little slip of a thing sit up at table and take part in the conversation of the grown people, capably and with ease and tranquillity. Poor Jean was obliged to keep still, for the subjects discussed never happened to hit her level, but at last the talk fell within her limit and she had her chance to contribute to it. "Tom Sawyer" was mentioned. Jean spoke gratefully up and said,

"I know who wrote that book — Harriet Beecher Stowe!"

One evening Susy had prayed, Clara was curled up for sleep; she was reminded that it was her turn to pray now. She said "Oh! one's enough," and dropped off to slumber.

Clara five years old. — We were in Germany. The nurse, Rosa, was not allowed to speak to the children otherwise than in German. Clara grew very tired of it; by and by the little creature's patience was exhausted, and she said "Aunt Clara, I wish God had made Rosa in English."

Clara four years old, Susy six. — This morning when Clara discovered that this is my birthday, she was greatly troubled because she had provided no gift for me, and repeated her sorrow several times. Finally she went musing to the nursery and presently returned with her newest and dearest treasure, a large toy horse, and said, "You shall have this horse for your birthday, papa."

I accepted it with many thanks. After an hour she was racing up and down the room with the horse, when Susy said,

"Why Clara, you gave that horse to papa, and now you've tooken it again."

Clara. —"I never give it to him for always; I give it to him for his birthday."

In Geneva, in September, I lay abed late one morning, and as Clara was passing through the room I took her on my bed a moment. Then the child went to Clara Spaulding and said,

"Aunt Clara, papa is a good deal of trouble to me."

"Is he? Why?"

"Well, he wants me to get in bed with him, and I can't do that with jelmuls [gentlemen]—I don't like jelmuls anyway."

"What, you don't like gentlemen! Don't you like Uncle Theodore Crane?"

"Oh yes, but he's not a jelmul, he's a friend."

CHAPTER XX

[*Notes on "Innocents Abroad." Dictated in Florence, Italy, April, 1904*][1]— I will begin with a note upon the dedication. I wrote the book in the months

(1868) of March and April, 1868, in San Francisco.[2] It was published in August, 1869.[3] Three years afterward Mr. Goodman, of Virginia City, Nevada, on whose newspaper I had served ten years before, came East, and we were walking down Broadway one day when he said: "How did you come to steal Oliver Wendell Holmes's[4] dedication and put it in your book?"

I made a careless and inconsequential answer, for I supposed he was joking. But he assured me that he was in earnest. He said: "I'm not discussing the question of whether you stole it or didn't — for that is a question that can be settled in the first bookstore we come to — I am only asking you *how* you came to steal it, for that is where my curiosity is focalized."

I couldn't accommodate him with this information, as I hadn't it in stock. I could have made oath that I had not stolen anything, therefore my vanity was not hurt nor my spirit troubled. At bottom I supposed that he had mistaken another book for mine, and was now getting himself into an untenable place and preparing sorrow for himself and triumph for me. We entered a bookstore and he asked for "The Innocents Abroad" and for the dainty little blue and gold edition of Dr. Oliver Wendell Holmes's poems. He opened the books, exposed their dedications and said: "Read them. It is plain that the author of the second one stole the first one, isn't it?"

I was very much ashamed, and unspeakably astonished. We continued our walk, but I was not able to throw any gleam of light upon that origi-

North American Review, vol. 186, no. 618 (July 5, 1907): 465–74.

nal question of his. I could not remember ever having seen Dr. Holmes's dedication. I knew the poems, but the dedication was new to me.

I did not get hold of the key to that secret until months afterward, then it came in a curious way, and yet it was a natural way; for the natural way provided by nature and the construction of the human mind for the discovery of a forgotten event is to employ another forgotten event for its resurrection.

I received a letter from the Rev. Dr. Rising,[5] who had been rector of the Episcopal church in Virginia City in my time, in which letter Dr. (1866) Rising made reference to certain things which had happened to us in the Sandwich Islands six years before; among things he made casual mention of the Honolulu Hotel's poverty in the matter of literature. At first I did not see the bearing of the remark, it called nothing to my mind. But presently it did — with a flash! There was but one book in Mr. Kirchhof's hotel, and that was the first volume of Dr. Holmes's blue and gold series. I had had a fortnight's chance to get well acquainted with its contents, for I had ridden around the big island (Hawaii) on horseback and had brought back so many saddle boils that if there had been a duty on them it would have bankrupted me to pay it. They kept me in my room, unclothed, and in persistent pain for two weeks, with no company but cigars and the little volume of poems. Of course I read them almost constantly; I read them from beginning to end, then read them backwards, then began in the middle and read them both ways, then read them wrong end first and upside down. In a word, I read the book to rags, and was infinitely grateful to the hand that wrote it.

Here we have an exhibition of what repetition can do, when persisted in daily and hourly over a considerable stretch of time, where one is merely reading for entertainment, without thought or intention of preserving in the memory that which is read. It is a process which in the course of years dries all the juice out of a familiar verse of Scripture, leaving nothing but a sapless husk behind. In that case you at least know the origin of the husk, but in the case in point I apparently preserved the husk but presently forgot whence it came. It lay lost in some dim corner of my memory a year or two, then came forward when I needed a dedication, and was promptly mistaken by me as a child of my own happy fancy.

I was new, I was ignorant, the mysteries of the human mind were a sealed book to me as yet, and I stupidly looked upon myself as a tough and unforgivable criminal. I wrote to Dr. Holmes and told him the whole disgraceful affair, implored him in impassioned language to believe that I had never intended to commit this crime, and was unaware that I had committed it until I was confronted with the awful evidence. I have lost his answer, I could better have afforded to lose an uncle. Of these I had a surplus, many of them of no real value to me, but that letter was beyond price, beyond uncledom, and unsparable. In it Dr. Holmes laughed the kindest and heal-ingest laugh over the whole matter, and at considerable length and in happy phrase assured me that there was no crime in unconscious plagiarism; that I committed it every day, that he committed it every day, that every man alive on the earth who writes or speaks commits it every day and not merely once or twice but every time he opens his mouth; that all our phrasings are spiritualized shadows cast multitudinously from our readings; that no happy phrase of ours is ever quite original with us, there is nothing of our own in it except some slight change born of our temperament, character, environment, teachings and associations; that this slight change differenti-ates it from another man's manner of saying it, stamps it with our special style, and makes it our own for the time being; all the rest of it being old, moldy, antique, and smelling of the breath of a thousand generations of them that have passed it over their teeth before!

In the thirty-odd years which have come and gone since then, I have sat-isfied myself that what Dr. Holmes said was true.[6]

I wish to make a note upon the preface of the "Innocents." In the last paragraph of that brief preface, I speak of the proprietors of the "Daily Alta California" having "waived their rights" in certain letters which I wrote for that journal while absent on the "Quaker City" trip.[7] I was young then, I am white-headed now, but the insult of that word rankles yet, now that I am reading that paragraph for the first time in many years, reading it for the first time since it was written, perhaps. There were rights, it is true — such rights as the strong are able to acquire over the weak and the ab-sent. Early in '66 George Barnes invited me to resign my reportership on his paper, the San Francisco "Morning Call," and for some months ther-eafter I was without money or work; then I had a pleasant turn of fortune.[8] The proprietors of the "Sacramento Union," a great and influential daily journal, sent me to the Sandwich Islands to write four letters a month at twenty dollars apiece. I was there four or five months,[9] and returned to find myself about the best known honest man on the Pacific Coast. Thomas McGuire,[10] proprietor of several theatres, said that now was the time to make my fortune — strike while the iron was hot! — break into the lecture field! I did it. I announced a lecture on the Sandwich Islands, closing the advertisement with the remark, "Admission one dollar; doors open at half-past 7, the trouble begins at 8." A true prophecy. The trouble certainly did begin at 8, when I found myself in front of the only audience I had ever faced, for the fright which pervaded me from head to foot was paralyzing. It lasted two minutes and was as bitter as death, the memory of it is indestructible, but it had its compensations, for it made me immune from timidity before audiences for all time to come.[11] I lectured in all the principal Californian towns and in Nevada, then lectured once or twice more in San Francisco, then retired from the field rich — for me — and laid out a plan to sail Westward from San Francisco, and go around the world.[12] The proprietors of the "Alta" engaged me to write an account of the trip for that paper — fifty letters of a column and a half each, which would be about two thousand words per letter, and the pay to be twenty dollars per letter.

I went East to St. Louis to say good-bye to my mother, and then I was bitten by the prospectus of Captain Duncan of the "Quaker City" excursion, and I ended by joining it.[13] During the trip I wrote and sent the fifty letters; six of them miscarried, and I wrote six new ones to complete my contract. Then I put together a lecture on the trip and delivered it in San Francisco at great and satisfactory pecuniary profit, then I branched out into the country and was aghast at the result: I had been entirely forgotten, I never had people enough in my houses to sit as a jury of inquest on my lost reputation! I inquired into this curious condition of things and found that the thrifty owners of that prodigiously rich "Alta" newspaper had *copyrighted* all those poor little twenty-dollar letters, and had threatened with prosecution any journal which should venture to copy a paragraph from them!

And there I was! I had contracted to furnish a large book, concerning the excursion, to the American Publishing Co. of Hartford, and I supposed I should need all those letters to fill it out with. I was in an uncomfortable situation — that is, if the proprietors of this stealthily acquired copyright should refuse to let me use the letters. That is just what they did; Mr. Mac — something — I have forgotten the rest of his name — said his firm were going to make a book out of the letters in order to get back the thousand dollars which they had paid for them.[14] I said that if they had acted fairly and honorably, and had allowed the country press to use the letters or portions of them, my lecture-skirmish on the coast would have paid me ten thousand dollars, whereas the "Alta" had lost me that amount. Then he offered a compromise: he would publish the book and allow me ten per cent. royalty on it. The compromise did not appeal to me, and I said so. I was now quite unknown outside of San Francisco, the book's sale would be confined to that city, and my royalty would not pay me enough to board me three months; whereas my Eastern contract, if carried out, could be profitable to me, for I had a sort of reputation on the Atlantic seaboard acquired through the publication of six excursion-letters in the New York "Tribune" and one or two in the "Herald."

In the end Mr. Mac agreed to suppress his book, on certain conditions: in my preface I must thank the "Alta" for waiving its "rights" and granting me permission. I objected to the thanks. I could not with any large degree of sincerity thank the "Alta" for bankrupting my lecture-raid. After considerable debate my point was conceded and the thanks left out.

Noah Brooks[15] was editor of the "Alta" at the time, a man of sterling character and equipped with a right heart, also a good historian where facts were not essential. In biographical sketches of me written many years afterward (1902), he was quite eloquent in praises of the generosity of the "Alta" (1902) people in giving to me without compensation a book which, as history had afterward shown, was worth a fortune. After all the fuss, I did not levy heavily upon the "Alta" letters. I found that they were newspaper matter, not book matter. They had been written here and there and yonder, as opportunity had given me a chance working-moment or two during our feverish flight around about Europe or in the furnace-heat of my state-room on board the "Quaker City," therefore they were loosely constructed, and needed to have some of the wind and water squeezed out of them. I used several of them — ten or twelve, perhaps. I wrote the rest of "The Innocents Abroad" in sixty days, and I could have added a fortnight's labor with the pen and gotten along without the letters altogether. I was very young in those days, exceedingly young, marvellously young, younger than I am now, younger than I shall ever be again, by hundreds of years. I worked every night from eleven or twelve until broad day in the morning, and as I did two hundred thousand words in the sixty days, the average was more than three thousand words a day — nothing for Sir Walter Scott,[16] nothing for Louis Stevenson, nothing for plenty of other people, but quite (1897) handsome for me. In 1897, when we were living in Tedworth Square, London, and I was writing the book called "Following the Equator"[17] my average was eighteen hundred words a day; here in Florence (1904), (1904) my average seems to be fourteen hundred words per sitting of four or five hours.*

I was deducing from the above that I have been slowing down steadily

---

*With the pen, I mean. This Autobiography is dictated, not written.

in these thirty-six years, but I perceive that my statistics have a defect: three thousand words in the spring of 1868 when I was working seven or eight or nine hours at a sitting has little or no advantage over the sitting of to-day, covering half the time and producing half the output. Figures often beguile me, particularly when I have the arranging of them myself; in which case the remark attributed to Disraeli would often apply with justice and force:

"There are three kinds of lies: lies, damned lies, and statistics."

[*Dictated, January 23, 1907*]—The proverb says that Providence protects children and idiots. This is really true. I know it because I have tested it. It did not protect George through the most of his campaign, but it saved him in his last inning, and the veracity of the proverb stood confirmed.

I have several times been saved by this mysterious interposition, when I was manifestly in extreme peril. It has been common, all my life, for smart people to perceive in me an easy prey for selfish designs, and I have walked without suspicion into the trap set for me, yet have often come out unscathed, against all the likelihoods. More than forty years ago, in San Francisco, the (1865) office staff adjourned, upon conclusion of its work at two o'clock in the morning, to a great bowling establishment where there were twelve alleys. I was invited, rather perfunctorily, and as a matter of etiquette—by which I mean that I was invited politely, but not urgently. But when I diffidently declined, with thanks, and explained that I knew nothing about the game, those lively young fellows became at once eager and anxious and urgent to have my society. This flattered me, for I perceived no trap, and I innocently and gratefully accepted their invitation. I was given an alley all to myself. The boys explained the game to me, and they also explained to me that there would be an hour's play, and that the player who scored the fewest ten-strikes in the hour would have to provide oysters and beer for the combination. This disturbed me very seriously, since it promised me bankruptcy, and I was sorry that this detail had been overlooked in the beginning. But my pride would not allow me to back out now, so I stayed in, and did what I could to look satisfied and glad I had come. It is not likely that I looked as contented as I wanted to, but the others looked glad enough to make up for it, for they were quite unable to hide their evil joy. They showed me how to stand, and how to stoop, and how to aim the ball, and how to let fly; and then the game began. The results were astonishing. In my ignorance I delivered the balls in apparently every way except the right one; but no matter—during half an hour I never started a ball down the alley that didn't score a ten-strike, every time, at the other end. The others lost their grip early, and their joy along with it. Now and then one of them got a ten-strike, but the occurrence was so rare that it made no show alongside of my giant score. The boys surrendered at the end of the half-hour, and put on their coats and gathered around me and in courteous, but sufficiently definite, language expressed their opinion of an experience-worn and seasoned expert who would stoop to lying and deception in order to rob kind and well-meaning friends who had put their trust in him under the delusion that he was an honest and honorable person. I was not able to convince them that I had not lied, for now my character was gone, and they refused to attach any value to anything I said. The proprietor of the place stood by for a while saying nothing, then he came to my defence. He said: "It looks like a mystery, gentlemen, but it isn't a mystery after it's explained. That is a *grooved* alley; you've only to start a ball down it any way you please and the groove will do the rest; it will slam the ball against the northeast curve of the head pin every time, and nothing can save the ten from going down."

It was true. The boys made the experiment and they found that there was no art that could send a ball down that alley and fail to score a ten-strike with it. When I had told those boys that I knew nothing about that game I was speaking only the truth; but it was ever thus, all through my life: whenever I have diverged from custom and principle and uttered a truth, the rule has been that the hearer hadn't strength of mind enough to believe it.

A quarter of a century ago I arrived in London to lecture a few weeks under the management of George Dolby, who had conducted the Dickens readings in America five or six years before. He took me to the Albemarle and fed me, and in the course of the dinner he enlarged a good deal, and with great satisfaction, upon his reputation as a player of fifteen-ball pool, and when he learned by my testimony that I had never seen the game played, and knew nothing of the art of pocketing balls, he enlarged more and more, and still more, and kept on enlarging, until I recognized that I was either in the presence of the very father of fifteen-ball pool or in the presence of his most immediate descendant. At the end of the dinner Dolby was eager to introduce me to the game and show me what he could do. We adjourned to the billiard-room and he framed the balls in a flat pyramid and told me to fire at the apex ball and then go on and do what I could toward pocketing the fifteen, after which he would take the cue and show me what a past-master of the game could do with those balls. I did as required. I began with the diffidence proper to my ignorant

(1873)

estate, and when I had finished my inning all the balls were in the pockets and Dolby was burying me under a volcanic irruption of acid sarcasms.

So I was a liar in Dolby's belief. He thought he had been sold, and at a cheap rate; but he divided his sarcasms quite fairly and quite equally between the two of us. He was full of ironical admiration of his childishness and innocence in letting a wandering and characterless and scandalous American load him up with deceptions of so transparent a character that they ought not to have deceived the house cat. On the other hand, he was remorselessly severe upon me for beguiling him, by studied and discreditable artifice, into bragging and boasting about his poor game in the presence of a professional expert disguised in lies and frauds, who could empty more balls in billiard pockets in an hour than he could empty into a basket in a day.

In the matter of fifteen-ball pool I never got Dolby's confidence wholly back, though I got it in other ways, and kept it until his death. I have played that game a number of times since, but that first time was the only time in my life that I have ever pocketed all the fifteen in a single inning.

My unsuspicious nature has made it necessary for Providence to save me from traps a number of times. Thirty years ago, a couple of Elmira bankers invited me to play the game of "Quaker" with them. I had never (1876) heard of the game before, and said that if it required intellect, I should not be able to entertain them. But they said it was merely a game of chance, and required no mentality — so I agreed to make a trial of it. They appointed four in the afternoon for the sacrifice. As the place, they chose a ground-floor room with a large window in it. Then they went treacherously around and advertised the "sell" which they were going to play upon me.

I arrived on time, and we began the game — with a large and eager free-list to superintend it. These superintendents were outside, with their noses pressed against the window-pane. The bankers described the game to me. So far as I recollect, the pattern of it was this: they had a pile of Mexican dollars on the table; twelve of them were of even date, fifty of them were of odd dates. The bankers were to separate a coin from the pile and hide it under a hand, and I must guess "odd" or "even." If I guessed correctly, the coin would be mine; if incorrectly, I lost a dollar. The first guess I made was "even," and was right. I guessed again, "even," and took the money. They fed me another one and I guessed "even" again, and took the money. I guessed "even" the fourth time, and took the money. It seemed to me that "even" was a good guess, and I might as well stay by it, which I did. I guessed

"even" twelve times, and took the twelve dollars. I was doing as they secretly desired. Their experience of human nature had convinced them that
any human being as innocent as my face proclaimed me to be, would repeat his first guess if it won, and would go on repeating it if it should continue to win. It was their belief that an innocent would be almost sure at
the beginning to guess "even," and not "odd," and that if an innocent should
guess "even" twelve times in succession and win every time, he would go
on guessing "even" to the end — so it was their purpose to let me win those
twelve even dates and then advance the odd dates, one by one, until I
should lose fifty dollars, and furnish those superintendents something to
laugh about for a week to come.

But it did not come out in that way; for by the time I had won the twelfth
dollar and last even date, I withdrew from the game because it was so one-
sided that it was monotonous, and did not entertain me. There was a burst
of laughter from the superintendents at the window when I came out of
the place, but I did not know what they were laughing at nor whom they
were laughing at, and it was a matter of no interest to me anyway. Through
that incident I acquired an enviable reputation for smartness and penetration, but it was not my due, for I had not penetrated anything that the cow
could not have penetrated.

CHAPTER XXI

From Susy's Biography of Me

Feb. 12, '86.

Mamma and I have both been very much troubled of late because papa since he has been publishing Gen. Grant's book has seemed to forget his own books and work entirely, and the other evening as papa and I were promonading up and down the library he told me that he didn't expect to write but one more book, and then he was ready to give up work altogether, die, or do anything, he said that he had written more than he had ever expected to, and the only book that he had been pertickularly anxious to write was one locked up in the safe down stairs, not yet published.*

But this intended future of course will never do, and although papa usually holds to his own opinions and intents with outsiders, when mamma realy desires anything and says that it must be, papa allways gives up his plans (at least so far) and does as she says is right (and she is usually right, if she dissagrees with him at all). It was because he knew his great tendency to being convinced by her, that he published without her knowledge that article in the "Christian Union" concerning the government of children. So judging by the proofs of past years, I think that we will be able to persuade papa to go back to work as before, and not leave off writing with the end of his next story. Mamma says that she sometimes feels, and I do too, that she would rather have papa depend on his writing for a living than to have him think of giving it up.

[*Dictated, November 8, 1906*] I have a defect of a sort which I think is not common; certainly I hope it isn't: it is rare that I can call before my mind's eye the form and face of either friend or enemy. If I should make a list, now, of persons whom I know in America and abroad — say to the number of even an entire thousand — it is quite unlikely that I could re-

*It isn't yet. Title of it, "Captain Stormfield's Visit to Heaven."⎯S. L. C.

North American Review, vol. 186, no. 620 (August 2, 1907): 689–98.

produce five of them in my mind's eye. Of my dearest and most intimate friends, I could name eight whom I have seen and talked with four days ago, but when I try to call them before me they are formless shadows. Jean has been absent, this past eight or ten days, in the country, and I wish I could reproduce her in the mirror of my mind, but I can't do it.

It may be that this defect is not constitutional, but a result of lifelong absence of mind and indolent and inadequate observation. Once or twice in my life it has been an embarrassment to me. Twenty years ago, in the days of Susy's Biography of Me, there was a dispute one morning at the breakfast-table about the color of a neighbor's eyes. I was asked for a verdict, but had to confess that if that valued neighbor and old friend had eyes I was not sure that I had ever seen them. It was then mockingly suggested that perhaps I didn't even know the color of the eyes of my own family, and I was required to shut my own at once and testify. I was able to name the color of Mrs. Clemens's eyes, but was not able to even suggest a color for Jean's, or Clara's, or Susy's.

All this talk is suggested by Susy's remark: "The other evening as papa and I were promonading up and down the library." Down to the bottom of my heart I am thankful that I can see *that* picture! And it is not dim, but stands out clear in the unfaded light of twenty-one years ago. In those days Susy and I used to "promonade" daily up and down the library, with our arms about each other's waists, and deal in intimate communion concerning affairs of State, or the deep questions of human life, or our small personal affairs.

It was quite natural that I should think I had written myself out when I was only fifty years old, for everybody who has ever written has been smitten with that superstition at about that age. Not even yet have I really written myself out. I have merely stopped writing because dictating is pleasanter work, and because dictating has given me a strong aversion to the pen, and because two hours of talking per day is enough, and because— But I am only damaging my mind with this digging around in it for pretexts where no pretext is needed, and where the simple truth is for this one time better than any invention, in this small emergency. I shall never finish my five or six unfinished books, for the reason that by forty years of slavery to the pen I have earned my freedom. I detest the pen and I wouldn't use it again to sign the death warrant of my dearest enemy.

[*Dictated, March 8, 1906*] For thirty years, I have received an average of a dozen letters a year from strangers who remember me, or whose fathers remember me as boy and young man. But these letters are almost always disappointing. I have not known these strangers nor their fathers. I have not heard of the names they mention; the reminiscences to which they call attention have had no part in my experience; all of which means that these strangers have been mistaking me for somebody else. But at last I have the refreshment, this morning, of a letter from a man who deals in names that were familiar to me in my boyhood. The writer encloses a newspaper clipping which has been wandering through the press for four or five weeks, and he wants to know if Capt. Tonkray, lately deceased, was (as stated in the clipping) the original of "Huckleberry Finn."[2]

I have replied that "Huckleberry Finn" was Frank F.[3] As this inquirer evidently knew the Hannibal of the forties, he will easily recall Frank. Frank's father was at one time Town Drunkard, an exceedingly well-defined and unofficial office of those days. He succeeded "General" Gaines, and for a time he was sole and only incumbent of the office; but afterward Jimmy Finn proved competency and disputed the place with him, so we had two town drunkards at one time — and it made as much trouble in that village as Christendom experienced in the fourteenth century when there were two Popes at the same time.

In "Huckleberry Finn" I have drawn Frank exactly as he was. He was ignorant, unwashed, insufficiently fed; but he had as good a heart as ever any boy had. His liberties were totally unrestricted. He was the only really independent person — boy or man — in the community, and by consequence he was tranquilly and continuously happy, and was envied by all the rest of us. We liked him; we enjoyed his society. And as his society was forbidden us by our parents, the prohibition trebled and quadrupled its value, and therefore we sought and got more of his society than of any other boy's. I heard, four years ago, that he was Justice of the Peace in a remote village in the State of _____,[4] and was a good citizen and was greatly respected.

During Jimmy Finn's term he (Jimmy) was not exclusive; he was not finical; he was not hypercritical; he was largely and handsomely democratic — and slept in the deserted tan-yard with the hogs. My father tried to reform him once, but did not succeed.[5] My father was not a professional reformer. In him the spirit of reform was spasmodic. It only broke out now and then, with considerable intervals between. Once he tried to reform Injun Joe. That also was a failure. It was a failure, and we boys were glad. For Injun Joe, drunk, was interesting and a benefaction to us, but Injun Joe, sober, was a dreary spectacle. We watched my father's experiments upon him with a good deal of anxiety, but it came out all right and we were satisfied. Injun Joe got drunk oftener than before, and became intolerably interesting.

I think that in "Tom Sawyer" I starved Injun Joe to death in the cave. But that may have been to meet the exigencies of romantic literature. I can't remember now whether the real Injun Joe died in the cave or out of it, but I do remember that the news of his death reached me at a most unhappy time — that is to say, just at bedtime on a summer night when a prodigious storm of thunder and lightning accompanied by a deluging rain that turned the streets and lanes into rivers, caused me to repent and resolve to lead a better life. I can remember those awful thunder-bursts and the white glare of the lightning yet, and the wild lashing of the rain against the window-panes. By my teachings I perfectly well knew what all that wild riot was for — Satan had come to get Injun Joe. I had no shadow of doubt about it. It was the proper thing when a person like Injun Joe was required in the under world, and I should have thought it strange and unaccountable if Satan had come for him in a less impressive way. With every glare of lightning I shrivelled and shrunk together in mortal terror, and in the interval of black darkness that followed I poured out my lamentings over my lost condition, and my supplications for just one more chance, with an energy and feeling and sincerity quite foreign to my nature.

But in the morning I saw that it was a false alarm and concluded to resume business at the old stand and wait for another reminder.

The axiom says "History repeats itself." A week or two ago Mr. Blank-Blank[6] dined with us. At dinner he mentioned a circumstance which flashed me back over about sixty years and landed me in that little bedroom on that tempestuous night, and brought to my mind how creditable to me was my conduct through the whole night, and how barren it was of moral spot or fleck during that entire period: he said Mr. X[7] was sexton, or something, of the Episcopal church in his town,[8] and had been for many years the competent superintendent of all the church's worldly affairs, and was regarded by the whole congregation as a stay, a blessing, a priceless treasure. But he had a couple of defects — not large defects, but they seemed large when flung against the background of his profoundly religious character: he drank a good deal, and he could outswear a brakeman. A movement arose to persuade him to lay aside these vices, and after consulting with his pal, who occupied the same position as himself in the other Episcopal church, and whose defects were duplicates of his own and had inspired regret in the congregation he was serving, they concluded to try for reform — not wholesale, but half at a time. They took the liquor pledge and waited for results. During nine days the results were entirely satisfactory, and they were recipients of many compliments and much congratulation. Then on New-year's eve they had business a mile and a half out of town, just beyond the State line. Everything went well with them that evening in the bar-room of the inn — but at last the celebration of the occasion by those villagers came to be of a burdensome nature. It was a bitter cold night and the multitudinous hot toddies that were circulating began by and by to exert a powerful influence upon the new prohibitionists. At last X's friend remarked,

"X, does it occur to you that we are *outside the diocese?*"

That ended reform No. 1. Then they took a chance in reform No. 2. For a while that one prospered, and they got much applause. I now reach the incident which sent me back a matter of sixty years, as I have remarked a while ago.

One morning Mr. Blank-Blank met X on the street and said,

"You have made a gallant struggle against those defects of yours. I am aware that you failed on No. 1, but I am also aware that you are having better luck with No. 2."

"Yes," X said; "No. 2 is all right and sound up to date, and we are full of hope."

Blank-Blank said, "X, of course you have your troubles like other people, but they never show on the outside. I have never seen you when you were not cheerful. Are you always cheerful? Really always cheerful?"

"Well, no," he said, "no, I can't say that I am always cheerful, but — well, you know that kind of a night that comes: *say* — you wake up 'way in the night and the whole world is sunk in gloom and there are storms and earthquakes and all sorts of disasters in the air threatening, and you get cold and clammy; and when that happens to me I recognize how sinful I am and it all goes clear to my heart and wrings it and I have such terrors and terrors! — oh, they are indescribable, those terrors that assail me, and I slip out of bed and get on my knees and pray and pray and promise that I *will* be good, if I can only have another chance. And then, you know, in the morning the sun shines out *so* lovely, and the birds sing and the whole world is so beautiful, and — *b' God, I rally!*"

Now I will quote a brief paragraph from this letter which I have a minute ago spoken of. The writer says:

You no doubt are at a loss to know who I am. I will tell you. In my younger days I was a resident of Hannibal, Mo., and you and I were schoolmates attending Mr. Dawson's school along with Sam and Will Bowen and Andy Fuqua and others whose names I have forgotten. I was then about the smallest boy in school, for my age, and they called me little Aleck for short.

I only dimly remember him, but I knew those other people as well as I knew the town drunkards. I remember Dawson's schoolhouse perfectly. If I wanted to describe it I could save myself the trouble by conveying the description of it to these pages from "Tom Sawyer." I can remember the drowsy and inviting summer sounds that used to float in through the open windows from that distant boy-Paradise, Cardiff Hill (Holliday's Hill), and mingle with the murmurs of the studying pupils and make them the more dreary by the contrast. I remember Andy Fuqua, the oldest pupil — a man of twenty-five. I remember the youngest pupil, Nannie Owsley, a child of seven. I remember George Robards, eighteen or twenty years old, the only pupil who studied Latin. I remember — in some cases vividly, in others vaguely — the rest of the twenty-five boys and girls. I remember Mr. Dawson very well. I remember his boy, Theodore, who was as good as he could be. In fact, he was inordinately good, extravagantly good, offensively good, detestably good — and he had pop-eyes — and I would have drowned him if I had had a chance. In that school we were all about on an equality, and, so far as I remember, the passion of envy had no place in our hearts, except in the case of Arch Fuqua — the other one's brother. Of course we all went barefoot in the summer-time. Arch Fuqua was about my own age — ten or eleven. In the winter we could stand him, because he wore shoes then, and his great gift was hidden from our sight and we were enabled to forget it. But in the summer-time he was a bitterness to us. He was our envy, for he could double back his big toe and let it fly and you could hear it snap thirty yards. There was not another boy in the school that could approach this feat. He had not a rival as regards a physical distinction — except in Theodore Eddy, who could work his ears like a horse. But he was no real rival, because you couldn't hear him work his ears; so all the advantage lay with Arch Fuqua.

I am not done with Dawson's school; I will return to it in a later chapter.

[*Dictated at Hamilton, Bermuda, January 6, 1907*] "That reminds me." In conversation we are always using that phrase, and seldom or never noticing how large a significance it bears. It stands for a curious and interesting fact, to wit: that sleeping or waking, dreaming or talking, the thoughts which swarm through our heads are almost constantly, almost continuously, accompanied by a like swarm of reminders of incidents and episodes of our past. A man can never know what a large traffic this commerce of association carries on in our minds until he sets out to write his autobiography; he then finds that a thought is seldom born to him that does not immediately remind him of some event, large or small, in his past experience. Quite naturally these remarks remind me of various things, among others this: that sometimes a thought, by the power of association, will bring back to your mind a lost word or a lost name which you have not been able to recover by any other process known to your mental equipment. Yesterday we had an instance of this. Rev. Joseph H. Twichell is with me on this flying trip to Bermuda. He was with me on my last visit to Bermuda, and to-day we were trying to remember when it was. We thought it was somewhere in the neighborhood of thirty years ago, but that was as near as we could get at the date. Twichell said that the landlady in whose boarding-house we sojourned in that ancient time could doubtless furnish us the date, and we must look her up. We wanted to see her, anyway, because she and her blooming daughter of eighteen were the only persons whose acquaintance we had made at that time, for we were travelling under fictitious names, and people who wear aliases are not given to seeking society and bringing themselves under suspicion. But at this point in our talk we encountered an obstruction: we could not recall the landlady's name. We hunted all around through our minds for that name, using all the customary methods of research, but without success; the name was gone from us, apparently permanently. We finally gave the matter up, and fell to talking about something else. The talk wandered from one subject to another, and finally arrived at Twichell's school-days in Hartford — the Hartford of something more than half a century ago — and he mentioned several of his schoolmasters, dwelling with special interest upon the peculiarities of an aged one named Olney. He remarked that Olney, humble village schoolmaster as he was, was yet a man of superior parts, and had published text-books which had enjoyed a wide currency in America in their day. I said I remembered those books, and had studied Olney's Geography in school when I was a boy. Then Twichell said,

"That reminds me — our landlady's name was a name that was associated with school-books of some kind or other fifty or sixty years ago. I wonder what it was. I believe it began with K."

Association did the rest, and did it instantly. I said,

"Kirkham's Grammar!"

That settled it. Kirkham was the name; and we went out to seek for the owner of it. There was no trouble about that, for Bermuda is not large, and is like the earlier Garden of Eden, in that everybody in it knows everybody else, just as it was in the serpent's headquarters in Adam's time. We easily found Miss Kirkham — she that had been the blooming girl of a generation before — and she was still keeping boarders; but her mother had passed from this life. She settled the date for us, and did it with certainty, by help of a couple of uncommon circumstances, events of that ancient time. She said we had sailed from Bermuda on the 24th of May, 1877, which was the day on which her only nephew was born—and he is now thirty years of age. The other unusual circumstance—she called it an unusual circumstance, and I didn't say anything—was that on that day the Rev. Mr. Twichell (bearing the assumed name of Peters) had made a statement to her which she regarded as a fiction. I remembered the circumstance very well. We had bidden the young girl good-by and had gone fifty yards, perhaps, when Twichell said he had forgotten something (I doubted it) and must go back. When he rejoined me he was silent, and this alarmed me, because I had not seen an example of it before. He seemed quite uncomfortable, and I asked him what the trouble was. He said he had been inspired to give the girl a pleasant surprise, and so had gone back and said to her—

"That young fellow's name is not Wilkinson—that's Mark Twain."

She did not lose her mind; she did not exhibit any excitement at all, but said quite simply, quite tranquilly,

"Tell it to the marines, Mr. Peters—if that should happen to be *your* name."

It was very pleasant to meet her again. We were white-headed, but she was not; in the sweet and unvexed spiritual atmosphere of the Bermudas one does not achieve gray hairs at forty-eight.

I had a dream last night, and of course it was born of association, like nearly everything else that drifts into a person's head, asleep or awake. On board ship, on the passage down, Twichell was talking about the swiftly developing possibilities of aerial navigation, and he quoted those striking verses of Tennyson's[9] which forecast a future when air-borne vessels of war shall meet and fight above the clouds and redden the earth below with a rain of blood. This picture of carnage and blood and death reminded me of something which I had read a fortnight ago—statistics of railway accidents compiled by the United States Government, wherein the appalling fact was set forth that on our 200,000 miles of railway we annually kill 10,000 persons outright and injure 80,000. The war-ships in the air suggested the railway horrors, and three nights afterward the railway horrors suggested my dream. The work of association was going on in my head, unconsciously, all that time. It was an admirable dream, what there was of it.

In it I saw a funeral procession; I saw it from a mountain peak; I saw it crawling along and curving here and there, serpentlike, through a level vast plain. I seemed to see a hundred miles of the procession, but neither the beginning of it nor the end of it was within the limits of my vision. The procession was in ten divisions, each division marked by a sombre flag, and the whole represented ten years of our railway activities in the accident line; each division was composed of 80,000 cripples, and was bearing its own year's 10,000 mutilated corpses to the grave: in the aggregate 800,000 cripples and 100,000 dead, drenched in blood!

CHAPTER XXII

[*Dictated, October 10, 1906*] Susy has named a number of the friends who were assembled at Onteora at the time of our visit, but there were others —

(1890) among them Laurence Hutton, Charles Dudley Warner, and Carroll Beckwith, and their wives.[1] It was a bright and jolly company. Some of those choice spirits are still with us; the others have passed from this life: Mrs. Clemens, Susy, Mr. Warner, Mary Mapes Dodge, Laurence Hutton, Dean Sage[2] — peace to their ashes! Susy is in error in thinking Mrs. Dodge was not there at that time; we were her guests.

We arrived at nightfall, dreary from a tiresome journey; but the dreariness did not last. Mrs. Dodge had provided a home-made banquet, and the happy company sat down to it, twenty strong, or more. Then the thing happened which always happens at large dinners, and is always exasperating: everybody talked to his elbow-mates and all talked at once, and gradually raised their voices higher, and higher, and higher, in the desperate effort to be heard. It was like a riot, an insurrection; it was an intolerable volume of noise. Presently I said to the lady next me —

"I will subdue this riot, I will silence this racket. There is only one way to do it, but I know the art. You must tilt your head toward mine and seem to be deeply interested in what I am saying; I will talk in a low voice; then, just because our neighbors won't be able to hear me, they will *want* to hear me. If I mumble long enough — say two minutes — you will see that the dialogues will one after another come to a standstill, and there will be silence, not a sound anywhere but my mumbling."

Then in a very low voice I began:

"When I went out to Chicago, eleven years ago, to witness the Grant

North American Review, vol. 186, no. 622 (September 8, 1907): 8–21.

festivities, there was a great banquet on the first night, with six hundred ex-soldiers present.[3] The gentleman who sat next me was Mr. X. X. He was very hard of hearing, and he had a habit common to deaf people of shouting his remarks instead of delivering them in an ordinary voice. He would handle his knife and fork in reflective silence for five or six minutes at a time and then suddenly fetch out a shout that would make you jump out of the United States."

By this time the insurrection at Mrs. Dodge's table — at least that part of it in my immediate neighborhood — had died down, and the silence was spreading, couple by couple, down the long table. I went on in a lower and still lower mumble, and most impressively —

"During one of Mr. X. X.'s mute intervals, a man opposite us approached the end of a story which he had been telling his elbow-neighbor. He was speaking in a low voice — there was much noise — I was deeply interested, and straining my ears to catch his words, stretching my neck, holding my breath, to hear, unconscious of everything but the fascinating tale. I heard him say, 'At this point he seized her by her long hair — she shrieking and begging — bent her neck across his knee, and with one awful sweep of the razor —'

"HOW DO YOU LIKE CHICA-A-AGO?!!!"

That was X. X.'s interruption, hearable at thirty miles. By the time I had reached that place in my mumblings Mrs. Dodge's dining-room was so silent, so breathlessly still, that if you had dropped a thought anywhere in it you could have heard it smack the floor.* When I delivered that yell the entire dinner company jumped as one person, and punched their heads through the ceiling, damaging it, for it was only lath and plaster, and it all came down on us, and much of it went into the victuals and made them gritty, but no one was hurt. Then I explained why it was that I had played that game, and begged them to take the moral of it home to their hearts and be rational and merciful thenceforth, and cease from screaming in mass, and agree to let one person talk at a time and the rest listen in grateful and unvexed peace. They granted my prayer, and we had a happy time all the rest of the evening; I do not think I have ever had a better time in my life. This was largely because the new terms enabled me to keep the floor — now that I had it — and do all the talking myself. I do like to hear myself talk. Susy has exposed this in her Biography of me.

Dean Sage was a delightful man, yet in one way a terror to his friends,

*This was tried. I well remember it. — M. T., *October, '06.*

for he loved them so well that he could not refrain from playing practical jokes on them. We have to be pretty deeply in love with a person before we can do him the honor of joking familiarly with him. Dean Sage was the best citizen I have known in America. It takes courage to be a good citizen, and he had plenty of it. He allowed no individual and no corporation to infringe his smallest right and escape unpunished. He was very rich, and very generous, and benevolent, and he gave away his money with a prodigal hand; but if an individual or corporation infringed a right of his, to the value of ten cents, he would spend thousands of dollars' worth of time and labor and money and persistence on the matter, and would not lower his flag until he had won his battle or lost it.

He and Rev. Mr. Harris[4] had been classmates in college, and to the day of Sage's death they were as fond of each other as an engaged pair. It follows, without saying, that whenever Sage found an opportunity to play a joke upon Harris, Harris was sure to suffer.

Along about 1873 Sage fell a victim to an illness which reduced him to a skeleton, and defied all the efforts of the physicians to cure it. He went to the Adirondacks and took Harris with him. Sage had always been an active man, and he couldn't idle any day wholly away in inanition, but walked every day to the limit of his strength. One day, toward nightfall, the pair came upon a humble log cabin which bore these words painted upon a shingle: "Entertainment for Man and Beast." They were obliged to stop there for the night, Sage's strength being exhausted. They entered the cabin and found its owner and sole occupant there, a rugged and sturdy and simple-hearted man of middle age. He cooked supper and placed it before the travellers — salt junk, boiled beans, corn bread and black coffee. Sage's stomach could abide nothing but the most delicate food, therefore this banquet revolted him, and he sat at the table unemployed, while Harris fed ravenously, limitlessly, gratefully; for he had been chaplain in a fighting regiment all through the war, and had kept in perfection the grand and uncritical appetite and splendid physical vigor which those four years of tough fare and activity had furnished him. Sage went supperless to bed, and tossed and writhed all night upon a shuck mattress that was full of attentive and interested corn-cobs. In the morning Harris was ravenous again, and devoured the odious breakfast as contentedly and as delightedly as he had devoured its twin the night before. Sage sat upon the porch, empty, and contemplated the performance and meditated revenge. Presently he beckoned to the landlord and took him aside and had a confidential talk with him. He said,

"I am the paymaster. What is the bill?"

"Two suppers, fifty cents; two beds, thirty cents; two breakfasts, fifty cents—total, a dollar and thirty cents."

Sage said, "Go back and make out the bill and fetch it to me here on the porch. Make it thirteen dollars."

"Thirteen dollars! Why, it's impossible! I am no robber. I am charging you what I charge everybody. It's a dollar and thirty cents, and that's all it is."

"My man, I've got something to say about this as well as you. It's thirteen dollars. You'll make out your bill for that, and you'll *take* it, too, or you'll not get a cent."

The man was troubled, and said, "I don't understand this. I can't make it out."

"Well, I understand it. I know what I am about. It's thirteen dollars, and I want the bill made out for that. There's no other terms. Get it ready and bring it out here. I will examine it and be outraged. You understand? I will dispute the bill. You must stand to it. You must refuse to take less. I will begin to lose my temper; you must begin to lose yours. I will call you hard names; you must answer with harder ones. I will raise my voice; you must raise yours. You must go into a rage—foam at the mouth, if you can; insert some soap to help it along. Now go along and follow your instructions."

The man played his assigned part, and played it well. He brought the bill and stood waiting for results. Sage's face began to cloud up, his eyes to snap, and his nostrils to inflate like a horse's; then he broke out with—

"*Thirteen dollars!* You mean to say that you charge thirteen dollars for these damned inhuman hospitalities of yours? Are you a professional buccaneer? Is it your custom to—"

The man burst in with spirit: "Now, I don't want any more out of you—that's a plenty. The bill is thirteen dollars and you'll *pay* it—that's all; a couple of characterless adventurers bilking their way through this country and attempting to dictate terms to a gentleman! a gentleman who received you supposing you were gentlemen yourselves, whereas in my opinion hell's full of—"

Sage broke in—

"Not another word of that!—I won't have it. I regard you as the lowest-down thief that ever—"

"Don't you use that word again! By _____, I'll take you by the neck and—"

Harris came rushing out, and just as the two were about to grapple he pushed himself between them and began to implore—

"Oh, Dean, don't, *don't*—now, Mr. Smith, control yourself! Oh, think of your family, Dean!—think what a scandal—"

But they burst out with maledictions, imprecations and all the hard names they could dig out of the rich accumulations of their educated memories, and in the midst of it the man shouted—

"When *gentlemen* come to this house, I treat them *as* gentlemen. When people come to this house with the ordinary appetites of gentlemen, I charge them a dollar and thirty cents for what I furnished you; but when a man brings a hell-fired Famine here that gorges a barrel of pork and four barrels of beans at two sittings—"

Sage broke in, in a voice that was eloquent with remorse and self-reproach, "I never thought of that, and I ask your pardon; I am ashamed of myself and of my friend. Here's your thirteen dollars, and my apologies along with it."

[*Dictated March 12, 1906*] I have always taken a great interest in other people's duels. One always feels an abiding interest in any heroic thing which has entered into his own experience.

In 1878, fourteen years after my unmaterialized duel, Messieurs Fortu and Gambetta fought a duel which made heroes of both of them in France, (1878) but made them rather ridiculous throughout the rest of the world. I was living in Munich that fall and winter, and I was so interested in that funny tragedy that I wrote a long account of it, and it is in one of my books, somewhere—an account which had some inaccuracies in it, but as an exhibition of the *spirit* of that duel, I think it was correct and trustworthy.[5] And when I was living in Vienna, thirty-four years after my ineffectual duel, my interest in that kind of incident was still strong; and I find here among my Autobiographical manuscripts of that day a chapter which I began concerning it, but did not finish. I wanted to finish it, but held it open in the hope that the Italian ambassador, M. Nigra, would find time to furnish me the *full* history of Señor Cavalotti's adventures in that line. But he was a busy man; there was always an interruption before he could get well started; so my hope was never fulfilled. The following is the unfinished chapter:

As concerns duelling. This pastime is as common in Austria to-day as it is in France. But with this difference, that here in the Austrian States the duel is dangerous, while in France it is not. Here it is tragedy, in France it is comedy; (1898) here it is a solemnity, there it is monkey-shines; here the duellist risks his life, there he does not even risk his shirt. Here he fights with pistol or sabre, in

France with a hairpin—a blunt one. Here the desperately wounded man tries to walk to the hospital; there they paint the scratch so that they can find it again, lay the sufferer on a stretcher, and conduct him off the field with a band of music.

At the end of a French duel the pair hug and kiss and cry, and praise each other's valor; then the surgeons make an examination and pick out the scratched one, and the other one helps him on to the litter and pays his fare; and in return the scratched one treats to champagne and oysters in the evening, and then "the incident is closed," as the French say. It is all polite, and gracious, and pretty, and impressive. At the end of an Austrian duel the antagonist that is alive gravely offers his hand to the other man, utters some phrases of courteous regret, then bids him good-by and goes his way, and that incident also is closed. The French duellist is painstakingly protected from danger, by the rules of the game. His antagonist's weapon cannot reach so far as his body; if he get a scratch it will not be above his elbow. But in Austria the rules of the game do not provide against danger, they carefully provide *for* it, usually. Commonly the combat must be kept up until one of the men is disabled; a non-disabling slash or stab does not retire him.

For a matter of three months I watched the Viennese journals, and whenever a duel was reported in their telegraphic columns I scrap-booked it. By this record I find that duelling in Austria is not confined to journalists and old maids, as in France, but is indulged in by military men, journalists, students, physicians, lawyers, members of the legislature, and even the Cabinet, the Bench and the police. Duelling is forbidden by law; and so it seems odd to see the makers and administrators of the laws dancing on their work in this way. Some months ago Count Bodeni, at that time Chief of the Government, fought a pistol-duel here in the capital city of the Empire with representative Wolf, and both of those distinguished Christians came near getting turned out of the Church—for the Church as well as the State forbids duelling.

In one case, lately, in Hungary, the police interfered and stopped a duel after the first innings. This was a sabre-duel between the chief of police and the city attorney. Unkind things were said about it by the newspapers. They said the police remembered their duty uncommonly well when their own officials were the parties concerned in duels. But I think the underlings showed good bread-and-butter judgment. If their superiors had carved each other well, the public would have asked, Where were the police? and their places would have been endangered; but custom does not require them to be around where mere unofficial citizens are explaining a thing with sabres.

There was another duel—a double duel—going on in the immediate neighborhood at the time, and in this case the police obeyed custom and did not disturb it. Their bread and butter was not at stake there. In this duel a physician fought a couple of surgeons, and wounded both—one of them lightly, the other seriously. An undertaker wanted to keep people from interfering, but that was quite natural again.

Selecting at random from my record, I next find a duel at Tarnopol between military men. An officer of the Tenth Dragoons charged an officer of the Ninth Dragoons with an offence against the laws of the card-table. There was a defect or a doubt somewhere in the matter, and this had to be examined and passed upon by a Court of Honor. So the case was sent up to Lemberg for this purpose. One would like to know what the defect was, but the newspaper does not say. A man here who has fought many duels and has a graveyard, says that probably the matter in question was as to whether the accusation was true or not; that if the charge was a very grave one — cheating, for instance — proof of its truth would rule the guilty officer out of the field of honor; the Court would not allow a gentleman to fight with such a person. You see what a solemn thing it is; you see how particular they are; any little careless act can lose you your privilege of getting yourself shot, here. The Court seems to have gone into the matter in a searching and careful fashion, for several months elapsed before it reached a decision. It then sanctioned a duel and the accused killed his accuser.

Next I find a duel between a prince and a major; first with pistols — no result satisfactory to either party; then with sabres, and the major badly hurt.

Next, a sabre-duel between journalists — the one a strong man, the other feeble and in poor health. It was brief; the strong one drove his sword through the weak one, and death was immediate.

Next, a duel between a lieutenant and a student of medicine. According to the newspaper report these are the details. The student was in a restaurant one evening: passing along, he halted at a table to speak with some friends; near by sat a dozen military men; the student conceived that one of these was "staring" at him; he asked the officer to step outside and explain. This officer and another one gathered up their caps and sabres and went out with the student. Outside — this is the student's account — the student introduced himself to the offending officer and said, "You seemed to stare at me"; for answer, the officer struck at the student with his fist; the student parried the blow; both officers drew their sabres and attacked the young fellow, and one of them gave him a wound on the left arm; then they withdrew. This was Saturday night. The duel followed on Monday, in the military riding-school — the customary duelling-ground all over Austria, apparently. The weapons were pistols. The duelling terms were somewhat beyond custom in the matter of severity, if I may gather that from the statement that the combat was fought "*unter sehr schweren Bedingungen*"— to wit, "Distance, 15 steps — with 3 steps advance." There was but one exchange of shots. The student was hit. "He put his hand on his breast, his body began to bend slowly forward, then collapsed in death and sank to the ground."

It is pathetic. There are other duels in my list, but I find in each and all of them one and the same ever-recurring defect — the *principals* are never present, but only their sham representatives. The *real* principals in any duel are not the duellists themselves, but their families. They do the mourning, the suffering, theirs is the loss and theirs the misery. They stake all that, the duellist stakes nothing but his life, and that is a trivial thing compared with what his death must cost those whom he leaves behind him. Challenges should not mention the duellist; he has nothing much at stake, and the real vengeance cannot reach him. The challenge should summon the offender's old gray mother, and his young wife and his little children,— these, or any to whom he is a dear and worshipped possession — and should say, "You have done me no harm, but I am the meek slave of a custom which requires me to crush the happiness out of your hearts and condemn you to years of pain and grief, in order that I may wash clean with your tears a stain which has been put upon me by another person."

The logic of it is admirable: a person has robbed me of a penny; I must beggar ten innocent persons to make good my loss. Surely nobody's "honor" is worth all that.

Since the duellist's family are the real principals in a duel, the State ought to compel them to be present at it. Custom, also, ought to be so amended as to require it; and without it no duel ought to be allowed to go on. If that student's unoffending mother had been present and watching the officer through her tears as he raised his pistol, he — why, he would have fired in the air. We know that. For we know how we are all made. Laws ought to be based upon the ascertained facts of our nature. It would be a simple thing to make a duelling law which would stop duelling.

As things are now, the mother is never invited. She submits to this; and without outward complaint, for she, too, is the vassal of custom, and custom requires her to conceal her pain when she learns the disastrous news that her son must go to the duelling-field, and by the powerful force that is lodged in habit and custom she is enabled to obey this trying requirement — a requirement which exacts a miracle of her, and gets it. Last January a neighbor of ours who has a young son in the army was wakened by this youth at three o'clock one morning, and she sat up in bed and listened to his message:

"I have come to tell you something, mother, which will distress you, but you must be good and brave, and bear it. I have been affronted by a fellow officer, and we fight at three this afternoon. Lie down and sleep, now, and think no more about it."

She kissed him good night and lay down paralyzed with grief and fear, but said nothing. But she did not sleep; she prayed and mourned till the first streak of dawn, then fled to the nearest church and implored the Virgin for help; and from that church she went to another and another and another; church after church, and still church after church, and so spent all the day until three o'clock on her knees in agony and tears; then dragged herself home and sat down comfortless and desolate, to count the minutes, and wait, with an outward show of calm, for what had been ordained for her — happiness, or endless misery. Presently she heard the clank of a sabre — she had not known before what music was in that sound! — and her son put his head in and said:

"X was in the wrong, and he apologized."

So that incident was closed; and for the rest of her life the mother will always find something pleasant about the clank of a sabre, no doubt.

In one of my listed duels — however, let it go, there is nothing particularly striking about it except that the seconds interfered. And prematurely, too, for neither man was dead. This was certainly irregular. Neither of the men liked it. It was a duel with cavalry sabres, between an editor and a lieutenant. The editor walked to the hospital, the lieutenant was carried. In this country an editor who can write well is valuable, but he is not likely to remain so unless he can handle a sabre with charm.

The following very recent telegram shows that also in France duels are humanely stopped as soon as they approach the (French) dangerpoint:

"*Reuter's Telegram.—* PARIS, *March* 5. —The duel between Colonels Henry and Picquart took place this morning in the Riding School of the Ecole Militaire, the doors of which were strictly guarded in order to prevent intrusion. The combatants, who fought with swords, were in position at ten o'clock.

"At the first reengagement Lieutenant-Colonel Henry was slightly scratched in the fore arm, and just at the same moment his own blade appeared to touch his adversary's neck. Senator Ranc, who was Colonel Picquart's second, stopped the fight, but as it was found that his principal had not been touched, the combat continued. A very sharp encounter ensued, in which Colonel Henry was wounded in the elbow, and the duel terminated."

After which, the stretcher and the band. In lurid contrast with this delicate flirtation, we have this fatal duel of day before yesterday in Italy, where the earnest Austrian duel is in vogue. I knew Cavalotti slightly, and this gives me a sort of personal interest in his duel. I first saw him in Rome several years ago. He was sitting on a block of stone in the Forum, and was writing something in his note-book—a poem or a challenge, or something like that—and the friend who pointed him out to me said, "That is Cavalotti—he has fought thirty duels; do not disturb him." I did not disturb him.

[*May 13, 1907*] It is a long time ago. Cavalotti—poet, orator, satirist, statesman, patriot—was a great man, and his death was deeply lamented by his countrymen: many monuments to his memory testify to this. In his duels he killed several of his antagonists and disabled the rest. By nature he was a little irascible. Once when the officials of the library of Bologna threw out his books the gentle poet went up there and challenged the whole fifteen! His parliamentary duties were exacting, but he proposed to keep coming up and fighting duels between trains until all those officials had been retired from the activities of life. Although he always chose the sword to fight with, he had never had a lesson with that weapon. When game was called he waited for nothing, but always plunged at his opponent and rained such a storm of wild and original thrusts and whacks upon him that the man was dead or crippled before he could bring his science to bear. But his latest antagonist discarded science, and won. He held his sword straight forward like a lance when Cavalotti made his plunge—with the result that he impaled himself upon it. It entered his mouth and passed out at the back of his neck. Death was instantaneous.

[*Dictated December 20, 1906*] Six months ago, when I was recalling early days in San Francisco, I broke off at a place where I was about to tell about Captain Osborn's odd adventure at the "What Cheer," or perhaps it was at another cheap feeding-place— the "Miners' Restaurant." It was a place where one could get good food on the cheapest possible terms, and its popularity was great among the multitudes whose purses were light. It was a good place to go to, to observe mixed humanity. Captain Osborn and Bret Harte went there one day and took a meal, and in the course of it Osborn fished up an interesting reminiscence of a dozen years before and told about it. It was to this effect:

He was a midshipman in the navy when the Californian gold craze burst upon the world and set it wild with excitement. His ship made the long journey around the Horn and was approaching her goal, the Golden Gate, when an accident happened.

"It happened to me," said Osborn. "I fell overboard. There was a heavy sea running, but no one was much alarmed about me, because we had on board a newly patented life-saving device which was believed to be competent to rescue anything that could fall overboard, from a midshipman to an anchor. Ours was the only ship that had this device; we were very proud of it, and had been anxious to give its powers a practical test. This thing was lashed to the garboard-strake of the main-to'gallant mizzen-yard amidships,* and there was nothing to do but cut the lashings and heave it over; it would do the rest. One day the cry of 'Man overboard!' brought all hands on deck. Instantly the lashings were cut and the machine flung joyously over. Damnation, it went to the bottom like an anvil! By the time that the ship was brought to and a boat manned, I was become but a bobbing speck on the waves half a mile astern and losing my strength very fast; but by good luck there was a common seaman on board who had practical ideas in his head and hadn't waited to see what the patent machine was going to do, but had run aft and sprung over after me the moment the alarm was cried through the ship. I had a good deal of a start of him, and the seas made his progress slow and difficult, but he stuck to his work and fought his way to me, and just in the nick of time he put his saving arms about me when I was about to go down. He held me up until the boat reached us and rescued us. By that time I was unconscious, and I was still unconscious when we arrived at the ship. A dangerous fever followed, and I was delirious for three days; then I came to myself and at once inquired for my benefactor, of course. He was gone. We were lying at anchor in the Bay and every man had deserted to the gold-mines except the commissioned officers. I found out nothing about my benefactor but his name—Burton Sanders—a name which I have held in grateful memory ever since. Every time I have been on the Coast, these twelve or thirteen years, I have tried

*Can this be correct? I think there must be some mistake—M. T.[6]

to get track of him, but have never succeeded. I wish I could find him and make him understand that his brave act has never been forgotten by me. Harte, I would rather see him and take him by the hand than any other man on the planet."

At this stage or a little later there was an interruption. A waiter near by said to another waiter, pointing,

"Take a look at that tramp that's coming in. Ain't that the one that bilked the house, last week, out of ten cents?"

"I believe it is. Let him alone — don't pay any attention to him; wait till we can get a good look at him."

The tramp approached timidly and hesitatingly, with the air of one un-sure and apprehensive. The waiters watched him furtively. When he was passing behind Harte's chair one of them said,

"He's the one!"— and they pounced upon him and proposed to turn him over to the police as a bilk. He begged piteously. He confessed his guilt, but said he had been driven to his crime by necessity — that when he had eaten the plate of beans and slipped out without paying for it, it was because he was starving, and hadn't the ten cents to pay for it with. But the waiters would listen to no explanations, no palliations; he must be placed in cus-tody. He brushed his hand across his eyes and said meekly that he would submit, being friendless. Each waiter took him by an arm and faced him about to conduct him away. Then his melancholy eyes fell upon Captain Osborn, and a light of glad and eager recognition flashed from them. He said,

"Weren't you a midshipman once, sir, in the old 'Lancaster'?"

"Yes," said Osborn. "Why?"

"Didn't you fall overboard?"

"Yes, I did. How do you come to know about it?"

"Wasn't there a new patent machine aboard, and didn't they throw it over to save you?"

"Why, yes," said Osborn, laughing gently, "but it didn't do it."

"No, sir, it was a sailor that done it."

"It certainly was. Look here, my man, you are getting distinctly inter-esting. Were you of our crew?"

"Yes, sir, I was."

"I reckon you may be right. You do certainly know a good deal about that incident. What is your name?"

"Burton Sanders."

The Captain sprang up, excited, and said,

"Give me your hand! Give me both your hands! I'd rather shake them than inherit a fortune!"—and then he cried to the waiters, "Let him go!—take your hands off! He is my guest, and can have anything and everything this house is able to furnish. I am responsible."

There was a love-feast, then. Captain Osborn ordered it regardless of expense, and he and Harte sat there and listened while the man told stirring adventures of his life and fed himself up to the eyebrows. Then Osborn wanted to be benefactor in his turn, and pay back some of his debt. The man said it could all be paid with ten dollars—that it had been so long since he had owned that amount of money that it would seem a fortune to him, and he should be grateful beyond words if the Captain could spare him that amount. The Captain spared him ten broad twenty-dollar gold pieces, and made him take them in spite of his modest protestations, and gave him his address and said he must never fail to give him notice when he needed grateful service.

Several months later Harte stumbled upon the man in the street. He was most comfortably drunk, and pleasant and chatty. Harte remarked upon the splendidly and movingly dramatic incident of the restaurant, and said,

"How curious and fortunate and happy and interesting it was that you two should come together, after that long separation, and at exactly the right moment to save you from disaster and turn your defeat by the waiters into a victory. A preacher could make a great sermon out of that, for it does look as if the hand of Providence was in it."

The hero's face assumed a sweetly genial expression, and he said,

"Well now, it wasn't Providence this time. I was running the arrangements myself."

"How do you mean?"

"Oh, I hadn't ever seen the gentleman before. I was at the next table, with my back to you the whole time he was telling about it. I saw my chance, and slipped out and fetched the two waiters with me and offered to give them a commission out of what I could get out of the Captain if they would do a quarrel act with me and give me an opening. So, then, after a minute or two I straggled back, and you know the rest of it as well as I do."

CHAPTER XXIII

[*Dictated March 9, 1906*] . . . I am talking of a time sixty years ago, and upwards. I remember the names of some of those schoolmates, and, by fit-
(1845) ful glimpses, even their faces rise dimly before me for a moment — only just long enough to be recognized; then they vanish. I catch glimpses of George Robards, the Latin pupil — slender, pale, studious, bending over his book and absorbed in it, his long straight black hair hanging down below his jaws like a pair of curtains on the sides of his face. I can see him give his head a toss and flirt one of the curtains back around his head — to get it out of his way, apparently; really to show off. In that day it was a great thing among the boys to have hair of so flexible a sort that it could be flung back in that way, with a flirt of the head. George Robards was the envy of us all. For there was no hair among us that was so competent for this exhibition as his — except, perhaps, the yellow locks of Will Bowen and John Robards. My hair was a dense ruck of short curls, and so was my brother Henry's. We tried all kinds of devices to get these crooks straightened out so that they would flirt, but we never succeeded. Sometimes, by soaking our heads and then combing and brushing our hair down tight and flat to our skulls, we could get it straight, temporarily, and this gave us a comforting moment of joy; but the first time we gave it a flirt it all shrivelled into curls again and our happiness was gone.[1]

John Robards was the little brother of George; he was a wee chap with silky golden curtains to his face which dangled to his shoulders and below, and could be flung back ravishingly. When he was twelve years old he crossed the plains with his father amidst the rush of the gold-seekers

North American Review, vol. 186, no. 623 (October 1907): 161–73 (the *North American Review* was now published monthly rather than fortnightly).

of '49; and I remember the departure of the cavalcade when it spurred westward. We were all there to see and to envy. And I can still see that proud little chap sailing by on a great horse, with his long locks streaming out behind. We were all on hand to gaze and envy when he returned, two years later, in unimaginable glory — *for he had travelled!* None of us had ever been forty miles from home. But he had crossed the Continent. He had been in the gold-mines, that fairyland of our imagination. And he had done a still more wonderful thing. He had been in ships — in ships on the actual ocean; in ships on three actual oceans. For he had sailed down the Pacific and around the Horn among icebergs and through snow-storms and wild wintry gales, and had sailed on and turned the corner and flown northward in the trades and up through the blistering equatorial waters — and there in his brown face were the proofs of what he had been through. We would have sold our souls to Satan for the privilege of trading places with him.

I saw him when I was out on that Missouri trip four years ago. He was old then — though not quite so old as I — and the burden of life was upon him. He said his granddaughter, twelve years old, had read my books and would like to see me. It was a pathetic time, for she was a prisoner in her room and marked for death. And John knew that she was passing swiftly away. Twelve years old — just her grandfather's age when he rode away on that great journey with his yellow hair flapping behind him. In her I seemed to see that boy again. It was as if he had come back out of that remote past and was present before me in his golden youth. Her malady was heart disease, and her brief life came to a close a few days later.

Another of those schoolboys was John Garth. He became a prosperous banker and a prominent and valued citizen; and a few years ago he died, rich and honored. *He died.* It is what I have to say about so many of those boys and girls. The widow still lives, and there are grandchildren. In her pantalette days and my barefoot days she was a schoolmate of mine. I saw John's tomb when I made that Missouri visit.

Her father, Mr. Kercheval,[2] had an apprentice in the early days when I was nine years old, and he had also a slave woman who had many merits. But I can't feel very kindly or forgivingly toward either that good apprentice boy or that good slave woman, for they saved my life. One day when I was playing on a loose log which I supposed was attached to a raft — but it wasn't — it tilted me into Bear Creek. And when I had been under water twice and was coming up to make the third and fatal descent my fingers appeared above the water and that slave woman seized them and pulled

me out. Within a week I was in again, and that apprentice had to come
along just at the wrong time, and he plunged in and dived, pawed around
on the bottom and found me, and dragged me out and emptied the water
out of me, and I was saved again. I was drowned seven times after that before I learned to swim — once in Bear Creek and six times in the Mississippi.
I do not now know who the people were who interfered with the intentions
of a Providence wiser than themselves, but I hold a grudge against them
yet. When I told the tale of these remarkable happenings to Rev. Dr. Burton of Hartford, he said he did not believe it. *He slipped on the ice the
very next year and sprained his ankle.*

Will Bowen was another schoolmate, and so was his brother, Sam, who
was his junior by a couple of years. Before the Civil War broke out, both
became St. Louis and New Orleans pilots. Both are dead, long ago.

[*Dictated March 16, 1906*] We will return to those schoolchildren of
sixty years ago. I recall Mary Miller. She was not my first sweetheart, but
(1845) I think she was the first one that furnished me a broken heart. I
fell in love with her when she was eighteen and I was nine, but she
scorned me, and I recognized that this was a cold world. I had not noticed
that temperature before. I believe I was as miserable as even a grown man
could be. But I think that this sorrow did not remain with me long. As I
remember it, I soon transferred my worship to Artimisia Briggs, who was
a year older than Mary Miller. When I revealed my passion to her she did
not scoff at it. She did not make fun of it. She was very kind and gentle
about it. But she was also firm, and said she did not want to be pestered
by children.

And there was Mary Lacy. She was a schoolmate. But she also was out
of my class because of her advanced age. She was pretty wild and determined and independent. But she married, and at once settled down and
became in all ways a model matron and was as highly respected as any matron in the town. Four years ago she was still living, and had been married
fifty years.

Jimmie McDaniel was another schoolmate. His age and mine about tallied. His father kept the candy-shop and he was the most envied little chap
in the town — after Tom Blankenship ("Huck Finn")[3] — for although we
never saw him eating candy, we supposed that it was, nevertheless, his ordinary diet. He pretended that he never ate it, and didn't care for it because there was nothing forbidden about it — there was plenty of it and he
could have as much of it as he wanted. He was the first human being to

whom I ever told a humorous story, so far as I can remember. This was about Jim Wolfe and the cats; and I gave him that tale the morning after that memorable episode. I thought he would laugh his teeth out. I had never been so proud and happy before, and have seldom been so proud and happy since. I saw him four years ago when I was out there. He wore a beard, gray and venerable, that came half-way down to his knees, and yet it was not difficult for me to recognize him. He had been married fifty-four years. He had many children and grandchildren and great-grandchildren, and also even posterity, they all said — thousands — yet the boy to whom I had told the cat story when we were callow juveniles was still present in that cheerful little old man.

Artimisia Briggs got married not long after refusing me. She married Richmond, the stone mason, who was my Methodist Sunday-school teacher in the earliest days, and he had one distinction which I envied him: at some time or other he had hit his thumb with his hammer and the result was a thumb nail which remained permanently twisted and distorted and curved and pointed, like a parrot's beak. I should not consider it an ornament now, I suppose, but it had a fascination for me then, and a vast value, because it was the only one in the town. He was a very kindly and considerate Sunday-school teacher, and patient and compassionate, so he was the favorite teacher with us little chaps. In that school they had slender oblong pasteboard blue tickets, each with a verse from the Testament printed on it, and you could get a blue ticket by reciting two verses. By reciting five verses you could get three blue tickets, and you could trade these at the bookcase and borrow a book for a week. I was under Mr. Richmond's spiritual care every now and then for two or three years, and he was never hard upon me. I always recited the same five verses every Sunday. He was always satisfied with the performance. He never seemed to notice that these were the same five foolish virgins that he had been hearing about every Sunday for months. I always got my tickets and exchanged them for a book. They were pretty dreary books, for there was not a bad boy in the entire bookcase. They were *all* good boys and good girls and drearily uninteresting, but they were better society than none, and I was glad to have their company and disapprove of it.

Twenty years ago Mr. Richmond had become possessed of Tom Sawyer's cave in the hills three miles from town, and had made a tourist-resort of it. In 1849 when the gold-seekers were streaming through our little town of Hannibal, many of our grown men got the gold fever, and I think that

all the boys had it. On the Saturday holidays in summer-time we used
(1849) to borrow skiffs whose owners were not present and go down the
river three miles to the cave hollow (Missourian for "valley"), and
there we staked out claims and pretended to dig gold, panning out half
a dollar a day at first; two or three times as much, later, and by and by
whole fortunes, as our imaginations became inured to the work. Stupid
and unprophetic lads! We were doing this in play and never suspecting.
Why, that cave hollow and all the adjacent hills were made of gold! But
we did not know it. We took it for dirt. We left its rich secret in its own
peaceful possession and grew up in poverty and went wandering about
the world struggling for bread—and this because we had not the gift of
prophecy. That region was all dirt and rocks to us, yet all it needed was
to be ground up and scientifically handled and it was gold. That is to say,
the whole region was a cement-mine—and they make the finest kind of
Portland cement there now, five thousand barrels a day, with a plant that
cost $2,000,000.

For a little while Reuel Gridley attended that school of ours. He was an
elderly pupil; he was perhaps twenty-two or twenty-three years old. Then
came the Mexican War[4] and he volunteered. A company of infantry was
raised in our town and Mr. Hickman, a tall, straight, handsome athlete of
twenty-five, was made captain of it and had a sword by his side and a
broad yellow stripe down the leg of his gray pants. And when that company
marched back and forth through the streets in its smart uniform—which
it did several times a day for drill—its evolutions were attended by all the
boys whenever the school hours permitted. I can see that marching company yet, and I can almost feel again the consuming desire that I had to
join it. But they had no use for boys of twelve and thirteen, and before I
had a chance in another war the desire to kill people to whom I had not
been introduced had passed away.

I saw the splendid Hickman in his old age. He seemed about the oldest
man I had ever seen—an amazing and melancholy contrast with the showy
young captain I had seen preparing his warriors for carnage so many, many
years before. Hickman is dead—it is the old story. As Susy said, "What is
it all for?"

Reuel Gridley went away to the wars and we heard of him no more for
fifteen or sixteen years. Then one day in Carson City while I was having
a difficulty with an editor on the sidewalk—an editor better built for war
than I was—I heard a voice say, "Give him the best you've got, Sam, I'm

at your back." It was Reuel Gridley. He said he had not recognized me by my face but by my drawling style of speech.

He went down to the Reese River mines about that time and presently he lost an election bet in his mining camp, and by the terms of it he was obliged to buy a fifty-pound sack of self-raising flour and carry it through the town, preceded by music, and deliver it to the winner of the bet. Of course the whole camp was present and full of fluid and enthusiasm. The winner of the bet put up the sack at auction for the benefit of the United States Sanitary Fund, and sold it. The excitement grew and grew. The sack was sold over and over again for the benefit of the Fund. The news of it came to Virginia City by telegraph. It produced great enthusiasm, and Reuel Gridley was begged by telegraph to bring the sack and have an auction in Virginia City. He brought it. An open barouche was provided, also a brass band. The sack was sold over and over again at Gold Hill, then was brought up to Virginia City toward night and sold—and sold again, and again, and still again, netting twenty or thirty thousand dollars for the Sanitary Fund. Gridley carried it across California and sold it at various towns. He sold it for large sums in Sacramento and in San Francisco. He brought it East, sold it in New York and in various other cities, then carried it out to a great Fair at St. Louis, and went on selling it; and finally made it up into small cakes and sold those at a dollar apiece. First and last, the sack of flour which had originally cost ten dollars, perhaps, netted more than two hundred thousand dollars for the Sanitary Fund. Reuel Gridley has been dead these many, many years—it is the old story.[5]

In that school were the first Jews I had ever seen. It took me a good while to get over the awe of it. To my fancy they were clothed invisibly in the damp and cobwebby mould of antiquity. They carried me back to Egypt, and in imagination I moved among the Pharaohs and all the shadowy celebrities of that remote age. The name of the boys was Levin. We had a collective name for them which was the only really large and handsome witticism that was ever born in that Congressional district. We called them "Twenty-two"—and even when the joke was old and had been worn threadbare we always followed it with the explanation, to make sure that it would be understood, "Twice Levin—twenty-two."

There were other boys whose names remain with me. Irving Ayres—but no matter, he is dead. Then there was George Butler, whom I remember as a child of seven wearing a blue leather belt with a brass buckle, and hated and envied by all the boys on account of it. He was a nephew of General Ben Butler[6] and fought gallantly at Ball's Bluff and in several other actions of the Civil War. He is dead, long and long ago.

Will Bowen (dead long ago), Ed Stevens (dead long ago) and John Briggs were special mates of mine. John is still living.

In 1845, when I was ten years old, there was an epidemic of measles in the town and it made a most alarming slaughter among the little people. (1845) There was a funeral almost daily, and the mothers of the town were nearly demented with fright. My mother was greatly troubled. She worried over Pamela and Henry and me, and took constant and extraordinary pains to keep us from coming into contact with the contagion. But upon reflection I believed that her judgment was at fault. It seemed to me that I could improve upon it if left to my own devices. I cannot remember now whether I was frightened about the measles or not, but I clearly remember that I grew very tired of the suspense I suffered on account of being continually under the threat of death. I remember that I got so weary of it and so anxious to have the matter settled one way or the other, and promptly, that this anxiety spoiled my days and my nights. I had no pleasure in them. I made up my mind to end this suspense and be done with it. Will Bowen was dangerously ill with the measles and I thought I would go down there and catch them. I entered the house by the front way and slipped along through rooms and halls, keeping sharp watch against discovery, and at last I reached Will's bed-chamber in the rear of the house on the second floor and got into it uncaptured. But that was as far as my victory reached. His mother caught me there a moment later and snatched me out of the house and gave me a most competent scolding and drove me away. She was so scared that she could hardly get her words out, and her face was white. I saw that I must manage better next time, and I did. I hung about the lane at the rear of the house and watched through cracks in the fence until I was convinced that the conditions were favorable; then I slipped through the back yard and up the back way and got into the room and into the bed with Will Bowen without being observed. I don't know how long I was in the bed. I only remember that Will Bowen, as society, had no value for me, for he was too sick to even notice that I was there. When I heard his mother coming I covered up my head, but that device was a failure. It was dead summer-time — the cover was nothing more than a limp blanket or sheet, and anybody could see that there were two of us under it. It didn't remain two very long. Mrs. Bowen snatched me out of the bed and conducted me home herself, with a grip on my collar which she never loosened until she delivered me into my mother's hands along with her opinion of that kind of a boy.

It was a good case of measles that resulted. It brought me within a shade of death's door. It brought me to where I no longer took any interest in anything, but, on the contrary, felt a total absence of interest — which was most placid and enchanting. I have never enjoyed anything in my life any more than I enjoyed dying that time. I *was*, in effect, dying. The word had been passed and the family notified to assemble around the bed and see me off. I knew them all. There was no doubtfulness in my vision. They were all crying, but that did not affect me. I took but the vaguest interest in it, and that merely because I was the centre of all this emotional attention and was gratified by it and vain of it.

When Dr. Cunningham had made up his mind that nothing more could be done for me he put bags of hot ashes all over me. He put them on my breast, on my wrists, on my ankles; and so, very much to his astonishment — and doubtless to my regret — he dragged me back into this world and set me going again.

[*Dictated July 26, 1907*] In an article entitled "England's Ovation to Mark Twain," Sydney Brooks — but never mind that, now.

I was in Oxford by seven o'clock that evening (June 25, 1907), and trying on the scarlet gown which the tailor had been constructing, and found it right — right and surpassingly becoming.[7] At half past ten the next morning we assembled at All Souls College and marched thence, gowned, mortar-boarded and in double file, down a long street to the Sheldonian Theatre, between solid walls of the populace, very much hurrah'd and limitlessly kodak'd. We made a procession of considerable length and distinction and picturesqueness, with the Chancellor, Lord Curzon, late Viceroy of India,[8] in his rich robe of black and gold, in the lead, followed by a pair of trim little boy train-bearers, and the train-bearers followed by the young Prince Arthur of Connaught, who was to be made a D.C.L.[9] The detachment of D.C.L.'s were followed by the Doctors of Science, and these by the Doctors of Literature, and these in turn by the Doctors of Music. Sidney Colvin[10] marched in front of me; I was coupled with Sidney Lee,[11] and Kipling followed us; General Booth,[12] of the Salvation Army, was in the squadron of D.C.L.'s.

Our journey ended, we were halted in a fine old hall whence we could see, through a corridor of some length, the massed audience in the theatre. Here for a little time we moved about and chatted and made acquaintanceships; then the D.C.L.'s were summoned, and they marched through that corridor and the shouting began in the theatre. It would be some time before the Doctors of Literature and of Science would be called for, because each of those D.C.L.'s had to have a couple of Latin speeches made over him before his promotion would be complete — one by the Regius Professor of Civil Law, the other by the Chancellor. After a while I asked Sir William Ramsay[13] if a person might smoke here and not get shot. He said, "Yes," but that whoever did it and got caught would be fined a guinea, and perhaps hanged later. He said he knew of a place where we could accomplish at least as much as half of a smoke before any informers would be likely to chance upon us, and he was ready to show the way to any who might be willing to risk the guinea and the hanging. By request he led the way, and Kipling, Sir Norman Lockyer[14] and I followed. We crossed an unpopulated quadrangle and stood under one of its exits — an archway of massive masonry — and there we lit up and began to take comfort. The photographers soon arrived, but they were courteous and friendly and gave us no trouble, and we gave them none. They grouped us in all sorts of ways and photographed us at their diligent leisure, while we smoked and talked. We were there more than an hour; then we returned to headquarters, happy, content, and greatly refreshed. Presently we filed into the theatre, under a very satisfactory hurrah, and waited in a crimson column, dividing the crowded pit through the middle, until each of us in his turn should be called to stand before the Chancellor and hear our merits set forth in sonorous Latin. Meantime, Kipling and I wrote autographs until some good kind soul interfered in our behalf and procured for us a rest.

I will now save what is left of my modesty by quoting a paragraph from Sydney Brooks's "Ovation."

.   .   .   .

Let those stars take the place of it for the present. Sydney Brooks has done it well. It makes me proud to read it; as proud as I was in that old day, sixty-two years ago, when I lay dying, the centre of attraction, with one eye piously closed upon the fleeting vanities of this life — an excellent effect — and the other open a crack to observe the tears, the sorrow, the admiration — all for me — all for me!

Ah, that was the proudest moment of my long life — until Oxford!

.   .   .   .

Most Americans have been to Oxford and will remember what a dream of the Middle Ages it is, with its crooked lanes, its gray and stately piles of ancient architecture and its meditation-breeding air of repose and dignity and unkinship with the noise and fret and hurry and bustle of these modern days. As a dream of the Middle Ages Oxford was not perfect until Pageant day arrived and furnished certain details which had been for generations lacking. These details began to appear at mid-afternoon on the 27th. At that time singles, couples, groups and squadrons of the three thousand five hundred costumed characters who were to take part in the Pageant began to ooze and drip and stream through house doors, all over the old town, and wend toward the meadows outside the walls. Soon the lanes were thronged with costumes which Oxford had from time to time seen and been familiar with in bygone centuries—fashions of dress which marked off centuries as by dates, and mile-stoned them back, and back, and back, until history faded into legend and tradition, when Arthur was a fact and the Round Table a reality. In this rich commingling of quaint and strange and brilliantly colored fashions in dress the dress-changes of Oxford for twelve centuries stood livid and realized to the eye; Oxford as a dream of the Middle Ages was complete now as it had never, in our day, before been complete; at last there was no discord; the mouldering old buildings, and the picturesque throngs drifting past them, were in harmony; soon—astonishingly soon!—the only persons that seemed out of place, and grotesquely and offensively and criminally out of place were such persons as came intruding along clothed in the ugly and odious fashions of the twentieth century; they were a bitterness to the feelings, an insult to the eye.

The make-ups of illustrious historic personages seemed perfect, both as to portraiture and costume; one had no trouble in recognizing them. Also, I was apparently quite easily recognizable myself. The first corner I turned brought me suddenly face to face with Henry VIII,[15] a person whom I had been implacably disliking for sixty years; but when he put out his hand with royal courtliness and grace and said, "Welcome, well-beloved stranger, to my century and to the hospitalities of my realm," my old prejudices vanished away and I forgave him. I think now that Henry the Eighth has been over-abused, and that most of us, if we had been situated as he was, domestically, would not have been able to get along with as limited a graveyard as he forced himself to put up with. I feel now that he was one of the nicest men in history. Personal contact with a king is more effective in removing baleful prejudices than is any amount of argument drawn from tales and histories. If I had a child I would name it Henry the Eighth, regardless of sex.

Do you remember Charles the First?—and his broad slouch with the plume in it? and his slender, tall figure? and his body clothed in velvet doublet with lace sleeves, and his legs in leather, with long rapier at his side and his spurs on his heels? I encountered him at the next corner, and knew him in a moment — knew him as perfectly and as vividly as I should know the Grand Chain in the Mississippi if I should see it from the pilot-house after all these years. He bent his body and gave his hat a sweep that fetched its plume within an inch of the ground, and gave me a welcome that went to my heart. This king has been much maligned; I shall understand him better hereafter, and shall regret him more than I have been in the habit of doing these fifty or sixty years. He did some things in his time, which might better have been left undone, and which cast a shadow upon his name — we all know that, we all concede it — but our error has been in regarding them as crimes and in calling them by that name, whereas I perceive now that they were only indiscretions. At every few steps I met persons of deathless name whom I had never encountered before outside of pictures and statuary and history, and these were most thrilling and charming encounters. I had hand-shakes with Henry the Second,[16] who had not been seen in the Oxford streets for nearly eight hundred years; and with the Fair Rosamond,[17] whom I now believe to have been chaste and blameless, although I had thought differently about it before; and with Shakespeare, one of the pleasantest foreigners I have ever gotten acquainted with; and with Roger Bacon;[18] and with Queen Elizabeth, who talked five minutes and never swore once[19]—a fact which gave me a new and good opinion of her and moved me to forgive her for beheading the Scottish Mary, if she really did it, which I now doubt; and with the quaintly and anciently clad young King Harold Harefoot,[20] of near nine hundred years ago, who came flying by on a bicycle and smoking a pipe, but at once checked up and got off to shake with me; and also I met a bishop who had lost his way because this was the first time he had been inside the walls of Oxford for as much as twelve hundred years or thereabouts. By this time I had grown so used to the obliterated ages and their best-known people that if I had met Adam I should not have been either surprised or embarrassed; and if he had come in a racing automobile and a cloud of dust, with nothing on but his fig-leaf, it would have seemed to me all right and harmonious.

CHAPTER XXIV

From Susy's Biography of Me [1885–6]
Mamma and papa have returned from Onteora and they have had a delightful visit. Mr. Frank Stockton was down in Virginia and could not reach Onteora in time, so they did not see him, and Mrs. Mary Mapes Dodge was ill and couldn't go to Onteora, but Mrs. General Custer was there, and mamma said that she was a very attractive, sweet appearing woman.

[*Dictated October 9, 1906*] Onteora was situated high up in the Catskill Mountains, in the centre of a far-reaching solitude. I do not mean that the region was wholly uninhabited; there were farmhouses here and there, at generous distances apart. Their occupants were descendants of ancestors who had built the houses in Rip Van Winkle's time, or earlier; and those ancestors were not more primitive than were this posterity of theirs. The city people were as foreign and unfamiliar and strange to them as monkeys would have been, and they would have respected the monkeys as much as they respected these elegant summer-resorters. The resorters were a puzzle to them, their ways were so strange and their interests so trivial. They drove the resorters over the mountain roads and listened in shamed surprise at their bursts of enthusiasm over the scenery. The farmers had had that scenery on exhibition from their mountain roosts all their lives, and had never noticed anything remarkable about it. By way of an incident: a pair of these primitives were overheard chatting about the resorters, one day, and in the course of their talk this remark was dropped:

"I was a-drivin' a passel of 'em round about yisterday evenin', quiet ones, you know, still and solemn, and all to wunst they busted out to make your

North American Review, vol. 186, no. 624 (November 1970): 327–36.

hair lift and I judged hell was to pay. Now what do you reckon it was? It wa'n't anything but jest one of them common damned yaller sunsets."

In those days—

[*Tuesday, October 16, 1906*] . . . Warner is gone. Stockton is gone. I attended both funerals. Warner was a near neighbor, from the autumn of '71 until his death, nineteen years afterward. It is not the privilege of the most of us to have many intimate friends—a dozen is our aggregate—but I think he could count his by the score. It is seldom that a man is so beloved by both sexes and all ages as Warner was. There was a charm about his spirit, and his ways, and his words, that won all that came within the sphere of its influence. Our children adopted him while they were little creatures, and thenceforth, to the end, he was "Cousin Charley" to them. He was "Uncle Charley" to the children of more than one other friend. Mrs. Clemens was very fond of him, and he always called her by her first name— shortened. Warner died, as she died, and as I would die—without premonition, without a moment's warning.

Uncle Remus still lives, and must be over a thousand years old. Indeed, I know that this must be so, because I have seen a new photograph of him in the public prints within the last month or so, and in that picture his aspects are distinctly and strikingly geological, and one can see he is thinking about the mastodons and plesiosaurians that he used to play with when he was young.

It is just a quarter of a century since I have seen Uncle Remus. He visited us in our home in Hartford and was reverently devoured by the big eyes of Susy and Clara, for I made a deep and awful impression upon the little creatures—who knew his book by heart through my nightly declamation of its tales to them—by revealing to them privately that he was the real Uncle Remus whitewashed so that he could come into people's houses the front way.

He was the bashfulest grown person I have ever met. When there were people about he stayed silent, and seemed to suffer until they were gone. But he was lovely, nevertheless; for the sweetness and benignity of the immortal Remus looked out from his eyes, and the graces and sincerities of his character shone in his face.

It may be that Jim Wolf was as bashful as Harris. It hardly seems possible, yet as I look back fifty-six years and consider Jim Wolf, I am almost persuaded that he was. He was our long slim apprentice in my brother's printing-office in Hannibal. He was seventeen, and yet he was as much as four times as bashful as I was, though I was only fourteen. He boarded and slept in the house, but he was always tongue-tied in the presence of my sister, and when even my gentle mother spoke to him he could not answer save in frightened monosyllables. He would not enter a room where a girl was; nothing could persuade him to do such a thing. Once when he was in our small parlor alone, two majestic old maids entered and seated themselves in such a way that Jim could not escape without passing by them. He would as soon have thought of passing by one of Harris's plesiosaurians ninety feet long. I came in presently, was charmed with the situation, and sat down in a corner to watch Jim suffer, and enjoy it. My mother followed a minute later and sat down with the visitors and began to talk. Jim sat upright in his chair, and during a quarter of an hour he did not change his position by a shade — neither General Grant nor a bronze image could have maintained that immovable pose more successfully. I mean as to body and limbs; with the face there was a difference. By fleeting revealments of the face I saw that something was happening — something out of the common. There would be a sudden twitch of the muscles of the face, an instant distortion, which in the next instant had passed and left no trace. These twitches gradually grew in frequency, but no muscle outside of the face lost any of its rigidity, or betrayed any interest in what was happening to Jim. I mean if something *was* happening to him, and I knew perfectly well that that was the case. At last a pair of tears began to swim slowly down his cheeks amongst the twitchings, but Jim sat still and let them run; then I saw his right hand steal along his thigh until half-way to his knee, then take a vigorous grip upon the cloth.

That was a *wasp* that he was grabbing! A colony of them were climbing up his legs and prospecting around, and every time he winced they stabbed him to the hilt — so for a quarter of an hour one group of excursionists after another climbed up Jim's legs and resented even the slightest wince or squirm that he indulged himself with, in his misery. When the entertainment had become nearly unbearable, he conceived the idea of gripping them between his fingers and putting them out of commission. He succeeded with many of them, but at great cost, for, as he couldn't see the wasp, he was as likely to take hold of the wrong end of him as he was the right; then the dying wasp gave him a punch to remember the incident by.

If those ladies had stayed all day, and if all the wasps in Missouri had come and climbed up Jim's legs, nobody there would ever have known it but Jim and the wasps and me. There he would have sat until the ladies left.

When they finally went away we went up-stairs and he took his clothes

off, and his legs were a picture to look at. They looked as if they were
mailed all over with shirt buttons, each with a single red hole in the centre.
The pain was intolerable — no, would have been intolerable, but the pain
of the presence of those ladies had been so much harder to bear that the
pain of the wasps' stings was quite pleasant and enjoyable by comparison.

Jim never could enjoy wasps. I remember once —

From Susy's Biography of Me [1885–6]

Mamma has given me a very pleasant little newspaper scrap about papa, to copy.
I will put it in here.

[*Thursday, October 11, 1906*] It was a rather strong compliment; I think
I will leave it out. It was from James Redpath.

The chief ingredients of Redpath's make-up were honesty, sincerity, kind-
liness, and pluck. He wasn't afraid. He was one of Ossawatomie Brown's[1]
right-hand men in the bleeding Kansas days; he was all through that struggle. He carried his life in his hands, and from one day to another it wasn't
worth the price of a night's lodging. He had a small body of daring men
under him, and they were constantly being hunted by the "jayhawkers,"
who were proslavery Missourians, guerillas, modern free lances.

[*Friday, October 12, 1906*] . . . I can't think of the name of that dare-
devil guerilla who led the jayhawkers and chased Redpath up and down
the country, and, in turn, was chased by Redpath. By grace of the chances
of war, the two men never met in the field, though they several times came
within an ace of it.

Ten or twelve years later, Redpath was earning his living in Boston as
chief of the lecture business in the United States. Fifteen or sixteen years
after his Kansas adventures I became a public lecturer, and he was my
agent. Along there somewhere was a press dinner, one November night, at
the Tremont Hotel in Boston, and I attended it. I sat near the head of the
table, with Redpath between me and the chairman; a stranger sat on my
other side. I tried several times to talk with the stranger, but he seemed to
be out of words and I presently ceased from troubling him. He was manifestly a very shy man, and, moreover, he might have been losing sleep the
night before.

The first man called up was Redpath. At the mention of the name the
stranger started, and showed interest. He fixed a fascinated eye on Redpath,
and lost not a word of his speech. Redpath told some stirring incidents of
his career in Kansas, and said, among other things:

"Three times I came near capturing the gallant jayhawker chief, and once he actually captured *me*, but didn't know me and let me go, because he said he was hot on Redpath's trail and couldn't afford to waste time and rope on inconsequential small fry."

My stranger was called up next, and when Redpath heard his name he, in turn, showed a startled interest. The stranger said, bending a caressing glance upon Redpath and speaking gently—I may even say sweetly:

"You realize that I was that jayhawker chief. I am glad to know you now and take you to my heart and call you friend"—then he added, in a voice that was pathetic with regret, "but if I had only known you then, what tumultuous happiness I should have had in your society!—while it lasted."

The last quarter of a century of my life has been pretty constantly and faithfully devoted to the study of the human race—that is to say, the study of myself, for, in my individual person, I am the entire human race compacted together. I have found that there is no ingredient of the race which I do not possess in either a small way or a large way. When it is small, as compared with the same ingredient in somebody else, there is still enough of it for all the purposes of examination. In my contacts with the species I find no one who possesses a quality which I do not possess. The shades of difference between other people and me serve to make variety and prevent monotony, but that is all; broadly speaking, we are all alike; and so by studying myself carefully and comparing myself with other people, and noting the divergences, I have been enabled to acquire a knowledge of the human race which I perceive is more accurate and more comprehensive than that which has been acquired and revealed by any other member of our species. As a result, my private and concealed opinion of myself is not of a complimentary sort. It follows that my estimate of the human race is the duplicate of my estimate of myself.

I am not proposing to discuss all of the peculiarities of the human race, at this time; I only wish to touch lightly upon one or two of them. To begin with, I wonder why a man should prefer a good billiard-table to a poor one; and why he should prefer straight cues to crooked ones; and why he should prefer round balls to chipped ones; and why he should prefer a level table to one that slants; and why he should prefer responsive cushions to the dull and unresponsive kind. I wonder at these things, because when we examine the matter we find that the essentials involved in billiards are as competently and exhaustively furnished by a bad billiard outfit as they are by the best one. One of the essentials is amusement. Very well, if there is any more amusement to be gotten out of the one outfit than out of the other, the facts are in favor of the bad outfit. The bad outfit will always furnish thirty per cent. more fun for the players and for the spectators than will the good outfit. Another essential of the game is that the outfit shall give the players full opportunity to exercise their best skill, and display it in a way to compel the admiration of the spectators. Very well, the bad outfit is nothing behind the good one in this regard. It is a difficult matter to estimate correctly the eccentricities of chipped balls and a slanting table, and make the right allowance for them and secure a count; the finest kind of skill is required to accomplish the satisfactory result. Another essential of the game is that it shall add to the interest of the game by furnishing opportunities to bet. Very well, in this regard no good outfit can claim any advantage over a bad one. I know, by experience, that a bad outfit is as valuable as the best one; that an outfit that couldn't be sold at auction for seven dollars is just as valuable for all the essentials of the game as an outfit that is worth a thousand.

I acquired some of this learning in Jackass Gulch, California, more than forty years ago.[2] Jackass Gulch had once been a rich and thriving surface-mining camp. By and by its gold deposits were exhausted; then the people began to go away, and the town began to decay, and rapidly; in my time it had disappeared. Where the bank, and the city hall, and the church, and the gambling-dens, and the newspaper office, and the streets of brick blocks had been, was nothing now but a wide and beautiful expanse of green grass, a peaceful and charming solitude. Half a dozen scattered dwellings were still inhabited, and there was still one saloon of a ruined and rickety character struggling for life, but doomed. In its bar was a billiard outfit that was the counterpart of the one in my father-in-law's garret. The balls were chipped, the cloth was darned and patched, the table's surface was undulating, and the cues were headless and had the curve of a parenthesis — but the forlorn remnant of marooned miners played games there, and those games were more entertaining to look at than a circus and a grand opera combined. Nothing but a quite extraordinary skill could score a carom on that table — a skill that required the nicest estimate of force, distance, and how much to allow for the various slants of the table and the other formidable peculiarities and idiosyncrasies furnished by the contradictions of the outfit. Last winter, here in New York, I saw Hoppe and Schaefer and Sutton[3] and the three or four other billiard champions of world-wide fame contend against each other, and certainly the art and science displayed were a wonder to see; yet I saw nothing there in the way of science and art that was more wonderful than shots which I had seen Texas Tom make on the wavy surface of that poor old wreck in the perishing saloon at Jack-ass Gulch forty years before. Once I saw Texas Tom make a string of seven points on a single inning! — all calculated shots, and not a fluke or a scratch among them. I often saw him make runs of four, but when he made his great string of seven, the boys went wild with enthusiasm and admiration. The joy and the noise exceeded that which the great gathering at Madison Square produced when Sutton scored five hundred points at the eighteen-inch game, on a world-famous night last winter. With practice, that cham-pion could score nineteen or twenty on the Jackass Gulch table; but to start with, Texas Tom would show him miracles that would astonish him; also it might have another handsome result: it might persuade the great experts to discard their own trifling game and bring the Jackass Gulch outfit here and exhibit their skill in a game worth a hundred of the discarded one, for profound and breathless interest, and for displays of almost superhuman skill.

In my experience, games played with a fiendish outfit furnish ecstacies of delight which games played with the other kind cannot match. Twenty-seven years ago my budding little family spent the summer at Bateman's Point, near Newport, Rhode Island. It was a comfortable boarding-place, well stocked with sweet mothers and little children, but the male sex was scarce; however, there was another young fellow besides myself, and he and I had good times — Higgins was his name, but that was not his fault. He was a very pleasant and companionable person. On the premises there was what had once been a bowling-alley. It was a single alley, and it was esti-mated that it had been out of repair for sixty years — but not the balls, the balls were in good condition; there were forty-one of them, and they ranged in size from a grapefruit up to a lignum-vitae sphere that you could hardly lift. Higgins and I played on that alley day after day. At first, one of us lo-cated himself at the bottom end to set up the pins in case anything should happen to them, but nothing happened. The surface of that alley consisted of a rolling stretch of elevations and depressions, and neither of us could, by any art known to us, persuade a ball to stay on the alley until it should accomplish something. Little balls and big, the same thing always hap-pened — the ball left the alley before it was half-way home and went thun-dering down alongside of it the rest of the way and made the gamekeeper climb out and take care of himself. No matter, we persevered, and were rewarded. We examined the alley, noted and located a lot of its peculiari-ties, and little by little we learned how to deliver a ball in such a way that it would travel home and knock down a pin or two. By and by we succeeded in improving our game to a point where we were able to get all of the pins with thirty-five balls — so we made it a thirty-five-ball game. If the player did not succeed with thirty-five, he had lost the game. I suppose that all the balls, taken together, weighed five hundred pounds, or maybe a ton — or along there somewhere — but anyway it was hot weather, and by the time that a player had sent thirty-five of them home he was in a drench of perspiration, and physically exhausted.

Next, we started cocked hat — that is to say, a triangle of three pins, the other seven being discarded. In this game we used the three smallest balls and kept on delivering them until we got the three pins down. After a day or two of practice we were able to get the chief pin with an output of four balls, but it cost us a great many deliveries to get the other two; but by and by we succeeded in perfecting our art — at least we perfected it to our limit. We reached a scientific excellence where we could get the three pins down with twelve deliveries of the three small balls, making thirty-six shots to conquer the cocked hat.

Having reached our limit for daylight work, we set up a couple of candles and played at night. As the alley was fifty or sixty feet long, we couldn't see the pins, but the candles indicated their locality. We continued this game until we were able to knock down the invisible pins with thirty-six shots. Having now reached the limit of the candle game, we changed and played it left-handed. We continued the left-handed game until we conquered its limit, which was fifty-four shots. Sometimes we sent down a succession of fifteen balls without getting anything at all. We easily got out of that old alley five times the fun that anybody could have gotten out of the best alley in New York.

One blazing hot day, a modest and courteous officer of the regular army appeared in our den and introduced himself. He was about thirty-five years old, well built and militarily erect and straight, and he was hermetically sealed up in the uniform of that ignorant old day — a uniform made of heavy material, and much properer for January than July. When he saw the venerable alley, and glanced from that to the long procession of shining balls in the trough, his eye lit with desire, and we judged that he was our meat. We politely invited him to take a hand, and he could not conceal his gratitude; though his breeding, and the etiquette of his profession, made him try. We explained the game to him, and said that there were forty-one balls, and that the player was privileged to extend his inning and keep on playing until he had used them all up — repeatedly — and that for every ten-strike he got a prize. We didn't name the prize — it wasn't necessary, as no prize would ever be needed or called for. He started a sarcastic smile, but quenched it, according to the etiquette of his profession. He merely remarked that he would like to select a couple of medium balls and one small one, adding that he didn't think he would need the rest.

Then he began, and he was an astonished man. He couldn't get a ball to stay on the alley. When he had fired about fifteen balls and hadn't yet reached the cluster of pins, his annoyance began to show out through his clothes. He wouldn't let it show in his face; but after another fifteen balls he was not able to control his face; he didn't utter a word, but he exuded mute blasphemy from every pore. He asked permission to take off his coat, which was granted; then he turned himself loose, with bitter determination, and although he was only an infantry officer he could have been mistaken for a battery, he got up such a volleying thunder with those balls. Presently he removed his cravat; after a little he took off his vest; and still he went bravely on. Higgins was suffocating. My condition was the same, but it would not be courteous to laugh; it would be better to burst, and we came near it. The officer was good pluck. He stood to his work without uttering a word, and kept the balls going until he had expended the outfit four times, making four times forty-one shots; then he had to give it up, and he did; for he was no longer able to stand without wobbling. He put on his clothes, bade us a courteous good-by, invited us to call at the Fort, and started away. Then he came back, and said,

"What is the prize for the ten-strike?"

We had to confess that we had not selected it yet.

He said, gravely, that he thought there was no occasion for hurry about it.

I believe Bateman's alley was a better one than any other in America, in the matter of the essentials of the game. It compelled skill; it provided opportunity for bets; and if you could get a stranger to do the bowling for you, there was more and wholesomer and delightfuler entertainment to be gotten out of his industries than out of the finest game by the best expert, and played upon the best alley elsewhere in existence.

CHAPTER XXV

January 11, 1906. Answer to a letter received this morning:

DEAR MRS. H.,—I am forever your debtor for reminding me of that curious passage in my life.[1] During the first year or two after it happened, I could not bear to think of it. My pain and shame were so intense, and my sense of having been an imbecile so settled, established and confirmed, that I drove the episode entirely from my mind—and so all these twenty-eight or twenty-nine years I have lived in the conviction that my performance of that time was coarse, vulgar and destitute of humor. But your suggestion that you and your family found humor in it twenty-eight years ago moved me to look into the matter. So I commissioned a Boston typewriter to delve among the Boston papers of that bygone time and send me a copy of it.

It came this morning, and if there is any vulgarity about it I am not able to discover it. If it isn't innocently and ridiculously funny, I am no judge. I will see to it that you get a copy.

Address of Samuel L. Clemens ("Mark Twain")
From a report of the dinner given by the Publishers
of the Atlantic Monthly in honor of the
Seventieth Anniversary of the
Birth of John Greenleaf Whittier, at the Hotel Bruns-
wick, Boston, December 17, 1877,
as published in the
BOSTON EVENING TRANSCRIPT,
December 18, 1877

Mr. Chairman—This is an occasion peculiarly meet for the digging up of pleasant reminiscences concerning literary folk; therefore I will drop lightly into history myself. Standing here on the shore of the Atlantic and contemplating certain of its largest literary billows, I am reminded of a thing which happened to me thirteen years ago, when I had just succeeded in stirring up a little Nevadian literary

North American Review, vol. 186, no. 625 (December 1907): 481–94.

puddle myself, whose spume-flakes were beginning to blow thinly Californiawards. I started an inspection tramp through the southern mines of California. I was callow and conceited, and I resolved to try the virtue of my *nom de guerre*. I very soon had an opportunity. I knocked at a miner's lonely log cabin in the foothills of the Sierras just at nightfall. It was snowing at the time. A jaded, melancholy man of fifty, barefooted, open the door to me. When he heard my *nom de guerre* he looked more dejected than before. He let me in — pretty reluctantly, I thought — and after the customary bacon and beans, black coffee and hot whiskey, I took a pipe. This sorrowful man had not said three words up to this time. Now he spoke up and said, in the voice of one who is secretly suffering, "You're the fourth — I'm going to move." "The fourth what?" said I. "The fourth littery man that has been here in twenty-four hours — I'm going to move." "You don't tell me!" said I; "who were the others?" "Mr. Longfellow, Mr. Emerson and Mr. Oliver Wendell Holmes — consound the lot!"

You can easily believe I was interested. I supplicated — three hot whiskeys did the rest — and finally the melancholy miner began. Said he —

"They came here just at dark yesterday evening, and I let them in of course. Said they were going to the Yosemite. They were a rough lot, but that's nothing; everybody looks rough that travels afoot. Mr. Emerson was a seedy little bit of a chap, red-headed. Mr. Holmes was as fat as a balloon; he weighed as much as three hundred, and had double chins all the way down to his stomach. Mr. Longfellow was built like a prize-fighter. His head was cropped and bristly, like as if he had a wig made of hair-brushes. His nose lay straight down his face, like a finger with the end joint tilted up. They had been drinking, I could see that. And what queer talk they used! Mr. Holmes inspected this cabin, then he took me by the buttonhole, and says he —

"'Through the deep caves of thought
I hear a voice that sings,
Build thee more stately mansions,
O my soul!'

"Says I, 'I can't afford it, Mr. Holmes, and moreover I don't want to.' Blamed if I liked it pretty well, either, coming from a stranger, that way. However, I started to get out my bacon and beans, when Mr. Emerson came and looked on awhile, and then *he* takes me aside by the buttonhole and says —

"'Give me agates for my meat;
Give me cantharids to eat;
From air and ocean bring me foods,
From all zones and altitudes.'

"Says I, 'Mr. Emerson, if you'll excuse me, this ain't no hotel.' You see it sort of riled me — I warn't used to the ways of littery swells. But I went on a-sweating over my work, and next comes Mr. Longfellow and buttonholes me, and interrupts me. Says he,

"'Honor be to Mudjekeewis!
You shall hear how Pau-Puk-Keewis —'

"But I broke in, and says I, 'Beg your pardon, Mr. Longfellow, if you'll be so kind as to hold your yawp for about five minutes and let me get this grub ready, you'll do me proud.' Well, sir, after they'd filled up I set out the jug. Mr. Holmes looks at it and then he fires up all of a sudden and yells—

"'Flash out a stream of blood-red wine!
For I would drink to other days.'

"By George, I was getting kind of worked up. I don't deny it, I was getting kind of worked up. I turns to Mr. Holmes, and says I, 'Looky here, my fat friend, I'm a-running this shanty, and if the court knows herself, you'll take whiskey straight or you'll go dry.' Them's the very words I said to him. Now I don't want to sass such famous littery people, but you see they kind of forced me. There ain't nothing onreasonable 'bout me; I don't mind a passel of guests a-treadin' on my tail three or four times, but when it comes to *standing* on it it's different, 'and if the court knows herself,' I says, 'you'll take whiskey straight or you'll go dry.' Well, between drinks they'd swell around the cabin and strike attitudes and spout; and pretty soon they got out a greasy old deck and went to playing euchre at ten cents a corner—on trust. I began to notice some pretty suspicious things. Mr. Emerson dealt, looked at his hand, shook his head, says—

"'I am the doubter and the doubt—'

and ca'mly bunched the hands and went to shuffling for a new layout. Says he—

"'They reckon ill who leave me out;
They know not well the subtle ways I keep.
I pass and deal *again!*'

Hang'd if he didn't go ahead and do it, too! O, he was a cool one! Well, in about a minute, things were running pretty tight, but all of a sudden I see by Mr. Emerson's eye he judged he had 'em. He had already corralled two tricks and each of the others one. So now he kind of lifts a little in his chair and says—

"'I tire of globes and aces!—
Too long the game is played!'

—and down he fetched a right bower. Mr. Longfellow smiles as sweet as pie and says—

"'Thanks, thanks to thee, my worthy friend,
For the lesson thou hast taught,'

—and blamed if he didn't down with *another* right bower! Emerson claps his hand on his bowie, Longfellow claps his on his revolver, and I went under a bunk. There was going to be trouble; but that monstrous Holmes rose up, wobbling his double chins, and says he, 'Order, gentlemen; the first man that draws, I'll lay down on him and smother him!' All quiet on the Potomac, you bet!

"They were pretty how-come-you-so, by now, and they begun to blow. Emerson says, 'The nobbiest thing I ever wrote was Barbara Frietchie.' Says Longfellow, 'It don't begin with my Biglow Papers.' Says Holmes, 'My Thanatopsis lays over 'em both.[2] They mighty near ended in a fight. Then they wished they had some more company — and Mr. Emerson pointed to me and says —

> "'Is yonder squalid peasant all
> That this proud nursery could breed?'

He was a-whetting his bowie on his boot — so I let it pass. Well, sir, next they took it into their heads that they would like some music; so they made me stand up and sing 'When Johnny Comes Marching Home' till I dropped — at thirteen minutes past four this morning. That's what I've been through, my friend. When I woke at seven, they were leaving, thank goodness, and Mr. Longfellow had my only boots on, and his'n under his arm. Says I, 'Hold on, there, Evangeline, what are you going to do with *them*?' He said, 'Going to make tracks with 'em; because —

> "'Lives of great men all remind us
> We can make our lives sublime;
> And, departing, leave behind us
> Footprints on the sands of time.'

As I said, Mr. Twain, you are the fourth in twenty-four hours — and I'm going to move; I ain't suited to a littery atmosphere."

I said to the miner, "Why, my dear sir, *these* were not the gracious singers to whom we and the world pay loving reverence and homage; these were impostors."

The miner investigated me with a calm eye for a while; then said he, "Ah! impostors, were they? Are *you?*"

I did not pursue the subject, and since then I have not travelled on my *nom de guerre* enough to hurt. Such was the reminiscene I was moved to contribute, Mr. Chairman. In my enthusiasm I may have exaggerated the details a little, but you will easily forgive me that fault, since I believe it is the first time I have ever deflected from perpendicular fact on an occasion like this.

What I have said to Mrs. H. is true. I did suffer during a year or two from the deep humiliations of that episode. But at last, in 1888, in Venice, my wife and I came across Mr. and Mrs. A. P. C., of Concord, Massachusetts,[3] and a friendship began then of the sort which nothing but death terminates. The C.'s were very bright people and in every way charming and companionable. We were together a month or two in Venice and several months in Rome, afterwards, and one day that lamented break of mine was mentioned. And when I was on the point of lathering those people for bringing it to my mind when I had gotten the memory of it almost squelched, I perceived with joy that the C.'s were indignant about the way that my performance had been received in Boston. They poured out their opinions most freely and frankly about the frosty attitude of the people who were present at that performance, and about the Boston newspapers for the position they had taken in regard to the matter. That position was that I had been irreverent beyond belief, beyond imagination. Very well, I had accepted that as a fact for a year or two, and had been thoroughly miserable about it whenever I thought of it—which was not frequently, if I could help it. Whenever I thought of it I wondered how I ever could have been inspired to do so unholy a thing. Well, the C.'s comforted me, but they did not persuade me to continue to think about the unhappy episode. I resisted that. I tried to get it out of my mind, and let it die, and I succeeded. Until Mrs. H.'s letter came, it had been a good twenty-five years since I had thought of that matter; and when she said that the thing was funny I wondered if possibly she might be right. At any rate, my curiosity was aroused, and I wrote to Boston and got the whole thing copied, as above set forth.

I vaguely remember some of the details of that gathering—dimly I can see a hundred people—no, perhaps fifty—shadowy figures sitting at tables feeding, ghosts now to me, and nameless forever more. I don't know who they were, but I can very distinctly see, seated at the grand table and facing the rest of us, Mr. Emerson,[4] supernaturally grave, unsmiling; Mr. Whittier,[5] grave, lovely, his beautiful spirit shining out of his face; Mr. Longfellow,[6] with his silken white hair and his benignant face; Dr. Oliver Wendell Holmes, flashing smiles and affection and all good-fellowship everywhere like a rose-diamond whose facets are being turned toward the light first one way and then another—a charming man, and always fascinating, whether he was talking or whether he was sitting still (what *he* would call still, but what would be more or less motion to other people). I can see those figures with entire distinctness across this abyss of time.

One other feature is clear—Willie Winter[7] (for these past thousand years dramatic editor of the "New York Tribune," and still occupying that high post in his old age) was there. He was much younger then than he is now, and he showed it. It was always a pleasure to me to see Willie Winter at a banquet. During a matter of twenty years I was seldom at a banquet where Willie Winter was not also present, and where he did not read a charming poem written for the occasion. He did it this time, and it was up to standard: dainty, happy, choicely phrased, and as good to listen to as music, and sounding exactly as if it was pouring unprepared out of heart and brain.

Now at that point ends all that was pleasurable about that notable celebration of Mr. Whittier's seventieth birthday—because *I* got up at that point and followed Winter, with what I have no doubt I supposed would be the gem of the evening—the gay oration above quoted from the Boston paper. I had written it all out the day before and had perfectly memorized it, and I stood up there at my genial and happy and self-satisfied ease, and began to deliver it. Those majestic guests, that row of venerable and still active volcanoes, listened, as did everybody else in the house, with attentive interest. Well, I delivered myself of — we'll say the first two hundred words of my speech. I was expecting no returns from that part of the speech, but this was not the case as regarded the rest of it. I arrived now at the dialogue: 'The old miner said, "You are the fourth, I'm going to move." "The fourth what?" said I. He answered, "The fourth littery man that has been here in twenty-four hours. I am going to move." "Why, you don't tell me," said I. "Who were the others?" "Mr. Longfellow, Mr. Emerson, Mr. Oliver Wendell Holmes, consound the lot — "'

Now then the house's *attention* continued, but the expression of interest in the faces turned to a sort of black frost. I wondered what the trouble was. I didn't know. I went on, but with difficulty — I struggled along, and entered upon that miner's fearful description of the bogus Emerson, the bogus Holmes, the bogus Longfellow, always hoping — but with a gradually perishing hope — that somebody would laugh, or that somebody would at least smile, but nobody did. I didn't know enough to give it up and sit down, I was too new to public speaking, and so I went on with this awful performance, and carried it clear through to the end, in front of a body of people who seemed turned to stone with horror. It was the sort of expression their faces would have worn if I had been making these remarks about the Diety and the rest of the Trinity; there is no milder way in which to describe the petrified condition and the ghastly expression of those people.

When I sat down it was with a heart which had long ceased to beat. I shall never be as dead again as I was then. I shall never be as miserable again as I was then. I speak now as one who doesn't know what the condition of things may be in the next world, but in this one I shall never be as wretched again as I was then. Howells, who was near me, tried to say a comforting word, but couldn't get beyond a gasp. There was no use — he understood the whole size of the disaster. He had good intentions, but the words froze before they could get out. It was an atmosphere that would freeze anything. If Benvenuto Cellini's salamander had been in that place he would not have survived to be put into Cellini's autobiography. There was a frightful pause. There was an awful silence, a desolating silence. Then the next man on the list had to get up — there was no help for it. That was Bishop — Bishop had just burst handsomely upon the world with a most acceptable novel, which had appeared in the "Atlantic Monthly," a place which would make any novel respectable and any author noteworthy.[8] In this case the novel itself was recognized as being, without extraneous help, respectable. Bishop was away up in the public favor, and he was an object of high interest, consequently there was a sort of national expectancy in the air; we may say our American millions were standing, from Maine to Texas and from Alaska to Florida, holding their breath, their lips parted, their hands ready to applaud when Bishop should get up on that occasion, and for the first time in his life speak in public. It was under these damaging conditions that he got up to "make good," as the vulgar say. I had spoken several times before, and that is the reason why I was able to go on without dying in my tracks, as I ought to have done — but Bishop had had no experience. He was up facing those awful deities — facing those other people, those strangers — facing human beings for the first time in his life, with a speech to utter. No doubt it was well packed away in his memory, no doubt it was fresh and usable, until I had been heard from. I suppose that after that, and under the smothering pall of that dreary silence, it began to waste away and disappear out of his head like the rags breaking from the edge of a fog, and presently there wasn't any fog left. He didn't go on — he didn't last long. It was not many sentences after his first before he began to hesitate, and break, and lose his grip, and totter, and wobble, and at last he slumped down in a limp and mushy pile.

Well, the programme for the occasion was probably not more than one-third finished, but it ended there. Nobody rose. The next man hadn't strength enough to get up, and everybody looked so dazed, so stupefied, paralyzed, it was impossible for anybody to do anything, or even try. Nothing could go on in that strange atmosphere. Howells mournfully, and without words, hitched himself to Bishop and me and supported us out of the room. It was very kind — he was most generous. He towed us tottering away into some room in that building, and we sat down there. I don't know what my remark was now, but I know the nature of it. It was the kind of remark you make when you know that nothing in the world can help your case. But Howells was honest — he had to say the heart-breaking things he did say: that there was no help for this calamity, this shipwreck, this cataclysm; that this was the most disastrous thing that had ever happened in anybody's history — and then he added, "That is, for *you* — and consider what you have done for Bishop. It is bad enough in your case, you deserve to suffer. You have committed this crime, and you deserve to have all you are going to get. But here is an innocent man. Bishop had never done you any harm, and see what you have done to him. He can never hold his head up again. The world can never look upon Bishop as being a live person. He is a corpse."

That is the history of that episode of twenty-eight years ago, which pretty nearly killed me with shame during that first year or two whenever it forced its way into my mind.

Now, then, I take that speech up and examine it. As I said, it arrived this morning, from Boston. I have read it twice, and unless I am an idiot, it hasn't a single defect in it from the first word to the last. It is just as good as good can be. It is smart; it is saturated with humor. There isn't a suggestion of coarseness or vulgarity in it anywhere. What could have been the matter with that house? It is amazing, it is incredible, that they didn't shout with laughter, and those deities the loudest of them all. Could the fault have been with me? Did I lose courage when I saw those great men up there whom I was going to describe in such a strange fashion? If that happened, if I showed doubt, that can account for it, for you can't be successfully funny if you show that you are afraid of it. Well, I can't account for it, but if I had those beloved and revered old literary immortals back here now on the platform at Carnegie Hall I would take that same old speech, deliver it, word for word, and melt them till they'd run all over that stage. Oh, the fault must have been with *me*, it is not in the speech at all.

[*Dictated October 3, 1907*] In some ways, I was always honest; even from my earliest years I could never bring myself to use money which I had acquired in questionable ways; many a time I tried, but principle was always stronger than desire. Six or eight months ago, Lieutenant-General Nelson A. Miles[9] was given a great dinner-party in New York, and when he and I were chatting together in the drawing-room before going out to dinner he said,

"I've known you as much as thirty years, isn't it?"

I said, "Yes, that's about it, I think."

He mused a moment or two and then said,

"I wonder we didn't meet in Washington in 1867; you were there at that time, weren't you?"

I said, "Yes, but there was a difference; I was not known then; I had not begun to bud — I was an obscurity; but you had been adding to your fine Civil War record; you had just come back from your brilliant Indian campaign in the Far West, and had been rewarded with a brigadier-generalship in the regular army, and everybody was talking about you and praising you. If you had met me, you wouldn't be able to remember it now — unless some unusual circumstance of the meeting had burnt it into your memory. It is forty years ago, and people don't remember nobodies over a stretch of time like that."

I didn't wish to continue the conversation along that line, so I changed the subject. I could have proven to him, without any trouble, that we did meet in Washington in 1867, but I thought it might embarrass one or the other of us, so I didn't do it. I remember the incident very well. This was the way of it:

I had just come back from the Quaker City Excursion, and had made a contract with Bliss of Hartford to write "The Innocents Abroad." I was out of money, and I went down to Washington to see if I could earn enough there to keep me in bread and butter while I should write the book. I came across William Clinton, brother of the astronomer, and together we invented a scheme for our mutual sustenance; we became the fathers and origina- tors of what is a common feature in the newspaper world now — the syndi- cate. We became the old original first Newspaper Syndicate on the planet; it was on a small scale, but that is usual with untried new enterprises. We had twelve journals on our list; they were all weeklies, all obscure and poor, and all scattered far away among the back settlements. It was a proud thing for those little newspapers to have a Washington correspondence, and a for- tunate thing for us that they felt in that way about it. Each of the twelve took two letters a week from us, at a dollar per letter; each of us wrote one letter per week and sent off six duplicates of it to these benefactors, thus acquiring twenty-four dollars a week to live on — which was all we needed, in our cheap and humble quarters.

Clinton was one of the dearest and loveliest human beings I have ever known, and we led a charmed existence together, in a contentment which knew no bounds. Clinton was refined by nature and breeding; he was a gentleman by nature and breeding; he was highly educated; he was of a beautiful spirit; he was pure in heart and speech. He was a Scotchman, and a Presbyterian; a Presbyterian of the old and genuine school, being honest and sincere in his religion, and loving it, and finding serenity and peace in it. He hadn't a vice — unless a large and grateful sympathy with Scotch whiskey may be called by that name. I didn't regard it as a vice, because he was a Scotchman, and Scotch whiskey to a Scotchman is as in- nocent as milk is to the rest of the human race. In Clinton's case it was a virtue, and not an economical one. Twenty-four dollars a week would re- ally have been riches to us if we hadn't had to support that jug; because of the jug we were always sailing pretty close to the wind, and any tardi- ness in the arrival of any part of our income was sure to cause us some in- convenience.

I remember a time when a shortage occurred; we had to have three dol- lars, and we had to have it before the close of the day. I don't know now how we happened to want all that money at one time; I only know we had to have it. Clinton told me to go out and find it—and he said he would also go out and see what he could do. He didn't seem to have any doubt that we would succeed, but I knew that that was his religion working in him; I hadn't the same confidence; I hadn't any idea where to turn to raise all that bullion, and I said so. I think he was ashamed of me, privately, because of my weak faith. He told me to give myself no uneasiness, no concern; and said in a simple, confident, and unquestioning way, "the Lord will provide." I saw that he fully believed the Lord would provide, but it seemed to me that if he had had my experience—

But never mind that; before he was done with me his strong faith had had its influence, and I went forth from the place almost convinced that the Lord really would provide.

I wandered around the streets for an hour, trying to think up some way to get that money, but nothing suggested itself. At last I lounged into the big lobby of the Ebbitt House, which was then a new hotel, and sat down. Presently a dog came loafing along. He paused, glanced up at me and said, with his eyes, "Are you friendly?" I answered, with my eyes, that I was. He gave his tail a grateful little wag and came forward and rested his jaw on my knee and lifted his brown eyes to my face in a winningly affectionate way. He was a lovely creature—as beautiful as a girl, and he was made all of silk and velvet. I stroked his smooth brown head and fondled his drooping ears, and we were a pair of lovers right away. Pretty soon Brigadier-General Miles, the hero of the land, came strolling by in his blue and gold splendors, with everybody's admiring gaze upon him. He saw the dog and stopped, and there was a light in his eye which showed that he had a warm place in his heart for dogs like this gracious creature; then he came forward and patted the dog and said,

"He is very fine—he is a wonder; would you sell him?"

I was greatly moved; it seemed a marvellous thing to me, the way Clinton's prediction had come true. I said,

"Yes."

The General said,

"What do you ask for him?"

"Three dollars."

The General was manifestly surprised. He said,

"Three dollars? Only three dollars? Why, that dog is a most uncommon dog; he can't possibly be worth less than fifty. If he were mine, I wouldn't take a hundred for him. I'm afraid you are not aware of his value. Reconsider your price if you like, I don't wish to wrong you."

But if he had known me he would have known that I was no more capable of wronging him than he was of wronging me. I responded with the same quiet decision as before,

"No—three dollars. That is his price."

"Very well, since you insist upon it," said the General, and he gave me three dollars and led the dog away, and disappeared up-stairs.

In about ten minutes a gentle-faced middle-aged gentleman came along, and began to look around here and there and under tables and everywhere, and I said to him,

"Is it a dog you are looking for?"

His face was sad, before, and troubled; but it lit up gladly now, and he answered,

"Yes—have you seen him?"

"Yes," I said, "he was here a minute ago, and I saw him follow a gentleman away. I think I could find him for you if you would like me to try."

I have seldom seen a person look so grateful—and there was gratitude in his voice, too, when he conceded that he would like me to try. I said I would do it with great pleasure, but that as it might take a little time I hoped he would not mind paying me something for my trouble. He said he would do it most gladly—repeating that phrase "most gladly"—and asked me how much. I said—

"Three dollars."

He looked surprised, and said,

"Dear me, it is nothing! I will pay you ten, quite willingly."

But I said,

"No, three is the price"—and I started for the stairs without waiting for any further argument, for Clinton had said that that was the amount that the Lord would provide, and it seemed to me that it would be sacrilegious to take a penny more than was promised.

I got the number of the General's room from the office-clerk, as I passed by his wicket, and when I reached the room I found the General there caressing his dog, and quite happy. I said,

"I am sorry, but I have to take the dog again."

He seemed very much surprised, and said,

"Take him again? Why, he is my dog; you sold him to me, and at your own price."

"Yes," I said, "it is true—but I have to have him, because the man wants him again."

"What man?"

"The man that owns him; he wasn't my dog."

The General looked even more surprised than before, and for a moment he couldn't seem to find his voice; then he said,

"Do you mean to tell me that you were selling another man's dog — and knew it?"

"Yes, I knew it wasn't my dog."

"Then why did you sell him?"

I said,

"Well, that is a curious question to ask. I sold him because you wanted him. You offered to buy the dog; you can't deny that. I was not anxious to sell him — I had not even thought of selling him, but it seemed to me that if it could be any accommodation to you —"

He broke me off in the middle, and said,

"*Accommodation* to me? It is the most extraordinary spirit of accommodation I have ever heard of — the idea of your selling a dog that didn't belong to you —"

I broke him off there, and said,

"There is no relevancy about this kind of argument; you said yourself that the dog was probably worth a hundred dollars, I only asked you three; was there anything unfair about that? You offered to pay more, you know you did. I only asked you three; you can't deny it."

"Oh, what in the world has that to do with it! The crux of the matter is that you didn't own the dog — can't you see that? You seem to think that there is no impropriety in selling property that isn't yours provided you sell it cheap. Now, then —"

I said,

"Please don't argue about it any more. You can't get around the fact that the price was perfectly fair, perfectly reasonable — considering that I didn't own the dog — and so arguing about it is only a waste of words. I have to have him back again because the man wants him; don't you see that I haven't any choice in the matter? Put yourself in my place. Suppose you had sold a dog that didn't belong to you; suppose you —"

"Oh," he said, "don't muddle my brains any more with your idiotic reasonings! Take him along, and give me a rest."

So I paid back the three dollars and led the dog down-stairs and passed him over to his owner, and collected three for my trouble.

I went away then with a good conscience, because I had acted honorably; I never could have used the three that I sold the dog for, because it was not rightly my own, but the three I got for restoring him to his rightful owner was righteously and properly mine, because I had earned it. That man might never have gotten that dog back at all, if it hadn't been for me. My principles have remained to this day what they were then. I was always honest; I know I can never be otherwise. It is as I said in the beginning— I was never able to persuade myself to use money which I had acquired in questionable ways.

Now, then, that is the tale. Some of it is true.[10]

MARK TWAIN.

Appendices
Notes
Selected Bibliography
Index

Appendix A:
"The Death of Jean"

Clemens wrote "The Death of Jean" during the two days immediately following Jean Clemens' unexpected death on 24 December 1909. The essay presents a final example of just how important the act of writing, of composition, was to Clemens. Although he had come to hate the pen, it provided him a much-needed outlet and a much-needed comfort.

Jean's death was only the latest in a line of crises that had led Clemens to seek the solace of work. As he had years earlier when Susy Clemens and then Olivia Clemens died, Clemens turned once again to composing—and once again to the pen—to ease his troubled spirit: "I am setting it down . . . everything. It is a relief to me to write it. It furnishes me an excuse for thinking" (*MTB*, 1549).

The essay does begin the close of Clemens' life. Its occasion is Jean's death, but its topic is Clemens' attempt to come to terms with her death and with his loneliness. Jean's homecoming was important to Clemens, and the six months they spent together before her death helped him become reacquainted with his daughter, whom he now included among the parade of dead family and friends: Susy, Livy, and Langdon, George, the Clemenses' man-servant, Henry Rogers, and Charles Dudley Warner. Clemens' longevity now seemed a curse.

Jean's death left Clemens more alone: Clara had married in October and had sailed to Europe in early December. Clemens lamented, "How poor I am, who was once so rich!" And later, "Why did I build this house, two years ago? To shelter this vast emptiness? How foolish I was! But I shall stay in it. The spirits of the dead hallow a house, for me." He did not, however, stay in that house long. He sailed for Bermuda on 5 January 1910. Clemens returned to Redding on 14 April 1910, only seven days before his own death. "The Death of Jean" was published in *Harper's Monthly Magazine* in January 1911 (vol. 122, no. 728:210–15).

STORMFIELD, CHRISTMAS EVE, *11* A.M., *1909.*[1]

Jean is dead!

Has any one ever tried to put upon paper all the little happenings connected with a dear one—happenings of the twenty-four hours preceding the sudden and unexpected death of that dear one? Would a book contain them? would two books

245

contain them? I think not. They pour into the mind in a flood. They are little things that have been always happening every day, and were always so unimportant and easily forgettable before—but now! Now, how different! how precious they are, how dear, how unforgettable, how pathetic, how sacred, how clothed with dignity!

Last night Jean, all flushed with splendid health, and I the same, from the wholesome effects of my Bermuda holiday, strolled hand in hand from the dinner table and sat down in the library and chatted, and planned, and discussed, cheerily and happily (and how unsuspectingly!) until nine—which is late for us—then went upstairs, Jean's friendly German dog following. At my door Jean said, "I can't kiss you good night, father: I have a cold, and you could catch it." I bent and kissed her hand. She was moved—I saw it in her eyes—and she impulsively kissed my hand in return. Then with the usual gay "Sleep well, dear!" from both, we parted.

At half past seven this morning I woke, and heard voices outside my door. I said to myself, "Jean is starting on her usual horseback flight to the station for the mail." Then Katy* entered, stood quaking and gasping at my bedside a moment, then found her tongue:

"Miss Jean is dead!"

Possibly I know now what the soldier feels when a bullet crashes through his heart.

In her bath-room there she lay, the fair young creature, stretched upon the floor and covered with a sheet. And looking so placid, so natural, and as if asleep. We knew what had happened. She was an epileptic: she had been seized with a convulsion and heart failure in her bath. The doctor had to come several miles. His efforts, like our previous ones, failed to bring her back to life.

It is noon, now. How lovable she looks, how sweet and how tranquil! It is a noble face, and full of dignity; and that was a good heart that lies there so still.

In England, thirteen years ago, my wife and I were stabbed to the heart with a cablegram which said, "Susy was mercifully released to-day." I had to send a like shock to Clara, in Berlin, this morning. With the peremptory addition, "You must not come home." Clara and her husband sailed from here on the 11th of this month.[2] How will Clara bear it? Jean, from her babyhood, was a worshipper of Clara.

Four days ago I came back from a month's holiday in Bermuda in perfected health; but by some accident the reporters failed to perceive this. Day before yesterday, letters and telegrams began to arrive from friends and strangers which indicated that I was supposed to be dangerously ill. Yesterday Jean begged me to explain my case through the Associated Press. I said it was not important enough; but she was distressed and said I must think of Clara. Clara would see the report in the German papers, and as she had been nursing her husband day and night for four months† and was worn out and feeble, the shock might be disastrous. There was reason in that; so I sent a humorous paragraph by telephone to the Associated Press denying the "charge" that I was "dying," and saying "I would not do such a thing at my time of life."

Jean was a little troubled, and did not like to see me treat the matter so lightly;

---

*Katy Leary, who had been in the service of the Clemens family for twenty-nine years.
†Mr. Gabrilowitsch had been operated on for appendicitis.

but I said it was best to treat it so, for there was nothing serious about it. This morning I sent the sorrowful facts of this day's irremediable disaster to the Associated Press. Will both appear in this evening's papers?— the one so blithe, the other so tragic.

I lost Susy thirteen years ago; I lost her mother—her incomparable mother!— five and a half years ago; Clara has gone away to live in Europe; and now I have lost Jean. How poor I am, who was once so rich! Seven months ago Mr. Rogers[3] died—one of the best friends I ever had, and the nearest perfect, as man and gentleman, I have yet met among my race; within the last six weeks Gilder has passed away, and Laffan—old, old friends of mine.[4] Jean lies yonder, I sit here; we are strangers under our own roof; we kissed hands good-by at this door last night— and it was forever, we never suspecting it. She lies there, and I sit here—writing, busying myself, to keep my heart from breaking. How dazzlingly the sunshine is flooding the hills around! It is like a mockery.

Seventy-four years old, twenty-four days ago. Seventy-four years old yesterday. Who can estimate my age to-day?

I have looked upon her again. I wonder I can bear it. She looks just as her mother looked when she lay dead in that Florentine villa so long ago. The sweet placidity of death! it is more beautiful than sleep.

I saw her mother buried. I said I would never endure that horror again; that I would never again look into the grave of any one dear to me. I have kept to that. They will take Jean from this house to-morrow, and bear her to Elmira, New York, where lie those of us that have been released, but I shall not follow.

Jean was on the dock when the ship came in, only four days ago. She was at the door, beaming a welcome, when I reached this house the next evening. We played cards, and she tried to teach me a new game called "Mark Twain." We sat chatting cheerily in the library last night, and she wouldn't let me look into the loggia, where she was making Christmas preparations. She said she would finish them in the morning, and then her little French friend would arrive from New York — the surprise would follow; the surprise she had been working over for days. While she was out for a moment I disloyally stole a look. The loggia floor was clothed with rugs and furnished with chairs and sofas; and the uncompleted surprise was there: in the form of a Christmas tree that was drenched with silver film in a most wonderful way; and on a table was a prodigal profusion of bright things which she was going to hang upon it to-day. What desecrating hand will ever banish that eloquent unfinished surprise from that place? Not mine, surely. All these little matters have happened in the last four days. "Little." Yes—*then*. But not now. Nothing she said or thought or did is little now. And all the lavish humor!—what is become of it? It is pathos, now. Pathos, and the thought of it brings tears.

All these little things happened such a few hours ago—and now she lies yonder. Lies yonder, and cares for nothing any more. Strange—marvellous —incredible! I have had this experience before; but it would still be incredible if I had had it a thousand times.

"Miss Jean is dead!"

That is what Katy said. When I heard the door open behind the bed's head without a preliminary knock, I supposed it was Jean coming to kiss me good morning, she being the only person who was used to entering without formalities.

And so —

I have been to Jean's parlor. Such a turmoil of Christmas presents for servants and friends! They are everywhere; tables, chairs, sofas, the floor — everything is occupied, and over-occupied. It is many and many a year since I have seen the like. In that ancient day Mrs. Clemens and I used to slip softly into the nursery at midnight on Christmas Eve and look the array of presents over. The children were little then. And now here is Jean's parlor looking just as that nursery used to look. The presents are not labelled — the hands are forever idle that would have labelled them to-day. Jean's mother always worked herself down with her Christmas preparations. Jean did the same yesterday and the preceding days, and the fatigue has cost her her life. The fatigue caused the convulsion that attacked her this morning. She had had no attack for months.

Jean was so full of life and energy that she was constantly in danger of overtaxing her strength. Every morning she was in the saddle by half past seven, and off to the station for her mail. She examined the letters and I distributed them: some to her, some to Mr. Paine, the others to the stenographer and myself. She despatched her share and then mounted her horse again and went around superintending her farm and her poultry the rest of the day. Sometimes she played billiards with me after dinner, but she was usually too tired to play, and went early to bed.

Yesterday afternoon I told her about some plans I had been devising while absent in Bermuda, to lighten her burdens. We would get a housekeeper; also we would put her share of the secretary-work into Mr. Paine's hands.

No — she wasn't willing. She had been making plans herself. The matter ended in a compromise. I submitted. I always did. She wouldn't audit the bills and let Paine fill out the checks — she would continue to attend to that herself. Also, she would continue to be housekeeper, and let Katy assist. Also, she would continue to answer the letters of personal friends for me. Such was the compromise. Both of us called it by that name, though I was not able to see where any formidable change had been made.

However, Jean was pleased, and that was sufficient for me. She was proud of being my secretary, and I was never able to persuade her to give up any part of her share in that unlovely work.

In the talk last night I said I found everything going so smoothly that if she were willing I would go back to Bermuda in February and get blessedly out of the clash and turmoil again for another month. She was urgent that I should do it, and said that if I would put off the trip until March she would take Katy and go with me. We struck hands upon that, and said it was settled. I had a mind to write to Bermuda by to-morrow's ship and secure a furnished house and servants. I meant to write the letter this morning. But it will never be written, now.

For she lies yonder, and before her is another journey than that.

Night is closing down; the rim of the sun barely shows above the sky-line of the hills.

I have been looking at that face again that was growing dearer and dearer to me every day. I was getting acquainted with Jean in these last nine months. She had been long an exile from home when she came to us three-quarters of a year ago. She had been shut up in sanitariums, many miles from us. How eloquently glad and grateful she was to cross her father's threshold again!

Would I bring her back to life if I could do it? I would not. If a word would do it, I would beg for strength to withhold the word. And I would have the strength; I am sure of it. In her loss I am almost bankrupt, and my life is a bitterness, but I am content: for she has been enriched with the most precious of all gifts — that gift which makes all other gifts mean and poor — death. I have never wanted any released friend of mine restored to life since I reached manhood. I felt in this way when Susy passed away; and later my wife, and later Mr. Rogers. When Clara met me at the station in New York and told me Mr. Rogers had died suddenly that morning, my thought was, Oh, favorite of fortune — fortunate all his long and lovely life — fortunate to his latest moment! The reporters said there were tears of sorrow in my eyes. True — but they were for *me*, not for him. He had suffered no loss. All the fortunes he had ever made before were poverty compared with this one.

Why did I build this house, two years ago? To shelter this vast emptiness? How foolish I was! But I shall stay in it. The spirits of the dead hallow a house, for me. It was not so with other members of my family. Susy died in the house we built in Hartford. Mrs. Clemens would never enter it again. But it made the house dearer to me. I have entered it once since, when it was tenantless and silent and forlorn, but to me it was a holy place and beautiful. It seemed to me that the spirits of the dead were all about me, and would speak to me and welcome me if they could: Livy, and Susy, and George, and Henry Robinson,[5] and Charles Dudley Warner. How good and kind they were, and how lovable their lives! In fancy I could see them all again, I could call the children back and hear them romp again with George — that peerless black ex-slave and children's idol who came one day — a flitting stranger — to wash windows, and stayed eighteen years. Until he died. Clara and Jean would never enter again the New York hotel which their mother had frequented in earlier days. They could not bear it. But I shall stay in this house. It is dearer to me to-night than ever it was before. Jean's spirit will make it beautiful for me always. Her lonely and tragic death — but I will not think of that now.

Jean's mother always devoted two or three weeks to Christmas shopping, and was always physically exhausted when Christmas Eve came. Jean was her very own child — she wore herself out present-hunting in New York these latter days. Paine has just found on her desk a long list of names — fifty, he thinks — people to whom she sent presents last night. Apparently she forgot no one. And Katy found there a roll of bank-notes, for the servants.

Her dog has been wandering about the grounds to-day, comradeless and forlorn. I have seen him from the windows. She got him from Germany. He has tall ears and looks exactly like a wolf. He was educated in Germany, and knows no language but the German. Jean gave him no orders save in that tongue. And so, when the burglar-alarm made a fierce clamor at midnight a fortnight ago, the butler, who is French and knows no German, tried in vain to interest the dog in the supposed burglar. Jean wrote me, to Bermuda, about the incident. It was the last letter I was ever to receive from her bright head and her competent hand. The dog will not be neglected.

There was never a kinder heart than Jean's. From her childhood up she always spent the most of her allowance on charities of one kind and another. After she became secretary and had her income doubled she spent her money upon these things with a free hand. Mine too, I am glad and grateful to say.

She was a loyal friend to all animals, and she loved them all, birds, beasts, and everything — even snakes — an inheritance from me. She knew all the birds: she was high up in that lore. She became a member of various humane societies when she was still a little girl — both here and abroad — and she remained an active member to the last. She founded two or three societies for the protection of animals, here and in Europe.

She was an embarrassing secretary, for she fished my correspondence out of the waste-basket and answered the letters. She thought all letters deserved the courtesy of an answer. Her mother brought her up in that kindly error.

She could write a good letter, and was swift with her pen. She had but an indifferent ear for music, but her tongue took to languages with an easy facility. She never allowed her Italian, French, and German to get rusty through neglect.

The telegrams of sympathy are flowing in, from far and wide, now, just as they did in Italy five years and a half ago, when this child's mother laid down her blameless life. The cannot heal the hurt, but they take away some of the pain. When Jean and I kissed hands and parted at my door last, how little did we imagine that in twenty-two hours the telegraph would be bringing words like these:

"From the bottom of our hearts we send our sympathy, dearest of friends."

For many and many a day to come, wherever I go in this house, remembrancers of Jean will mutely speak to me of her. Who can count the number of them?

She was in exile two years with the hope of healing her malady — epilepsy. There are no words to express how grateful I am that she did not meet her fate in the hands of strangers, but in the loving shelter of her own home.

"Miss Jean is dead!"
It is true. Jean is dead.
A month ago I was writing bubbling and hilarious articles for magazines yet to appear, and now I am writing — this.

Christmas Day. Noon. — Last night I went to Jean's room at intervals, and turned back the sheet and looked at the peaceful face, and kissed the cold brow, and remembered that heart-breaking night in Florence so long ago, in that cavernous and silent vast villa, when I crept down-stairs so many times, and turned back a sheet and looked at a face just like this one — Jean's mother's face — and kissed a brow that was just like this one. And last night I saw again what I had seen then — that strange and lovely miracle — the sweet soft contours of early maidenhood restored by the gracious hand of death! When Jean's mother lay dead, all trace of care, and trouble, and suffering, and the corroding years had vanished out of the face, and I was looking again upon it as I had known and worshipped it in its young bloom and beauty a whole generation before.

About three in the morning, while wandering about the house in the deep silences, as one does in times like these, when there is a dumb sense that something has been lost that will never be found again, yet must be sought, if only for the employment the useless seeking gives, I came upon Jean's dog in the hall downstairs, and noted that he did not spring to greet me, according to his hospitable habit, but came slow and sorrowfully; also I remembered that he had not visited Jean's apartment since the tragedy. Poor fellow, did he know? I think so. Always when Jean was abroad in the open he was with her; always when she was in the house he was with her, in the night as well as in the day. Her parlor was his bedroom. Whenever I happened upon him on the ground floor he always followed me about, and when I went up-stairs he went too — in a tumultuous gallop. But now it was different: after patting him a little I went to the library — he remained behind; when I went up-stairs he did not follow me, save with his wistful eyes. He has wonderful eyes — big, and kind, and eloquent. He can talk with them. He is a beautiful creature, and is of the breed of the New York police-dogs. I do not like dogs, because they bark when there is no occasion for it; but I have liked this one from the beginning, because he belonged to Jean, and because he never barks except when there is occasion — which is not oftener than twice a week.

In my wanderings I visited Jean's parlor. On a shelf I found a pile of my books, and I knew what it meant. She was waiting for me to come home from Bermuda and autograph them, then she would send them away. If I only knew whom she intended them for! But I shall never know. I will keep them. Her hand has touched them — it is an accolade — they are noble, now.

And in a closet she had hidden a surprise for me — a thing I have often wished I owned: a noble big globe. I couldn't see it for the tears. She will never know the pride I take in it, and the pleasure. To-day the mails are full of loving remembrances for her: full of those old, old kind words she loved so well, "Merry Christmas to Jean!" If she could only have lived one day longer!

At last she ran out of money, and would not use mine. So she sent to one of those New York homes for poor girls all the clothes she could spare — and more, most likely.

Christmas Night. —This afternoon they took her away from her room. As soon as I might, I went down to the library, and there she lay, in her coffin, dressed in exactly the same clothes she wore when she stood at the other end of the same room on the 6th of October last, as Clara's chief bridesmaid. Her face was radiant with happy excitement then; it was the same face now, with the dignity of death and the peace of God upon it.

They told me the first mourner to come was the dog. He came uninvited, and stood up on his hind legs and rested his fore paws upon the trestle, and took a last long look at the face that was so dear to him, then went his way as silently as he had come. *He knows.*

At mid-afternoon, it began to snow. The pity of it—that Jean could not see it! She so loved the snow.

The snow continued to fall. At six o'clock the hearse drew up to the door to bear away its pathetic burden. As they lifted the casket, Paine began playing on the orchestrelle Schubert's *Impromptu*, which was Jean's favorite. Then he played the Intermezzo; that was for Susy; then he played the Largo; that was for their mother. He did this at my request. Elsewhere in this Autobiography I have told how the Intermezzo and the Largo came to be associated in my heart with Susy and Livy in their last hours in this life.

From my windows I saw the hearse and the carriages wind along the road and gradually grow vague and spectral in the falling snow, and presently disappear. Jean was gone out of my life, and would not come back any more. Jervis,[6] the cousin she had played with when they were babies together—he and her beloved old Katy —were conducting her to her distant childhood home, where she will lie by her mother's side once more, in the company of Susy and Langdon.

December 26th. —The dog came to see me at eight o'clock this morning. He was very affectionate, poor orphan! My room will be his quarters hereafter.

The storm raged all night. It has raged all the morning. The snow drives across the landscape in vast clouds, superb, sublime—and Jean not here to see.

2.30 p.m.—It is the time appointed. The funeral has begun. Four hundred miles away, but I can see it all, just as if I were there. The scene is the library, in the Langdon homestead. Jean's coffin stands where her mother and I stood, forty years ago, and were married; and where Susy's coffin stood thirteen years ago; where her mother's stood, five years and a half ago; and where mine will stand, after a little time.

Five o'clock. —It is all over.

When Clara went away two weeks ago to live in Europe, it was hard, but I could bear it, for I had Jean left. I said *we* would be a family. We said we would be close comrades and happy—just we two. That fair dream was in my mind when Jean met me at the steamer last Monday; it was in my mind when she received me at the door last Tuesday evening. We were together; *we were a family!* the dream had come true—oh, preciously true, contentedly true, satisfyingly true! and remained true two whole days.

And now? Now Jean is in her grave!

In the grave—if I can believe it. God rest her sweet spirit![7]

Appendix B:
Mark Twain's Experiments
in Autobiography

1870	The Tennessee Land
1871	*Mark Twain's (Burlesque) Autobiography*
	"An Autobiography," in *The Aldine*
1873	Autobiographical Sketch
1877	Early Years in Florida, Missouri
1885	The Grant Dictations
1890	The Machine Episode
	Jane Lampton Clemens
1897–98	Ancestors
	Playing "Bear"
	Herrings
	Old Lecture Days
	Ralph Keeler
	Beauties of the German Language
	A Viennese Procession
	Comment on Tautology and Grammar
	Jim Wolf and the Cats
1900	The Private History of a MS that Came to Grief
1901	The Last Napoleon
	Comments related to Susy's biography
1901(?)	Interpreting the Deity
1904	Villa Quarto
	John Hay
	Notes on "Innocents Abroad"
	Henry H. Rogers
1904(?)	Stevens, Aldrich, etc.
	Hunting the Deceitful Turkey
	Untitled pages on the definition of a sainthood
	The Rhodes Scholar's Club, & similar benefactors

1906	Begins autobiographical dictations: will continue until 1909
	"Chapters from My Autobiography" in *North American Review*
1907(?)	The Oxford Pageant
1909	The Ashcroft-Lyon MS
	The Death of Jean

Appendix C:
The Editions and the Chronology
of Composition

Clemens' comment, "In this autobiography it is my purpose to wander whenever I please and come back when I get ready" (*MTA* 2:128), focuses on his haphazard process and on his desire to present material in the order in which it was composed. But it is clear that Clemens himself violated that rule when preparing the chapters for the *North American Review* and, ironically, that Paine seems to be the only editor who attempted to publish the materials in the order in which they were composed.

What follows is a list of materials as they have been used in the four editions of the autobiography: "Chapters from My Autobiography" (*NAR*), Paine's *Mark Twain's Autobiography* (*MTA*), DeVoto's *Mark Twain in Eruption* (*MTE*), and Neider's *The Autobiography of Mark Twain* (*AMT*). The material is identified by name or date wherever possible, to give an idea of the sequence imposed on the variety of written fragments and dictations.

NAR	*MTA*	*MTE*[a]	*AMT*[b]
3/26/06	Tennessee Land	**Roosevelt**	Early Years
Early Days	Early Years	7/16/08	Early Days
Playing "Bear"	The Grant Dictations	11/1/07	Tennessee Land
Herrings	The Machine Episode	10/18/07	Jane Lampton Clemens
Florence Dictations	Early Days	10/21/07	Playing "Bear"
2/1/06	Jane Lampton Clemens	9/7/07	Herrings
2/2/06	Playing "Bear"	5/29/07	Jim Wolf and the Cats
2/5/06	Herrings	5/30/07	Jim Wolf and the Wasps

[a]Headings in bold type in this column indicate the categories DeVoto used to separate the materials.

[b]Neider's edition does not identify material by the dates of composition. Many of the dates he gives serve as markers for a series of dictations which cover similar material. This list presents clearly identifiable materials or those which Neider identifies in the notes in his text. Neider's text, of course, offers a great deal more than what is identified here: he included text from the *North American Review*, the early fragments and dictations, and some 30,000 words which had not appeared in any other edition.

NAR	MTA	MTE	AMT
2/7/06	Jim Wolf and the Cats	7/14/08	12/26/06
2/8/06	Macfarlane	4/3/06	3/8/06
2/9/06	Old Lecture Days	9/12/08	7/30/06
2/12/06	Ralph Keeler	**Carnegie**	8/31/06
2/26/06	Beauties of the German	8/11/06	3/23/06
3/7/06	Language	12/2/07	3/29/06
3/22/06	A Viennese Procession	12/10/07	3/26/06
3/5/06	Comment on Tautology	**Plutocracy**	10/12/06
3/6/06	and Grammar	12/13/06	5/26/07
3/23/06	Private History of a MS	1/15/07	4/11/06
1/19/06	that Came to Grief	1/28/07	2/1/06
12/13/06	Villa Quarto	2/16/06	4/5/06
12/1/06	A Memory of John Hay	1/30/07	4/6/06
12/2/06	Notes on "Innocents	3/20/06	5/26/06
3/28/06	Abroad"	1/30/07	Henry H. Rogers
3/28/06	Stevenson, Aldrich, etc.	5/21/08	8/30/06
7/3/08	Henry H. Rogers	**Hannibal Days**	7/31/06
4/5/06	Henry H. Rogers (1909)	8/15/06	2/7/06
Florence dictations	1/9/06	11/30/06	8/11/06
Early Days	1/10/06	12/1/06	Stevenson, Aldrich, etc.
12/6/06	1/12/06	12/2/06	2/4/07
12/17/06	1/13/06	12/3/06	Villa Quarto
2/10/07	1/15/06	10/16/06	6/4/06
2/12/07	1/16/06	10/30/06	5/23/07
1/17/06	1/17/06	**Two Halos**	1/13/08
10/8/06	1/18/06	5/21/06	7/3/08
1/22/07	1/19/06	5/23/06	The Death of Jean
1/12/05	1/23/06	5/24/06	
10/15/06	1/24/06	5/26/06	
Jim Wolf and the	2/1/06	5/28/06	
Cats	2/2/06	5/29/06	
12/21/06	2/5/06	6/1/06	
3/28/07	2/6/06	6/2/06	
12/22/06	2/7/06	**In a Workshop**	
11/19/06	2/8/06	8/30/06	
11/30/06	2/9/06	7/31/06	
9/5/06	2/12/06	12/5/06	
Florence dictations	2/13/06	10/10/07	
1/23/07	2/14/06	9/10/06	
11/8/06	2/15/06	9/4/07	
3/8/06	2/16/06	8/29/06	
1/6/07	2/20/06	2/15/06	
10/10/06	2/21/06	4/3/06	
3/12/06	2/23/06	**Literary People**	
3/13/06	2/26/06	6/13/06	
12/20/06	3/5/06	6/14/06	
3/9/06	3/6/06	2/4/07	
3/16/06	3/7/06	7/3/08	
7/26/07	3/8/06	7/8/08	

NAR	MTA	MTE	AMT
10/9/06	3/9/06	8/11/06	
10/16/06	3/12/06	8/13/06	
10/11/06	3/14/06	1/13/08	
10/12/06	3/15/06	**Last Visit to**	
1/11/06	**3/16/06**	**England**	
10/3/07	3/21/06	7 & 8/07	
	3/22/06	White and Red	
	3/23/06	Marie Corelli	
	3/26/06	Winston Churchill	
	3/27/06	Sidney Lee	
	3/28/06	The Holy Grail	
	3/29/06	**Miscellany**	
	3/30/06	Grover Cleveland	
	4/2/06	Horace Greeley	
	4/4/06	John Wanamaker	
	4/5/06	10/31/08	
	4/6/06	10/3/07	
	4/9/06	11/24/06	
	4/10/06	9/7/06	
	4/11/06	10/2/06	

Appendix D:
A Sample of Letters

This sample of nine letters sheds light on both the early Sam Clemens as well as the older Clemens as he begins his life with Olivia Langdon and, still later, as he navigates the losses of Susy, Livy, and Jean. Each letter opens a small window through which it is possible to take a snapshot of Clemens at a particular time and in a particular place.[1]

The contrasting images of Clemens here are striking. From his earliest letters home to his mother from New York in 1853, we see a young man on an adventure. The New York letters were published by Orion Clemens in his local newspaper, and young Sam would have known that publication was likely.[2] Not all the images here flatter Clemens or conform to the icon of Mark Twain. In these letters he affirms the social conventions—and, indeed, the racism and nativist prejudice—of antebellum Hannibal. At seventeen, Clemens is certainly regurgitating the lessons he had learned about those who are different. Perhaps as a way to reinforce a brand of frontier superiority (and to reinforce that even in New York he remains a citizen of the South and West), he dismisses abolition and notions of racial equality with snide comments and decries the influx of the poor (and especially children) as reason to shudder.[3]

Juxtaposed to the concerns of an older Clemens, we marvel at the shift in tone and attitude as Clemens moves into adult responsibilities. He worries early in his career about how best to nurture and develop his talent for humorous writing—a talent that he is none too impressed with, until, of course, others see his promise. That tendency to depend on the accolades of others, on the benefit of wiser and more worldly opinion, comes to the fore again as he reflects on his marriage. The post-wedding letter to Will Bowen offers a wealth of reminiscences, many of which will later find their way into Clemens' Mississippi-based novels. This is Clemens as he comes to terms with a notion of the past as grist for a literary present. More importantly, however, is Clemens' shift out of that past into the present of his life with Livy. That movement opens an entirely new and decidedly domestic context for Clemens' writing. He will become more pointed in his social criticism because of his education into the progressivism of the Langdon family and eventually of the host of friends and acquaintances he and Livy would collect in Hartford. But all that begins with setting aside the tales of childhood for the demands of domestic life.

Clemens used his autobiographical writing to renew his family ties and to seek some consolation for his long life, from the memories that flood in as he marks anniversaries, to the collaboration with Susy by using so much of the biography of him and the family that she wrote, to the ache that runs through the record of Jean's death. The sense of lost connections is also part of his letter writing. Though it is possible to overstress the momentous loss of family members and its toll on the aging Clemens, his letters marking the deaths of Susy, Livy, and Jean offer the authentic voice of grief. It is that grief that propels much of the material that he presents in "Chapters from My Autobiography." As he responds more immediately to each loss, his voice in the letters is especially clear and vibrates with a deep emotion that, if at times presented in the conventional language of mourning, demonstrates the depth of his grief. It's impossible to read the letters about these losses and not feel Clemens' devastation.

Though these brief glimpses into Clemens' private life are affecting, they are only a partial record of the life and times of Clemens and his literary, social, and domestic persona Mark Twain. Given the range of topics presented in the autobiographical "Chapters from My Autobiography," however, even these few letters make it possible to see the immediacy and authenticity of Clemens' reactions to events and the emotion with which he struggled.

To Jane Lampton Clemens[4]

New York
Wednesday, August 24th 1853

My Dear Mother: you will doubtless be a little surprised, and somewhat angry when you receive this, and find me so far from home; but you must bear a little with me, for you know I was always the best boy you had, and perhaps you remember the people used to say to their children—"Now don't do like Orion and Henry Clemens but take Sam for your guide!"

Well, I was out of work in St. Louis, and didn't fancy loafing in such a dry place, where there is no pleasure to be seen without paying well for it, and so I thought I might as well go to New York. I packed up my "duds" and left for this village, where I arrived, all right, this morning.

It took a day, by steamboat and cars, to go from St. Louis to Bloomington, Ill; another day by railroad, from there to Chicago, where I laid over all day Sunday; from Chicago to Monroe, in Michigan, by railroad, another day; from Monroe, across Lake Erie, in the fine Lake palace, "Southern Michigan," to Buffalo, another day; from Buffalo to Albany, by railroad, another day; and from Albany to New York, by Hudson river steamboat, another day—an awful trip, taking five days, where it should have been only three. I shall wait a day or so for my insides to get settled, after the jolting they received, when I shall look out for a sit; for they say there is plenty of work to be had for *sober* compositors.

The trip, however, was a very pleasant one. Rochester, famous on account of the "Spirit Rappings" was of course interesting; and when I saw the Court House in Syracuse, it called to mind the time when it was surrounded with chains and companies of soldiers, to prevent the rescue of McReynolds' nigger, by the infernal abolitionists. I reckon I had better black my face, for in these Eastern States niggers are considerably better than white people.

I saw a curiosity to-day, but I don't know what to call it. Two beings, about like common people, with the exception of their faces, which are more like the "phiz" of an orang-outang, than human. They are white, though, like other people. Imagine a person about the size of Harvel Jordan's oldest boy, with small lips and full breast, with a constant uneasy, fidgety motion, bright, intelligent eyes, that seems as if they would look through you, and you have these *things*. They were found in the Island of Borneo (the only ones of the species ever discovered,) about twenty years ago. One of them is twenty three, and the other twenty five years of age. They possess amazing strength; the smallest one would shoulder three hundred pounds as easily as I would a plug of tobacco; they are supposed to be a cross between man and orang-outang; one is the best natured being in the world, while the other would tear a stranger to pieces, if he did but touch him; they wear their hair "Samson" fashion, down to their waists. They have no apple in their throats, whatever, and can therefore scarcely make a sound; no memory either; what transpires to-day, they have forgotten before to-morrow; they look like one mass of muscle, and can walk either on all fours or upright; when let alone, they will walk to and fro across the room, thirteen hours out of the twenty-four; not a day passes but they walk twenty-five or thirty miles, without resting thirty minutes; I watched them about an hour and they were "tramping" the whole time. The little one bent his arm with the elbow in front, and the hand pointing upward, and no two strapping six footers in the room could pull it out straight. Their faces and eyes are those of the beast, and when they fix their glittering orbs on you with a steady, unflinching gaze, you instinctively draw back a step, and a very unpleasant sensation steals through your veins. They are both males and brothers, and very small, though I don't know their exact height. I have given you a very lengthy description of the animals, but I have nothing else to write about, and nothing from here would be interesting anyhow. The Crystal Palace is a beautiful building—so is the Marble Palace. If I can find nothing better to write about, I will say something about these in my next.

To Jane Lampton Clemens[5]

New York, Aug. 31, 1853

My dear Mother:

New York is at present overstocked with printers; and I supposed they are from the South, driven North by the yellow fever. I got a permanent situation on Monday morning, in a book and job office, and went to work. The printers here are badly organized, and therefore have to work for various prices. These prices are 23, 25, 28, 30, 32, and 35 cents per 1,000 ems. The price I get is 23 cents; but I did very well to get a place at all, for there are thirty or forty—yes, fifty good printers in the city with no work at all; besides, my situation is permanent, and I shall keep it till I can get a better one. The office I work in is John A. Gray's,

976 Cliff Street, and, next to Harper's, is the most extensive in the city. In the room in which I work I have forty compositors for company. Taking compositors, pressmen, sterotypers, and all, there about two hundred persons employed in the concern. The "Knickerbocker," "New York Recorder," "Choral Advocate," "Jewish Chronicle," "Littell's Living Age," "Irish ——," and a half dozen other papers and periodicals are printed here, besides an immense number of books. They are very particular about spacing, justification, proofs, etc., and even if I do not make much money, I will learn a great deal. I thought Ustick was particular enough, but acknowledge now that he was not old-maidish. Why, you must put exactly the same space between every two words, and *every line must be spaced alike.* They think it dreadful to space one line with three em spaces, and the next one with five ems. However, I expected this, and worked accordingly from the beginning; and out of all the proofs I saw, without boasting, I can say mine was by far the cleanest. In St. Louis, Mr. Baird said my proofs were the cleanest that were ever set in his office. The foreman of the Anzeiger told me the same—foreman of the Watchman the same; and with all this evidence, I believe I *do* set clean proof.

My boarding house is more than a mile from the office; and I can hear the signal calling the hands to work before I start down; they use a steam whistle for that purpose. I work in the fifth story; and from one window I have a pretty good view of the city, while another commands a view of the shipping beyond the Battery; and the "forests of masts," with all sorts of flags flying, is no mean sight. You have everything in the shape of water craft, from a fishing smack to the steamships and men-of-war; but packed so closely together for miles, that when close to them you can scarcely distinguish one from another.

Of all the commodities, manufacturers—or whatever you please to call it—in New York, trundle-bed trash—children I mean—take the lead. Why, from Cliff street, up Frankfort to Nassau street, six or seven squares—my road to dinner—I think I could count two hundred brats. Niggers, mulattoes, quadroons, Chinese, and some the Lord no doubt originally intended to be white, but the dirt on whose faces leaves one uncertain as to that fact, block up the little, narrow street; and to wade through this mass of human vermin, would raise the ire of the most patient person that ever lived. In going to and from my meals, I go by the way of Broadway—and to *cross* Broadway is the rub—but once across, it is *the* rub for two or three squares. My plan—and how could I choose another, when there *is* no other—is to get into the crowd; and when I get in, I am borne, and rubbed, and crowded along, and need scarcely trouble myself about using my own legs; and when I get out, it seems like I had been pulled to pieces and very badly put back together again.

Last night I was in what is known as one of *the* finest fruit saloons in the world. The whole length of the huge, glittering hall is filled with beautiful ornamented marble slab tables, covered with the finest fruit I ever saw in my life. I suppose the fruit could not be mentioned with which they could not supply you. It is a perfect palace. The gas lamps hang in clusters of half a dozen together—representing grapes, I suppose—all over the hall.

P.S. The printers have two libraries in town, entirely free to the craft; and in these I can spend my evenings most pleasantly. If books are not good company, where will I find it?

To Orion and Mollie Clemens[6]

San F.—Oct. 19, 1865

My Dear Bro & Sister:

Orion there was **genius**—true, unmistakable **genius**—in that sermon of yours. It was not the gilded base metal that passes for intellectual gold too generally in this world of ours. It is one of the few sermons that I have read with pleasure—I do not say profit, because I am beyond the reach of argument now. But seven or eight years ago that single sermon would have saved me. It even made me **think**—yea, & *regret*, for a while, as it was. (Don't preach from the above, text, next time.) Viewed as a **literary** production, that sermon was first-class.

And now let me preach *you* a sermon. I never had but two **powerful** ambitions in my life. One was to be a pilot, & the other a preacher of the gospel. I accomplished the one & failed in the other, **because** I could not supply myself with the necessary stock in trade—*i.e.* religion. I have given it up forever. I never had a "call" in that direction, anyhow, & my aspirations were the very ecstasy of presumption. But I *have* had "call" to literature, of a low order—*i.e.* humorous. It is nothing to be proud of, but it is my strongest suit, & if I were to listen to that maxim of stern *duty* which says that to do right you **must** multiply the one or the two or the three talents which the Almighty entrusts to your keeping, I would long ago have ceased to meddle with things for which I was by nature unfitted & turned my attention to seriously scribbling to excite the **laughter** of God's creatures. Poor, pitiful business! Though the Almighty did His part by me—for the talent is a mighty engine when supplied with the steam of **education**—which I have not got, & so its pistons & cylinders & shafts move feebly & for a holiday show & are useless for any good purpose.

. . . You see in me a talent for humorous writing, & urge me to cultivate it. But I always regarded it as brotherly partiality, on your part, & attached no value to it. It is only now, when editors of standard literary papers in the distant east give me high praise, & who do not know me & cannot of course be blinded by the glamour of partiality, that I really begin to believe there must be something in it. . . .

I read all your sermons—and I shall continue to read them, but of course as unsympathetically as a man of stone. I have a religion—but you will call it blasphemy. It is that there is a God for the rich man but none for the poor.

You are in trouble, & in debt—so am I. I am utterly miserable—so are you. Perhaps your religion will sustain you, will feed you—I place no dependence on mine. Our religions are alike, though, in one respect—neither can make a man happy when he is out of luck. If I do not get out of debt in 3 months,—pistols or poison for one—exit *me*. [There's a text for a sermon on Self-Murder—Proceed.]

P.S. You had better shove this in the stove—for if we strike a bargain I don't want any absurd "literary remains" & "unpublished letters of Mark Twain" published after I am planted.

To Will Bowen[7]

Sunday Afternoon,
At Home, 472 Delaware Avenue
Buffalo, Feb. 6 [18]70.

My First, & Oldest & Dearest Friend,

My heart goes out to you just the same as ever! Your letter has stirred me to the bottom. The fountains of my great deep are broken up & I have rained reminiscences for four & twenty hours. The old life has swept before me like a panorama; the old days have trooped by in their old glory, again; the old faces have looked out of the mists of the past; old footsteps have sounded in my listening ears; old hands have clasped mine, old voices have greeted me, & the songs I loved ages & ages ago have come wailing down the centuries! Heavens what eternities have swung their hoary cycles about us since those days were new! Since we tore down Dick Hardy's stable; since you had the measles & I went to your house purposely to catch them; since Henry Beebe kept that envied slaughter-house, & Joe Crain sold him cats to kill in it; since old General Gaines used to say, "Whoop! Bow your neck & spread!;" since Jimmy Finn was town drunkard & we stole his dinner while he slept in the vat & fed it to the hogs in order to keep them still till we could mount them and have a ride; since Clint Levering was drowned; since we taught that one-legged nigger, Higgins, to offend Bill League's dignity by hailing him in public with his exasperating "Hello, League!"—since we used to undress & play Robin Hood in our shirt-tails, with lath swords, in the woods on Holliday's Hill on those long summer days; since we used to go swimming above the still-house branch—& at mighty intervals wandered on vagrant fishing excursions clear up to "the Bay," & wondered what was curtained away in the great world beyond that remote point; since I jumped overboard from the ferry boat in the middle of the river that stormy day to get my hat, & swam two or three miles after it (& *got* it,) while all the town collected on the wharf & for an hour or so looked out across the angry waste of "white-caps" toward where people said Sam. Clemens was last seen before he went down; since we got up a rebellion against Miss Newcomb, under Ed. Stevens' leadership, (to force her to let us all go over to Miss Torry's side of the schoolroom,) & gallantly "sassed" Laura Hawkins when she came out the third time to call us in, & then afterward marched in in threatening & bloodthirsty array,—& meekly yielded, & took each his little thrashing, & resumed his old seat entirely "reconstructed;" since we used to indulge in that very peculiar performance on that old bench outside the school-house to drive good old Bill Brown crazy while he was eating his dinner; since we used to remain at school at noon & go hungry, in order to persecute Bill Brown in all possible ways—poor old Bill, who *could* be driven to such extremity of vindictiveness as to call us "You *infernal* fools!" & chase us round and round the school-house—& yet who never had the heart to hurt us when he caught us, & who always loved us & always took our part when the big boys wanted to thrash us; since we used to lay in wait for Bill Pitts at the pump & whale him; (I saw him two or three years ago, & was awful polite to his six feet two, & mentioned no reminiscences); since we used to be in Dave Garth's class in Sunday school & on week-days stole his leaf tobacco to run our miniature tobacco presses with; since Owsley shot Smar; since Ben Hawkins shot off his finger; since we accidentally burned up that poor fellow in the calaboose; since we used to shoot spool canons; & cannons made of keys, while that envied & hated Henry Beebe drowned out our poor little pop-guns with his booming brazen little artillery on wheels; since Laura Hawkins was my sweetheart ————

Hold! *That* rouses me out of my dream, & brings me violently back unto this day & this generation. For behold I have at this moment the only sweetheart I ever *loved*, & bless her old heart she is lying asleep upstairs in a bed that I sleep in every night, & for four whole days she has been *Mrs. Samuel L. Clemens*!

I am 34 & she is 24; I am young & very handsome (I make that statement with the fullest confidence, for I got it from her,) & she is much the most beautiful girl I ever saw (I said that before she was anything to me, & so it is worthy of all belief) & she is the *best* girl, & the sweetest, & the gentlest, & the daintiest, & the most modest & unpretentious, & the wisest in all things she should be wise in & the most ignorant in all matters it would not grace her to know, & she is sensible & quick, & loving & faithful, forgiving, full of charity—& her beautiful life is ordered by a religion that is all kindness & unselfishness. Before the gentle majesty of her purity all evil things & evil ways & evil deeds stand abashed,— then surrender. Wherefore without effort, or struggle, or spoken exorcism, all the old vices & shameful habits that have possessed me these many many years, are falling away, one by one, & departing into the darkness.

Bill, I know whereof I speak. I am too old & have moved about too much, & rubbed against too many people not to know human beings as well as we used to know "boils" from "breaks."

She is the very most perfect gem of womankind that ever I saw in my life—& I will stand by that remark till I die.

William, old boy, her father surprised us a little, the other night. We all arrived here in a night train (my little wife & I were going to board,) & under pretense of taking us to the private boarding house that had been selected for me while I was absent lecturing in New England, my new father-in-law & some old friends drove us in sleighs to the daintiest, darlingest, loveliest little palace in America—& when I said, "Oh, this won't do—people who can afford to live in this sort of style won't take boarders," that same blessed father-in-law let out the secret that this was all *our* property—a present from himself. House & furniture cost $40,000 in cash, (including stable, horse & carriage), & is a most exquisite little palace (I saw no apartment in Europe so lovely as our little drawing-room.)

Come along, you & Mollie, just whenever you can, & pay us a visit, (giving us a little notice beforehand,) & if we don't make you comfortable nobody in the world can.

[And now my princess has come down for dinner (bless me, isn't it cozy, nobody but just us two, & three servants to wait on us & respectfully call us "Mr." and "Mrs. Clemens" instead of "Sam." & "Livy!") It took me many a year to work up to where I can put on style, but now I'll do it. My book gives me an income like a small lord, & my paper is a good profitable concern.

Dinner's ready. Good bye & God bless you, old friend, & keep your heart fresh & your memory green for the old days that will never come again.

Yrs. always,
Sam. Clemens.

To William Dean Howells[8]

Elmira, Aug. 9 [1876]

My Dear Howells:

I was just about to write to you, when your letter came—& not one of those obscene postal cards, either, but reverently, upon paper. . . .

I am infringing on your patent—I started a record of our children's sayings, last night. Which reminds me that last week I sent down & got Susie a vast pair of shoes of a most villainous pattern, for I discovered that her feet were being twisted & cramped out of shape by a smaller & prettier article. She did not complain, but looked degraded & injured. At night her mamma gave her the usual admonition when she was about to say her prayers—to-wit:

"Now, Susie—think about God."

"Mamma, I can't, with these shoes."

The farm is perfectly delightful, this season. It is as quiet & peaceful as a South-sea island. Some of the sun-sets which we have witnessed from this commanding eminence were marvelous. One evening a rainbow spanned an entire range of hills with its mighty arch, & from a black hub resting upon the hill-top in the exact centre, *black* rays diverged upward in perfect regularity to the rainbow's arch & created a very strongly defined & altogether the most majestic, magnificent, & startling half-sunk wagon wheel you can imagine. After that, a world of tumbling & prodigious clouds came drifting up out of the west & took to themselves a wonderfully rich & brilliant *green* color—the decided green of new spring foliage. Close by them we saw the intense blue of the skies, through rents in the cloud-rack, & away off in another quarter were drifting clouds of a delicate pink color. In one place hung a pall of dense black clouds, like compacted pitch-smoke. And the stupendous wagon wheel was still in the supremacy of its unspeakable grandeur. So you see, the colors present in the sky at one & the same time were blue, green, pink, black, & the vari-colored splendors of the rainbow. All strong & decided colors, too. I don't know whether this weird & astounding spectacle most suggested heaven, or hell. The wonder with its constant, stately, & always surprising changes, lasted upwards of two hours, & we all stood on the top of the hill by my study till the final miracle was complete & the greatest day ended that we ever saw.

Our farmer, who is a grave man, watched that spectacle to the end, & then observed that it was "dam funny." . . .

I . . . began another boy's book—more to be at work than anything else. I have written 400 pages on it—therefore it is very nearly half done. It is Huck Finn's Autobiography. I like it only tolerably well, as far as I have got, & may possibly pigeon-hole or burn the MS when it is done. . . .

To William Dean Howells[9]

London, Sept. 24/[18]96

Dear Howells:

Yes, you two know what we feel—but no others among our friends. They have lost children, but the proportions were not the same.[10] As Mrs. Clemens says, "they have lost a daughter, but they have not lost a Susy Clemens." There was not a detail in Susy's make-up that was commonplace.

To me our loss is bitter, bitter, bitter. Then what must it be to my wife. It would bankrupt the vocabularies of all the languages to put in into words. For the relation between Susy and her mother was not merely & only the relation of mother & child, but that of sweethearts, lovers also. "Do you love me, mamma?" "No, I don't love you, Susy, I worship you."

What a ghastly tragedy it was; how cruel it was; how exactly & precisely it was planned; & how remorselessly every detail of the dispensation was carried out. Susy stood on the platform at Elmira at half past ten on the 14th of July, 1895, in the glare of electric lights, waving her good-byes as our train moved westward on the long trip; & she was brimming with life & the joy of it. That is what I saw; & it was what her mother saw through her tears. One year, one month, & one week later, Livy & Clara had completed the circuit of the globe, arriving at Elmira at the same hour in the evening, and by the same train, & *in the same car*—& Susy was there to meet them—lying white & fair in her coffin in the house she was born in.

They were flying on the wings of steam & in the torture of dread & anxiety; & if three little days could have been spared them out of the rich hoard laid up for the building of the coming ages, poor Susy would have died in her mother's arms—& the poor three days were denied; they could not be afforded.

(Blank to be filled some day)

We send our love to both of you. Mrs. Clemens asks me to thank Mr. Howells for his note, & to say that it was a comfort to her, coming as it did from a heart that had suffered the same bruise as her own.

Good-bye. Will healing ever come, or life have value again?

And shall we see Susy? Without doubt! without *shadow* of doubt, if it can furnish opportunity to break our hearts again.

SL Clemens

To Joseph H. Twichell[11]

Permanent address:
C/o Chatto & Windus
111 T. Martin's Lane, London
Sept. 27, [18]96

Through Livy and Katy I have learned, dear old Joe, how loyally you stood poor Susy's friend, and mine, and Livy's: how you came all the way down, twice, from your summer refuge on your merciful errands to bring the peace and comfort of your beloved presence, first to that poor child, and again to the broken heart of her poor desolate mother. It was like you; like your good great heart, like your matchless and unmatchable self. It was no surprise to me to learn that you stayed by Susy long hours, careless of fatigue and heat, it was no surprise to me to learn that you could still the storms that swept her spirit when no other could; for she loved you, revered you, trusted you, and "Uncle Joe" was no empty phrase upon her lips! I am grateful to you, Joe, grateful to the bottom of my heart, which has always been filled with love for you, and respect and admiration; and I would have chosen you out of all the world to take my place at Susy's side and Livy's in those black hours.

Susy was a rare creature; the rarest that has been reared in Hartford this generation. And Livy knew it, and you knew it, and Charley Warner and George, and Harmony . . . and perhaps others. And I also was of the number, but not in the same degree—for she was above my duller comprehension. I merely knew that she was my superior in fineness of mind, in the delicacy and subtlety of her intellect, but to fully measure her I was not competent. I know her better now; for I have read her private writings and sounded the deeps of her mind; and I know better, now, the treasure that was mine than I knew it when I had it. But I have this consolation: that dull as I was, I always knew enough to be proud that she commended me or my work—as proud as if Livy had done it herself—and I took it as the accolade from the hand of genius. I see now—as Livy always saw—that she had greatness in her; and that she herself was dimly conscious of it.

And now she is dead—and I can never tell her.

God bless you Joe—and all of your house.

S.L.C.

To William Dean Howells[12]

Villa Quarto, Florence, June 6/[19]04

Dear Howells:

Last night at 9:20 I entered Mrs. Clemens's room to say the usual goodnight—& she was dead! tho' no one knew it. She had been cheerfully talking, a moment before. She was sitting up in bed—she had not lain down for months—& Katie & the nurse were supporting her. They supposed she had fainted, & they were holding the oxygen pipe to her mouth, expecting to revive her. I bent over her & looked in her face, & I think I spoke—I was surprised and troubled that she did not notice me. Then we understood, & our hearts broke. How poor we are to-day!

But how thankful I am that her persecutions are ended. I would not call her back if I could.

To-day, treasured in her worn old Testament, I found a dear & gentle letter from you, dated Far Rockaway, Sept. 13, 1896, about our poor Susy's death.[13] I am tired & old; I wish I were with Livy.

I send my love—& hers—and to you all.

SLC

To Clara Clemens Gabrilowitsch[14]

Redding, Conn.,
Dec. 29, [19]09

O, Clara, Clara dear, I am so glad she is out of it and safe—safe! I am not melancholy; I shall never be melancholy again, I think. You see, I was in such distress when I came to realize that you were gone far away and no one stood between her and danger but me—and I could die at any moment, and *then*—oh then what would become of her! For she was willful, you know, and would not have been governable.

You can't imagine what a darling she was, that last two or three days; and how *fine*, and good, and sweet, and noble—and *joyful*, thank Heaven!—and how intellectually brilliant. I never had been acquainted with Jean before. I recognize that.

But I mustn't try to write about her—I *can't*. I have already poured my heart out with the pen, recording that last day or two. I will send you that—and you must let no one but Ossip read it.[15]

Good-bye. I love you so! And Ossip.

Father

Notes

INTRODUCTION

1. For a full picture of Clemens' childhood see Albert Bigelow Paine's *Mark Twain: A Biography*, Dixon Wecter's *Sam Clemens of Hannibal*, and Ron Powers' *Dangerous Water: A Biography of the Boy Who Became Mark Twain*.

2. Perhaps the most interesting source for biographical information on this part of Clemens' life is *Mark Twain's Letters*, vol. 1: *1853–1866*. The literary material that Clemens produced can be found in *Early Tales and Sketches*, vol. 1: *1851–1864* and *Early Tales and Sketches*, vol. 2: *1864–1865*. Clemens' evolution as a writer has been discussed by Henry Nash Smith in *Mark Twain: The Development of a Writer*; DeLancey Ferguson in *Mark Twain: Man and Legend*; William M. Gibson in *The Art of Mark Twain*; Jeffrey Steinbrink in *Getting to Be Mark Twain*; Everett Emerson in *The Authentic Mark Twain: A Literary Biography of Samuel L. Clemens* and *Mark Twain: A Literary Life*; Laura Skandera Trombley in *Mark Twain in the Company of Women*; and Leland Krauth in *Mark Twain & Company: Six Literary Relations*. Clemens' connection to the literary humorists has been traced by Constance Rourke in *American Humor: A Study of the National Character*; Walter Blair in *Native American Humor*; Pascal Covici in *Mark Twain's Humor: The Image of the World*; Kenneth S. Lynn in *Mark Twain and Southwestern Humor*; James Cox in *Mark Twain: The Fate of Humor*; Neil Schmitz in *of Huck and Alice: Humorous Writing in American Literature*; David E. E. Sloane in *Mark Twain as a Literary Comedian*; Don Florence in *Persona and Humor in Mark Twain's Early Writings*; Henry B. Wonham in *Mark Twain and the Art of the Tall Tale*; and by Bruce Michelson in *Mark Twain on the Loose: A Comic Writer and the American Self*. Also helpful is *Mark Twain's Humor: Critical Essays*, edited by David E. E. Sloane.

3. Robert D. Jerome and Herbert A. Wisbey, Jr., offer a look at the Langdon family and at the Clemens family's connection to Elmira in *Mark Twain in Elmira*. Additional material on the Clemenses' home life can be found in Caroline Thomas Harnsberger's *Mark Twain Family Man*; Edith Colgate Salsbury's *Susy and Mark Twain: Family Dialogues*; Susy Clemens' *Papa: An Intimate Biography of Mark Twain*, edited by Charles Neider; Clara Clemens Gabrilowitsch's *My Father Mark Twain*; and *The Love Letters of Mark Twain*, edited by Dixon Wecter.

4. See Kenneth R. Andrews' *Nook Farm: Mark Twain's Hartford Circle* for a description of the neighborhood. Steve Courtney describes the political, cultural, and religious atmosphere in Hartford in *Joseph Hopkins Twichell: The Life and Times of Mark Twain's Closest Friend*. Harold K. Bush also discusses Hartford's influence, and especially Twichell's, in *Mark Twain and the Spiritual Crisis of His Age*.

5. See Charles H. Gold's *"Hatching Ruin" or Mark Twain's Road to Bankruptcy*.

6. Twenty-five installments appeared in the *North American Review*, starting 7 September 1906. The magazine offered readers a variety of literature, politics, culture, and commentary. The issue in which the first installment of "Chapters from My Autobiography" appeared, for example, presented essays on Theodore Roosevelt's right to run for the presidency, on the British in India, on the practice of amassing private fortunes, and on Palestine, railroads, and world politics. Clemens used the same material for a series in the *New York Tribune Sunday Magazine* beginning on 27 October 1907 and running until 27 September 1908. The *Tribune* series mirrors the *North American Review* text, though it reverses the two final chapters.

7. The Mark Twain Papers at the University of California at Berkeley is planning to publish a three-volume edition that will present all of the autobiographical materials. Volume one should be available in 2010, which will mark the centennial of Mark Twain's death. An electronic edition is also planned.

8. For an introduction to the questions involved in the processes of autobiography and biography, see James Olney's collection of essays, *Autobiography: Essays Theoretical and Critical;* Marc Pachter's *Telling Lives: The Biographer's Art;* and Albert Stone's *Autobiographical Occasions and Original Acts*. Other useful sources on the theory and practice of autobiography include Roy Pascal's *Design and Truth in Autobiography;* William Spengemann's *The Forms of Autobiography: Episodes in the History of a Literary Genre;* Robert Sayre's *The Examined Self: Benjamin Franklin, Henry Adams, Henry James;* Janet Varner Gunn's *Autobiography: Towards a Poetics of Experience;* Susanna Egan's *Patterns and Experience in Autobiography;* Avrom Fleishman's *Figures of Autobiography: The Language of Self-Writing;* Paul John Eakin's collection *American Autobiography: Retrospect and Prospect* and his *How Our Lives Become Stories: Making Selves*. For a look at early American autobiography, see Daniel B. Shea's *Spiritual Autobiography in Early America* and Patricia Caldwell's *The Puritan Conversion Narrative: The Beginnings of American Experience*.

9. See Gary Scharnhorst's edited volume *Mark Twain: The Complete Interviews*. Other studies of Clemens' work to tailor his public image include Louis Budd's *Our Mark Twain: The Making of His Public Personality*, which examines the careful nurturing of that public persona. In *At Home Abroad: Mark Twain in Australasia*, Miriam Jones Shillingsburg examines the public relations efforts connected to Clemens' lecture tour of 1895 and 1896.

10. In *Mark Twain: The Fate of Humor*, James M. Cox suggests the "extract" as the most useful form for understanding Clemens' autobiography (304–6).

11. Albert Bigelow Paine published the first section as the preface for his edition of *Mark Twain's Autobiography* (xv–xvi). Sections II and III remain in typescript in the Mark Twain Papers.

12. The daughter-in-law of Henry H. Rogers, Clemens' friend and financial advisor.

13. Clemens used the money to build his home in Redding, Connecticut. That home was designed by John Mead Howells, William Dean Howells' son, and was known as "Autobiography House" for a time and then "Innocence at Home" before it was christened "Stormfield"; royalties from *Captain Stormfield's Visit to Heaven* helped to pay for the loggia wing of the house.

14. See Isabelle Budd, "'Twain's Will Be Done," *Mark Twain Journal* 22 (Spring 1984): 34–39. Also Isabelle Budd, "Clara Samossoud's Will," *Mark Twain Journal* 25 (Spring 1987): 17–29.

15. See *HHT* 2:41–53.

16. See Paul Baender's "Alias Macfarlane: A Revision of Mark Twains Biography," *American Literature* 38 (1966–67): 187–97.

17. The file of "Miscellaneous Autobiographical Manuscripts" also contains "Hunting the Deceitful Turkey" (undated); "The Rhodes Scholar's Club, & Similar Benefactions" (undated); "The Oxford Pageant" (undated); "Bible Teaching and Religious Practice" (1890); and "The Cholera Epidemic in Hamburg" (1892), both of which became part of *Europe and Elsewhere*, and "The Last Napoleon" (1901). There are other autobiographical pieces not linked to the autobiography. One is Clemens' disastrous *Mark Twain's (Burlesque) Autobiography*, which the publishers of *Galaxy* first brought out in 1871. Clemens' embarrassment over that piece was so acute that he destroyed the plates. Another is "Wapping Alice," which was among the autobiographical materials until Clemens changed the narrator and offered it as a short story. See William R. MacNaughton, *Mark Twain's Last Years as a Writer* (94); see also Linda A. Morris, *Gender Play in Mark Twain: Cross-Dressing and Transgression*. John Cooley's collection *How Nancy Jackson Married Kate Wilson and Other Tales of Rebellious Girls & Daring Young Women* is also useful.

18. For example, a nasty description of a countess in Florence excised from the material composed in Florence (MTP, 117–18), a sharp criticism of Jay Gould removed from Clemens' dictation of 16 February 1906, and an energetic damnation of Elisha Bliss cut from Clemens' dictation of 21 February 1906. This process of cleansing can also be seen in Clara's biography of her father, *My Father Mark Twain*.

19. DeLancey Ferguson, "The Uncollected Portions of Mark Twain's Autobiography," *American Literature* 8 (1936): 37–46.

20. Clemens' last years have been examined in detail by Hamlin Hill in *Mark Twain: God's Fool* and William R. MacNaughton in *Mark Twains Last Years as a Writer*. In his section focusing on the autobiography in *The Authentic Mark Twain* (261–71), Everett Emerson points out that dictating "had a significant effect on the remainder of Mark Twain's career: it all but stopped him from writing anything for some time" (266). It does seem that dictating took over Clemens' creative life at a time when he was quite willing to lay the pen aside. This, though, still led to the creative push to complete the collection of the *North American Review* chapters. It is also helpful to examine William M. Gibson's *Mark Twain's Mysterious Stranger Manuscripts*, and John S. Tuckey's *Mark Twain's "Which Was the Dream" and Other Symbolic Writings of the Later Years*. For a close look at the chaotic year of 1908–9, see Laura Skandera Trombley's "Mark Twain's *Annus Horribilis* of 1908–1909," *ALR* 40, no. 2 (Winter 2008): 114–36. For an extended look at Clemens' home and family

life during the final years, see Karen Lystra's *Dangerous Intimacy: The Untold Story of Mark Twain's Final Years.*

21. See *MTLs* vol. 1.

22. See Edgar M. Branch's *Clemens of the "Call": Mark Twain in San Francisco.*

23. See *Mark Twain's Letters from Hawaii*, edited by A. Grove Day.

24. Bernard DeVoto describes the Mississippi Valley during the time immediately before and throughout Clemens' childhood in *Mark Twain's America.*

25. For an extended discussion of Clemens' focus on childhood in his fiction, see Albert E. Stone, Jr.'s *The Innocent Eye: Childhood in Mark Twain's Imagination.*

26. For a discussion of Clemens' dictations see Jennifer L. Zaccara's "Mark Twain, Isabel Lyon, and the 'Talking Cure'" in *Constructing Mark Twain: New Directions in Scholarship* and Michael J. Kiskis' "Dead Man Talking: Mark Twain's Autobiographical Deception." Also useful is Forrest Robinson's discussion of Clemens' autobiography and the autobiographical impulse in the fiction; see *The Author Cat: Clemens's Life in Fiction.*

27. This is treated most starkly in Clemens' "gospel" *What Is Man*, but is also a major theme in *A Connecticut Yankee in King Arthur's Court* and a source for the tension in *Pudd'nhead Wilson.*

28. During the summer of 1885, rumors surfaced regarding Clemens' role in the negotiations between Grant and the publishers of *Century* magazine (*MTA* 1:55–57). One rumor claimed that Clemens gave Jesse Grant, General Grant's son, a partnership in the publishing business as part of the deal to get the contract for the general's memoirs. In fact, stories based on that rumor were published in the *New York World* and the *New York Tribune.* Another report claimed that Grant's book was actually written by General Adam Badeau. That charge was published in a letter to the *New York World* on 29 April 1885. Grant denounced the rumor in a letter to the paper on 2 May 1885.

29. This section is also an example of how Clemens could use his art to escape present conditions. That creative movement is examined by Susan K. Harris in *Mark Twain's Escape from Time: A Study of Patterns and Images.*

30. Hamlin Hill presents an extensive discussion of the Ashcroft-Lyon MS in *Mark Twain: God's Fool.* Also, see Lystra's *Dangerous Intimacies.*

31. See John C. Gerber, "Mark Twain's Use of the Comic Pose," *PMLA* 77 (1962): 297–304. Poses also come into play in Leland Krauth's discussion in *Proper Mark Twain.*

32. See Forrest Robinson's *The Author Cat: Clemens's Life in Fiction* for a discussion of this aspect of bad faith. Also, see Robinson's *In Bad Faith: The Dynamics of Deception in Mark Twain's America* for the initial discussion that serves as the foundation for the position in *The Author Cat.*

33. See the preface to *Mark Twain's Autobiography*, vol. 1.

34. In "Autobiography as Anti-Biography: The Case for Twain vs. Paine," *Auto/Biography Studies* 3, no. 3 (Fall 1987): 13–20, G. Thomas Couser makes a case for a major battle between the two men as Clemens used the dictations and his control over documents to subvert the work of the biographer.

35. It is also taking part in the tradition of the tall tale in American fiction. See

Carolyn S. Brown, *The Tall Tale in American Folklore and Literature*, 108–21. Also, see Henry B. Wonham's *Mark Twain and the Art of the Tall Tale*.

36. Clemens' reliance on the echoes of slave voices is explored by Shelley Fisher Fishkin in *Was Huck Black? Mark Twain and African American Voices*.

37. "The Death of Jean" was originally published in *Harper's Monthly Magazine* in January 1910. Because Clemens considered that it completed his autobiography it has been included as Appendix A in this volume.

38. Two of the more prominent examples are "The Facts Behind the Recent Carnival of Crime in Connecticut," in which Clemens confronts his conscience, and *Adventures of Huckleberry Finn*, in which Huck is constantly plagued by his conscience as he flees St. Petersburg in the company of Jim. The adult narrator of "Carnival of Crime" eventually succeeds at shredding his conscience; Huck, on the other hand, never is able to escape conscience's demands.

39. This was a complicated time that pushed Clemens not only to attempt to find solace from Susy's loss but also to become intimately involved and interested in Austrian politics. See Carl Dolmetch's *"Our Famous Guest": Mark Twain in Vienna*.

40. See *Life on the Mississippi*, chapters XVIII, XIX, XX

41. For a contemporary account of Henry's suffering and death, see Clemens' 18 June 1858 letter to his sister-in-law Mollie (*MTLs* 1:80–85).

42. For a detailed description of Sam's and Orion's relationship, see Philip Ashley Fanning's *Mark Twain and Orion Clemens: Brothers, Partners, Strangers*.

43. For the original passage see "Jane Lampton Clemens" (*HHT*, 50).

44. For a discussion of the collaborative nature of Clemens' process, see Michael J. Kiskis, "Mark Twain and Collaborative Autobiography," *Studies in the Literary Imagination* 29, no. 2 (Fall 1996): 27–40. In the autobiographical dictations during 1907, Clemens turned for inspiration to the journal kept by Ralph Ashcroft during Clemens' trip to Oxford to receive an honorary degree.

45. Sam and Olivia were married on 2 February 1870. The dictation would, then, be from 1 February 1906.

46. See Michael J. Kiskis' "Susy Clemens as the Fire for Mark Twain's Autobiography" *Mid-Hudson Language Studies* 10 (1987): 43–50.

47. See Harold K. Bush, Jr. "'Broken Idols': Mark Twain's Elegies for Susy and a Critique of Freudian Grief Theory," *Nineteenth-Century Literature* 57, no. 2 (Sept. 2002): 237–68.

CHAPTER I

1. This prefatory note appeared at the head of each chapter. It has been deleted from subsequent chapters so that the presentation will not be unduly interrupted. No alterations have been made in the text of the chapters; the typography of the subheads has been slightly modified. The first three chapters were subdivided with roman numerals; after that, the practice was abandoned.

2. Clemens celebrated his arrival at "Pier No. 70" at a dinner given in his honor on 5 December 1905, at Delmonico's in New York City. The dinner was hosted by Colonel George Harvey, publisher of the *North American Review*. The guests—

including more than sixty women, a distinct break with the banquet tradition of the time—heard an array of speakers, and each received a foot-high bust of Mark Twain. William Dean Howells was toastmaster.

3. This introduction is taken from Clemens' dictation of 26 March 1906.

4. William Dean Howells (1837–1920) played a major role in the development of American realism as a writer of essays and novels, as an editor (for *The Atlantic Monthly* from 1871 to 1881), and as a critic (for *Harper's Monthly Magazine* from 1886 to 1892). He first met Clemens in Boston in 1869 in the office of James T. Fields, editor of *The Atlantic Monthly*, soon after Howells' review of Clemens' *The Innocents Abroad* appeared in the magazine.

5. This section is taken from "Ancestors" (1897–98).

6. An account of the Virginia line of Clemens' family can be found in chapter 1 of Albert Bigelow Paine's *Mark Twain: A Biography* and the first three chapters of Dixon Wecter's *Sam Clemens of Hannibal*.

7. Elizabeth I ruled England from 1558 to 1603.

8. Sir Francis Drake (1540?–96) and Sir John Hawkins (1532–95) became famous and infamous privateers during the years of undeclared war between England and Spain prior to the outbreak of formal hostilities in 1588 which resulted in the defeat of the Spanish Armada. Drake is perhaps best known for his circumnavigation of the globe (1577–80).

9. James I, the first Stuart king, ruled England between 1603 and 1625. Charles I ascended the throne in 1625 and ruled until his execution in 1649, which marked the beginning of the Cromwellian protectorate. The protectorate came to an end in 1660 with the restoration of Charles II.

10. Albert Bigelow Paine identifies this ancestor as Gregory Clemens, who was a member of Cromwell's parliament and who signed the death warrant of Charles I. Paine tells us that "afterward he was tried as a regicide, his estates were confiscated, and his head was exposed on a pole on the top of Westminster Hall" (*MTB*, 1).

11. Perhaps Alexander Jaffray, a Scot, who served in the Barbones Parliament and opposed a number of Cromwell's policies. He was later prominent in the radical opposition to Charles II.

12. James II—a Catholic—ascended the throne upon the death of Charles II in 1685 and ruled until 1688, when he was deposed in a bloodless revolution (The Glorious Revolution) which transferred power to William of Orange, the husband of James's Protestant daughter Mary.

13. In "Jane Lampton Clemens" (*HHT*, 43–53) Clemens characterizes his mother as a "Friend of Satan." He describes her asking, "Who prays for Satan? Who, in eighteen centuries, has had the common humanity to pray for the one sinner that needed it most, our one fellow and brother who most needed a friend yet had not a single one, the one sinner among us all who had the highest and clearest *right* to every Christian's daily and nightly prayers for the plain and unassailable reason that his was the first and greatest need, he being among sinners the supremest?" (44–45).

14. William Walter Phelps was United States minister in Berlin when the Clemens family spent the winter of 1891 in that city. The emperor was William II of Germany.

15. Jeremiah Clemens (1814–65), Clemens' third cousin, served as Democratic senator from Alabama between 1849 and 1853. He authored several historical romances and spent time as a newspaper editor.

16. Sherrard Clemens (1820–80), Clemens' third cousin, served as a Democratic congressman from Virginia during 1852–53 and again during 1857–61.

17. James Clemens, Jr. (1791–1878), of St. Louis was a distant cousin. In 1855, Orion Clemens sent his younger brother to James Clemens, Jr., with a letter of introduction, hoping James would be able to help Sam become a cub pilot on the Mississippi. Illness apparently prevented James Clemens from helping (*N&J* 1:36).

18. Senator Joseph R. Hawley (1826–1905) rose to the rank of brevet major general in the Civil War, was a governor of Connecticut, served as president of the United States Centennial Commission, and was a neighbor of Clemens in Hartford. He edited the Hartford *Courant* with Charles Dudley Warner.

19. A more complete description of Jane Lampton's family can be found in chapter 1 of Albert Bigelow Paine's *Mark Twain: A Biography* and chapter 2 of Dixon Wecter's *Sam Clemens of Hannibal*.

20. It is likely that Jane married John Marshall on the rebound after a failed relationship. This might be one reason for the reported coolness between the pair. For a description of the marriage, see Ron Powers' *Mark Twain: A Life* (16–44).

21. Samuel Clemens was the sixth child of John Marshall and Jane Clemens. There were seven children in all: Orion (1825–97), Pamela Ann (1827–1904), Pleasant Hannibal (1828 or 1829; lived three months), Margaret (1830–39), Benjamin (1832–42), Samuel Langhorne (1835–1910), and Henry (1838–58). Samuel and Henry were born in Florida, Missouri.

22. *The Gilded Age: A Tale of Today* (1873) introduced the character Colonel Beriah Sellers, Clemens' quintessential optimist, and offered a hard look at the problems caused by speculation in the post–Civil War West.

23. John Marshall Clemens died on 24 March 1847 after a brief bout with pneumonia.

24. John T. Raymond (John O'Brien, 1836–87) was a well-known and successful comic actor. He portrayed Colonel Sellers in Clemens' play *Colonel Sellers: A Drama in Five Acts*, which was loosely based on *The Gilded Age* and which opened in New York's Park Theater on 16 September 1874. In 1884 Clemens tried to enlist Raymond in a production of *Colonel Sellers as a Scientist*, a collaboration between Clemens and William Dean Howells. Raymond was not satisfied with the script and did not take on the project.

25. Frank Mayo gained a reputation from his portrayal of Davy Crockett. His dramatization of *Pudd'nhead Wilson* opened in Hartford on 8 April 1895 and in New York on April 15. After he returned from Europe Clemens attended a performance at which he gave a brief speech praising Mayo's work (*Mark Twain Speaking*, 276–77).

26. Charles Dudley Warner (1829–1900) was Clemens' neighbor in Hartford and editor of the Hartford *Courant*.

27. The American Publishing Company of Hartford published seven of Clemens' books: *The Innocents Abroad* (1869), *Roughing It* (1872), *The Gilded Age* (1873),

Sketches New and Old (1875), *Tom Sawyer* (1876), *A Tramp Abroad* (1880), and *Following the Equator* (1897).

28. George Washington Cable (1844–1925) published stories and novels important in southern local-color literature. During 1884 and 1885 Cable and Clemens joined for a fifteen-week reading tour which took them to seventy cities—including Rochester, New York, where Cable introduced Clemens to Malory's *Morte d'Arthur.*

CHAPTER II

1. Charles H. Webb was founder and editor of the *Californian,* the literary journal to which Clemens contributed while in San Francisco during 1864 and 1865.

2. "Jim Smiley and His Jumping Frog" was first published in the New York *Saturday Press* of 18 November 1865.

3. Artemus Ward (Charles Farrar Browne, 1834–67) was a popular American humorist and editor of *Vanity Fair,* a New York humor magazine. During his lecture tour on the Pacific Coast during 1863 and 1864, he spent about ten days in Virginia City, Nevada. Clemens was then a reporter for the Virginia City *Enterprise.*

4. Henry Clapp was publisher of the *Saturday Press.* Clapp published both Clemens' "Jim Smiley and His Jumping Frog" and Walt Whitman's "O Captain! My Captain!" just two weeks before the *Press* ceased operations in 1865.

5. *The Celebrated Jumping Frog of Calaveras County and Other Sketches* was offered to the public on 25 April 1867. The cost was $1. 50.

6. The *Quaker City,* a side-wheel steamer, sailed on 8 June and returned to New York on 19 November 1867. The excursion was a precursor to today's luxury cruise, with an ambitious itinerary (it navigated the Mediterranean with an extended stay in the Holy Land) and a prohibitive cost ($1,250). The *Alta California* paid Clemens' way in exchange for letters describing the journey.

7. Elisha Bliss (1822–80) was president of the American Publishing Company, which dealt exclusively in subscription publishing. He directed the company from 1869 until his death.

8. Albert Dean Richardson was one of Bliss' more popular writers. Subscription sales of two of Richardson's books, *The Secret Service* (1865) and *Beyond the Mississippi* (1866), totaled nearly 200,000 copies during a six-year period.

9. Possibly Sidney Drake.

10. There may have been a telegram. There is a letter to Bliss from Clemens dated 22 July 1869 which mentions Clemens' hurt at being treated badly by the repeated delays and asks if Bliss will take responsibility if sales are affected by them. The letter mentions no twenty-four-hour deadline, no threat of a suit (*Mark Twain's Letters to His Publishers,* 22–24).

11. By the end of the first year, 67,000 copies of *The Innocents Abroad* had been sold (at a price of $3.50 each); 85,000 copies were sold within sixteen months; and 100,000 copies were sold in two years.

12. This section combines "Playing 'Bear'" and "Herrings" (1897–98).

13. The world tour began on 14 July 1895 when Clemens left Elmira accompanied by Olivia and Clara. Susy and Jean remained in the United States. The tour ended

when the Clemenses reached England 31 July 1896. Eighteen days later, Clemens received word that Susy had died from Spinal Meningitis.

14. This section is one of the reminiscences Clemens composed in Florence, Italy, in 1904. Others focused on John Hay and Henry H. Rogers.

15. Robert Louis Stevenson (1850–94) is best known for three novels: *Kidnapped* (1886), *Dr. Jekyll and Mr. Hyde* (1886), and *Treasure Island* (1883).

16. Bret Harte (1836–1902) became an immediate success with the publication of "The Luck of Roaring Camp" in 1870. As editor of the *Californian*, he accepted a number of Clemens' contributions, which marked the beginning of a long and eventually stormy relationship. In 1876, Clemens collaborated with Harte on a play, *Ah Sin*, which opened in New York on 31 July 1877. It closed soon afterwards (*MTB*, 587–90). Their relationship deteriorated in the years that followed, and Clemens developed a strong and active dislike for Harte (*Mark Twain in Eruption*, 254–92). For more on the relationship between Harte and Clemens, see Margaret Duckett's *Mark Twain & Bret Harte*, Axel Nissen's *Bret Harte: Prince and Pauper*, and Gary Scharnhorst's *Bret Harte: Opening the American Literary West*.

17. Thomas Bailey Aldrich (1836–1907) and Clemens first corresponded in 1871 when Aldrich, then editor of *Every Saturday*, criticized a poem which appeared in the Buffalo *Express* and mistakenly identified Clemens as its author. Clemens wrote Aldrich to correct that error (*MTL* 1:181–82; also Clemens' January 28 letter, *MTL* 1:182–84). Aldrich's novel *The Story of a Bad Boy* (1869) probably had an influence on Clemens' *The Adventures of Tom Sawyer* (1876).

18. Thomas Nast (1840–1902) created the donkey, the elephant, and the tiger as symbols for the Democratic Party, the Republican Party, and New York City's Tammany Hall, respectively.

19. Ulysses S. Grant (1822–85). Clemens' Charles L. Webster & Co. published Grant's memoirs in two volumes during 1885 and 1886. More than 300,000 sets were sold, and over $400,000 was paid to Grant's family (*MTB*, 799–816).

CHAPTER III

1. This section is taken from Clemens' dictation of 1 February 1906.

2. The Clemenses were married in the Langdon home in Elmira, New York, on 2 February 1870.

3. Olivia Clemens died in Florence, Italy, on 5 June 1904. Her last long bout with illness actually began in August 1902 while the Clemenses were spending time at York Harbor, Maine. She was buried in Woodlawn Cemetery in Elmira on 14 July 1904.

4. Charles Jervis Langdon (1849–1916) was the Langdons' youngest child.

5. Clemens was introduced to Olivia Langdon in New York City on 27 December 1867. On New Year's Eve, he accompanied the Langdons to Charles Dickens' public reading in Steinway Hall.

6. This refers to the death of John Marshall Clemens and his single kiss for his daughter Pamela when he was on his deathbed. The scene appears in chapter 14 of *Mark Twain: A Biography*, 72–73.

7. The Reverend Thomas K. Beecher, the younger brother of Henry Ward

Beecher and pastor of the Park Congregational Church in Elmira, conducted the ceremony with the Reverend Joseph Twichell of Hartford, with whom Clemens had already formed a friendship during his trips to discuss arrangements for publication of *The Innocents Abroad.*

8. Before his marriage, Clemens considered investing in a number of newspapers: the Cleveland *Herald,* New York *Tribune,* Toledo *Blade,* and Hartford *Courant.* When a deal with the *Herald* collapsed, Jervis Langdon offered to lend Clemens $25,000 to buy a one-third interest in the Buffalo *Express.* Clemens took ownership on 14 August 1869.

9. Jervis Langdon (1809–70) made his fortune in coal and lumber. He settled in Elmira in 1845; he was a founder of Park Church, which began as an antislavery church, and worked for the underground railroad.

10. Patrick McAleer (1846–1906) worked for Clemens from 1870 to 1891, when the family left for Europe, and then again in the summer of 1905, in Dublin, New Hampshire.

11. Langdon Clemens (1870–72) was born prematurely and lived only eighteen months. Never a strong child, he contracted diphtheria and died on 2 June 1872. He was buried in Woodlawn Cemetery, Elmira.

12. Olivia Susan Clemens (1872–96), the Clemenses' second child, was known to her family as Susy. She was buried in Woodlawn Cemetery in Elmira on 23 August 1896.

13. Jane Lampton Clemens (1880–1909), the Clemenses' youngest child, was always known as Jean. Jean suffered from epilepsy and spent much of her adult life shuttling in and out of various sanitariums. She died on 24 December 1909 in the house Clemens built in Redding, Connecticut ("Stormfield"). She was buried in Woodlawn Cemetery in Elmira on 26 December 1909.

14. Katy Leary (1856–1934), an Elmira girl, joined the Clemens household in October 1880 as a maid for Olivia Clemens and spent thirty years in the family's employ.

15. John O'Neill was Clemens' gardener in Hartford. He and his wife took charge of the Hartford home when the Clemenses moved to Europe in 1891.

16. Clara Clemens (1874–1962), Clemens' second daughter, was the only family member to survive Clemens. She married Ossip Gabrilowitsch, an accomplished pianist and orchestra conductor, at Stormfield in October 1909, and they had one daughter—Nina Gabrilowitsch—who was born in August 1910, too late for Clemens to see his only grandchild. After Gabrilowitsch died in 1936, Clara married Jacques Alexander Samossoud (1894–1966). Nina died in 1966. She, her mother, and her father are buried in Woodlawn Cemetery in Elmira.

17. They had left Elmira on 14 July 1895.

18. This section is from Clemens' dictation of 2 February 1906.

19. Olivia and Clara were met by the Reverend Joseph Twichell and Dr. Clarence C. Rice.

20. The Reverend Joseph Twichell (1838–1918) was pastor of the Asylum Hill Congregational Church in Hartford—Clemens dubbed it the "Church of the Holy Speculators." He and Clemens met in 1869. Twichell accompanied Clemens on a walking tour of Europe during 1878 to help him gather material for *A Tramp Abroad*

(1880). He later presided at Clara Clemens' wedding and at the funerals of Olivia Clemens and Samuel Clemens. Steve Courtney's *Joseph Hopkins Twichell: The Life and Times of Mark Twain's Closest Friend* describes the long friendship.

21. Theodore W. Crane (1831–89) and Susan Langdon Crane (1836–1924). Susan Crane was Olivia Clemens' sister.

22. In her fever, Susy Clemens scratched out a few pages of notes, about 1,000 words, which reveal the extent of her delusions. Charles Neider has published those notes in his introduction to *Papa: An Intimate Biography of Mark Twain*, 43–51.

23. Quarry Farm is located about two miles from the center of Elmira. Jervis Langdon originally purchased the small farmhouse in 1869; Susan Langdon Crane took possession after his death in 1870. It was placed on the National Register of Historic Places in 1975. Jervis Langdon, Jr., presented the house to Elmira College, and it now serves as the site of the Center for Mark Twain Studies at Quarry Farm.

24. Lilly G. Foote (1860–1932) joined Clemens' Hartford household in 1880.

25. The manuscript is "A Record of the Small Foolishnesses of Susie and 'Bay' Clemens (Infants)." It is housed at the University of Virginia.

26. This section is taken from Clemens' dictation of 5 February 1906.

27. Genesis 37:1–36.

28. Solomon (ca. 970–931 B.C.) ascended to the throne of the Israelites after David. His reign lasted forty years; he oversaw the building of the temple in Jerusalem. His story is told in I Kings 1–11.

CHAPTER IV

1. This section is taken from Clemens' dictation of 7 February 1906.

2. Clemens often returned to this idea, most often in a political context; for example, see "Corn Pone Opinions" and "As Regards Patriotism" (*CTSSE* 2:507–11; 476–78).

3. Clemens wrote chapters 1 through 11, as well as chapters 24, 25, 27, 28, 30, 32, 33, 34, 36, 37, 42, 43, 45, 51, 52, 53, 57, 59, 60, 61, 62, and portions of chapters 35, 49, and 56. Charles Dudley Warner wrote chapters 12 to 23, 26, 29, 31, 38, 39, 40, 41, 44, 46, 47, 48, 50, 54, 55, 58, 63, and portions of chapters 35, 49, and 56.

4. Like Artemus Ward and Josh Billings, Petroleum V. Nasby (David Ross Locke, 1833–88) based his humor on conflicts between the pretentious and the common. His verbal humor is characterized by incongruous spellings, inappropriate and erratic grammar, and malapropisms, all of which give the presentation a local, vernacular sound. He met Clemens in 1869 when they both employed James Redpath of Boston as a lecture agent.

5. This section is taken from Clemens' dictation of 8 February 1906.

6. Elihu Vedder (1836–1923) was an American painter and illustrator.

7. Ralph W. Ashcroft was hired by Clemens to act as secretary for the 1907 trip to Oxford, England. He later became Clemens' business manager and was given power of attorney in 1908. Ashcroft and Isabel Lyon—Clemens' secretary—were married in early 1909. The Ashcrofts resigned from Clemens' service in mid-1909 after a raucous series of suits and countersuits was filed over control of Clemens' affairs.

8. The suit was over control of the financial affairs of the American Plasmon Company.

9. Franklin G. Whitmore (1846–1926) was Clemens' business agent during the 1880s.

10. Clemens used the tale for "The McWilliamses and the Burglar Alarm" (*CTSSE* 1:837–43).

CHAPTER V

1. This section is taken from Clemens' dictation of 9 February 1906.

2. George Griffin (d. 1897) was the Clemenses' black servant. He worked for the family from 1875 to 1891, when they closed the Hartford house and moved to Europe.

3. *The Prince and the Pauper* (1881) was published by James R. Osgood of Boston.

4. *Adventures of Huckleberry Finn* (1885) was published by Charles L. Webster & Co., Clemens' own publishing firm, which began operation in early 1884 and closed with Clemens' bankruptcy in 1894. For a detailed look at Clemens' business affairs and his relationship with Charlie Webster, see Charles H. Gold's *"Hatching Ruin" or Mark Twain's Road to Bankruptcy.*

5. F.F.V.—First Families of Virginia.

6. Sherrard Clemens was the congressman from Virginia who fought that duel. O. Jennings Wise was one of the editors of the Richmond *Enquirer* and had accused Clemens of political trickery. Wise wounded Clemens in the thigh.

7. In 1879, Clemens proposed that a monument to Adam be erected in Elmira, New York. Clemens created the Adam Monument Association of Elmira and distributed a petition to present to Congress. Ninety-four of Elmira's citizens—as well as the governor of New York, Lucius D. Robinson—signed the petition. The project was halted when Joseph Hawley, then a member of Congress, decided not to present the petition to the House of Representatives. The text of the petition and the identification of the signatories can be found in *Mark Twain in Elmira*, 83–91.

8. This section is taken from Clemens' dictation of 12 February 1906.

9. *The Adventures of Tom Sawyer* (1876) was published by the American Publishing Company of Hartford.

10. That pledge was actually taken before Clemens left Hannibal for the East in June 1853 (*MTB*, 93). During that journey, Clemens supported himself by working as a journeyman printer in New York and Philadelphia; he may have returned home as early as April 1854.

CHAPTER VI

1. This section is taken from Clemens' dictation of 26 February 1906.

2. Vassar College is located in Poughkeepsie, New York.

3. Clara Spaulding (1849–1935) was a friend of Olivia Clemens. She accompanied the Clemenses on a number of their family trips abroad and was a frequent guest and companion in Hartford.

4. Colonel Frederick Grant (1850–1912), son of Ulysses S. Grant, served as commissioner of police of New York City from 1895 to 1897 and held military posts from Georgia to the Philippines.

5. Charles L. Webster (1851–91) was Clemens' business manager. In 1884 Clemens named him head of his publishing firm—Charles L. Webster & Co.—which was based in New York. That company published *Huckleberry Finn, A Connecticut Yankee in King Arthur's Court,* and *Tom Sawyer Abroad.* It also published Ulysses S. Grant's *Memoirs.*

6. James B. Pond (1838–1903) was the manager of the 1884–85 lecture tour by Clemens and G. W. Cable. He also managed Clemens' world tour of 1895 and 1896.

7. Clemens may have become interested in dictating at least in part because of Grant's success—Grant dictated a good deal of his *Memoirs.* The Grant dictations figure prominently as the longest section of autobiography Clemens composed prior to the later dictations of 1906 to 1909.

8. General Robert E. Lee surrendered to General Ulysses S. Grant on 9 April 1865. The signing took place in the McLean house in Appomattox, Virginia.

9. General William T. Sherman began his drive to Atlanta on 5 May 1864. Jumping off from Chattanooga, he took Atlanta on 1 September 1864. The march to the sea began from Atlanta on October 17. Sherman's troops cut a sixty-mile-wide swath and destroyed whatever could be used to support the Confederate armies. The Union forces reached the coast near Savannah on December 10 and took the city before Christmas.

10. General John Bell Hood (1831–79) of the Confederate army was involved in the campaigns at Antietam, Gettysburg, Chickamauga, and Atlanta. His forces were defeated at Nashville in December 1864, and he was removed from command. His career later focused on assignments in Texas and New Orleans.

11. Clemens expressed this sentiment in the days immediately following Susy's death. As he would after Jean's death, he kept a running commentary of his feelings over the days following the news. See his 19 August 1896 letter to Livy (*Love Letters of Mark Twain,* 320–23).

12. This section is taken from Clemens' dictation of 7 March 1906.

13. John Hay (1838–1905) was assistant private secretary to Abraham Lincoln between 1861 and 1865. He also served as the secretary to the United States legation in Paris (1865–67), worked for the New York *Tribune,* and became assistant secretary of state in 1878. In 1897 President McKinley appointed him ambassador to Great Britain; in 1898 he became secretary of state, a post he held until 1905. He was responsible for the Open Door Policy in China and negotiated a treaty which gave the United States control of the territory where the Panama Canal was later built.

14. *Liebes Geschenk on die mamma.*—Dear treasure, mama.

15. *O heilige maria Mutter Jesus!*—Oh holy Mary mother of Jesus!

16. *Ach Gott!*—Oh God!

17. *Gott sei Dank ich bin fertig mit'm Gott verdammtes Haar!*—Thank God I am finished with this God-damned hair!

18. This section is taken from Clemens' dictation of 22 March 1906.

19. Emma Nye was a friend of Olivia Clemens. She stayed with the Clemenses in

Buffalo during the fall of 1870 on her way from North Carolina to a teaching position in Detroit. While a guest she contracted typhoid fever and died on September 29 in the Clemens home.

20. Clemens does not come back to Langdon's death again; in fact, he rarely mentioned Langdon's death in his correspondence in the months after the child's death. For an account of the days surrounding Langdon's death see *MTLs* 5:97–101. Also in the same volume, see Clemens' letters to Louise Chandler Moulton (18 June 1872, 108–109); Mary Mason Fairbanks (11 August 1872, 146–47); and Will Bowen (17 January 1873, 273–74).

21. The men Susy mentions were all prominent in British literary, social, and political circles: Dr. John Brown (1810–82) was a prominent physician and essayist. Sir Henry Morton Stanley (1841–1910), a journalist and explorer, is best remembered for his 1871 search for and rescue of David Livingstone (1813–73), an explorer of the African continent. Sir Thomas Hardy (1840–1928), novelist and poet, is best known for his novels *Tess of the D'Urbervilles* (1891) and *Jude the Obscure* (1895). Viscount Horatio Nelson (1758–1805) was victor of the Battle of Trafalgar, a defeat for Napoleon's navy which assured that France would not mount an attack across the English Channel. Sir Henry Irving (1838–1905) was a successful actor known for his productions of Shakespeare's works. His management of the Lyceum theater between 1878 and 1902 effectively revived public interest in Shakespeare. Robert Browning (1812–89) is known for his use of dramatic monologue in poetry. His best-known collections of poetry are *Men and Women* (1864), *Dramatis Personae* (1864), and the major epic, *The Ring and the Book* (1868–69). He married Elizabeth Barrett in 1846. Sir Charles Wentworth Dilke (1843–1911) was a radical statesman and member of Parliament. Charles Reade (1814–84) had careers as both theater manager and reformer/novelist. He is chiefly remembered for *The Cloister and the Hearth* (1861), which dealt with abusive practices in lunatic asylums, and *Griffith Gaunt* (1866), which sparked a series of legal battles because of its frank and open attitude towards sexuality. William Black (1841–98) was a well-known and prolific Scottish novelist. (Richard) Monckton Milnes—Baron Houghton (1809–85)—a reformist politician well known in literary circles, worked to improve the British copyright laws and wrote and published poetry, sociological treatises, and biography—*Life and Letters of John Keats* (1848) is among his best known. Francis Trevelyan Buckland (1826–80) was a surgeon as well as a writer. He published a number of natural history texts. Thomas Hughes (1822–96), a liberal politician, was active on behalf of educating the working man and of the cooperative movements. He advocated "muscular christianity," which touted physical courage, self-reliance, love of sport, school loyalty, and patriotism. Anthony Trollope (1815–82), who started his literary career late in life after serving in Egypt, West Indies, and the United States as an official of the British Post Office, is known for his "Barsetshire" series of novels, which includes *Barchester Towers* (1857), and his "Palliser" novels, which include *Phineas Finn* (1869) and *The Prime Minister* (1876). Thomas Hood the Younger (1835–74) founded *Tom Hood's Comic Annual* in 1867. He was a novelist and humorist and wrote and illustrated a number of children's books. Dr. George MacDonald (1824–1905) is known for his children's stories, such as *At the Back of the North Wind* (1871),

and his adult fantasies, *Phantasies* (1858) and *Lilith* (1895). William Harrison Ains-worth's (1805–82) thirty-nine novels are predominantly tales of swashbucklers and highwaymen.

22. Charles Lutwidge Dodgson (1832–1898) is most famous for *Alice's Adventures in Wonderland* (1865) and *The Hunting of the Snark* (1876). Dodgson was a lecturer in mathematics at Christ Church, Oxford: he was also an accomplished amateur photographer.

23. Joel Chandler Harris (1848–1908) used the persona of the former slave "Uncle Remus" to offer a variety of sketches to his newspaper readers. The tales brought Harris a national audience, and he introduced that audience to the complexities of the black dialect and folklore. Five collections of the Uncle Remus sketches were published.

24. George W. Smalley.

25. Herbert Spencer (1820–1903) worked as a civil engineer and later turned to philosophy. Inspired by Darwin, he developed an idea for the unification of all knowledge based on the principles of evolution. In *Education, Intellectual, Moral and Physical* (1861) he urged that more science and social science studies be taught.

26. Sir Arthur Helps (1813–75) served in a variety of posts, including secretary to the Chancellor of the Exchequer and clerk of the Privy Council. He also authored several volumes of history and politics and a few novels.

27. Francis Wemyss Charteris Douglas (1818–1914) founded the volunteer movement. As Lord Elcho he served as Lord of the Treasury from 1852 to 1855.

CHAPTER VII

1. This section is taken from Clemens' dictation of 5 March 1906.

2. On 17 and 19 March 1888, Clemens took part in a series of public readings in Washington in support of the American Copyright League. The reception was held on March 19.

3. Grover Cleveland was elected president in 1884. His honesty shook his supporters during the campaign when he admitted the possibility that he had fathered an illegitimate son. He ran again on the Democratic ticket in 1888, but lost to Benjamin Harrison. In 1892 he was elected to a second term as president.

4. Cleveland was a bachelor when he took office on 5 March 1885. He married Frances Folsom in June 1886.

5. Ruth Cleveland, the president's daughter.

6. This section is taken from Clemens' dictation of 6 March 1906.

7. The mugwumps were originally a group of disaffected Republicans who bolted the party when James G. Blaine was picked as the Republican nominee for president in 1884. The name was initially a pejorative title.

8. This section is taken from Clemens' dictation of 23 March 1906.

9. Harriet Beecher Stowe (1811–96) is perhaps best known for the antislavery novel *Uncle Tom's Cabin* (1852). She was, however, an amazingly dedicated and prolific writer whose books covered a range of subjects from slavery to New England life and theological disputes. Her better known works are *Dred: A Tale of the Great*

Dismal Swamps (1856), *The Minister's Wooing* (1859), *Pearl of Orr's Island* (1862), and *Old Town Folks* (1869). Her last years, unfortunately, were marred by senility.

10. Calvin Stowe was a professor of Biblical literature. When he retired from teaching in 1864, the Stowes moved to Hartford, Connecticut, where Harriet had spent her youth.

11. Charles Stowe, one of the Stowes' seven children, became a Congregational minister and settled in Hartford in a parsonage paid for by his mother.

CHAPTER VIII

1. This section is taken from Clemens' dictation of 19 January 1906.

2. Clemens joined the paper in August 1862. Joe Goodman was co-owner and publisher of the paper, the *Territorial Enterprise*. William H. Barstow also showed an interest in Clemens because of the series of "Josh" letters Clemens wrote for the paper (none of those letters has survived). Barstow was interested in reprinting Clemens' letters that had appeared in the Keokuk *Gate City*.

3. Rollin M. Daggett (1831–1901) had a varied and active career as a journalist (he founded the San Francisco *Golden Era* in 1852 and the *Evening Mirror* in 1860), the owner of a brokerage house in Virginia City, and later as a reporter and editor for the *Territorial Enterprise*.

4. The Virginia City *Union* started in 1862 when the paper was transplanted to Virginia City from Carson City.

5. Thomas Fitch (1838–1923) was a newspaper editor in Milwaukee and in California and served as a lawyer and state assemblyman in California before settling in Virginia City. In 1863 he became an editor for the Virginia City *Union;* he also served a term as a Republican congressman from Nevada.

6. That encounter took place in California on 28 September 1863. Clemens reported on an earlier aborted duel in the *Territorial Enterprise* for 2 August 1863 ("A Duel Prevented," *Early Tales and Sketches* 1:262–66).

7. William Walker conducted a series of military expeditions into Mexico and Nicaragua during the mid-1850s and planned to establish a Central American federation. Walker seized control of Nicaragua in 1856 and declared himself president. He was overthrown in 1857 but made a number of attempts to return. He was executed by firing squad in Honduras in 1866.

8. The father was Angus Gillis (1800–1870).

9. Stephen E. Gillis (1838–1918) was the Virginia City *Territorial Enterprise*'s foreman when Clemens started to work for the paper in 1862. George Gillis is perhaps William Gillis (1840–1929). He and James Gillis (1830–1907) set up a homestead in Angels Camp, California, where Clemens stayed during January and February of 1865.

10. Robert Muir Howland (1838–90) was superintendent of several mines in the territory and was co-owner of the Pride of Esmeralda Gold and Silver Mining Company and the Miners' Foundry. He was also marshal of Aurora and warden of the territorial prison in Carson City. In 1883 he was appointed United States deputy marshal for California.

11. James L. Laird was a partner in John Church and Co., publishers of the *Virginia City Union*. The exchange between Laird and Clemens can be found in *MTLs* 1:290–96.

12. The law had been in effect since November 1861; potential duelists sought to avoid the law by crossing into California.

13. Perhaps John W. North (1815–90), who served as an associate justice of the territorial supreme court from 1862 to 1864.

14. The exchange of letters and challenges between Laird and Clemens took place between 21 and 24 May 1864. Clemens left for California on May 29.

15. William A. Cutler was the husband of Ellen Cutler, the president of the Sanitary Ball committee. A challenge did pass between the two men. Clemens had insulted the ladies on the committee by publishing a scathing article in the May 24 edition of the *Territorial Enterprise* which suggested that monies raised by the charity were to be diverted to a miscegenation society in the East. Though Clemens apologized both publicly and privately, the story certainly hastened his departure from Virginia City. In a letter to his sister Mollie dated 20 May 1864, Clemens writes that the offending comments were merely a joke undertaken "in drunken jest and no harm was meant by them" (*MTLs* 1:287).

CHAPTER IX

1. Individual dictations are now identified with specific dates; however, this can be deceiving. In *Mark Twain in Eruption*, Bernard DeVoto comments on this first entry: "The *Autobiography* has no entry under this date. All but the first three paragraphs of this section were written about a year earlier, under the title 'Comment on Mr. Root's Utterances.' Mark Twain apparently decided to insert the passage in the *Autobiography* when he published portions in the *North American Review*, where, with the introductory two paragraphs and the date as given, it appears in the issue of January 4, 1907" (61).

2. Elihu Root served as a United States senator from Washington State, was secretary of war under President McKinley, and held that same position under Theodore Roosevelt for a time. He split from Roosevelt during the 1912 presidential campaign.

3. Ship-money was a tax levied on English ports, maritime towns, cities, and counties during war in order to finance the king's fleet. An ancient tax, it was reinstituted by Charles I and extended to the inland counties. The tax was abolished in 1640.

4. Urban E. Hicks, whom Clemens mentions in "Villagers of 1840–3," "Saw Jenny Lind. Went to Oregon; served in Indian War" (*HHT*, 33).

5. Dr. Humphrey Peake, "Dr. Peake" in "Villagers of 1840–3" (*HHT*, 28).

6. Clemens made his final visit to Hannibal in 1902 on his way to receive an honorary LL.D. from the University of Missouri (chapter 221 of *Mark Twain: A Biography*). The discrepancy "I saw it a year ago . . ." suggests that this section was composed in 1903 rather than in 1906.

7. Dr. Orville Grant also treated the murdered "Uncle Sam" Smarr—the killing formed the basis for Boggs' murder in *Huckleberry Finn*, 210–18.

8. Thomas Carlyle (1795–1881), author of *Sartor Resartus* (1833), *The French Revolution* (1837), and *Past and Present* (1843). Some of Clemens' later comments about the conflict between public acts and private thought in biography and autobiography seem intimately connected with Carlyle's "clothes" philosophy in *Sartor Resartus*.

CHAPTER X

1. Orion was the oldest child of John Marshall and Jane Clemens. Pamela Clemens Moffett died in Greenwich, Connecticut. Samuel E. Moffett (1860–1908) influenced the impression the world would have of his uncle when, as an editorial writer for the San Francisco *Examiner,* he declared that in his uncle's bankruptcy, "honor knows no statute of limitations." He also prepared a biographical sketch which appeared as part of the "Autograph Edition" of the writings of Mark Twain (1899 and 1900). Moffett drowned in the surf off the New Jersey shore in August 1908.

2. Abraham Lincoln (1809–65) held office from 1860 until his assassination in 1865. Edward Bates (1793–1869) was Lincoln's attorney general. It was Bates who helped secure Orion's appointment as secretary of the Nevada Territory.

3. The Whig party, formed in 1834, combined the National Republicans with other groups opposed to the Democrats. It was succeeded in 1856 by the Republican party. The Democratic party was first known as the Anti-Federal (and later as the Democratic-Republican) party. Its original philosophy favored a strict interpretation of the Constitution and little interference with individual liberties.

4. The family's physician was Dr. Hugh Meredith. He had moved to Florida, Missouri, at the same time as the Clemenses and later followed them to Hannibal. He is mentioned in "Villagers of 1840–3" (*HHT,* 28).

5. This section is taken from Clemens' dictation of 29 March 1906.

6. In fact, Clemens was not taken out of school immediately. In *Sam Clemens of Hannibal,* Dixon Wecter points out that the *Courier* was not established in Hannibal until 1848. Clemens may have mixed memories: the delivery of "extras" for the *Gazette* which heralded the 1847 Battle of Chapultepec in the Mexican War and his later apprenticeship to Joseph P. Ament (*SCH,* 122–23; 200–202).

7. This apprentice is Wales McCormick. Ralph, whom Clemens mentions, appears to have left little but his name behind.

8. The journeyman was Pet McMurray.

9. Joseph P. Ament married Sarah J. Ruff on 12 April 1849, only a year after moving to Hannibal.

CHAPTER XI

1. This section is taken from Clemens' dictation of 29 March 1906.

2. Orion Clemens began publishing the Hannibal *Western Union* in January 1851; he revived the Hannibal *Journal* a few months after that.

3. Orion sold the *Journal* on 22 September 1853. He entered into an agreement with John Mahin to edit the Muscatine *Journal* and published his first issue on 30 September 1853.

4. Orion married Mary Eleanor Stotts of Keokuk on 19 December 1854.

5. The couple moved to Keokuk on 6 June 1855; Orion sold his share in the Muscatine *Journal* to James W. Logan. On June 11 Orion opened shop as the owner of the Benjamin Franklin Book and Job Office.

6. Clemens began this journey in August 1853; he arrived in New York on August 24.

7. John A. Gray's printing house was at 95–97 Cliff Street. Clemens boarded on Duane Street, some ten blocks from Gray's establishment. His letters back home can be found in *MTLs* 1:3–18.

8. Clemens stayed in New York until October 1853. While in Philadelphia, Clemens worked for the *Pennsylvania Inquirer and National Gazette* and the Philadelphia *Public Ledger.* As a "sub" he was paid on a piecework basis.

9. The trip to Washington during February 1854 may have lasted no more than a weekend. Clemens returned to Philadelphia and then moved on to New York, where the possibilities for employment were severely limited because fires had destroyed Harper and Brothers and George F. Cooledge and Brothers publishing houses in December 1853. It is possible that Clemens returned west as early as April 1854.

10. Richard Higham was an apprentice printer in Orion's shop in 1856. He was killed at Fort Donelson on 15 February 1862.

11. T. Wrightson and Company was one of Cincinnati's leading printing houses. Clemens made this trip in October 1856, not in midwinter as is suggested in the description above. The trip to Cincinnati is presented in chapter 5 of *Life on the Mississippi.*

12. There were two volumes of *Exploration of the Valley of the Amazon, Made Under Direction of the Navy Department (1853–54).* The first volume was written by William Lewis Herndon; the other was written by Lardner Gibbon.

13. Coca, of course, is the plant from which cocaine is derived. The South American Indians would often chew coca leaves as they worked; the drug would stimulate them and remove the sensation of hunger, thus allowing them to work harder and longer—they could go without food for two or three days at a time. Clemens had heard of the effects of coca and the potential for investment obviously interested him. This is an early example of his extravagant financial schemes.

14. Horace E. Bixby (1826–1912) was the pilot of the *Paul Jones,* the boat on which Clemens traveled from Cincinnati to New Orleans. That journey began on 15 April 1857. In New Orleans, Clemens and Bixby came to terms: Bixby would teach Clemens to become a river pilot for $500—$100 down and the balance to be paid out of Clemens' earnings. Clemens borrowed the $100 down payment from his brother-in-law, James A. Moffett (1816–65), Pamela's husband, during a stop in St. Louis. When Bixby and Clemens left St. Louis on the *Crescent City,* Clemens was a cub pilot. The two met for a final time when Clemens returned to the river during his 1902 trip west.

15. Clemens was awarded his pilot's license on 9 April 1859. He left piloting after his May 1861 trip from New Orleans to St. Louis on the *Nebraska,* which was the last boat to pass through the Union blockade at Memphis. A calendar of Clemens' piloting assignments can be found in *MTLs* 1:385–90.

16. This tale is told in more detail in chapter 4 of *Roughing It.*

17. This section is taken from Clemens' dictation of 2 April 1906.

18. James W. Nye (1815–76) was a district attorney and judge in New York State before heading west. His service as governor of the territory was a stepping stone for a position as a United States senator when Nevada gained statehood. He served as a Republican senator from Nevada between 1864 and 1873.

19. Nye made a number of extended trips to California, New York, and Washington, D.C. Orion served as governor during these absences; the longest absence lasted from December 1862 to July 1863.

20. Nevada became the thirty-sixth state on 31 October 1864.

21. For an extended discussion of Orion's accomplishments in Nevada, see Philip Ashley Fanning's *Mark Twain and Orion Clemens: Brothers, Partners, Strangers.*

CHAPTER XII

1. This section is taken from Clemens' dictation of 5 April 1906.

2. The Republican candidate, Chauncey N. Noteware, was nominated. Orion was later elected to the state assembly in November 1865. He served from 1 January to 1 March 1866.

3. Clemens moved on to San Francisco in 1864.

4. Herman Camp was a speculator in mining stocks. Clemens knew him from Virginia City.

5. The Hale and Norcross Silver Mining Company. When Clemens arrived in San Francisco the company stock was quoted at $915 per share; by the end of June 1864 it rose to over $2,000 per share. It later fell to $500 per share and then to $300. The rapid rise and fall continued: in August the stock was quoted at $200; in November it boomed to $1,000; by December 1, 1864, it had fallen to $310.

6. John Marshall Clemens bought the land for $400 around 1830. There were some 75,000 acres located in Fentress County, near Jamestown, Tennessee. Clemens wrote to Orion about the possible sale on 13 December 1865 (*MTLs* 1:326–27).

7. Clemens sailed from San Francisco on 15 December 1866.

8. Orion and Mollie Clemens left Carson City in March 1866. Because of financial difficulties, they did not sail from San Francisco until August 10.

9. Orion, in fact, moved to Hartford earlier than Clemens. In 1870, with Clemens' urgings and intervention, Orion took a position with the American Publishing Company; he performed various office duties and edited *The American Publisher,* a trade paper—he also succeeded in angering his brother with an advertisement that Clemens would be a regular contributor to the paper (SLC to OC, 11 March 1871; *Mark Twain's Letters to His Publishers,* 56–60).

10. The paper was in Rutland, Vermont.

11. Orion and Mollie Clemens moved back to Keokuk in 1872 after Orion had a falling-out with Elisha Bliss.

12. William Stotts (1799–1888).

13. This section is taken from Clemens' dictation of 6 April 1906.

14. Jane Lampton Clemens died in Keokuk on 27 October 1890; she was eighty-six when she died.

15. Clemens was enthusiastic about the project and wrote Orion on 6 May 1880, calling the manuscript "a model autobiography" (*MTL* 1:378).

16. After reading a part of Orion's manuscript, William Dean Howells wrote to Clemens: "It wrung my heart, and I felt haggard after I had finished it. . . . The best touches in it are those which make us acquainted with *you*; and they will be valuable material hereafter. But the writer's soul is laid *too* bare: it is shocking. I can't risk the paper in the *Atlantic*; and if you print it anywhere, I hope you wont let your love of the naked truth prevent you from striking out some of the most intimate passages. Don't let any one else even see those passages about the autopsy. The light on your father's character is most pathetic" (WDH to SLC, 14 June 1880; *SMTHL*, 155–56). This mention of the autopsy along with a reference in "Villagers of 1840–3" (*HHT* 40) and a 1903 notebook entry form the basis for Dixon Wecter's argument that Clemens had somehow managed to witness the post-mortem examination performed on his father (*SCH*, 116–17).

17. There is no indication that Clemens quoted Orion. Albert Bigelow Paine did use some of Orion's manuscript when preparing *Mark Twain: A Biography*.

18. Orion Clemens died on 11 December 1897.

19. This section is taken from sections Clemens composed in 1904 in Florence, Italy.

20. Whitelaw Reid (1837–1912) was United States minister to France between 1889 and 1892 and ambassador to Great Britain between 1905 and 1912.

21. Horace Greeley (1811–72) was editor of the New York *Tribune* and is most remembered for his frequently quoted advice, "Go West, young man, go West." Greeley championed a wide variety of reforms: land reform (Greeley introduced the first homestead bill in Congress in 1848), changes in labor laws, and dynamic opposition to slavery. He was an early supporter of women's rights.

22. By 1875 Clemens had published *The Celebrated Jumping Frog of Calaveras County and Other Sketches*, *The Innocents Abroad*, *Roughing It*, and *The Gilded Age*. His best work did indeed lie before him.

CHAPTER XIII

1. This section is taken from "Ancestors" (1897–98).

2. See Chapter XII, in which Clemens describes being approached by a gentleman from Tennessee who offered evidence that the Clemens family still owned about 1,000 acres.

3. *The Gilded Age* (1873).

4. The play was *Colonel Sellers: A Play in Five Acts*.

5. John Marshall and Jane Clemens were married on 6 May 1823 and had settled in Gainsborough, Tennessee, about a year after their marriage. They then moved on to Jamestown, Tennessee, where several of their children—Orion, Pamela, Pleasant, Margaret, and Benjamin—were born. The family moved to Florida, Missouri, in 1835.

6. On 30 November 1835.

7. There is a reference to a similar occurrence in a letter from Jane Lampton

Clemens to Orion Clemens: "Henrys nurse was a negro boy they were playing in the yard. Henry was high enough to hold the top of the kettle and peep over. This time there was hot embers he ran into the hot embers bare footed. I set on one chair with a wash bowl on another & held Henry in my arms & his feet in the cold water, or he would have gone into spasms before your father got there from the store with the Dr . . ." (JLC to OC, 25 April 1880; MTP‡).

8. In Book 1, Chapter 4 of his autobiography, *The Life of Benvenuto Cellini*, Cellini describes two incidents from his early years: taking hold of a large scorpion when he was three years of age, and then getting his ears boxed at five to ensure that he would remember the day a salamander darted among fiery coals (Cellini, 8–9).

9. Helen Adams Keller (1880–1968) was a famous deaf and blind American author and educator of the blind. After she had been taught to read braille by Anne Sullivan, she attended Radcliffe College and graduated *magna cum laude*. The Pulitzer Prize–winning play *The Miracle Worker* was based on Keller's early life.

10. There is an important change in this version of Clemens' rationalization. In *Mark Twain's Autobiography* the passage reads: "I am grown old and my memory is not as active as it used to be. When I was younger I could remember anything, whether it had happened or not; but my faculties are decaying now, and soon I shall be so I cannot remember any but the things that *never* happened. It is sad to go to pieces like this, but we all have to do it" (96; emphasis added).

11. John A. Quarles was married to Jane Clemens' sister, Patsey Lampton. He helped convince John Marshall Clemens to make the move to Florida, Missouri, and was his partner in keeping store in Florida. The elder Clemens seems to have prospered for a time in Florida, but his fortunes began to change when he withdrew from the partnership with Quarles.

12. *Adventures of Huckleberry Finn* (1885); *Tom Sawyer Detective* (1896).

13. *Tom Sawyer Abroad* (1894).

14. His name was Jim. The episode is chapter 2 of *The Adventures of Tom Sawyer.*

15. The following passage is notable for its movement into and then out of the past. The movement is highlighted by the variations in phrasing, from "I can call back" to "I can see" to "I can feel" to "I know." That ascending order demonstrates Clemens' transition from his present—a present that in 1897 vibrates with the still fresh loss of Susy—into his past—a past that helps him reconnect with an idyllic and peaceful experience. And all of that moves him toward the moment of reconciliation as the "grey dawn" lights the darkness and life begins anew.

CHAPTER XIV

1. Jean was nine years old in 1889; the family was still in Hartford at that time. After moving to Europe, they did spend time in Berlin during 1891.

2. This dinner is described in chapter 179 of *Mark Twain: A Biography*. Mention is also made in *MTN*, 223–24.

3. Prince Heinrich was the brother of Kaiser Wilhelm II.

4. *Life on the Mississippi* (1882). "Old Times on the Mississippi" was the title used for chapters 4 through 27 when they appeared in the *Atlantic Monthly* between

January and July 1875. "Old Times" ostensibly tells the story of Clemens' apprenticeship as a river pilot and is firmly focused on the Mississippi; the remainder of the book grew out of Clemens' return to the river in 1882 and reflects the changes both in Clemens and in post–Civil War America.

5. Prince Otto von Bismarck (1815–98), known as the Iron Chancellor, was given the title of chancellor by Wilhelm I. Bismarck was mainly responsible for the formation of the German Empire in 1871 and was its first chancellor.

6. Chancellor Georg Leo von Caprivi succeeded Bismarck as chancellor of the German Empire.

7. According to the guest list in *Mark Twain: A Biography* (940), this was probably Rudolf Lindau.

8. Clemens gives the date as 1892 in his notebook.

9. *A Tramp Abroad* (1880).

10. Albert Bigelow Paine published his highly selective two-volume *Mark Twain's Autobiography* in 1924. Clemens may have been using comments like this to titillate his audience. Clemens often alluded to his autobiography in interviews with reporters. See Gary Scharnorst's *Mark Twain: The Complete Interviews*.

11. "The Awful German Language" appears in the appendix for *A Tramp Abroad*.

12. *The Innocents Abroad* (1869).

13. Harris is Joseph H. Twichell. General Daniel Edgar Sickles (1819–1914) was Joseph Twichell's commanding officer during the Civil War. Twichell served as chaplain to Sickles' brigade and was present when surgeons amputated the general's leg after he was struck by a ball at Gettysburg. Sickles was military governor of South Carolina when military rule replaced civilian administrators in March 1867 with passage of the first Reconstruction Act. President Grant eventually replaced Sickles because of the general's arbitrary acts and the developing unrest of the population under his control.

14. This is merely a jumble of personages and books of the Old and New Testaments. It mimics the pattern of generations in Genesis; for example, Genesis 5:1–32; 10:1–32; 11:10–32.

CHAPTER XV

1. Karl Gerhardt (1853–1940) was a struggling sculptor when Clemens met him in 1881 and decided to finance his study abroad for three years. He eventually did busts of both General Grant and Clemens. Candace Thurber Wheeler was one of the founders of the Onteora Club in the Catskill Mountains of New York State. The Clemenses spent the summer of 1890 there. Dora Wheeler was Candace Wheeler's daughter. Frank Richard Stockton (1834–1902) was an editor of *St. Nicholas* magazine. Mary Mapes Dodge was editor of *St. Nicholas* magazine and a member of the Onteora Club. Clemens had considered allowing Dodge to serialize *The Prince and the Pauper* in 1880 but finally chose not to out of fear that a serial would cut into book profits. She did publish *Tom Sawyer Abroad* as a six-part serial which ran from November 1893 through April 1894. General George A. Custer (1839–76) led a column of soldiers against the Sioux and Northern Cheyenne at the Little Big Horn River in

Montana. The Indian force of 2,500 led by Crazy Horse killed Custer and his entire command of 265.

2. Clemens was dictating this in Dublin, New Hampshire. Those days of dictating are described in chapters 246 and 247 of *Mark Twain: A Biography*.

3. Joseph H. Choate (1832–1917) served as ambassador to Great Britain (1897–1905) and ambassador to the Hague peace conference (1907). Clemens and Choate had shared the dais numerous times ranging back to the 1870s. Choate often joined Clemens to raise funds for a variety of worthy causes; for example, in 1906 they both presided over a gathering at Carnegie Hall in New York City for the benefit of Booker T. Washington's Tuskegee Institute and later joined again at a meeting in support of the New York State Association for Promoting the Interests of the Blind (the texts of Clemens' speeches can be found in *Mark Twain Speaking*, 478–82; 506–11).

4. Edmund C. Stedman (1833–1908) was active in both business and literary circles. He edited the eleven-volume *Library of American Literature* (1889–90) and a ten-volume edition of the works of Edgar Allan Poe (1894–95).

5. William Wilfred Campbell (1858–1918) was an Anglican minister who wrote poetry, travel books, and fiction. *Beyond the Hills of Dream* was published in 1899.

6. The inscription reads:

> Warm summer sun
>> Shine kindly here,
> Warm southern wind
>> Blow gently here
> Green sod above
>> Lie light, lie light
> Good night, dear heart,
>> Good night, good night.
>>> Robert Richardson

7. Finley Peter Dunne (1867–1936) published a number of volumes of humorous sketches using an Irish saloonkeeper, Mr. Dooley, as the primary character and making ample use of dialect.

8. The walk took place in November 1874 (chapter 97 in *MTB*). Clemens' full description of the encounter at the inn can be found in *Mark Twain in Eruption*, 366–72.

CHAPTER XVI

1. This should read January 12, 1906.

2. The Reverend Francis Goodwin was an Episcopal rector in Hartford and the cousin of J. P. Morgan.

3. The Monday Evening Club was founded by Calvin Stowe, J. Hammond Trumbull (a noted historian, bibliographer, and philologist who wrote a number of monographs on Indian language and culture), and the Reverend Horace Bushnell. The club was formed to offer its members an opportunity to meet and discuss a wide range of intellectual topics.

4. Horace Bushnell was pastor of Hartford's Park Church and was an important leader in Hartford's religious community. His ideas influenced a host of nineteenth-century preachers, including Henry Ward Beecher and Phillips Brooks. In 1865, Bushnell helped Joseph Twichell become the pastor of the First Congregational Church in Hartford.

5. Clemens' "The Facts Behind the Recent Carnival of Crime in Connecticut" was first presented as an essay to the Monday Evening Club in 1876.

6. See *Mark Twain Speaking*, 462–67.

7. Edwin Pond Parker came to Hartford in 1860 as minister of the Second Church, where he preached for the next sixty years. On 24 December 1860 his was the first New England Congregational Church to celebrate Christmas.

8. Nathaniel Burton was the eldest of the small group of Hartford preachers that had connections to the Nook Farm neighborhood (the others were Edwin Pond Parker and Joseph H. Twichell). Burton came to Hartford in 1857 when he became minister of the Fourth Congregational Church. With Horace Bushnell's retirement, Burton took over the leadership of Park Church, which he held until his death. After Burton's death, Clemens saw to it that a collection of a dozen of Burton's lectures to the Yale Divinity School was published.

9. This section is taken from Clemens' dictation of 13 January 1906.

10. Clemens served on the *Pennsylvania* from time to time during 1857 and 1858. The captain was John S. Klinefelter (1810–85).

11. William Brown. Brown died in the aftermath of the explosion which destroyed the *Pennsylvania*.

12. Clemens began his service under Brown in November 1857.

13. *Life on the Mississippi*, chapters 18, 19, and 20. The explosion of the *Pennsylvania* is described in chapter 20.

14. *Life on the Mississippi* was published in 1883; Jane Clemens died in 1890.

15. See "Villagers, 1840–3" (*HHT*, 39–40).

16. *Life on the Mississippi*, chapter 19.

17. *Life on the Mississippi*, chapter 20. Clemens also described the events surrounding Henry's death in a letter to his sister Mollie dated 18 June 1858 (*MTLs* 1:80–85).

18. Thomas F. Peyton attended patients in the third ward of the Memphis Exchange.

19. There is no mention of the morphine dose in the letter to Mollie Clemens of 18 June 1858.

20. This section is taken from Clemens' dictation of 15 January 1906.

21. Henry Clemens was buried beside John Marshall Clemens in Hannibal's Baptist cemetery on 25 June 1858, the same day his body arrived in Hannibal. Both bodies were moved to the Mount Olivet Cemetery in 1876.

CHAPTER XVII

1. See Clemens' "Taming the Bicycle" (*CTSSE* 1:892–99).

2. This version of "Jim Wolf and the Cats" was composed by Clemens in Vienna during 1897 and 1898.

3. In *The Adventures of Tom Sawyer* the boys do offer matches and tobacco to Muff Potter, who is awaiting trial in jail, but there is no fire (167–72). The burning of Jimmy Finn is a part of Clemens' reminiscence in chapter 66 of *Life on the Mississippi*.

4. The killing of Boggs in chapter 21 of *Adventures of Huckleberry Finn*.

5. See "Villagers, 1840–3" (*HHT*, 31).

6. The house and its owner appear a number of times in *The Adventures of Tom Sawyer*. Injun Joe's raid on the Widow Douglas' house in chapter 29 of *The Adventures of Tom Sawyer* may be connected to this anecdote.

7. Chapter 33 of *The Adventures of Tom Sawyer*.

8. Jim Wolf (or Wolfe) was first a printer's devil and later an apprentice printer for Orion's Hannibal *Western Union* (the *Journal*). He came to the paper in 1851 and lived with the Clemens family much of the time. The first sketch that Clemens ever published—"A Gallant Fireman"—told of Wolf's rather slow-witted efforts during a Hannibal fire (*Early Tales and Sketches* 1:62–63).

9. The New York *Sunday Mercury*. "Jim Wolf and the Tom-Cats" was Clemens' first extended use of his past for publication.

10. Artemus Ward (Charles Farrar Browne) often changed and distorted spelling to give his writing the appearance and "sound" of dialect.

11. Clemens traveled to England in the fall of 1872 for a whirlwind tour and discussions with his British publisher, George Routledge. He returned to America in November 1872 and, with his family, left again for England in May 1873. They stayed abroad until October 1873, when Clemens accompanied Livy and Susy to America and then turned around and went back to England to continue his speaking tour. That tour ended in January 1874.

12. George Dolby was Clemens' lecture agent for the British tour. He also managed Charles Dickens' last series of reading tours in America. Dolby scheduled six lectures for Clemens from October 13 to October 18. The success of those lectures brought Clemens and Dolby together again for another series of lectures from November 1873 to January 1874.

13. Charles Warren Stoddard (1843–1901) was a poet and essayist and an old friend of Clemens from the days in California. His *South Sea Idylls* (1873) is a series of sketches tied to his wanderings in Polynesia, which he had financed through newspaper correspondence.

14. Arthur Orton claimed that he was Sir Richard Tichborne, a missing heir to a large fortune. The claim was proved a fabrication with Orton's 1895 confession. Clemens apparently met Orton during the 1873 visit to England (*MTN*, 243).

15. *Tom Hood's Comic Annual*.

CHAPTER XVIII

1. The New York *Christian Union*.

2. Clemens' letter was published in the *Christian Union* for 16 July 1885 under the title "'What Ought He To Have Done?': Mark Twain's Opinion."

3. That letter, dated 21 July 1885, came from Thomas Twain. Clemens believed

Twain wrote the original article and was the father of the child mentioned in that piece.

4. Scipio Africanus (ca. 234–183 B.C.), also known as Publius Cornelius Scipio Africanus or Scipio the Elder, defeated the Carthaginian armies to end the Punic Wars (202 B.C.). Hannibal was the leader of the Carthaginian forces against Rome during the Second Punic War (218–201 B.C.).

5. Alexander the Great (356–323 B.C.), king of Macedonia, widened his kingdom by conquest; it eventually included southwest Asia and Egypt and spread as far east as the Indus River and Khyber Pass.

6. Pyrrhus (ca. 318–272 B.C.), king of Epirus, conducted a masterful military campaign throughout southern Italy and Sicily between 280 and 275 B.C. His name has come down to us in the expression "Pyrrhic victory"—a victory at tremendous and prohibitive expense.

7. Laurence Barrette (1838–91) was a well-known Shakespearean actor; he produced and acted in the plays based on William Dean Howells' *A Counterfeit Presentment* and *Yorick's Love.*

8. Laurence Hutton (1843–1904) was an editor for *Harper's Monthly* and also wrote a number of books dealing with the theater.

9. George Henry Warner (1833–1919) was the brother of Charles Dudley Warner. Mrs. Warner was Elizabeth Hooker Gillette. Warner was something of an expert on Oriental rugs and used his connections with importers to purchase items for his neighbors, especially Olivia Clemens.

10. *The Prince and the Pauper* (1881).

11. Clemens and William Dean Howells, however, did begin work on a collection of American humor. They collaborated on the project during the mid-1880s until Howells' agreements with Harper & Brothers forced him to dissociate himself from the book (WDH to SLC, 16 October 1885; *SMTHL*, 252–53). Clemens published *Mark Twain's Library of Humor* in 1887.

12. "What Is Man," 124–214. Clemens had 250 copies printed in 1906 for private circulation. He sent anonymous copies to a variety of readers, from Andrew Carnegie to the New York *Times*, and he received a variety of responses, from shock and agreement to quick dismissal. During the years of composition, Clemens probably shared some of the ideas with those around him: Olivia, Joe Twichell, and later his secretary Isabel Lyon.

CHAPTER XIX

1. The second son of Ulysses S. Grant.

2. The neighborhood children first performed their version of *The Prince and the Pauper* in 1884 as a surprise for Clemens when he came home for the Christmas holidays, a break from his tour with G. W. Cable. The performance was repeated a number of times later, with Clemens standing in as Miles Hendon.

3. Margaret (Daisy) Warner was the daughter of George Henry and Elizabeth Warner.

4. Mary Queen of Scots (1542–87), Catholic queen of Scotland, was a cousin of

Elizabeth I. Elizabeth ordered her execution in 1587 because of mounting fears that the Protestant Reformation in England would be undone if Mary ascended to the throne. Her execution was one factor in Spain's declaring war on England in 1587. Her son, James VI of Scotland, became James I of England in 1603.

5. Sir Francis Bacon (1561–1626) is considered the first English essayist; his first edition of *Essays* was published in 1597. His devotion to scientific study led to the formation of the Royal Society, which was chartered thirty years after his death. He was a counsel to James I.

6. Susan Lee Warner, wife of Charles Dudley Warner.

7. Their "literary" relationship began with reading the proofs for *The Innocents Abroad* while courting.

8. Andrew Carnegie (1835–1919), founder of the iron and steel industry in the United States, funneled his wealth into a variety of philanthropic causes—most notably town libraries and a number of trusts still in operation today.

9. Brander Matthews (1852–1929) taught at Columbia University from 1892 to 1924 and served as president of the National Institute of Arts and Letters from 1913 to 1914.

10. A number of the names mentioned—Billy Rice, Billy Birch, David Wambold, Backus—were connected to the minstrel shows which were a part of American entertainment from the antebellum period to the 1920s. Such shows began as farce with whites in blackface performing an organized show. As years passed, the shows became larger and eventually took on the shape of watered-down variety shows. Some were run by black owners and employed black performers.

11. The manuscript is "A Record of the Small Foolishnesses of Susie and 'Bay' Clemens (Infants)." "Bay" was the family's nickname for Clara.

12. *Was hast du gesagt?*—What did you say?

13. William Hooker Gillette (1855–1937) became one of America's great actors, most remembered for his portrayal of Sherlock Holmes. Clemens helped the young Gillette financially during the early days of his acting career. One of his early roles was in the stage version of *The Gilded Age* performed in Hartford in 1875.

14. Elsie Leslie played the double role of Tom Canty and the Prince in the stage version of *The Prince and the Pauper* which opened in 1889.

CHAPTER XX

1. Clemens took up work on the autobiography in Florence as a diversion during Livy's illness. His dictating, though, was hampered because his amanuensis wrote only longhand. He also became ill, which ended the experiment.

2. Clemens went to San Francisco in an attempt to procure the letters which were in the hands of the owners of the *Alta California*.

3. By the American Publishing Company.

4. Oliver Wendell Holmes (1809–94), a professor of anatomy and physiology at Harvard, became well known as a writer of poetry, much of it occasional verse. He also wrote prose. His series of *Breakfast Table* books was very popular; *The Autocrat of the Breakfast Table* (1858) was the courting book for Clemens and Livy.

5. The Reverend Franklin S. Rising (1833?–68), pastor of Virginia City's St. Paul's Episcopal Church, sailed to Hawaii in 1866 and arrived in Honolulu two days before Clemens.

6. In his letter to Helen Keller dated 17 April 1903 (*MTL* 2:730–33), Clemens says he talked to Dr. Holmes about the unintentional plagiarism.

7. The owners originally denied him use of the materials by claiming the rights to the letters which had appeared in their newspaper, rights which they had advertised in a printed notice. They planned to publish the letters in a book which would help them recoup some of their expenses connected with Clemens' *Quaker City* trip.

8. George E. Barnes (d. 1897) was editor as well as one of the proprietors of the paper. The invitation to resign was given after Clemens had already taken on a diminished workload, and they parted on good terms. See chapter 58 in *Roughing It*, as well as *MTLs* 1:309–19.

9. Clemens was in the islands between April and August 1866.

10. Clemens' first lecture was given with the encouragement of John McComb (1829–96). The performance took place in Maguire's Academy of Music in San Francisco on 2 October 1866. The tour of Californian and Nevada was arranged by Dennis E. McCarthy (1841–85), whom Clemens knew at the Virginia City *Enterprise*.

11. See chapter 78 of *Roughing It*.

12. The plan to travel to the Far East, most notably China, was hatched during conversations Clemens had with Anson Burlingame, the United States minister to China.

13. See *The Innocents Abroad*, chapters 1 and 2.

14. Frederick MacCrellish was owner of the *Alta*.

15. Noah Brooks (1830–1903) was an editor for the New York *Tribune* from 1871 to 1876 and for the New York *Times* from 1876 to 1884.

16. Sir Walter Scott (1771–1832), perhaps the most popular writer of the nineteenth century, was known for both his poetry and his novels; among the better known novels are *Waverley* (1814), *The Black Dwarf* (1816), *Rob Roy* (1817), and *Ivanhoe* (1819). Scott and Clemens also shared the pain of bankruptcy. Scott's publisher declared bankruptcy in 1825 and left Scott carrying a great debt; by 1827 Scott had paid off some 28,000 pounds. The struggle to do so ruined his health.

17. *Following the Equator* (1897).

CHAPTER XXI

1. *Captain Stormfield's Visit to Heaven* was never finished. Clemens did publish a piece from it in *Harper's Monthly Magazine* in 1907 and 1908. Two other versions have been published: one in 1952, the other in 1970.

2. The letter-writer was Tonkray's brother.

3. This should be Tom Blankenship. Clemens describes the family in "Villagers of 1840–3" (*HHT*, 31).

4. Montana.

5. Mirrored in chapter 4 of *Huckleberry Finn* when Judge Thatcher attempts to reform Pap.

6. Edward Loomis (1864–1937) was Clemens' nephew by marriage, the son-in-law of Olivia's brother, Charles Langdon.

7. Mr. Buckley. The code names are consistent throughout this section.

8. Elmira, New York.

9. Alfred, Lord Tennyson (1809–92), succeeded William Wordsworth as poet laureate of England in 1850. His *The Idylls of the King* (1859–85) was another of the works which influenced *A Connecticut Yankee in King Arthur's Court.*

CHAPTER XXII

1. James Carroll Beckwith (1852–1917), from Hannibal, Missouri, was a very popular painter in New York City; he helped to organize the Art Students League.

2. Dean Sage (1841–1902), a New York businessman, found success in the lumber industry.

3. In 1879, Clemens attended the reunion of the Army of the Tennessee in Chicago. The banquet was held in the Palmer House and was attended by some 600 veterans, including Generals Grant, Sherman, and Sheridan. Clemens delivered his toast "The Babies" to that crowd (*Mark Twain Speaking*, 131–34).

4. Joseph H. Twichell.

5. See chapter 8 in *A Tramp Abroad* (1880); chapters 5 through 8 are devoted to duelling.

6. This is gibberish. The objects and positions refer to different parts and locations on a sailing vessel: "garboard" is planking on a ship's bottom, near the keel; "strake" is planking on a ship's side, the breadth of which is used to calculate measurements; "main-to'gallant" is the small sail located above the main sail; the "mizzenyard" is the foremost sail on a three-sail vessel; "amidships" is the middle area of a ship.

CHAPTER XXIII

1. The affliction was also Tom Sawyer's: "He privately smoothed out the curls, with labor and difficulty, and plastered his hair close down to his head; for he held curls to be effeminate, and his own filled his life with bitterness" (*Adventures of Tom Sawyer*, 59).

2. "Old Kercheval the tailor" in "Villagers of 1840–3." He also mentions the apprentice's action, though Clemens calls himself Simon Carpenter in the passage (*HHT*, 37).

3. The parenthetical mention of Huckleberry Finn here contrasts with Clemens' earlier hesitancy to identify Blankenship with the character (see Chapter XXI).

4. Hostilities between the United States and Mexico broke out in 1846. The United States had annexed Texas and had designs on the California territory, which was still under Mexican control. The war ended in 1848 with the United States gaining control of Texas, New Mexico (which included Arizona), and upper California. This set up the next controversy—whether the new territories would be free or slaveholding.

5. The Sanitary Fund was established to help subsidize work to establish sanitary conditions within the Union Army's training camps. The tale of the flour sack is told in chapter 45 of *Roughing It*.

6. General Benjamin Franklin Butler (1818–93), a prominent Massachusetts politician, was commissioned a major general by Lincoln in 1861. He did not enjoy much military success and was removed as the commander of the occupation army in New Orleans.

7. Clemens was in Oxford to receive an honorary doctor of literature degree. One of the side benefits of the degree was the scarlet academic gown. Clemens so fancied it that he wore it for Clara's wedding later in 1909.

8. George Nathaniel, Lord Curzon, served as viceroy of India from 1899 to 1905. He was chancellor of Oxford University in 1907 and served as secretary of state for foreign affairs from 1918 to 1922.

9. Prince Arthur of Connaught received a doctor of civil law degree.

10. Sir Sidney Colvin (1845–1927) published articles on history and art criticism as well as biographies of W. S. Lander and Keats. He edited the Edinburgh edition of Robert Louis Stevenson's works (1894–97) and Stevenson's letters (1899–1911).

11. Sir Sidney Lee (1859–1926) was a Shakespearean scholar whose work examined the life and times of the playwright. He also wrote about the history and personages of the Elizabethan and Renaissance periods.

12. William "General" Booth (1829–1912) was the leader of the Salvation Army, which he founded in 1865.

13. Sir William Ramsay (1852–1916) was a British chemist. He won the Nobel Prize in 1906 for discovering four inert gases and recognizing their place in the periodic table.

14. Sir Joseph Norman Lockyer (1836–1920) was an astronomer. He discovered helium in the sun before it was known to exist on earth.

15. Henry VIII ruled England between 1509 and 1547. His rule was marked by controversy with the Roman Catholic Church. Although he was given the title "Defender of the Faith" by Pope Leo X for opposing Martin Luther's reformist views, Henry soon split with Rome because his attempts to obtain a divorce in order to assure a male heir met stiff papal opposition. His third union, with Jane Seymour, finally produced a son, Edward VI, who ruled from 1547 to 1553. After Edward's death Henry's daughter Mary ("Bloody Mary") reigned briefly; in 1558 his younger daughter, Elizabeth I, acceded to the throne.

16. Henry II, Duke of Normandy and leader of the Angevin Empire, ruled England between 1154 and 1189 and is most celebrated for his work to stabilize the kingdom by establishing clear boundaries between ecclesiastic and civil authorities and codifying English law. From Henry's system came the beginnings of English common law.

17. Rosamond Clifford—The Fair Rosamond—was most probably the mistress of Henry II in 1174. A ballad offers a story of her seclusion from the queen in a house constructed as a maze so only the king could find her. Eleanor of Aquitaine, the queen, was able to find her by following a thread.

18. Roger Bacon (1220–92) was a Franciscan of Oxford. He challenged the prevailing thought of the time by advocating the scientific method—making observa-

tions, using mathematics, and conducting experiments to check results—rather than the usual prolonged study of established texts. He foresaw the development of telescopes, submarines, automobiles, and flying machines.

19. Clemens' comment here may be an allusion to his privately published sketch "[Date, 1601.] Conversation, as it Was by the Social Fireside, in the Time of the Tudors" which presented a highly profane account of a conversation in the Court of Queen Elizabeth. See *CTSSE* 1:661–66.

20. Harold assumed the throne after the death of Edward the Confessor. He was defeated by William the Conqueror at the Battle of Hastings in 1066.

CHAPTER XXIV

1. This was John Brown, the antislavery activist and leader of the bloody and disastrous raid on the federal arsenal at Harper's Ferry, Virginia, on 16 October 1859. Brown was hanged on 2 December 1859. The reference here is to an earlier raid and massacre at Pottawatomie, Kansas, during the battle between pro- and antislavery factions in the Kansas territory in 1854.

2. Clemens spent time at Jackass Hill in Tuolumne County, California, from December 1864 to February 1865.

3. Two of these men were considered the greatest billiard players to have lived: Jacob "Wizzard" Schaefer began his long career in the 1870s. William Hoppe succeeded Schaefer as champion; he was international champion at the age of sixteen (in 1903) and world champion three years later.

CHAPTER XXV

1. What follows grew out of Clemens' experience after his speech at the birthday celebration for John Greenleaf Whittier on 17 December 1877. Whittier, Ralph Waldo Emerson, and Oliver Wendell Holmes were at that dinner, and the program was introduced by William Dean Howells. Both Clemens and Howells later convinced themselves that the speech had insulted the three New England poets; that feeling may have contributed to Clemens' plans to visit Europe during 1878. Clemens' reaction is clearly seen in his letter to Howells dated 23 December 1877. See *Selected Mark Twain–Howells Letters: 1872–1910*, 102–6, for the series of letters which dealt with that dinner and *Mark Twain Speaking*, 110–15, for the text.

2. Clemens mixes the attributions: "Barbara Frietchie" (1863) was written by Whittier, "The Biglow Papers" (1848) by James Russell Lowell (1819–91), and "Thanatopsis" (1817) by William Cullen Bryant (1794–1878).

3. Mr. and Mrs. Augustus P. Chamberlaine of Concord, Massachusetts. The Clemenses met the Chamberlaines in 1878 during a European tour.

4. Ralph Waldo Emerson (1803–82), poet and essayist, was most influential as the leader of the Transcendental movement in American literature, which was centered in Concord, Massachusetts.

5. John Greenleaf Whittier (1807–92) gained respect and reputation as a poet and a supporter of various reform movements, most notably abolition.

6. Henry Wadsworth Longfellow (1807–82) gained fame from his numerous poems which aimed at a patriotic spirit and which contributed to the development of an American mythology. His "The Song of Hiawatha" (1855) and "Paul Revere's Ride" (1860) have become an enduring part of the American national consciousness.

7. William Winter was a poet and essayist. His 1881 *The Trip to England* was a collection of travel letters he had written for the *Tribune*.

8. William H. Bishop's *Detmold: A Romance* was serialized in the *Atlantic Monthly* beginning in the December 1877 edition (vol. 40, no. 242). There were seven installments in all, from December 1877 to June 1878.

9. Lieutenant General Nelson Appleton Miles (1839–1925) served with distinction at the battles of Antietam, Fredericksburg, Chancellorsville, the Wilderness, and Petersburg. He also served in the Indian Wars and commanded the troops who quelled the Pullman Riots in Chicago in 1894.

10. This final comment is added by Clemens when he prepares the typescript for the *North American Review:* the tale originally ends with the paragraph above. The final statement, then, may been seen as the closing of the frame for the autobiography, a frame that begins with the introductory comments in the first paragraphs of the first chapter and ends with this final observation on the whole of the autobiography.

APPENDIX A: "THE DEATH OF JEAN"

1. Stormfield was the name of Clemens' home in Redding, Connecticut.

2. Clara and Ossip Gabrilowitsch were married at Stormfield on 6 October 1909.

3. Henry Huttleston Rogers.

4. Richard Watson Gilder was an editor for *The Century*. A long-time friend of Clemens, he was among those who attended Clara's wedding. William M. Laffan was the publisher of the New York *Sun*.

5. Henry C. Robinson was a Hartford lawyer and a member of the Monday Evening Club.

6. Jervis Langdon (1875–1952) was the son of Charles Jervis Langdon and Ida Clark.

7. For a discussion of Jean's situation in the household, see Karen Lystra's *Dangerous Intimacy: The Untold Story of Mark Twain's Final Years*. Lystra challenges Hamlin Hill's interpretation of Clemens' last decade in *Mark Twain: God's Fool*. For a view of Jean's condition, see Laura Skandera Trombley's "'She Wanted to Kill': Jean Clemens and Postictal Psychosis." In a contrast to Lystra's view, Skandera Trombley looks at the state of the Clemens household in the final years in "Mark Twain's *Annus Horribilis* of 1908–1909."

APPENDIX D: A SAMPLE OF LETTERS

1. All told, there exists roughly eleven thousand letters (originals or copies) written by Samuel Clemens or members of his immediate family. There are also some seventeen thousand letters (originals and copies) written by others to the Clemenses.

The texts of the letters published here are taken from three primary sources. Letters 1, 2, 3, and 4 are taken from *Mark Twain's Letters*, volumes 1 and 4. Volume 1 is edited by Edgar Marques Branch, Michael B. Frank, and Kenneth M. Sanderson; volume 4 is edited by Victor Fischer and Michael B. Frank; both volumes are published by University of California Press. Letters 5, 6, and 8 are taken from *Selected Mark Twain–Howells Letters*, edited by Frederick Anderson, William M. Gibson, and Henry Nash Smith, published by Harvard University Press. Letters 7 and 9 are taken from *Mark Twain's Letters*, edited by Albert Bigelow Paine, published by Harper & Brothers Publishers.

2. A number of Clemens' letters from the West also saw print in local papers, but Clemens sent letters with different intentions. Some of the letters written to friends or family members also allowed him to fine tune his storytelling; for examples, see his letters to Mollie Clemens (29, 30, and 31 January 1862, *MTLs* 1:143–46) and Jane Clemens (30 January 1862, *MTLs* 1:146–52). An earlier letter to Ann E. Taylor is also helpful (21 and 25 May 1856, *MTLs* 1:59–62).

3. Clemens had already played with the idea of the triumphant frontier in an early humorous sketch, "The Dandy Frightening the Squatter" (*Early Tales and Sketches* 1:63–65). His unease with the numbers of seemingly homeless children was common in New York in the 1850s, a decade that saw the rise of aid societies aimed, at their most ambitious and perhaps ominous, at "placing out" children to rural locations. This was especially important to the work of Charles Loring Brace and the Children's Aid Society of New York.

4. *MTLs* 1:3–9.

5. *MTLs* 1:9–12.

6. *MTLs* 1:322–25.

7. *MTLs* 4:50–55.

8. *SMTHL*, 74–76.

9. *SMTHL*, 311–12; Clemens repeats the chronology and the image of Susy on the platform in a letter to Henry C. Robinson dated 28 September [18]96; *MTL* 2:636–37.

10. Howells' daughter Winnifred died on 2 March 1889. She was under the care of Dr. S. Weir Mitchell. Mitchell's misdiagnosis and treatment likely led to Winnie's death (she may have been anorexic, a disease not at all understood in the nineteenth century). Mitchell's "rest cure" would later become the target of Charlotte Perkins Gilman in "The Yellow Wallpaper."

11. *MTL* 2:635–36.

12. *SMTHL*, 375.

13. See *SMTHL*, 310–11.

14. *MTL* 2:835–36. Clara had married Ossip Gabrilowitsch on 6 October 1909.

15. Clemens refers here to "The Death of Jean."

Selected Bibliography

THE WORKS OF SAMUEL CLEMENS

Adventures of Huckleberry Finn. Edited by Walter Blair and Victor Fischer. Berkeley: University of California Press, 1985.

Adventures of Huckleberry Finn. Edited by Walter Blair and Victor Fischer, with the assistance of Dahlia Armon and Harriet Elinor Smith. Berkeley: University of California Press, 1988.

Adventures of Hucklberry Finn. Edited by Victor Fischer and Lin Salamo, with Walter Blair. Berkeley: University of California Press, 2003.

The Adventures of Tom Sawyer, Tom Sawyer Abroad, Tom Sawyer Detective. Edited by John C. Gerber, Paul Baender, and Terry Firkins. Berkeley: University of California Press, 1980.

The Autobiography of Mark Twain. Edited by Charles Neider. New York: Harper & Row, 1959.

"Chapters from My Autobiography." *North American Review* 183 (1906), 184, 185, 186 (1907): various issues.

Clemens of the Call: Mark Twain in San Francisco. Edited by Edgar M. Branch. Berkeley: University of California Press, 1969.

Collected Tales, Sketches, Speeches, & Essays, vol. 1: *1852–1890.* Edited by Louis J. Budd. New York: The Library of America, 1992.

Collected Tales, Sketches, Speeches, & Essays, vol. 2: *1891–1910.* Edited by Louis J. Budd. New York: The Library of America, 1992.

A Connecticut Yankee in King Arthur's Court. Edited by Bernard L. Stein. Berkeley: University of California Press, 1979.

"The Death of Jean." *Harper's Monthly Magazine* vol. 122, 728 (January 1911): 210–15.

Early Tales and Sketches, vol. 1: *1851–1864.* Edited by Edgar M. Branch and Robert H. Hirst. Berkeley: University of California Press, 1979.

Early Tales and Sketches, vol. 2: *1864–1865.* Edited by Edgar M. Branch and Robert H. Hirst. Berkeley: University of California Press, 1981.

Europe and Elsewhere. The Writings of Mark Twain: Definitive Edition 29. New York: Gabriel Wells, 1923.

Following the Equator. The Writings of Mark Twain: Definitive Edition 20 and 21. New York: Gabriel Wells, 1923.

The Gilded Age: A Tale of Today. The Writings of Mark Twain: Definitive Edition 5 and 6. New York Gabriel Wells, 1922.

How Nancy Jackson Married Kate Wilson and Other Tales of Rebellious Girls & Daring Young Women. Edited by John Cooley. Lincoln: University of Nebraska Press, 2001.

The Innocents Abroad or the New Pilgrim's Progress. The Writings of Mark Twain: Definitive Edition 1 and 2. New York Gabriel Wells, 1922.

Life on the Mississippi. The Writings of Mark Twain: Definitive Edition 12. New York: Gabriel Wells, 1923.

The Love Letters of Mark Twain. Edited by Dixon Wecter. New York: Harper and Brothers, 1949.

Mark Twain: The Complete Interviews. Edited by Gary Scharnhorst. Tuscaloosa: University of Alabama Press, 2006.

Mark Twain Businessman. Edited by Samuel Charles Webster. Boston: Little, Brown and Company, 1946.

Mark Twain in Eruption: Hitherto Unpublished Pages About Men and Events. Edited by Bernard DeVoto. New York: Harper and Brothers, 1940.

Mark Twain Speaking. Edited by Paul Fatout. Iowa City: University of Iowa Press, 1976.

Mark Twain's Autobiography. 2 vols. Edited by Albert Bigelow Paine. New York: Harper and Brothers, 1924.

Mark Twain's (Burlesque) Autobiography. Norwood: Norwood Editions, 1975.

Mark Twain's Correspondence with Henry Huttleston Rogers, 1893–1909. Edited by Lewis Leary. Berkeley: University of California Press, 1969.

Mark Twain's Hannibal, Huck, and Tom. Edited by Walter Blair. Berkeley: University of California Press, 1969.

Mark Twain's Letters. 2 vols. Edited by Albert Bigelow Paine. New York: Harper & Brothers Publishers, 1917.

Mark Twain's Letters. Edited by Albert Bigelow Paine. The Writings of Mark Twain: Definitive Edition 34 and 35. New York: Gabriel Wells, 1923.

Mark Twain's Letters, vol. 1: *1853–1866.* Edited by Edgar Marquess Branch, Michael B. Frank, and Kenneth M. Sanderson. Berkeley: University of California Press, 1988.

Mark Twain's Letters, vol. 2: *1867–1868.* Edited by Harriet Elinor Smith, Richard Bucci, and Lin Salamo. Berkeley: University of California Press, 1990.

Mark Twain's Letters, vol. 3: *1869.* Edited by Victor Fischer and Michael B. Frank. Berkeley: University of California Press, 1992.

Mark Twain's Letters, vol. 4: *1870–1871.* Edited by Victor Fischer and Michael B. Frank. Berkeley: University of California Press, 1995.

Mark Twain's Letters, vol. 5: *1872–1873.* Edited by Lin Salamo and Harriet Elinor Smith. Berkeley: University of California Press, 1997.

Mark Twain's Letters, vol. 6: *1874–1875.* Edited by Michael B. Frank and Harriet Elinor Smith. Berkeley: University of California Press, 2002.

Mark Twain's Letters from Hawaii. Edited by A. Grove Day. New York: Meredith Press, 1966.

Mark Twain's Letters to His Publishers, 1867–1894. Edited with an introduction by Hamlin Hill. Berkeley: University of California Press, 1967.

Mark Twain's Letters to Mary. Edited by Lewis Leary. New York: Columbia University Press, 1961.

Mark Twain's Mysterious Stranger Manuscripts. Edited by William M. Gibson. Berkeley: University of California Press, 1969.

Mark Twain's Notebook. Edited by Albert Bigelow Paine. New York: Harper and Brothers, 1935.

Mark Twain's Notebooks & Journals, vol. 1: *1855–1873*. Edited by Frederick Anderson, Michael B. Frank, and Kenneth M. Sanderson. Berkeley: University of California Press, 1975.

Mark Twain's Notebooks & Journals, vol. 2: *1877–1883*. Edited by Frederick Anderson, Lin Salamo, and Bernard L. Stein. Berkeley: University of California Press, 1975.

Mark Twain's Notebooks & Journals, vol. 3: *1883–1891*. Edited by Robert Pack Browning, Michael B. Frank, and Lin Salamo. Berkeley: University of California Press, 1979.

Mark Twain's "Which Was the Dream" and Other Symbolic Writings of the Later Years. Edited by John S. Tuckey. Berkeley: University of California Press, 1966.

"Miscellaneous Autobiographical Manuscripts." Mark Twain Papers, Bancroft Library, University of California, Berkeley.

The Prince and the Pauper. Edited by Victor Fischer and Lin Salamo. Berkeley: University of California Press, 1979.

Pudd'nhead Wilson. The Writings of Mark Twain: Definitive Edition 16. New York: Gabriel Wells, 1923.

Roughing It. Edited by Franklin R. Rogers. Berkeley: University of California Press, 1972.

Selected Mark Twain–Howells Letters, 1872–1910. Edited by Frederick Anderson, William M. Gibson, and Henry Nash Smith. Cambridge: The Belknap Press of Harvard University Press, 1967.

Selected Shorter Writing of Mark Twain. Edited by Walter Blair. Boston: Houghton Mifflin Company, 1962.

A Tramp Abroad. The Writings of Mark Twain: Definitive Edition 9 and 10. New York: Gabriel Wells, 1923.

"What Is Man?" and Other Essays. The Writings of Mark Twain: Definitive Edition 26. New York: Gabriel Wells, 1923.

"What Is Man?" and Other Philosophical Writings. Edited by Paul Baender. Berkeley: University of California Press, 1973.

SECONDARY SOURCES

Agan, Robert E. "Katie Leary: She's Always There . . ." *Mark Twain Society Bulletin* 2, no. 2 (June 1979).

Andrews, Kenneth R. *Nook Farm: Mark Twain's Hartford Circle*. Seattle: University of Washington Press, 1969.

Baender, Paul. "Alias Macfarlane: A Revision of Mark Twain's Autobiography." *American Literature* 38 (1966–67): 187–97.

Baetzhold, Howard G. *Mark Twain and John Bull: The British Connection.* Bloomington: Indiana University Press, 1970.

Blair, Walter. *Native American Humor.* 1937. Reprint. San Francisco: Chandler, 1960.

Branch, Edgar M. *The Literary Apprenticeship of Mark Twain.* Urbana: University of Illinois Press, 1950.

Branch, Edgar M., ed. *Clemens of the Call: Mark Twain in San Francisco.* Berkeley and Los Angeles: University of California Press, 1969.

Bridgman, Richard. *Traveling in Mark Twain.* Berkeley: University of California Press, 1987.

Brooks, Van Wyck. *The Ordeal of Mark Twain.* New York: E. P. Dutton & Company, 1920.

Brown, Carolyn S. *The Tall Tale in American Folklore and Literature.* Knoxville: University of Tennessee Press, 1987.

Budd, Isabelle. "Twain's Will Be Done." *Mark Twain Journal* 22 (Spring 1984): 34–35.

Budd, Isabelle. "Clara Samossoud's Will." *Mark Twain Journal* 25 (Spring 1987): 17–29.

Budd, Louis. *Our Mark Twain: The Making of His Public Personality.* Philadelphia: University of Pennsylvania Press, 1983.

Bush, Harold K., Jr. "'Broken Idols': Mark Twain's Elegies for Susy and a Critique of Freudian Grief Theory." *Nineteenth-Century Literature* 57, no. 2 (Sept. 2002): 237–68.

Bush, Harold K., Jr. *Mark Twain and the Spiritual Crisis of His Age.* Tuscaloosa: University of Alabama Press, 2007.

Caldwell, Patricia. *The Puritan Conversion Narrative: The Beginnings of American Expression.* Cambridge: Cambridge University Press, 1983.

Camfield, Gregg. *The Oxford Companion to Mark Twain.* New York: Oxford University Press, 2003.

Cellini, Benvenuto. *The Autobiography of Benvenuto Cellini.* Translated by John Addington Symonds. 1888. Reprint. New York: Modern Library, 1985.

Clemens, Olivia Susan. *Papa: An Intimate Biography of Mark Twain.* Edited by Charles Neider. Garden City: Doubleday & Company, Inc., 1985.

Clemens, Samuel L., William Dean Howells, and Charles Hopkins Clark, eds. *Mark Twain's Library of Humor.* 1888. Reprint. New York: Bonanza Books, 1969.

Courtney, Steve. *Joseph Hopkins Twichell: The Life and Times of Mark Twain's Closest Friend.* Athens: University of Georgia Press, 2008.

Couser, G. Thomas. "Autobiography as Anti-biography: The Case of Twain vs. Paine." *Auto/Biography Studies* 3, no. 3 (Fall 1987): 13–20.

Covici, Pascal. *Mark Twain's Humor: The Image of the World.* Dallas: Southern Methodist University Press, 1962.

Cox, James M. *Mark Twain: The Fate of Humor.* Princeton: Princeton University Press, 1966.

Davis, Sara deSaussure, and Philip D. Beidler, eds. *The Mythologizing of Mark Twain.* University: University of Alabama Press, 1984.

De Eulis, Marilyn Davis. "Mark Twain's Experiments in Autobiography." *American Literature* 53, no. 2 (May 1981): 202–13.

DeVoto, Bernard. *Mark Twain's America*. Boston: Little, Brown, and Company, 1932.

DeVoto, Bernard. *Mark Twain at Work*. Cambridge: Harvard University Press, 1942.

Dolmetsch, Carl. *"Our Famous Guest": Mark Twain in Vienna*. Athens: University of Georgia Press, 1992.

Duckett, Margaret. *Mark Twain & Bret Harte*. Norman: University of Oklahoma Press, 1964.

Eakin, Paul John, ed. *American Autobiography: Retrospect and Prospect*. Madison: University of Wisconsin Press, 1991.

Eakin, Paul John. *How Our Lives Become Stories: Making Selves*. Ithaca, NY: Cornell University Press, 1999.

Eble, Kenneth E. *Old Clemens and W. D. H.: The Story of a Remarkable Friendship*. Baton Rouge: Louisiana State University Press, 1985.

Egan, Susanna. *Patterns of Experience in Autobiography*. Chapel Hill: The University of North Carolina Press, 1984.

Emerson, Everett. *The Authentic Mark Twain: A Literary Biography of Samuel L. Clemens*. Philadelphia: University of Pennsylvania Press, 1984.

Emerson, Everett. *Mark Twain: A Literary Life*. Philadelphia: University of Pennsylvania Press, 1999.

Fanning, Philip Ashley. *Mark Twain and Orion Clemens: Brothers, Partners, Strangers*. Tuscaloosa: University of Alabama Press, 2003.

Ferguson, DeLancey. *Mark Twain: Man and Legend*. New York: The Bobbs-Merrill Company, 1943.

Ferguson, DeLancey. "The Uncollected Portions of Mark Twain's Autobiography." *American Literature* 8 (1936): 37–46.

Fishkin, Shelley Fisher. *Was Huck Black? Mark Twain and African American Voices*. New York: Oxford University Press, 1993.

Fleishman, Avrom. *Figures of Autobiography: The Language of Self-Writing*. Berkeley: University of California Press, 1983.

Florence, Don. *Persona and Humor in Mark Twain's Early Writings*. Columbia: University Press of Missouri, 1995.

Foner, Philip S. *Mark Twain Social Critic*. New York: International Publishers, 1958.

Gabrilowitsch, Clara Clemens. *My Father Mark Twain*. New York: Harper and Brothers, 1931.

Gerber, John C. *Mark Twain*. Boston: Twayne Publishers, 1988.

Gerber, John C. "Mark Twain's Use of the Comic Pose." *PMLA* 77 (1962): 297–304.

Gibson, William M. *The Art of Mark Twain*. New York: Oxford University Press 1976.

Giddings, Robert, ed. *Mark Twain: A Sumptuous Variety*. London: Vision Press Ltd., 1985.

Gold, Charles H. *"Hatching Ruin" or Mark Twain's Road to Bankruptcy*. Columbia: University of Missouri Press, 2003.

Gribben, Alan. *Mark Twain's Library: A Reconstruction*. 2 vols. Boston: G. K. Hall and Co., 1980.

Gunn, Janet Warner. *Autobiography: Towards a Poetics of Experience.* Philadelphia: University of Pennsylvania Press, 1982.

Harnsberger, Caroline Thomas. *Mark Twain Family Man.* New York: The Citadel Press, 1960.

Harris, Susan K. *The Courtship of Olivia Langdon and Mark Twain.* New York: Cambridge University Press, 1996.

Harris, Susan K. *Mark Twain's Escape from Time: A Study of Patterns and Images.* Columbia: University of Missouri Press, 1982.

Harrison, Stanley R. "Mark Twain's Requiem for the Past." *Mark Twain Journal* 16, no. 2 (1972): 3–10.

Hill, Hamlin. *Mark Twain: God's Fool.* New York: Harper & Row Publishers, 1973.

Hoffman, Andrew. *Inventing Mark Twain: The Lives of Samuel Langhorne Clemens.* New York: William Morrow and Company, 1997.

Howells, William Dean. *My Mark Twain: Reminiscences and Criticisms.* New York: Harper and Brothers, 1910.

Howells, William Dean. *Literary Friends and Acquaintances.* New York: Harper and Brothers, 1901.

Jerome, Robert D., and Herbert A. Wisbey, eds. *Mark Twain in Elmira.* Elmira, N.Y.: Mark Twain Society, Inc., 1977.

Johnson, James L. *Mark Twain and the Limits of Power: Emerson's God in Ruins.* Knoxville: University of Tennessee Press, 1982.

Kaplan, Fred. *The Singular Mark Twain: A Biography.* New York: Doubleday, 2003.

Kaplan, Justin. *Mark Twain and His World.* New York: Crescent Books, 1982.

Kaplan, Justin. *Mr. Clemens and Mark Twain.* New York: Simon and Schuster, 1966.

Kazin, Alfred. *An American Procession: The Major American Writers from 1830 to 1930—The Crucial Century.* New York: Alfred A. Knopf, 1984.

Kiskis, Michael J. "Coming Back to Humor: The Comic Voice in Mark Twain's Autobiography." In *Mark Twain's Humor: Critical Essays,* edited by David E. E. Sloane, 541–69. New York: Garland Publishing, Inc., 1993.

Kiskis, Michael J. "Dead Man Talking: Mark Twain's Autobiographical Deception." *American Literary Realism* 40, no. 2 (Winter 2008): 95–113.

Kiskis, Michael J. "Mark Twain and Collaborative Autobiography." *Studies in the Literary Imagination* 24, no. 2 (Fall 1996): 27–40.

Kiskis, Michael J. "Susy Clemens as the Fire for Mark Twain's Autobiography." *Mid-Hudson Language Studies* 10 (1987): 43–50.

Krauth, Leland. *Mark Twain & Company: Six Literary Relations.* Athens: University of Georgia Press, 2003.

Krauth, Leland. *Proper Mark Twain.* Athens: University of Georgia Press, 1999.

Lauber, John. *The Making of Mark Twain.* New York: American Heritage Press, Inc., 1985.

Lawton, Mary. *A Lifetime with Mark Twain: The Memories of Katy Leary, for Thirty Years His Faithful and Devoted Servant.* New York: Harcourt, Brace and Company, 1925.

Lynn, Kenneth S. *Mark Twain and Southwestern Humor.* Westport, Conn.: Greenwood Press, Publishers, 1972.

Lystra, Karen. *Dangerous Intimacy: The Untold Story of Mark Twain's Final Years.*
Berkeley: University of California Press, 2004.

McCullough, David Willis, ed. *American Childhoods: An Anthology.* Boston: Little,
Brown and Company, 1987.

MacNaughton, William R. *Mark Twain's Last Years as a Writer.* Columbia: University
of Missouri Press, 1979.

Martin, Jay. *Harvests of Change: American Literature 1865–1914.* Englewood Cliffs,
N.J.: Prentice-Hall, 1967.

Michelson, Bruce. *Mark Twain on the Loose: A Comic Writer and the American Self.*
Amherst: University of Massachusetts Press, 1995.

Morris, Linda A. *Gender Play in Mark Twain: Cross-Dressing and Transgression.*
Columbia: University of Missouri Press, 2007.

Nissen, Axel. *Bret Harte: Prince and Pauper.* Jackson: University Press of Mississippi,
2000.

Olney, James, ed. *Autobiography: Essays Theoretical and Critical.* Princeton: Princeton University Press, 1980.

Pachter, Marc, ed. *Telling Lives: The Biographer's Art.* Philadelphia: University of
Pennsylvania Press, 1981.

Paine, Albert Bigelow. *Mark Twain: A Biography.* With author's note to the 1935 edition and introduction to the 1923 edition by William Lyon Phelps. 1912. Reprint.
New York: Chelsea House, 1980.

Pascal, Roy. *Design and Truth in Autobiography.* Cambridge: Harvard University
Press, 1960.

Pettit, Arthur G. *Mark Twain & The South.* Lexington: University of Kentucky Press,
1974.

Powers, Ron. *Dangerous Water: A Biography of the Boy who Became Mark Twain.*
New York: Basic Books, 1999.

Powers, Ron. *Mark Twain: A Life.* New York: Free Press, 2005.

Robinson, Forrest G. *The Author Cat: Clemens's Life in Fiction.* New York: Fordham
University Press, 2007.

Robinson, Forrest G. *In Bad Faith: The Dynamics of Deception in Mark Twain's
America.* Cambridge: Harvard University Press, 1986.

Rourke, Constance. *American Humor: A Study of the National Character.* New York:
Harcourt, Brace and Company, 1931.

Ryan, Ann M., and Joseph B. McCullough. *Cosmopolitan Twain.* Columbia: University of Missouri Press, 2008.

Salsbury, Edith Colgate, ed. *Susy and Mark Twain: Family Dialogues.* New York:
Harper & Row, 1965.

Sayre, Robert F. *The Examined Self: Benjamin Franklin, Henry Adams, Henry James.*
Princeton: Princeton University Press, 1964. Reprint. Madison: University of Wisconsin Press, 1988.

Scharnhorst, Gary. *Bret Harte: Opening the American Literary West.* Norman: University of Oklahoma Press, 2000.

Schinto, Jeanne M. "The Autobiographies of Mark Twain and Henry Adams: Life
Studies in Despair." *Mark Twain Journal* 17, no. 4 (1975): 5–7.

Schmitz, Neil. *Of Huck and Alice: Humorous Writing in American Literature.* Minneapolis: University of Minnesota Press, 1983.

Shea, Daniel B. *Spiritual Autobiography in Early America.* Princeton: Princeton University Press, 1968. Reprint. Madison: University of Wisconsin Press, 1988.

Shillingsburg, Miriam Jones. *At Home Abroad: Mark Twain in Australasia.* Jackson: University Press of Mississippi, 1988.

Shumaker, Wayne. *English Autobiography: Its Emergence, Materials, and Form.* Berkeley: University of California Press, 1954.

Skandera Trombley, Laura E. "Mark Twain's *Annus Horribilis* of 1908–1909." *American Literary Realism* 40, no. 2 (Winter 2008): 114–36.

Skandera Trombley, Laura E. *Mark Twain in the Company of Women.* Philadelphia: University of Pennsylvania Press, 1994.

Skandera Trombley, Laura E. "'She Wanted to Kill': Jean Clemens and Postictal Psychosis." *American Literary Realism* 37, no. 3 (Spring 2005): 225–37.

Skandera Trombley, Laura, and Michael J. Kiskis, eds. *Constructing Mark Twain: New Directions in Scholarship.* Columbia: University of Missouri Press, 2001.

Sloane, David E. E. *Mark Twain as a Literary Comedian.* Baton Rouge: Louisiana State University Press, 1979.

Sloane, David E. E., ed. *Mark Twain's Humor: Critical Essays.* New York: Garland Publishing, Inc., 1993.

Smith, Henry Nash. *Mark Twain: The Development of a Writer.* Cambridge: Harvard University Press, 1962.

Spengemann, William C. *The Forms of Autobiography: Episodes in the History of a Literary Genre.* New Haven: Yale University Press, 1980.

Steinbrink, Jeffrey. *Getting to Be Mark Twain.* Berkeley: University of California Press, 1991.

Stone, Albert E. *Autobiographical Occasions and Original Acts: Versions of Identity from Henry Adams to Nate Shaw.* Philadelphia: University of Pennsylvania Press, 1982.

Stone, Albert E., Jr. *The Innocent Eye: Childhood in Mark Twain's Imagination.* New Haven: Yale University Press, 1961.

Wagenknecht, Edward. *Mark Twain: The Man and His Work.* 1935. Reprint. Norman: University of Oklahoma Press, 1967.

Wecter, Dixon. *Sam Clemens of Hannibal.* Boston: Houghton Mifflin Company, 1952.

Willis, Resa. *Mark and Livy: The Love Story of Mark Twain and the Woman Who Almost Tamed Him.* New York: Atheneum Publishers, 1992.

Wonham, Henry B. *Mark Twain and the Art of the Tall Tale.* New York: Oxford University Press, 1993.

Zaccara, Jennifer L. "Mark Twain, Isabel Lyon, and the 'Talking Cure.'" In *Constructing Mark Twain: New Directions in Scholarship*, edited by Laura E. Skandera Trombley and Michael J. Kiskis, 101–21. Columbia: University of Missouri Press, 2001.

Index

Adam, 50, 195, 280n7
Agan, Robert, xv
Ainsworth, William Harrison, 63, 282n21
Aldrich, Thomas B., 19, 277n17
Alexander the Great, 295n5
Alta (Alta California), xxxii, 183–84, 296n2
Ament, Joseph P., 286n6, 289n9
American News Company, 14
American Publishing Company, 9, 14, 183, 275n27, 296n3
Andrews, Kenneth R., 270n4
Arthur of Connaught (prince), 217, 299n9
Ashcroft, Ralph W., 40, 279n7
Atlantic Monthly, 36, 37, 235, 274n4
Aunt Hannah, 115
Ayres, Irving, 215

Backus (minstrel), 175, 296n10
Bacon, Francis, 171, 296n5
Bacon, Roger, 220, 299n18
Badeau, Adam, 272n28
Baender, Paul, 271n16
Barnard College, 62
Barnes, George, 182, 297n8
Barrett, Elizabeth, 282n21
Barrette, Laurence, 167, 295n7
Barstow, William H., 284n2
Bates, Edward, 91, 99, 286n2
Beckwith, James Carroll, 198, 298n1
Beecher, Henry Ward, 24, 277n7, 293n4
Beecher, Thomas K., 24, 277n7
Billings, Josh, xlii, 279n4
Birch, Billy, 175, 296n10
Bishop, William H., 235–36, 301n8

Bismarck, Otto von, 125, 291nn5, 6
Bixby, Horace E., 98, 146, 287n14
Black, William, 63, 282n21
Blade (Toledo), 278n8
Blaine, James G., 283n7
Blair, Walter, 271n15
Blankenship, Tom, 191, 212, 297n3, 298n3
Bliss, Elisha, 14, 15, 238, 271n18, 276n7, 276n10, 288n11
Booth, William, 217, 299n12
Bowen, Sam, 193, 212
Bowen, Will, 193, 210, 212, 216, 258, 263–65, 282n20
Brace, Charles Loring, 302n3
Branch, Edgar M., 272n22
Briggs, Artimisia, 212, 213
Briggs, John, 155, 216
Brooks, Noah, 184, 297n15
Brooks, Phillips, 293n4
Brooks, Sydney, 217, 218
Brown, Carolyn S., 272n35
Brown, John, Dr., 63, 282n21
Brown, John ("Ossawatomie"), 50, 224, 300n1
Brown, William, 146, 147, 293nn11, 12
Browning, Robert, 63, 282n21
Bryant, William G., 300n2
Buckland, Francis ("Frank"), 63, 282n21
Budd, Isabelle, 271n13
Budd, Louis, 270n9
Bulletin, The, 12
Burton, Nathaniel, 145, 149, 212, 293n8
Bush, Harold, 270n4, 273n47
Bushnell, Horace, 143, 292n3, 293n4, 293n8

311

Loreta Janeta Velazquez
The Woman in Battle: The Civil War Narrative of Loreta Janeta Velazquez,
Cuban Woman and Confederate Soldier
Introduction by Jesse Alemán

Cathryn Halverson
Maverick Autobiographies:
Women Writers and the American West, 1900–1936

Jeffrey Brace
The Blind African Slave: Or Memoirs of Boyrereau Brinch,
Nicknamed Jeffrey Brace
as told to Benjamin F. Prentiss, Esq.
Edited with an introduction by Kari J. Winter

Colette Inez
The Secret of M. Dulong: A Memoir

Before They Could Vote: American Women's
Autobiographical Writing, 1819–1919
Edited by Sidonie Smith and Julia Watson

Bertram J. Cohler
Writing Desire: Sixty Years of Gay Autobiography

Philip Holden
Autobiography and Decolonization: Modernity, Masculinity,
and the Nation-State

Jing M. Wang
When "I" Was Born: Women's Autobiography in Modern China

Conjoined Twins in Black and White: The Lives of Millie-Christine McKoy
and Daisy and Violet Hilton
Edited by Linda Frost

Four Russian Serf Narratives
Translated, edited, and with an introduction by John MacKay

Mark Twain
Mark Twain's Own Autobiography:
The Chapters from the North American Review, second edition
Edited by Michael J. Kiskis